"This pot-stirring oral history reads like a backstory of how musical lightning comes to be. All of the surviving band members get to have their say."   —*Rolling Stone*

"Alan has a way with narrative that just draws you in without using the single-level story line used by other writers who have attempted telling the Allman Brothers Band's story. He gets right to the *hows* and *whys* that give his narrative real substance. Enjoy and become enlightened."

—Butch Trucks, the Allman Brothers Band
(from the Foreword)

"No journalist knows the ins and outs of the Allman Brothers Band better than Alan Paul."   —Warren Haynes, the Allman Brothers Band

"I learned so much reading *One Way Out*. If you want to know the real deal, read Alan Paul."   —Oteil Burbridge,
the Allman Brothers Band

"Allman Brothers, unvarnished . . . [Alan Paul]'s vast trove of interviews allows the band to tell its own story."   —*Atlanta Journal-Constitution*

"Alan Paul is one of America's foremost experts on the Allman Brothers Band. For the past twenty years, he has written informative, comprehensive articles on the band, and he truly understands the essence of their significance. It's great to see him release this chronicle."

—E. J. Devokaitis, curator/archivist, The Allman
Brothers Band Museum at the Big House

"Alan Paul's *One Way Out* is a brilliantly detailed all-access pass to the Allman Brothers Band. Using his numerous personal interviews with the band members themselves—both past and present—as well as an almost endless entourage of friends, family members, roadies, managers, promoters, booking agents, record label executives, and fellow musicians, Alan Paul has successfully created the definitive ABB biography." —Randy Poe, author of *Skydog: The Duane Allman Story*

"*One Way Out* is perhaps the most in-depth look at one of America's most beloved, but thoroughly dysfunctional ensembles. Engrossing reading . . . Alan Paul has written about the Allmans for the last twenty-five years, and his depth of knowledge shows. The stories are salty, unfiltered, and straight from the horse's mouth. The word 'definitive' gets tossed around so often it has lost some of its meaning, but this four-hundred-page journey into the heart of rock-and-roll darkness deserves the accolade." —*Guitar World* magazine

"No matter what you think you know about the Allman Brothers Band, *One Way Out* is bound to be revelatory on many levels. . . . This is essential reading that strips away the myth to expose all the moving parts in vivid detail." —*Seattle Post-Intelligencer*

"Music writer Paul catches up with the legendary band in this entertaining, compulsively readable oral history of the Allman Brothers. Duane's ghost haunts the book." —*Publishers Weekly*

"Perhaps no music journalist has written as extensively about the Allman Brothers Band as Paul, who has tracked the rock group's career for twenty-five years. And his deep familiarity with the band and its music shows everywhere in this fluid account. Augmented by photos and fascinating sidebars, this candid oral history has appeal beyond the Allman Brothers Band's loyal fan base." —*Booklist* (starred review)

"With this fine work, Alan Paul accomplishes the admirable feat of delving into the depths of the Allman Brothers, a great aggregation of talent and artistry. He puts together the sweeping picture of how these gifted individuals with their special Southern stylishness created something utterly unique to the world. Rock on."

—Billy F. Gibbons, ZZ Top

"Open this book to any page, start reading, and I dare you to stop. Alan Paul captures all the momentum and energy of the Allman Brothers' long, wild ride, which continues at a breakneck pace. *One Way Out?* There's no way out of this rollicking narrative until, with regret, you reach the end."

—Anthony DeCurtis, contributing editor, *Rolling Stone*

"I was struck by the similarities between The Doors and Allman Brothers, especially in our origins—the eureka moment of certainty amidst a jam. Alan lets the people who were actually there tell the story, and I couldn't put it down. Great read!"

—Robby Krieger, The Doors

"Like a master bandleader, Alan Paul orchestrates a bluesy, jazzy, rocking chorale of voices telling the tale of a brotherhood under stress and a band who got what they hardly realized they wanted, lost what they had, and fought a decades-long struggle to get it back."

—Charles Shaar Murray, author of *Crosstown Traffic: Jimi Hendrix and the Post-War Rock 'n' Roll Revolution* and *Boogie Man: The Adventures of John Lee Hooker in the American Twentieth Century*

"Paul's *One Way Out* is a fresh, intelligently arranged, and satisfyingly complete telling of the lengthy (and unlikely) history of the group that almost singlehandedly brought rock up to a level of jazz-like sophistication and virtuosity, introducing it as a medium worthy of the soloist's art. Oral histories can be tricky things: either penetrating, delivering information and backstories that get to the heart of how timeless music was made. Or too often, they lie flat on the page, a random retelling of repeated facts and reheated yarns. I'm happy to say that Paul's is in that first category."

—Ashley Kahn, author of *A Love Supreme: The Story of John Coltrane's Signature Album*

"Though enough tomes have been published about the Allmans' troubled history to deforest half of Brazil, only Paul's book gets all the principal figures assessing and confessing. However open and moving Gregg Allman's autobio from 2012 may have been, Paul's book gives a much fuller picture of the dynamics that drive every member—including why guitarist Dickey Betts remains so vexing."

—*The Daily News*

"Paul's book presents the most complete and detailed telling of the band's still-unfolding saga to date. Elizabeth Reed, Melissa, and Jessica would also probably agree." —*Houston Press*

ONE WAY OUT

ONE WAY OUT

The Inside History of the

ALLMAN BROTHERS BAND

ALAN PAUL

ST. MARTIN'S GRIFFIN ☙ NEW YORK

ONE WAY OUT. Copyright © 2014 by Alan Paul. Foreword copyright © 2014 by
Butch Trucks. Afterword copyright © 2014 by Jaimoe. All rights reserved.
Printed in the United States of America. For information, address St. Martin's
Press, 175 Fifth Avenue, New York, N.Y. 10010.

www.stmartins.com

Designed by Ellen Cipriano

TITLE PAGE PHOTO: The Allman Brothers Band, 1992: (from left) Jaimoe,
Allen Woody, Dickey Betts, Gregg Allman, Warren Haynes,
Marc Quiñones, and Butch Trucks. Courtesy of Kirk West,
www.kirkwestphotography.com

See page 461 for text photo credits.

THE LIBRARY OF CONGRESS HAS CATALOGED THE HARDCOVER
EDITION AS FOLLOWS:

Paul, Alan, 1966–
    One way out : the inside history of the Allman Brothers Band / Alan Paul.— 1st ed.
        p. cm.
    ISBN 978-1-250-04049-7 (hardcover)
    ISBN 978-1-4668-3586-3 (e-book)
    1. Allman Brothers Band.   2. Rock musicians—United States—Biography.   I. Title.
    ML3930.A43P38 2014
    782.42166092'2—dc23
    [B]

                                                                    2013030280

ISBN 978-1-250-04050-3 (trade paperback)

St. Martin's Griffin books may be purchased for educational, business, or
promotional use. For information on bulk purchases, please contact the
Macmillan Corporate and Premium Sales Department at 1-800-221-7945,
extension 5442, or write to specialmarkets@macmillan.com.

First St. Martin's Griffin Edition: February 2015

10 9 8 7 6 5 4

To my brother David, who handed me Eat a Peach,

then let me sit on that yellow shag carpet listening

to his stereo for hours on end.

And to Jacob, Eli, Anna, and Rebecca, of course.

CONTENTS

Author's Note

One Way Out is the culmination of thirty years trying to untangle the myths and legends surrounding the Allman Brothers Band. I have interviewed the members hundreds of times, shared meals, ridden buses, quietly watched rehearsals, and attended countless shows. Through it all, I have never lost sight of why this story matters: the music.

Any access I have gained has been in the service of trying to understand how this exotic brew came to be. I have viewed everything with the eyes and ears of a journalist but the heart and soul of a fan. The Allman Brothers Band, I believe, has no equal.

The original six-piece band, with Duane and Gregg Allman, Dickey Betts, Berry Oakley, Butch Trucks, and Jaimoe created inspired, utterly unique magic. From their remarkable self-titled debut album in 1969, the band succeeded in reinventing blues-based music in a way that was both visionary and true to the original material.

Their music was the result of true group collaboration. Butch Trucks and Jaimoe's pulsating drive provided unique depth and jazz swing. Dickey Betts and Duane Allman's guitar work expanded the blues melodically and harmonically, setting a new standard for touch and tone without ever lapsing into overplaying. Berry Oakley's bass wove between the other instruments, playing melodic lines that tied the music together into one cohesive package. Gregg's funky organ seasoned the mix, while his vocals sounded both ancient and modern, singing the blues in a legit fashion his peers could only fantasize about.

The instrumental majesty would not have meant much without a magnificent set of songs, written by Gregg Allman and Betts: "Whipping Post," "Dreams," "Midnight Rider," "Blue Sky," "Melissa," "In Memory of Elizabeth Reed," and "Jessica" are both timeless and wildly diverse with clear echoes of country, jazz, blues, and rock.

Given the rancor and turmoil that has often surrounded the group, it's easy to scoff at the notion of a musical brotherhood. But I believe that in its earliest years, the members and crew shared a bond that sustained them through perilous times. Since the early, devastating deaths of Duane Allman and Berry Oakley, the band has also managed to find brilliant new musical voices to keep them moving forward, including Chuck Leavell, Warren Haynes, and Derek Trucks.

The Allman Brothers' long history is equally tragic and uplifting, heroic and sad. I have spoken to virtually every living person who had a hand in this tale. When two people's recollections of an event differed, I present them here side-by-side.

Cast of Characters, in Order of Appearance

GREGG ALLMAN: Singer/keyboardist, founding member of the Allman Brothers Band (ABB); younger brother of guitarist Duane Allman.

JOHNNY SANDLIN: Longtime Allman friend and colleague. Bassist in the Allman Joys and Hour Glass. Produced *Brothers and Sisters* and other Allman Brothers releases.

RICK HALL: President, Fame Studios, Muscle Shoals, Alabama.

JON LANDAU: Writer for *Rolling Stone* and *Crawdaddy*; Bruce Springsteen's manager since 1978.

JAIMOE: Drummer and founding member of the ABB.

JACKIE AVERY JR.: Songwriter, friend of Jaimoe.

JOHN HAMMOND JR.: Guitarist/singer. Good friend of Duane Allman.

DICKEY BETTS: Guitarist/singer and founding member of the ABB. Has performed with his band Great Southern since an acrimonious 2000 departure from the ABB.

REESE WYNANS: Keyboardist in the Second Coming, with Dickey Betts and Berry Oakley. Participant in original jams that led to the ABB. Later a member of Stevie Ray Vaughan's Double Trouble.

THOM DOUCETTE: Harmonica player, Duane confidant, and unofficial member of the ABB.

BUTCH TRUCKS: Drummer and founding member of the ABB.

RICHARD PRICE: Florida bassist; played with Betts and Oakley and was there for the Jacksonville jams that birthed the Allman Brothers Band.

LINDA OAKLEY: Wife of Berry Oakley.

PHIL WALDEN: Original manager of the ABB and president of Capricorn Records. Died April 23, 2006.

KIM PAYNE: One of the band's original crew members; with the ABB 1969–73.

JOHN McEUEN: Founder, Nitty Gritty Dirt Band, brother of Bill McEuen, Hour Glass manager.

MIKE CALLAHAN: One of the band's original crew members; with the ABB 1969–73. Died September 2007.

RED DOG: One of the band's original crew members; with the ABB 1969–2000. Died February 21, 2011.

A.J. LYNDON: Twiggs's little brother, ABB crew member 1973–76.

MAMA LOUISE HUDSON: Cook and owner, H&H Soul Food Restaurant; mother figure to the band.

COL. BRUCE HAMPTON: Founder of the Hampton Grease Band, who often played with the ABB in Atlanta's Piedmont Park; friend of Duane Allman.

W. DAVID POWELL: Partner in Wonder Graphics, the duo that designed the ABB's mushroom logo and the iconic cover of *Eat a Peach*.

BUNKY ODOM: Vice President, Phil Walden and Associates; day-to-day management contact.

JOHN LYNDON: Twiggs's brother.

GARY ROSSINGTON: Lynyrd Skynyrd founder/guitarist.

DON LAW: Manager of the Boston Tea Party; major New England promoter for forty-five years.

STEPHEN PALEY: Photographer who took the pictures on the debut album cover.

WARREN HAYNES: Guitarist/singer who joined the ABB in 1989. Left in 1997. Rejoined in 2001.

SCOTT BOYER: Guitarist in the band Cowboy, friend of Duane Allman.

TOM DOWD: Producer of many ABB albums, including *Idlewild South, At Fillmore East*, and *Eat a Peach*. Also worked with Ray Charles, John Coltrane, Derek and the Dominos, and many others. Died October 27, 2000.

BOBBY WHITLOCK: Derek and the Dominos keyboardist; also worked with Duane in Delaney and Bonnie.

ERIC CLAPTON: Guitarist, rock legend. Worked with Duane Allman on Derek and the Dominos' *Layla and Other Assorted Love Songs*.

JONNY PODELL: ABB booking agent since 1969.

WILLIE PERKINS: ABB Road Manager, 1970–76.

BOB WEIR: Grateful Dead guitarist.

STEVE PARISH: Grateful Dead crew member.

DR. JOHN: Pianist, friend of Duane Allman.

DICK WOOLEY: Capricorn Vice President of Promotion, 1972–76.

CHUCK LEAVELL: Pianist, member of the ABB 1972–76.

SIDNEY SMITH: Photographer.

LES DUDEK: Guitarist, played on "Ramblin' Man" and "Jessica."

DAVID "ROOK" GOLDFLIES: Bassist, member of the ABB 1979–82.

MIKE LAWLER: Keyboardist/producer. Member of the ABB 1980–82.

JOHN SCHER: Promoter; ABB manager, 1981–82.

BERT HOLMAN: ABB manager since 1991.

MICHAEL CAPLAN: Epic Records A&R man who signed the Allman Brothers Band in 1989.

DANNY GOLDBERG: ABB manager 1989–91; has also worked with Led Zeppelin, Nirvana, and other rock icons.

JOHNNY NEEL: Keyboardist, member of the ABB, 1989–91.

ALLEN WOODY: Bassist, member of the ABB 1989–97. Died August 26, 2000.

MATT ABTS: Gov't Mule drummer.

DEREK TRUCKS: Guitarist, member of the ABB since 1999; nephew of Butch Trucks.

MARC QUIÑONES: Percussionist, member of the ABB since 1991.

KIRK WEST: ABB "Tour Magician" and logistical coordinator, 1989–2009.

DAVID GRISSOM: Guitarist. Toured with the ABB for nine shows in 1993, subbing for Dickey Betts.

ZAKK WYLDE: Ozzy Osbourne guitarist who played with the ABB for one gig, filling in for Dickey Betts in 1993.

JACK PEARSON: Guitarist, member of the ABB, 1997–99.

OTEIL BURBRIDGE: Bassist, member of the ABB since 1997.

JIMMY HERRING: Guitarist, summer tour 2000.

BILLY GIBBONS: ZZ Top guitarist.

BUDDY GUY: Blues guitarist.

Foreword by Butch Trucks

Early in 1969, I was living on the St. John's River with my first wife and on the verge of quitting what was, at the time, a very unprofitable and unsatisfying career in music. My not-too-well-thought-out plan was to return to college and get my degree in math, since that was what I seemed to be best at doing. My first attempt at "higher education" ended in 1966 when Florida State University asked me not to return for the fall trimester. It seems that the nonattendance that led to a great deal of F's was unacceptable even at the great party school of FSU. I joined up with two of my buddies from high school who happened to land in the same dorm as me and we decided to start a band and play this new stuff by the Byrds and the newly electric Bob Dylan among others, such as the Lovin' Spoonful. We called ourselves the Bitter Ind. and somehow going to class just didn't seem as important as rehearsing and playing for every frat at FSU.

In the summer of 1966 we packed our gear in the back of our guitar player and singer Scott Boyer's car and headed to Daytona Beach to make it big. Well, that bombed big-time. We auditioned at all of the clubs there and they all thought we were the best band they had ever heard, but the universal rejections came because "you can't dance to it." We were doing our last audition at a place called the Martinique when in walked the Beatles. Of course, it wasn't actually John, Paul, George, and Ringo, but the way people acted it may as well have been. It was a band called the Allman Joys, and walking in the lead was this dude with long blond hair followed closely by another dude with even longer and blonder hair. This was of course, Duane and Gregg Allman.

We played our set and got the usual "you guys are great but they can't dance to it" from the club owner. Waiting for us backstage, however, were those two blond guys, and they were blown away with what we had just played. We explained our predicament and got an invite to come hang out at 100 Van Avenue where they lived with their mother, Momma A.

After a few days we packed it up, stuck our tails between our legs, and headed back to Jacksonville, where a few weeks later I got a call from Duane asking me to come to a club in downtown Jacksonville, because their drummer had just quit. I, of course, said, "I'm on my way." I played with them for a night or two and Duane, knowing that this club's owner was a huge Dylan fan, got our band an audition and we took over the Allman Joys's gig. That lasted for around eight months. Then we hit the Southern club circuit, where we would run into Duane and Gregg from time to time.

Sometime in, I believe, 1967, we were in Daytona and stopped by 100 Van Avenue and found Duane and Gregg fresh from a run at the big time in L.A. as the Hour Glass. We decided to join forces and played for the next few months as the Bitter Ind., the Hour Glass, or the 31st of February. (We had signed a record contract with Vanguard Records and the Bitter End club in New York would not let us use that name).

We took this version to Miami to record our second record for Vanguard. You can hear two of those recordings on Duane's retrospective, *Skydog*. One of them was the very first recording of "Melissa." When we finished there, Gregg flew back to L.A. and found out that the Hour Glass's record company, Liberty, which has no relation to the current label of the same name, would release the rest of that band from their contracts if he would stay and record solo. I was with Duane in Daytona when he got the call from Gregg. I believe if Duane could have gotten through the phone he would have strangled Gregg on the spot. Well, Duane had been offered a gig as a studio player in Muscle Shoals and without Gregg he just didn't feel like our band was going to go anywhere, so he packed it up and headed to Alabama.

Back to my opening sentence: Luckily for me, before I enrolled in college again, there came a knock on my door and there was Duane with an incredible-looking black man. Duane, in his usual way, introduced us to each other as Jaimoe, his new drummer, and Butch, his old drummer. He hung around for a while and then took off to meet up with Berry Oakley at the house on Riverside Drive where Berry's then-band, Second Coming, was living. He left Jaimoe at my house and, for the first time in my middle-class white life I had to get to know and deal with a black man. It changed me profoundly. Over forty-four years later, Jaimoe and I are still best of friends and I am very proud to call him my brother.

I could go on with this story for several hundred pages, but that is what Alan Paul has written, and that is what I am writing a foreword for. I will let Alan tell the story of the Allman Brothers Band as he has been able to uncover it from many long interviews with me and everyone else that he could get to who was there during many of the band's incarnations.

There have been several attempts to write *the* epic rock and roll story but so far, I haven't read anything that really "gets it." They tend to be written by newspaper writers and the books wind up being very long articles that deal with who did what, where, and when. None have delved into the *how* and *why*.

I've read Alan Paul's articles about us going back many years. I've read his book *Big in China*, and the one thing that jumps from those pages is *how* and *why*. In *Big in China* Alan finds himself in as alien an environment as possible and still finds a way to assemble an extremely good band that he educates in American blues/jazz rock as exemplified by the Allman Brothers Band. Alan does an incredible job of telling his story from the very uneasy beginnings, when even communicating was difficult, other than through the music, up through the day that his group was selected as the top band in Beijing.

Alan has a way with narrative that just draws you in without using the single-level storyline used by other writers who have attempted telling the Allman Brothers Band's story. He gets right to the *hows* and *whys* that give his narrative real substance.

Enjoy and become enlightened.

—*West Palm Beach, Florida*

ONE WAY OUT

PROLOGUE

Howard Duane Allman was born in Nashville, Tennessee, on November 20, 1946. Baby brother Gregg arrived just over a year later, on December 8, 1947. Their father, Willis Turner Allman, an Army first lieutenant, was murdered on December 26, 1949, shot by a stranger whom he and a friend had met playing pool in a bar and offered a ride home. The widowed Geraldine Allman moved to Daytona Beach, Florida, where Duane and Gregg grew up as exceptionally close sole siblings.

It was thirteen-year-old Gregg who first brought music into the Allmans' Daytona, Florida, household when Geraldine bought him a Sears Silvertone guitar.

"I got the guitar and Duane got a motorcycle, a Harley 165, one of those tiny little ones where you mix the gas with the oil," Gregg recalls.

Before long, Duane was stealing the instrument and trying to steal his little brother's licks as well. Countless fights ensued until Duane traded in the remnants of the wrecked Harley for his own guitar.

"As soon as I got the guitar, he'd look at it and go, 'Now what you got there, baby brother?'" Gregg recalls with a laugh. "And I'd go, 'Now, all right, Duane, that's mine.' He would slip into my room and play it. We had more fights over that guitar than you'd believe. He drove the damned motorcycle into the ground and brought it home in a bag. Finally, to stop all the fights, my mom got him his own guitar in exchange for whatever was left of that motorcycle. Then there was not only peace in the family but we started playing together; we had a twosome. Within a few weeks, he could play it really good. It was pretty amazing.

"I just showed him the rudimentary map: E, A, and B, the three-chord turnaround, and he caught up with me very quickly. Then he started showing me some licks, and we would just help each other out. And that's how we learned. Neither of us ever learned to read music really, just chord charts."

Duane (left) and Gregg Allman, Seabreeze High.

The music bug bit Duane so hard that he dropped out of school after tenth grade and started playing constantly, Gregg recalls. "Then he passed me like I was standing still."

The brothers formed a band, and while Gregg was still in school, they were playing clubs up and down the Daytona Beach strip as the Escorts and then the Allman Joys. The music evolved rapidly, and by spring 1965 the Escorts had cut their own respectable versions of R&B hits like Bobby Bland's "Turn On Your Lovelight" and Ray Charles's "What'd I Say."

Young Gregg was still struggling to mimic his heroes, but he was already seizing his vocal identity.

"At first, we were playing what everyone else was—the Ventures and other surf music. You know, Surfer Joe stuff," Gregg says. "Then we met up with a group of black guys in Daytona Beach, including Floyd Miles, one of my best friends to this day, and they turned us on to so much great music and it was clear right away that [the surf music] just didn't have near the substance of the rhythm and blues stuff.

"When I was thirteen or fourteen, Floyd started taking me over across the tracks—literally. Blacks lived on the other side of the railroad tracks in Daytona. And it wasn't cool for either of us. It wasn't cool for me to be hanging out with him and going to that neighborhood and it wasn't cool for him to bring me there. We both caught hell from our friends and families, but we didn't care. He took me over there to this place, which was a convenience store/drug store/record store. I think you could have bought a car in there. And they had this big bin in the middle of the store just full of records. And he said, 'This is James Brown and this is B.B. King and this is Sonny Boy Williamson and this is Howlin' Wolf.' I'd get whatever I could afford. Every time I'd get two dollars I'd pedal my bicycle over there with Floyd, grab me a record, and get the hell out as quick as I could."

Back home, Duane was digesting the records his little brother brought home and learning to play the licks. By the time Gregg graduated in 1965, the brothers were already established as the best, most adventurous band on a burgeoning and competitive circuit.

"Duane was so confident we could make it and he always wanted me to drop out so we could just play all the time, but I was the Doubting Thomas," Gregg recalls. "I'd say, 'We're never gonna make enough playing music to pay the rent.' The Beatles had just come out and everybody had a band, so there was a lot of good competition out there. I wanted to finish school and become a dentist; I had my goal set to be a dental surgeon. And I was already accepted to college in Louisiana, so I figured I had that to fall back on. I graduated high school and thought, 'I'll give it a year. I'll go out and play these clubs and then I'll go on to college.' But after a year, I was so far in debt from trying to buy amps and guitars and everything else, that I had to do another year."

The brothers expanded their touring throughout the Southeast and began spending a fair amount of time in St. Louis, where they had established a following. The other members of the band changed with some frequency. By the spring of 1967, the group included two Alabama natives who would remain associated with the brothers for decades—drummer Johnny Sandlin and keyboardist Paul Hornsby. This group was playing a month-long gig in St. Louis when the fledgling Nitty Gritty Dirt Band came to town. Their manager, Bill

McEuen, happened upon the Allmans and was wowed, hearing tremendous potential in the blond brothers.

"He wandered into that bar and was so taken with them," recalls Bill's brother John, a founding member of the Nitty Gritty Dirt Band. "I'll never forget how excited he was after seeing them the first time."

Recalls Gregg: "We were playing a filthy little place and this L.A. manager happened to be in town and he came in and was impressed by what he heard—enough that he wanted us to come west. He actually said, 'Come to Hollywood and we'll make you the next Rolling Stones.' We laughed because this was the shit you see in the movies: 'Aw, c'mon with me, chickadee, I'll make you a big star.' As if anyone has the capacity to do that. If you ain't carrying your own fuel, I don't care how big of a building they shove you off of, you aren't going to fly.

"I would normally be the one to fall for this crap and my brother would be the one to slap me in the head, but I think he wanted to get out there and look at them pretty women in Hollywood and he said, 'Hey, let's do this.' I said, 'You're out of your goddamn mind.' He said, 'Come on, you know this ain't doing it.' And he had a point. So I thought, 'What the hell. If you do it, I'll do it.' It was one of them 'You jump in the lake first and I'll go in after you' deals. So we go."

They hoped that being discovered by McEuen was the big break they had been dreaming of, but the group did not find fame and fortune in Hollywood. Renamed the Hour Glass and signed to Liberty Records, they released an unsuccessful album, then found themselves bound by the label's dictates.

"All along they wanted to cut Gregg like Gerry and the Pacemakers, with him out front and the band being inconsequential," Sandlin says. "They hated anything we liked and we hated anything they liked."

On stage, the Hour Glass came to life, drawing the attention of the California rock elite, opening for the Doors at the Whisky a Go Go and Neil Young's Buffalo Springfield at San Francisco's Fillmore West. None of this seemed to have any impact on the people at Liberty Records, who dictated that they not overexpose themselves by playing too often.

"It was an awful time in my life," Gregg says. "I mean, they had us wearing *these Nehru clown suits. When I look at that today, I have to tell myself, 'Gregory, it was a long time ago, man. You were real naive and they were taking it from you hook, line, and sinker.'"*

Lacking a strong identity to match their well-developed skills, the restless brothers were struggling to find their own musical voices.

"They didn't know their position in the musical world yet—but they knew they were good," recalls John McEuen. "They would open their sets with an instrumental version of 'Norwegian Wood' and close it with a song by Buck Owens and the Buckaroos. It was all good, but all over the place. They were seeking their identity, but anyone who heard them understood how good they were. Duane had total command and authority of the guitar and Gregg was just a great singer who could make anything his own."

Gregg had written only a handful of songs he considered possible keepers. Duane had not yet begun to play the bottleneck slide guitar with which he would soon be closely associated.

GREGG ALLMAN: We had chops up the ass, but didn't have the originality thing down yet. We were stuck out in L.A. and we couldn't play anywhere because the label wanted to control everything we did. Duane wanted to split and go back south where we belonged and the label said, "You can't do that. We'll freeze you from signing anywhere or recording for anyone." He was in bad sorts over that.

Around this time, most of the members of the Hour Glass went to see Taj Mahal at the Magic Mushroom, a club near their apartments.

JOHNNY SANDLIN, *longtime Allman friend and colleague; bassist in the Allman Joys and Hour Glass:* Taj was great and so was his band, which included Jesse Ed Davis, playing slide guitar. Duane was knocked out by that slide playing and by "Statesboro Blues," which Taj had just cut on his first album.

I went by Duane's apartment a few days later and Duane was playing slide on "Statesboro Blues" and he was very excited about it.

"Statesboro Blues" was written and originally recorded by Blind Willie McTell in 1928, but it was a retake of Taj's version that would become intimately linked with the Allman Brothers. From the start, Duane was using an empty bottle of Coricidin cold medicine as a slide. Gregg says the original slide came from a bottle he had given his brother when Duane was suffering from a bad cold.

ALLMAN: A few days later we split up when he had just had it and left to go do sessions in Muscle Shoals while I stayed to try and fulfill the contract. We were apart for almost a year—and it seemed like three years to me. It was the only time he and I ever split up.

Duane and Gregg met up again briefly months later in Miami, where they cut an album-length demo with drummer Butch Trucks's band, the 31st of February, which included the first recorded version of "Melissa." These tracks were eventually released as an album with the misleading title Duane and Gregg Allman.

Following those sessions, Gregg returned to Los Angeles, while Duane made his way to Muscle Shoals, Alabama, which had a thriving recording scene. The Hour Glass had recorded some excellent demos at Rick Hall's Fame Studios in April 1968—blues-heavy tracks that were quickly rejected by Liberty.

When Duane appeared again looking for work, Fame was in the midst of producing a string of hit records by Aretha Franklin, Wilson Pickett, Percy Sledge, and other R&B greats.

RICK HALL: Duane showed up and said, "I understand you're cutting a lot of records. I'd like to be a studio picker." I said, "I don't need you. Guitar players are coming out my wazoo." He said, "OK, boss. Do you mind if I just hang around and maybe you can listen to me play some time?"

I told him to do what he wanted, but I was skeptical about him; he kind of spooked me. He had long white hair and looked like a junkie and I wasn't used to that type of person. But he put up a little pup tent on my property and slept there for two weeks. What turned me around on Duane was simply hearing him play; after seeing his determination, I thought I should give him a chance and I couldn't believe what I heard, which was different than anything I had ever experienced. I don't believe I had ever heard an electric bottleneck guitar and I know I had never recorded one.

Whatever reservations I had about Duane went away. I was a producer looking to make hit records and it was all about the music. I came to realize that Duane was actually a kind, courteous, gentle man, but his music was ragged and funky and dripping with sweat and stink. It smelled like it came out of the bottom of the Tennessee River. The other musicians were suspicious of him—they were clean-cut, clean-living guys and he was totally different, plus he was competition—but they had to put up with him because I wanted that funky guitar on my records.

SANDLIN: Duane looked like an absolute wild person for that time and place. In north Alabama in 1968 when you saw someone with long blond hair you expected them to be a girl. A bunch of rednecks were sure to give him trouble, but the music transcended that. He looked out of place, but he played right where he ought to play.

HALL: Duane did a Clarence Carter session and the next one was with Wilson Pickett. Wilson and I listened to every song the publishers had sent and agreed that we didn't have a hit, then Duane spoke up: "Why don't we do 'Hey Jude'?"

I said, "Are you nuts? 'Hey Jude' is number four with a bullet and it's probably going to be number one for the next month and you want to cover the Beatles with Wilson Pickett?"

Duane said, "That's absolutely what we need to do."

I said, "People will think we're just a bunch of crazy people down here."

But he stood his ground and argued with me and Pickett, who was also opposed. So I said, "Well, how are we going to do it?" He started plunking on his guitar like Chet Atkins playing one of those country-funk things and I said, "Hey that sounds pretty good. Wilson, why don't you sing along?" He starts singing and I ask, "Pickett, what are you singing there?" And he goes, "'Hey Jew.' That's what the record is, isn't it?" And I said, "No, it's Jude: J-U-D-E." Some people think to this day he actually did sing 'Jew.'"

When I sent it to Wexler, he called and said, "A fucking stroke of genius, Rick."

I said, "Really? Well, it wasn't my idea. It was Duane Allman's idea."

He said, "Whoever's idea it was, you produced a great record. I do believe it's going to number one."

Wilson Pickett and Duane Allman, Muscle Shoals, Alabama.

On one of his very first sessions, Allman had proven his value as both a guitarist and musical visionary, someone who could do much more than play his parts. He quickly began to be known as both "Skyman" and "Skydog." The nicknames would last forever, but there have been conflicting stories about their origins. Hall says neither is a mystery.

HALL: I called Duane "Dog" because he looked like an old hound dog with his big ears and hanging-down white hair. Then Wilson, who had a name for everyone, started calling Duane "Skyman" because he loved to have a toke. He'd go in the bathroom, then come back and play his ass off. "Skyman" and "Dog" kind of merged into "Skydog."

Duane wanted to start his own band and get back to performing, while Hall was looking to start working with groups in addition to recording individual artists. With their needs and desires lining up, a partnership was struck.

HALL: Given our relationship and the success we had, I signed Duane to a five-year recording contract, brought him into Studio B, and said, "Work up your songs and we'll put something down."

He was singing, too, though it was obvious to me that he was a guitarist, not a singer. When I'd say that, he'd go, "My brother's a great singer. If I got him to come with me, we'd have a great band."

And I said, "Well, get him here." And he said, "Oh, he don't want to come. He's got another band out in California." I just went, "Whatever." I wanted to get to work, not talk about guys who weren't there.

Hall could not quite see a way to turn his obviously talented charge into a successful recording artist, but Phil Walden immediately seemed to have a clearer vision. The manager of the late Otis Redding as well as several other R&B acts who had recorded in Muscle Shoals, Walden was looking to expand into rock acts when he visited Hall and discussed Allman.

HALL: Phil said, "This guy is gonna make you a million dollars. You just go in there, turn on the machine for eight hours, smoke a cigarette, drink a Pepsi, and when you get done, you'll have a million dollars. This guy's gonna be a superstar."

I said, "That's bullshit, man. Come on."

JON LANDAU, *then a writer for* Rolling Stone *and* Crawdaddy, *he has been Bruce Springsteen's manager since 1978:* I was in Macon with Phil [Walden] writing an article for *Rolling Stone* on the soul music world after Otis Redding, who had died in December 1967. I also wanted to go to Muscle Shoals and Phil took me there; we got two seats on a very early-in-the-morning mail plane. Phil was talking a lot about Duane Allman and was very anxious for me to meet him and hear him play. When I got there he was overdubbing for some session and I went to the studio and he was standing there by himself with his guitar and amp.

HALL: Duane had a little band together and they were sleeping in Studio B. I'd go wake them up and they would be high and covered in blankets. I'd say, "Let's record something, Duane." And he'd put his arm around me and say, "You know, Rick, the stars and moons are not lining up right. Let's wait around a day or two and once the signs are right, we'll be ready to go."

I said, "Bullshit. I can't put up with this crap."

SANDLIN: Hell no! We were all excited to record. Duane's band was me, [keyboardist] Paul Hornsby, and Berry [Oakley]. We weren't like Rick's regular musicians who came in and worked on a schedule every day, but we weren't sitting around. We were excited about this project; it just wasn't what Rick was expecting or used to dealing with.

HALL: I called Phil and said, "I can't do it. It's not me. I'm doing Aretha Franklin and Wilson Pickett and all these great people and I want to go in and get it on, not wait around for these guys. Do you want to buy the contract and the tracks we cut with him?"

LANDAU: Rick was a brilliant record producer, but a very dark person, very intense, very old school, very straight. There was no cultural connection between him and Duane. Phil was clearly a more appropriate fit. He was a very charismatic guy who just had it. He wanted to be big in the pop/rock world, and he saw Duane as the means to do that.

HALL: Phil and [Jerry] Wexler [of Atlantic Records] came down and asked how many sides I had cut. I said, "About seven or eight."

Wexler said, "What will you take for them and the contract?"

I said, "What will you give me?"

He goes, "How about eight thousand?"

Being a negotiator myself, I countered with, "It'll take ten."

Wexler said, "Fine," and wrote me a check for $10,000.

And the rest is history.

CHAPTER

Beginnings

*P*HIL WALDEN INTENDED *Duane's new band to be the center-piece artists on his new Atlantic-distributed label, Capricorn Records. He also signed Allman to a management contract. Duane now had a record label and a manager wrapped up in one charismatic figure.*

The first member of his new band was the drummer born in Ocean Springs, Mississippi, as Johnie Lee Johnson, then calling himself Jai Johanny Johanson and soon to be known by a single name: Jaimoe.

JAIMOE: I had been playing with rhythm and blues artists like Clarence Carter, Percy Sledge, and Arthur Conley and I was done with that whole scene. The people who became stars treated their musicians just like they were treated—like dogs. I decided that if I'm going to starve to death, at least I'm going to do it playing what I love: jazz music. I was moving to New York City.

I had played on a songwriting demo of songs written by my friend Jackie Avery, and he got them to Duane to consider, having heard he had signed with Phil and was putting together a band.

JACKIE AVERY JR., *songwriter:* I went to Muscle Shoals during a Wilson Pickett session and Duane was sitting in Studio B playing a dobro, with his legs crossed, one leg way up on the other kneecap, wearing big cowboy boots. I was struck by how different he was; he was a free spirit who just didn't give a damn. I played him this demo, with Johnny Jenkins singing "Voodoo in You" and two other songs.

He listened to the whole thing, then spit in a cup—I think he had some snuff—and all he asked was, "Who's the drummer?"

I went back to Georgia and Jai was playing at some roadhouse in the woods with [blues guitarist] Eddie Kirkwood and I told him that I thought he should get over to Muscle Shoals, that I thought this guy was going to be something.

JAIMOE: Avery said, "I ain't never heard nobody play guitar the way Duane does" and he had seen Guitar Slim and many other great ones, so that convinced me to go talk to Duane before going to New York and starving to death.

AVERY: Jaimoe packed up his drums and he and I scraped together $28 for a bus ticket and put those drums on a bus and off he went.

JAIMOE: I got to Muscle Shoals and rattling around my head was something my friend Honeyboy Otis had told me: "If you want to make some money, go play with those white boys. They'll pay you." I saw the guys getting ready to go to work. I knew them all from being there with Percy Sledge and I asked, "Hey, where's Skyman?"

"Oh, he's in Studio B getting ready to do a session."

I walk in and see this skinny little white boy hippie with long straight hair, and I said, "Excuse me, you must be the guy they call Skyman." He looked at me and said, "Yep, and you're Jai Johanny Johanson," and we shook hands. He went to do a session and I set up my drums in a little studio, playing along to albums on headphones. When Duane was free he rolled that [Fender] Twin in, cranked that bad boy up, and that was it, man. As soon as we played together I forgot all about moving to New York City. I moved into Duane's place on the Tennessee River and we just played constantly. Then Berry came and joined us.

Berry Oakley was the bassist in the popular Jacksonville band Second Coming, with a unique, melodic style; his wife-to-be Linda had introduced Berry and Duane in a Jacksonville club. The pair quickly became fast friends and musical admirers of each other. Allman invited Oakley to Muscle Shoals to jam with him and Jaimoe and test the chemistry of his potential rhythm section.

JAIMOE: I was excited when I started playing with Duane and more so when Berry joined us. As soon as the three of us played together, it was just, "Shit. This is all over with." It was like I had found the bass player I had been searching for since my friend Lamar [Williams] had joined the Army. We were playing some wild stuff.

JOHN HAMMOND JR., *guitarist/singer:* I asked Duane how he got so good and he said, "I took speed every day for three years and played every night all night." I think this was partly true and partly apocryphal but he really couldn't get enough. He was just phenomenal.

JAIMOE: Honestly, at the time, there were only a few white people I thought could play music: guys like Stan Getz and Buddy Rich. The biggest problem white musicians had was they were trying to imitate this or that person instead of letting themselves come out. Berry and Duane were themselves and they had strong voices.

It's been said that Duane was at first going to put together a power trio like Jimi Hendrix or Cream, but I would never have been the right guy for that—I was never a power drummer, and that's not what Duane was thinking. Duane had the idea for a different band right away. He was talking about two guitars and two drummers from the start. It was about finding the right guys. Berry was going back and forth between Muscle Shoals and Jacksonville.

SANDLIN: I didn't understand the two-drummer thing and I didn't want to do it. Jaimoe was there when we recorded those original sides for Rick, but I was playing, probably just because Duane and I had the history together and it was easier at that point to do things quickly, but Duane was talking about Jaimoe being in his band and me possibly as well.

JAIMOE: I was there when Duane cut those solo sides, and the reason Johnny played instead of me was simple: he knew how to make a record and I didn't. Johnny didn't really improvise; he learned parts and songs and he played them really well. I could not keep a straight beat and could not play a song exactly the same multiple times in a row.

One day, Duane said to me, "We're leaving. I'm sick of this. Pack up your stuff." We went to St. Louis for a few days so he could see his girl-friend. [*Donna Roosmann, who was soon to be the mother of Duane's daughter, Galadrielle.*] Then we made a beeline to Jacksonville. Duane drove straight through. We got there at two or three in the morning and Duane went around waking people up. People just had to hear that Duane was in town and they started coming around like termites in the spring.

Playing in the Band

*D*UANE'S VISION QUICKLY *began to be realized after he and Jai-moe arrived in Jacksonville during the first week of March 1969. The next two additions to his band were guitarist Dickey Betts, who played with Oakley in Second Coming, and Butch Trucks, the drummer whose group Duane and Gregg had recorded demos with less than a year earlier. With Gregg still in Los Angeles, the Second Coming's Reese Wynans, who would eventually join Stevie Ray Vaughan's Double Trouble, played keyboards. Duane, Oakley, and Betts handled most of the vocals.*

JAIMOE: Duane had been telling me about a lot of people he knew and thought would be good for the band and most of them were there, except Gregory. The whole thing was just about playing music—no agenda, no egos—and it was good.

DICKEY BETTS: It was fun and exciting, and the band just sort of happened. It was supposed to be a three-piece with Duane, Berry, and Jaimoe. Duane had no idea that he would end up with this very differ-ent thing, but he was open to seeing what happened. I was playing with Berry, and Duane and Jaimoe kept coming and sitting in with us and exciting stuff started happening really quickly and naturally. We all felt like we had discovered the very thing that we'd been looking for, even if we didn't know it beforehand. We all knew that something very, very good was happening.

REESE WYNANS, *Second Coming keyboardist:* I had never heard anything like Duane Allman and his slide guitar. He played it like a violin or saxophone. It was just the weirdest instrument and most unbelievable sound and his phrasing was impeccable and his ideas were over the top. When he sat in with us it lifted the whole thing up and I had an immediate, extremely positive reaction, as did everyone else.

JAIMOE: He was always on and up and pulling everyone along.

WYNANS: Sometimes when someone comes and sits in and they're hot shit, they get an attitude. Duane didn't have any of that; there was none of that diva attitude. He was one of us immediately. It became obvious in the jam sessions that something special was going on. We would play for hours and it was incredible. He was a really positive guy— outgoing, giving, and always handing out a lot of really positive thoughts and comments. Just hanging around him was exciting.

HALL: Duane always was an upper. He never had anything but praise for everybody. He was totally confident, but he also always had that little boy, down-home modesty about him. He was a good, good guy, which is why in time the musicians down here all fell in love with him, despite being leery at first.

HAMMOND: Duane was a phenomenal player, but the opposite of a headcutter. He wanted to include everyone and make him sound better. He had supreme confidence but he loved the music more than anything and was not on any kind of ego trip.

THOM DOUCETTE, *harmonica player, Duane confidant, and unofficial member of the ABB:* Duane had his arms wide open, and he was so fucking magnetic. This was a connected guy—connected to the higher order of the world. Just incredibly tuned in, and with absolute self-confidence but no ego. None. It was never about "me." That combination of total self-confidence and lack of ego with that kind of talent and fire is unheard of.

JAIMOE: The day after we got to Jacksonville, Duane took me over to meet Butch and said, "Butch, this is my new drummer, Jai Johanny Johanson. We're gonna jam tonight. Anyone who can be here, be there."

BUTCH TRUCKS: Duane called me when he came back to Jacksonville and was jamming with lots of different people. We played and it just worked and Jaimoe told Duane I was the guy they needed, because he wanted two drummers like James Brown had.

JAIMOE: I asked Duane why he wanted two drummers and he said, "Because Otis Redding and James Brown have two," and I never asked again.

BETTS: Jaimoe was a real good drummer, but more of a pocket guy, and once we all got in there, it was bigger and he wasn't really able to handle the power. It just wasn't his style and the drummer from Second Coming wasn't right. His name was "Nasty Lord John" [Meeks] and he played like Ginger Baker, hardly ever playing a straight beat. We needed Butch, who had that drive and strength, freight train, meat-and-potatoes thing. It set Jaimoe up perfectly.

RICHARD PRICE, *Florida bassist; played with Betts and Oakley and was there for the Jacksonville jams that birthed the Allman Brothers Band:* Jaimoe was always a great drummer in Duane's mind and that was clear from the minute they arrived together in Jacksonville. Butch was well known as a strong in-the-pocket player, while Jaimoe was more of an embellisher. He had great stick control and jazz chops and could do outside-the-box tempos up against the pocket.

AVERY: Duane loved Jai and Jai loved Duane. They were brothers first and more than anyone else.

PRICE: We had these big jams with a lot of drummers coming and going, but things started happening with Jaimoe and Butch as soon as they played together. Butch was doing the really strong foot/snare thing driving the beat and Jaimoe would do all these strange swells and fills in the open spaces that Butch left. They're not that similar and they could hear where to complement one another, which is what made them a great rhythm section. Right out of the box they listened really close to each other and tried to stay out of each other's way. They formed this strange symbiotic thing and melded into a terrific unit. Over a series of nights you could see something very substantial developing there.

BETTS: All of a sudden the trio had five pieces. We all were smart enough to say, "This guy's special" about one another.

AVERY: I'm agnostic, so I don't think I can call it the hand of God, but these people were meant to be together. I don't know how that all happened, but it had to happen.

DOUCETTE: You take any one of the guys out and the whole thing doesn't exist.

TRUCKS: I don't think Duane wanted me in the band. I fit musically but I was a bundle of insecurity and he didn't want that. He was such a strong person—very confident and totally sure of himself—and that's the kind of people he wanted around him.

BETTS: It says a lot that Duane's hero was Muhammad Ali. He had Ali's type of supreme confidence. If you weren't involved in what he thought was the big picture, he didn't have time for you. A lot of people really didn't like him for that. It's not that he was aggressive; it was more a super-positive, straight-ahead, I've-got-work-to-do kind of thing. If you didn't get it, see you later. He always seemed like he was charging ahead and it took a lot of energy to be with him.

DOUCETTE: I couldn't get enough of that Duane energy. If Duane put out his hand, you had a hand. There was no bullshit about him at all. None.

GREGG ALLMAN: My brother was a real pistol. He was a hell of a person . . . a firecracker. He knew how to push people's buttons and bring out the best.

SANDLIN: He was a personality you only see once in a lifetime. He could inspire you and challenge you, with eye contact, smiles . . . little things. It would just make you better and I think anyone who ever played with him would tell you the same thing. You knew he had your back, and that was the best feeling in the world.

TRUCKS: One day we were jamming on a shuffle going nowhere so I started pulling back and Duane whipped around, looked me in the eyes, and played this lick way up the neck like a challenge. My first reaction was to back up, but he kept doing it, which had everyone looking at me like the whole flaccid nature of this jam was my fault. The third time I got really angry and started pounding the drums like I was hitting him upside his head and the jam took off and I forgot about being self-conscious and started playing music, and he smiled at me, as if to say, "Now that's more like it."

It was like he reached inside me and flipped a switch and I've never been insecure about my drumming again. It was an absolute epiphany; it hit me like a ton of bricks. I swear if that moment had not happened I would probably have spent the past thirty years as a teacher. Duane was capable of reaching inside people and pulling out the best. He made us all realize that music will never be great if everyone doesn't give it all they have, and we all took on that attitude: Why bother to play if you're not going all in?

WYNANS: Dickey was the hottest guitar player in the area, the guy that everyone looked up to and wanted to emulate. Then Duane came and started sitting in with us and he was more mature and more fully formed, with total confidence, an incredible tone and that unearthly slide playing. But he and Dickey complemented each other—they didn't try to outgun one another—and the chemistry was obvious right away. It was just amazing that the two best lead guitarists around were teaming up. They were both willing to take chances rather than returning to parts they knew they could nail, and everything they tried worked.

PRICE: Dickey was already considered one of the hottest guitar players in the state of Florida. He was smoking in the Second Coming and always had a great ability to arrange.

WYNANS: I remember one time Duane came up to me with this sense of wonder and said, "Reese, I just learned how to play the highest note in the world. You put the slide on the harmonic and slide it up and all of a sudden it's birds chirping." And, of course, that became his famous "bird call." He was always playing and pushing and sharing his ideas and passions.

JAIMOE: Duane had talked about a lot of guitar players and when I heard some of them I said, "That dude can't tote your guitar case" and he was surprised. He loved jamming with everyone.

DOUCETTE: None of them could hold Duane's case except Betts.

PRICE: Berry basically told Duane that he would only form a new band with him if Dickey could be in it, too. After these jams, I don't think it was an issue because Duane and Dickey just hooked up in incredible ways. Their styles were so different and, like Jaimoe and Butch, they were able to complement one another.

LINDA OAKLEY, *Berry Oakley's wife:* Berry really liked playing with Dickey and felt bad about breaking up the Second Coming, but I don't recall him making any demands. It was up to Duane who would be in the new band. Berry had met Duane and thought, "This is my path right here."

JAIMOE: Duane loved guitar players. I only knew two people Duane didn't like: Jimmy Page and Sonny Sharrock. He played on the Herbie Mann *Push Push* sessions [in 1971] with Sonny and he hated him and the way nothing he played was ever really clear. He also didn't like Led Zeppelin, though I don't know why. Anyhow, Duane liked Dickey and the two of them clicked and started working on songs and parts immediately.

WYNANS: Berry was very dedicated to jamming and deeply into the Dead and the Airplane and these psychedelic approaches and always playing that music for us—and it was pretty exotic stuff to our ears, because there were no similar bands in the area. Dickey was a great blues player with a rock edge; he could play all these great Lonnie Mack licks, for instance. And then Duane arrived, and he was just on another planet. The power of all of it combined was immediately obvious.

BETTS: All of us were playing in good little bands, but Duane was the guy who had Phil Walden—Otis Redding's manager!—on his tail, anxious to get his career moving. And Duane was hip enough to say,

"Hey, Phil, instead of a three-piece, I have a six-piece and we need a hundred thousand dollars for equipment." And Phil was hip enough to have faith in this guy. If there was no Phil Walden and no Duane Allman there would have been no Allman Brothers Band.

The unnamed group began regularly playing free shows in Jacksonville's Willow Branch Park, joined by a large, rotating crop of musicians. They went on to play in several local parks.

PRICE: It was Berry's idea to play for free in the parks for the hippies.

TRUCKS: The six of us had this incredible jam and Duane went to the door and said, "If anyone wants to leave this room they're going to have to fight their way out." We were playing all the time and doing these free concerts in the park and we all knew we had something great going, but the keyboard player was Reese Wynans, not Gregg, and we didn't really have a singer.

Duane said, "I need to call my baby brother." I said, "Are you sure?" Because he was upset that Gregg had stayed out in L.A. to do his solo thing and I was upset that he had left when I thought we had something going with the 31st of February project the year before. He said, "I'm pissed at him, too, but he's the only one strong enough to sing with this band." And, of course, he was right. Whatever his issues, Gregg had the voice and he had the songs that we needed.

PHIL WALDEN, *original ABB manager; founder/president of Capricorn Records*: They had this great instrumental presence but no real vocalist. Berry, Dickey, and Duane were all doing a little singing. That was a lot of a little singing and no singer. So Duane called Gregg and asked him to come down.

JAIMOE: Duane was talking about Gregory being the singer in the band from the beginning. Very early on, Duane told me, "There's only one guy who can sing in this band and that's my baby brother." He told me that he was a womanizer. He said Gregg broke girls' hearts and all the rest of it, but that he's a hell of a singer and songwriter—which obviously was accurate and is to this day.

LINDA OAKLEY: We were all sitting in our kitchen late one night after one of these jams. They were all so psyched about what they were building and Duane said, "We've got to get my brother here, out of that bad situation. He's a great singer and songwriter and he's the guy who can finish this thing."

WYNANS: For a while, we were all just jamming and guys from other bands would be there singing, or Berry would sing, Duane would sing a little, "Rhino" Reinhardt would sing. [*Guitarist Larry "Rhino" Reinhardt, who was in the Second Coming and went on to play with Iron Butterfly.*] Then there was talk of this becoming a real band, and Duane was talking about getting his brother here to sing. Everyone was excited about it, but I knew Gregg played keyboards and figured that might be the end of it for me. It was personally disappointing, because the band was really going somewhere and obviously had a chance to do something great. It was kind of a drag but this was Duane's brother, so what can you say? You wish them good luck and move on to the next thing. It was a thrill to be a part of.

BETTS: We had all been bandleaders and we knew what we now had.

Gregg was still in Los Angeles, having stayed there after the breakup of the Hour Glass. Liberty Records had recorded and released a second album with Gregg backed by session musicians after Duane, Sandlin, and the rest of the band left California.

ALLMAN: I didn't have a band, but I was under contract to a label that had me cut two terrible records, including one with these studio cats in L.A. They had me do a blues version of Tammy Wynette's "D-I-V-O-R-C-E," which can't be done. It was really horrible. I hope you never hear it. They told us what to wear, what to play, everything. They dictated everything, including putting us in those clown suits. I hated it, but what are you gonna do when they're taking care of all your expenses? You end up feeling like some kind of kept man and it was fuckin' awful.

I was excited when my brother called and said he was putting a new band together and wanted me to join. I just wrote a note that said, "I'm gone. If you want to sue my ass, come on after me."

BETTS: We were all telling Duane to call Gregg. We knew we needed him. They were fighting or something, which they did all the time—just normal brotherly stuff.

JAIMOE: Duane finally called Gregg when he got everyone that he thought would work, because he needed to give him as much time as possible to resolve the contract issues with Liberty. Once everyone else was in place, Duane called him and said, "You've got to hear this band that I'm putting together. You need to be the singer."

KIM PAYNE, *one of the ABB's original crew members:* I met Gregory in L.A. when I was working for another band that played with him, and we became good friends, running around, staying with chicks until we got kicked out, and drinking cheap wine. Almost every day we were together, Gregg would bitch about his brother. He'd say, "He's calling me again asking him to join his band, but there ain't no way because I cannot get along with my brother in a band." He said that to me countless times.

LANDAU: When I was in Muscle Shoals I was sitting in the office with Duane, Rick, and Phil, and Duane picked up the phone, dialed a number, and said, "Brother, it's time for us to play together again." I was a fly on the wall and could obviously only hear one end of the conversation, but it seemed very positive.

ALLMAN: My brother only called me one time and I jumped on it.

JOHN McEUEN: As I recall, Duane kept calling Gregg, saying, "You got to get down here. The band has never sounded better." He called enough times and Gregg went. I have to give Duane credit for having the vision to do this thing. I know the L.A. years were not great ones for them, but I think it was something they had to go through to discover their path.

PAYNE: Gregg kept telling me, "I'm not going down and getting involved with that." You have to remember he was coming off a very bad band experience; he hated the way the Hour Glass went and how it ended up and he may have connected that with being Duane's fault. I think he also felt like Duane and the other guys turned on him and blamed him for staying in L.A., when he thought he had to.

SANDLIN: It kind of bothered me that Gregg stayed out in L.A., but I didn't know if he wanted to, or was being forced by management.

PAYNE: At the same time, he was looking at his future—he was driving an old Chevy with a fender held on by antenna wire. Whenever we ran out of money, he'd go down and sell a song. We were living hand to mouth.

ALLMAN: My brother said he was tired of being a robot on the staff down in Muscle Shoals, even though he had made some progress, and gotten a little known playing with great people like Aretha and Wilson Pickett. He wanted to take off and do his own thing. He said, "I'm ready to get back on the stage, and I got this killer band together. We got two drummers, a great bass player, and a hell of a lead guitar player, too." And I said, "Well, what do you do?" And he said, "Wait'll you get here and I'll show you."

I didn't know that he had learned to play slide so well. I thought he was out of his mind, but I was doing nothing, going nowhere. My brother sent me a ticket, but I knew he didn't have the money, so I put it in my back pocket, stuck out my thumb on the San Bernardino Freeway, and got a ride all the way to Jacksonville, Florida—and it was a bass player I got a ride from.

PAYNE: I know that Gregg remembers hitchhiking across the country, but the thing is, I'm the guy who drove him to the airport.

McEUEN: My brother bought a Chevy Corvair for Gregg to drive around L.A.—the most unsafe car ever invented. One day Gregg comes by the house, a little duplex in Laurel Canyon, looking for my brother, who wasn't there. He said, "Hey, John, the man pulled me over. You know how they are. He doesn't believe this is my car and is going to impound it. I got to take the pink slip to the judge." So I said, "I know where the pink slip is." I gave it to him and he took it and sold that car and bought a one-way ticket to Jacksonville. Maybe I'm responsible for the Allman Brothers Band! Gregg came back about six years later when the Brothers were playing the Forum, and gave my brother a check for the car.

TRUCKS: I don't know how he got there but a few days after Duane said he was calling Gregg, there was a knock on the door and there he was.

ALLMAN: I walked into rehearsal on March 26, 1969, and they played me the track they had worked up to Muddy Waters's "Trouble No More" and it blew me away. It was so intense.

BETTS: Gregg was floored when he heard us. We were really blowing; we'd been playing these free shows for a few weeks by that point.

ALLMAN: I got my brother aside and said, "I don't know if I can cut this. I don't know if I'm good enough." And he starts in on me: "You little punk, I told these people all about you and you don't come in here and let me down." Then I snatched the words out of his hand and said, "Count it off, let's do it." And with that, I did my damnedest. I'd never heard or sung this song before, but by God I did it. I shut my eyes and sang, and at the end of that there was just a long silence. At that moment we knew what we had. Duane kinda pissed me off and embarrassed me into singing my guts out. He knew which buttons to push.

The group played their first gig on March 30, 1969, at the Jacksonville Armory. Gregg had been in town for four days. The ABB on stage, with Dickey and Duane on guitar.

MIKE CALLAHAN, *one of the band's first crew members:* The original name of the band was Beelzebub. That's what the guys were calling it, or just "the band." When we played that first gig in Jacksonville, there was no name. It was just, "The boys are playing."

PRICE: We did a few shows with my band the Load, the Second Coming, and then what was becoming the Allman Brothers. Berry and Dickey would do double duty. At one of the first shows after Gregg arrived, Duane said, "I'm glad you really liked that. This is a new band. We don't have a name but we might be calling it Beelzebub." I don't think anyone liked it and it lasted about five minutes . . .

JAIMOE: Beelzebub was one name that was talked about, but it was never "the name." Lots of things were talked about. I do remember Jerry Wexler being worried because he said every brother band he had ever worked with had great conflicts over everything.

TRUCKS: I think we all knew that Beelzebub wasn't it, but we were at a loss as to what it should be—what *it* was. Phil Walden came up with the Allman Brothers due to the fact that Duane was the driving force. Duane absolutely would not allow it to be called the Duane Allman Band, but once Gregg joined the band, Phil sold the Brothers concept. Duane was at first very much against it. He felt that this was a band of equals and he did not want himself and his brother to become the focus of attention.

RED DOG, *early crew member:* The Allman Brothers Band name really was because of Duane, and Gregg used to say, "I'm lucky my name is Allman."

Joseph "Red Dog" Campbell was one of the band's first hardcore fans. A disabled Marine vet just home from Vietnam, he fell in love with Duane's playing after hearing the band play for free in a Jacksonville park, was drawn in by the guitarist's charisma, and begged for a job. Duane told him he could set up the drums, and Red Dog began hanging around the group, actually donating his monthly disability checks to the cause. He moved with the band to Macon and became their fourth crew member, hired as a driver and drum tech once the band started touring in earnest. He would remain with the group for more than thirty years.

JAIMOE: Red Dog loved Duane and started hanging around when we were playing in the park in Jacksonville. He was a vet who could score you a woman or some weed or whatever. He just wanted to be a part of what we were doing, so Duane said, "Go set up the drums." I would tell him to just take mine out of the case and I would set them up and he'd be kind of offended and ask to set them up and I'd say, "It's like waxing your car—some things you want to do yourself." After about six months, I said, "Go ahead and set them up," and he was so happy. Red Dog was a good man and he loved the band.

Georgia on a Fast Train

Y MAY 1, *the band had relocated to Macon, Georgia, where Walden was establishing Capricorn Records; his new band would be the label's first act. Walden's dual role as label head and band manager would eventually cause the members to complain about a serious conflict of interest, becoming the source of much rancor. Initially, however, it seemed to make everything much easier.*

The band moved together into Twiggs Lyndon's apartment on 309 College Street, which became the communal home of all six band members, as well as their original crew of Mike Callahan, Kim Payne, and Red Dog. Lyndon had worked for Walden as a trusted road manager of soul acts like Arthur Conley and Percy Sledge and was now given the job of shepherding this new band. Living on very little money, the group quickly found a patron of sorts in Louise Hudson, cook and proprietor of the H&H Soul Food Restaurant.

PAYNE: When I dropped Gregg off at the airport, he said, "If this turns out to be a good thing, I'll give you a call." I said, "Yeah, right," and never expected to hear from him again, but a few weeks later, he called me on the pay phone of the flophouse where I was staying and said, "This is just going to be an ass-kicking band and we need you. Come on down."

I didn't have any money so I asked if he could get me one of those plane tickets and he said he didn't think so. Eventually, he said the best he could do was some gas money so I could ride my bike. He sent me 50 dollars. I spent $37.50 getting my bike repaired and took off on the most insane three-thousand-mile trip anyone has ever taken. The $13.50 I had left got me to my parents' house in Alabama, where I almost collapsed in the driveway. My mother gave me five dollars to make it to Macon. I arrived at the pad, walked into a living room lined with end-to-end mattresses, collapsed on one of them, and slept for twenty-four hours.

RED DOG: We had mattresses across the floor and we had this Coke machine that had three beer selections and one Coke and it cost you a quarter.

A.J. LYNDON, *Twiggs's younger brother, ABB crew member 1973–76:* Everyone called that place the "Hippie Crash Pad." It was actually Twiggs's apartment and then everyone moved in as they arrived in town. One wall was painted purple, another bright yellow.

TRUCKS: We all moved into Twiggs's apartment when we arrived. He had the walls painted various psychedelic colors, including one that was squares of different colors. We bought some mattresses and threw them down and that was all that we ever had in there, along with the Coke machine.

A.J. LYNDON: I was just a kid in high school and I would go over there at lunchtime and they'd all be sleeping. I remember seeing a little blond head on Jaimoe's chest and thinking, "Well, this is different." I'd get my mom to give me four quarters for lunch, go over there, step over bodies sleeping end to end, get four PBRs out of the Coke machine, drink them for lunch, and head back to school.

TRUCKS: There were nine of us living in this little one-bedroom apartment, which made it real easy to spend all day rehearsing.

PAYNE: One of the first things I noticed was that no matter what Gregg said about Duane when he was away from him, when I saw them together, their love and closeness was immediately apparent.

RED DOG: Duane and Gregg lived separate lives and I don't think Duane had to ride herd on Gregg. I can only recall one time with Duane actually screaming and hollering at Gregg.

HAMMOND: What I admired about Duane is he was fearless. He had this vision of a mixed-race band in the Deep South in 1969. He was very adamant about including everyone. He didn't care what anyone said. He had his own vision of what was the right thing to do and he did it.

MAMA LOUISE HUDSON, *cook and owner, H&H Soul Food Restaurant:* Macon was just barely integrated. We didn't really have any white customers. And nobody around here had seen guys who looked like them. I had not. A lot of the white folk around here did not approve of them long-haired boys, or of them always having a black guy with them.

PAYNE: Having Jaimoe in the band was a very big issue in 1969 in the Deep South, where segregation was still pretty strict. That was one of the things that tightened up the brotherhood. It was us against the world, especially when we were traveling. Day-to-day life, you can live on your own, in your own world, but not on the road, where you have to stop and eat and sleep and get gas—where you have all this exposure to society. The long hair was enough to start shit in most places, but Jaimoe . . . that was enough to spark the gasoline.

COL. BRUCE HAMPTON, *founder of the Hampton Grease Band, who played many early shows with the ABB:* It was a different world. It was life or death. You'd stop at a gas station and you'd wonder if you were going to die. That's no joke. If you had long hair, you were a target.

MAMA LOUISE: One day I looked out the window and saw these long-haired boys walking around, looking in. Finally, Dickey and Berry came in. Dickey told Berry, "Ask that lady for some food."

He said, "I don't know nothing about her. You ask the lady." He said, "I don't know her. You ask the lady."

They got embarrassed and walked out. Then they came back in and started up again and I just said, "May I help you all, darlings?"

And one of them said, "May we please have two plates of food? We don't have any money, but we're going out on the road and when we come back, we'll pay you." I often helped people who didn't have no money, so I gave it to them, and they did come back and pay when they

The band at the H and H restaurant, 1969.

returned. Most people who said that never came back. Then they did that again, another time or two, and then one day they asked for those two plates and I said, "Well, there's five of y'all. Take five plates."

And they said, "Oh, thank you, ma'am. When we come back, we'll pay you." And they did—and we just got to be friends. They always treated me real respectful.

Fueled by Mama Louise's soul food and a steady diet of various drugs, the group began rehearsing for hours a day at Capricorn's new studio and rehearsal space. By July, Johnny Sandlin, Gregg and Duane's old Allman Joys and Hour Glass bandmate, was overseeing the studio.

The Allman Brothers Band was performing regularly around Macon, beginning with their first local show, May 2 at the College Discotheque. They often drove eighty miles north to perform free shows in Atlanta's Piedmont Park, where they grew their fan base and continued to perfect a unique, blues-based sound.

TRUCKS: We were busting to get out of that warehouse where we were rehearsing all the time and play for people. We loaded ourselves and our equipment into our Econoline and what other rides we could glom and headed to Atlanta. We went straight to Piedmont Park and found a perfect spot to set up. It was a large flat space at the top of some stairs with electrical outlets within reach. We didn't ask permission, we just set up and started pouring out all of this music.

There were a few hundred people within earshot and they all came running. Apparently many of them also went running to get friends and before long those few hundred turned into a few thousand. We played and played and it was amazing. It was church, it was electrifying, it was inspiring. It was so much fun that, if we hadn't formed the brotherhood of music before, that day galvanized it.

HAMPTON: They started coming up and playing these free shows in Piedmont Park and there started to be more and more of a local following. From the first time, they were just fantastic, and Duane especially was very supportive of many, many musicians and bands, including ours.

TRUCKS: The next Sunday we went back and there was a shitload more folks than were there the week before, as well as a couple of other Atlanta bands that wanted to play. This grew into a weekly event that went from that little place to a big flatbed stage set up on the end of a very large field that someone provided complete with a massive generator. The crowd grew to the level of around ten thousand after a few weeks, and a lot of other bands started coming and playing as well.

The band shared everything, including drugs, and legends have grown about the importance of psychedelic mushrooms. The Wonder Graphics team of Jim Flournoy Holmes and W. David Powell designed a mushroom logo for the band, which every original member had tattooed on their leg in 1971. The psychedelic 'shroom thus took on a legendary, mystical status, credited with helping the band forge both their music and their brotherhood. Not all agree with the drug's importance.

JAIMOE: To me, the mushrooms didn't really play that big a part in anything. It was just a cool thing that became a logo. We all lived together and I often stayed across the hall with this nice lady . . . , because the pad was too crazy to sleep. One morning, Duane came over and knocked and he was bouncing off the wall—full of energy, as he always was, but more so. He said, "What's up, my little chocolate drop?" He often called me that.

I said, "Nothing. Just waiting around until it's time to practice." And he said, "You want one of these?" He had a little container of something that I thought were blackberries, which were a kind of speed we took with some regularity. I said I was all right and he laughed and said, "Okay," and dashed off on his bike.

TRUCKS: Someone picked up a massive bag of psilocybin and it ended up getting us all in a very strange frame of mind.

JAIMOE: I went over to the pad to use the commode and sitting on the back of it was a little bottle of those pills—anytime someone got a little something they stored it there so that if the police came it could be flushed away. I looked at them and thought, "This is what Duane had. The way he was bouncing around, I'm gonna give it a try," and I popped three of them. God damn! They were psilocybin tablets and they slowly came on. They were real natural and earthy and pleasant, but I should not have taken three.

We got something to eat at Mama Louise's and went to practice like we did every day, but rehearsal was a waste. It had to be canceled because we had all taken some of those things. Butch couldn't play the drums because he said they were flying away. Gregory wasn't really into psychedelics so maybe he didn't take any, but the rest of us were flying, so we just called off practice and the day finally came to what it should have been: hanging out. There's been a lot of stories told about how we had this incredible jam, but we couldn't even play.

TRUCKS: We could not play on that stuff, which I don't think were real mushrooms. It was very, very intensely psychedelic. We had that failed rehearsal and I think that was the incident that led to us imposing a rule that we'd all stay straight until after rehearsal, because we knew we had work to do. After we'd come back, we'd take them and start raising hell all night. We'd be out front playing corkball at two or three in the morning. [*Corkball is a variant of baseball using a small ball and bat.*]

W. DAVID POWELL, *partner in Wonder Graphics:* I am pretty sure that the mushroom logo was our first paying job for Capricorn. I can't remember ever being given any real "art direction" by the label or the band. They certainly didn't specifically request a mushroom. It seems as though it didn't require much of a flight to land on the subject. Drug culture was pervasive throughout the music industry and the "hippie movement." Really, the Brothers were no more identified with it than other bands. The mushroom we rendered also has a strong reference to male and female genitalia.

TRUCKS: The real mystery is how we avoided ending up in jail or just having serious problems during that time and I can offer no explanations. There were five or six occupied apartments in the building with the Hippie Crash Pad and you would expect they would call the police on us because we were constantly raising hell at three or four in the morning, but they all just moved out. We came home from rehearsal one day and there was this family moving out. We lined up in the hallways and applauded, and boy they were pissed off. That guy wanted to kill us. I don't know how we got away with it.

I know that after we hit it big the police [received a memo] that basically said, "Keep these guys out of jail. Just keep them from killing themselves, they're bringing too much money into the local economy." But how we got away with it at the beginning when we had no money or influence and no one knew who we were . . . I have no idea.

While the band focused on making music and building their brotherhood, Twiggs Lyndon tended to their day-to-day business, making sure they made their gigs and that the gear was always top-notch and ready to go. Lyndon was a Macon native and a trusted Walden employee. It was Lyndon whom Walden sent to Wisconsin to identify Otis Redding's body following the December 10, 1967, plane crash that killed him and four members of his band.

BUNKY ODOM, *Vice president, Phil Walden and Associates; day-to-day management contact:* Twiggs Lyndon was the most intense, detail-oriented person I've ever met in my life. He came to the band through Phil Walden, whom he had been working for. He was somebody that Phil could absolutely trust. Twiggs and Duane understood each other and

Macon, Georgia, Spring 1969.

the intensity. Duane surrounded himself with good people and Twiggs fit right in with him.

JOHN LYNDON, *brother of Twiggs:* Twiggs was so excited from the moment he heard Duane. He said, "These guys love to play. It's all about the music." He had grown disillusioned with the R and B acts, who he said would walk off stage the second their allotted time was over. If they were contracted for forty-five minutes, they would not play forty-six.

JAIMOE: I'm not sure, but I think it was Twiggs who came up with the idea of "the Allman Brothers Band."

HAMPTON: To me, they were as good then as they ever got. They were on fire. The intent and the essence were there. It was just pure as hell.

You could feel the purity and the fire and intensity: Nobody was playing checkers or talking business. This was music for music's sake. The chemistry of putting all those guys together took them to a different level.

RED DOG: I said from the beginning that the band would be bigger than the Beatles. The music was just super hot. A live gig in the early days of the Allman Brothers was smoking.

Gregg was initially the band's sole songwriter, which was part of the reason they remade blues songs like "Trouble No More" and "One Way Out"; they needed more material. The band also began playing soaring, open-ended tunes like "Mountain Jam," an extended improv built off the melody of "There Is a Mountain" by the Scottish folksinger Donovan, which they were playing by May 1969 and which continued to be an open-ended highlight of their shows, even as their original repertoire quickly grew.

WALDEN: Aside from a true vocal presence, Gregg brought these really important foundation songs that the band was built around.

ALLMAN: They asked if I had any songs and I showed them twenty-two and they'd just go, "OK, what else you got?" They rejected them all and I got up to about the twelfth one and said, "Here's one I wrote on a Hammond organ" and that was "Dreams." Then I showed them "It's Not My Cross to Bear" and I was in like Flynn, but they told me to get busy writing.

McEUEN: I recorded Gregg's first demo of "Cross to Bear." It was in his apartment in L.A. I dragged over this giant ConcertTone tape recorder and said, "Hey, you want to hear what that song you just wrote sounded like?" He played it on a Wurlitzer piano with bass, drums, and guitar behind him and I thought it was incredible; to me, it was his first truly original direction. It was about half the tempo the Brothers eventually recorded it at, just almost painfully slow and very cool.

I had never heard a song like that, a very adult-sounding song from such a young person. It sounded as good as something you'd hear from Scrapper Blackwell or Robert Johnson. The lyrics were incredible, and that voice! It was probably the shittiest recording you could do, just totally bare in the room, but it's a master vocal. It was the sound of Gregg really finding himself.

ALLMAN: I remember years before having heard that Steve Winwood wrote "Gimme Some Loving" when he was sixteen, and that used to piss me off when I was struggling to write. Now I finally got it going.

After they told me to get busy, within the next five days I wrote "Whipping Post," "Black-Hearted Woman," and a few others. I stayed up night and day and got on a real roll there. That was a great summer, where I wrote one after another. Oakley had an old blue piano that he bought from some church for like fourteen bucks. I think he had to pay us more to carry it than he paid for the thing. And I wrote a lot of songs on that thing, let me tell you.

TRUCKS: Gregg would just come in with completed songs and we would work them up at rehearsal, and sometimes add whole instrumental sections.

ALLMAN: Before that, I'd only messed around a little on the electric piano, and I had a little Vox organ in the Allman Joys because the English guys had 'em, but I had mainly played rhythm guitar. That was my instrument, but the Allman Brothers had too many guitars, so they blindfolded me, took me in this room, sat me down, took the blindfold off and there sat a brand-new, 1969 B-3 Hammond and a 122-RV Leslie, with a few joints on it, and they said, "OK, we'll see you in a few days! Good luck! We'll bring you food and check back with you now and then. Learn how to play this thing."

That's only a slight exaggeration. The truth is, my brother knew I really, deep down, always wanted a Hammond. I always admired them when I saw them with blues bands and whatnot. But then I stayed up day and night, hour after hour, learning how to really play it.

BETTS: Duane and Gregg had a real "purist" blues thing together, but Oakley and I in our band would take a standard blues and re-arrange it. We were really trying to push the envelope. We loved the blues, but we wanted to play in a rock style, like what Cream and Hendrix were doing. Jefferson Airplane was also a big influence on us; Phil Lesh and Jack Casady were Oakley's favorite bassists. We liked to take some of that experimental stuff and put a harder melodic edge to it.

Duane was smart enough to see what ingredients were missing from both [of our previous] bands. We didn't have enough of the true, purist blues, and he didn't have enough of the avant-garde, psychedelic approach to the blues. So he tried to put the two sounds together, and that was the first step in finding the sound of the Allman Brothers Band. When the two things collided, by the grace of God it was something special. You can't say someone conceived of it all. It just happened and we all played a big part.

JAIMOE: We never tried to sound like anyone else and were always forging our own sound. I know for a fact that one of the greatest things that the Allman Brothers did was open that door for a lot of musicians, who thought, "If they can do that, we can do that." A whole lot of musicians wanted to do something original but were afraid to really try.

GARY ROSSINGTON, *Lynyrd Skynyrd founder/guitarist:* You can go way back to the Allman Joys playing in Daytona and they were different and a step above. They were unbelievable, playing the Yardbirds, Beatles, and Stones when everyone else was playing the Ventures and "Mustang Sally." They were like rock stars—skinny guys with long blond hair and leather jackets—and Duane and Gregg could both play the hell out of their guitars. We'd just stand there with our mouths open. They were that much better than everyone else, so it did not surprise me at all when they reappeared with the Allman Brothers Band and were so good. It was like we had been waiting.

Me and Allen [Collins, Skynyrd guitarist and co-founder] would go stand right in front of Duane. He was mesmerizing, and it's hard to describe the impact it had on us as young guitarists to stand there and see that guy play. They were all just tearing it up.

JAIMOE: The reason that Duane and Dickey played the way they did was because of who they had playing behind them, which was Butch and me. We wrote the book on double drumming, and we did things differently than anyone else—and then you had Berry, who was a guitar player who started playing bass because he had a chance to get a gig [with pop singer Tommy Roe] and get out of Chicago and onto the road. Nobody played bass like Berry. He, Butch, and I were just as important as Dickey or Duane in terms of what was going on in that band. That was fully appreciated when Duane was around.

RED DOG: Butch and Jaimoe and Dickey and Duane each played together like no one else ever had to my ears. You put those two combinations—drums and guitars—together with Oak moving around all of them, weaving musically and physically, roaming all over the stage and stomping his foot, and the results were magical and powerful. Then you have Gregg over there wailing away, which was just the icing on the cake. The combination of all this was religious—very spiritual and very deep.

JAIMOE: No one else was doing something similar to what Butch and I did. I had never heard the Grateful Dead until we did some gigs with them. We just played and played and worked stuff out that way.

TRUCKS: Jaimoe and I studied a bit of what [Bill] Kreutzmann and Mickey [Hart] were doing in the Dead, but it was much more contrived than what we did. I'm not criticizing, because it worked for them really well, but not for us. Our styles mesh in a way where we don't talk about it. We don't work it out. Jaimoe plays what he wants to play, I play what I want to play, and it just works.

JAIMOE: When we got to Jacksonville I lived over at Butch's house. My drums were set up in there, along with Gregory's organ once he finally came. I would sit in there and start practicing, Butch would come in, and we'd just play. We never said, "You play this part and I'll play that one."

Butch Trucks.

Living together in Macon, a new city, the group and their road crew forged an intense brotherhood, rehearsing for hundreds of hours and hanging out endlessly, as they continued to play local gigs. The group spent hours hanging out together and alone in Rose Hill, a hilly, Civil War–era cemetery overlooking the Ocmulgee River.

BETTS: Rose Hill is a beautiful, peaceful old place on the Ocmulgee River looking over the railroad tracks—trains would come by every now and then and rattle you. And there was an old part that was well kept and beautiful and had graves dating back to the 1800s. I know it sounds sappy romantic, but I would go down there day after day to the same spot and meditate and hang out and play my guitar because it was so quiet and peaceful.

The Allman Brothers Band's first performances outside the South were two nights opening for the Velvet Underground at the Boston Tea Party on May 30 and 31, 1969. Led Zeppelin had played their first Boston shows the preceding three nights.

DON LAW, *Tea Party manager:* That whole thing was really an off-shoot of my friendship with Jon Landau, who wrote for *Crawdaddy* and *Rolling Stone* and became good friends with Ahmet Ertegun and Jerry Wexler. They told him they had a relationship with Otis Redding's ex-manager to start a label in Macon, Georgia, and the first band included a guy who had done great session work in Muscle Shoals. They wanted to get them some exposure in the Northeast and Jon said, "Let me call my friend Don Law, who has the Boston Tea Party." Jon called me and said, "Ahmet and Jerry are really enthusiastic and feel this band has promise." I said, "Fine, let's bring them up."

LANDAU: Phil actually told me about the Allman Brothers and asked for help in getting them some exposure in the Northeast. I recommended them to Don, saying, "This guy Duane Allman is great. I don't know the band, but I'm sure it's very good."

They were still totally unknown up there when they played the Tea Party. Phil came up and he got Frank Barsalona, the head of Premier Talent, which was *the* rock and roll agency, to come up to check them out, which was something he did quite often. Phil wanted them to have that kind of agent.

LAW: We had them come up as support and the first thing available was the two nights with the Velvet Underground. It was not a great musical fit, but the Velvets were very popular in Boston, so we did get them a weekend in front of two sold-out crowds.

LANDAU: It wasn't them at their best. It didn't click. I knew when the set was going on that it was good but not great—that they could do better. I had led Frank and Don to believe that they were going to be knocked on their asses and it wasn't happening.

Afterwards, Frank, Phil, Don, and I went out. Frank was a great diplomat, with a very smooth style. Phil was a likably egotistical guy who believed in himself and had a charming way. Frank was saying that he sees potential but it's not quite there. He said, "Why don't I see what other shows I can get for them while they're up here?" They are going round and round and Phil was slightly defeated. Then he just said, "I would like you to work with this band. Do you want to or not?" Frank was not the kind of guy people spoke to in that way. I was amazed—both taken back and impressed—at how direct Phil was.

Wanting to put them on a more appropriate bill, Law booked the Allman Brothers Band for three nights opening for Dr. John on June 19–21. Unable to afford lodging, the band took over a squat, with many members also staying with Law at his apartment. Law, who has remained a major lynchpin of the Boston music scene for 40-plus years, helped the Allmans establish themselves in the market by playing free shows at the Boston and Cambridge commons during the long wait between Tea Party gigs.

JAIMOE: We stayed some nights at the crib of the promoter, sleeping on the floor, on whatever beds he had. A lot of it was just sitting up all night talking and listening to records. That's basically what we did wherever we went—them playing records for us and us playing records for them.

LAW: It was really exhilarating. I think it's the only band that I had live in my apartment. I certainly had friendly relationships with most bands we presented, but this was different and it was one of the great experiences of my life. We were all young and ready for anything and fueled by passion for the music.

JAIMOE: The way we lived, going around meeting all these great people who loved music like we did and sitting up listening and rapping about it, it was just the greatest thing in the world, man. It was like having your masters degree and you're working on your PhD—and you're doing it with Einstein. That was the Allman Brothers Band. We just hadn't got there yet. We were on the path, but we hadn't figured out what $E=MC^2$ was.

LAW: One night they all got the itch to rehearse in the middle of the night and wanted to get into the club but couldn't find me. Someone got the brilliant idea to go over to [progressive rock radio station] WBCN and put out an All Points Bulletin for me. They got the on-air guy to announce that the Allman Brothers Band was looking for Don Law, this is an APB, please meet them at the club. And it worked! Someone I knew heard it and found me and I met them and unlocked the club for them to rehearse.

TRUCKS: We had taken some kind of poison and we were up raging all night long. We were squatting in a real slum, with no electricity, no furniture, no hot water, floors covered thick in dirt. One of the roadies had talked to the girl across the way and she slipped an extension cord through our window so we could put on some music and her husband came home and saw that cord and just raised hell. He ripped it out and he threw a cherry bomb through the window, which, given our state of mind, was not well received.

We wandered the street for a while and were out messing around Boston and decided we should go to the Tea Party and rehearse. Duane gets on a pay phone, calls the radio station, and tells them to put out the word for Don Law to come to the club and let in the All-man Brothers Band, they want to rehearse. We just walk down there and stood waiting, oddly sure he would show up. He got out of his car, walked over, unlocked the door, turned around, got back in his car and left without saying a word or even looking at us. He was pissed, and I don't blame him.

And this is why we felt such an urgent need to rehearse: we went in and spent hours working up the sound of a Harley cranking up and go-ing through its gears, which was going to kick off our shows as an intro-duction to "Don't Want You No More/Cross to Bear." We were deadly serious about it, too. Once we straightened up, everyone realized how absurd it was. After we finished, we were walking across the Tea Party and this damn four-by-four fell from the roof and smashed Jaimoe's seat. If we had played for ten or fifteen minutes more, he would have been killed.

LAW: I felt privileged to have them there in that room. It was exciting and exhilarating. There was something magical happening and I think anyone who saw them realized that it was going to be pretty big. It was amazing to play them for free on the Commons. That was tre-mendously fun and it was a great way to expose somebody.

Duane's guitar playing was extraordinary. In my exposure to him, he was a very gentle, bright guy, and everybody understood that he was an incredible, unique talent. That was just obvious. He had a passion to play. He went and sat in with Frank Zappa and several other people at the Tea Party while they were in Boston.

CHAPTER

Dreams

*I*N AUGUST 1969, *the band went to New York City to record their self-titled debut. Their trip north was not without drama with their equipment truck breaking down in South Carolina. Lyndon rented a van. In New York, the band was to work with Cream's producer, Tom Dowd, but he was unavailable and Atlantic house engineer Adrian Barber was assigned to record the new band. Barber was an experienced engineer, having worked on sessions with Cream and a range of jazz greats, as well as with the Beatles in Hamburg, Germany, in 1963. This was his first producer's credit. A year later he would engineer and play most of the drums on the Velvet Underground's* Loaded.

The entire seven-song Allman Brothers Band *album was cut and mixed in two weeks, and virtually no outtakes exist from the sessions. The Brothers also played three nights at Ungano's, a Manhattan club; these were their first shows in the city that was to become their second home.*

JAIMOE: The best way to prepare to go into the studio is to play the songs you're going to record on gigs and then you should know if they're ready or not and judge from the crowd reaction what's clicking and what needs more work. We played them songs hard from May to August and walked into the studio having them down cold. We were not intimidated, even though me, Dickey, and Berry were not that experienced in studio work. Butch had more experience and Gregg and Duane had cut a few albums, in addition to all of Duane's session work.

TRUCKS: The whole experience of making the first album was absolutely wonderful. I felt comfortable in the studio, having recorded a bunch before, as did we all, and the music was great. We had played these songs so much and we were all just busting to get them down on record.

JAIMOE: They booked two weeks for us in Atlantic Studios—and that was just supposed to be laying down basic tracks, with overdubs coming later. We went in on Sunday night to get sounds, went back Monday night to start cutting, and came out Thursday with the whole thing done, overdubs and all. We went in there, played our asses off, and that was it; we were done in four days and they spent the rest of the time mixing.

TRUCKS: It all happened so fast. We did that whole record in two weeks beginning to end, from the time we set up to the time we mastered, and the only thing we got stuck on wound up being the high point of that whole record: Duane's solo on "Dreams." We tried playing it several times and couldn't get it to where it felt right to him. Finally, he said, "Let's not waste any more time. Let's record the song and leave a good long opening for me to solo." We were just jamming to give him some movement to play along with, and he was playing rhythm, leading us where he wanted to go, setting the track just how he wanted it.

And at the end of every day's sessions, he would go and give "Dreams" a shot, but never felt like it was happening. One night, we had finished what we were doing and he said, "Turn off all the lights," and he went way to the back corner, where his amp and baffle were, and sat down—on the floor, I think—and they rolled the track and he started playing that solo that's on the record. All of a sudden he was playing slide, which he had never done on the song before. He said that he just saw the slide sitting there, stuck it on, and played a lot of the same licks he had played, redone with the slide. Then he got to the end and started that rolling lick and built to an incredible climax. By the time he finished everybody in there was in tears. It was unbelievable. I still have a hard time listening to that solo without getting emotional. It was just magic. It's always been that the greatest music we played was from out of nowhere, that it wasn't practiced, planned, or discussed.

Just after the band returned to Macon from recording the album, Walden and Associates purchased them a Ford Econoline van from Riverside Ford, paying $2,751.55 for it on September 4, 1969. The members felt like they had hit the big time.

As they waited for the album to come out, Duane continued to travel to Muscle Shoals to play sessions, cutting great tracks with Ronnie Hawkins and others.

HALL: After Duane was in Macon and his band was going, he would keep driving in for sessions when he could, and talk about how excited he was about the band. He would drive up here in his little Ford and I was always happy to see him.

JAIMOE: It's unbelievable how much Duane accomplished, how many dates he played. One problem that a lot of us have is thinking about why we can't do something. Duane just did it. So many musicians will say, "Oh, I can't play with that guy." Well, why not? It's music—listen and play. That's what Duane did. He never, ever thought he couldn't play with someone, or didn't have time to do something.

DOUCETTE: He just never stopped. We'd be up until five in the morning, and at ten he was dressed and ready to go.

In November 1969, Duane showed up at Fame, excited to meet John Hammond Jr., one of his favorite blues guitarists.

HAMMOND: I was working with the Muscle Shoals session guys to record *Southern Fried* for Atlantic. No one there had heard of me and I was trying to forge some relationship with the band and it wasn't going well. Before I arrived, I thought they were all black and they thought I was black and we were both surprised and a little stand-offish. We were stumbling along together without much chemistry. Then Duane showed up after two days and said, "I want to meet John Hammond." They were so knocked out that he wanted to play with me. It earned me so much respect.

Eddie Hinton, the guitarist on the session, told me, "You got to hear this guy play." When I did, I flipped out. Duane was just a phenomenal guitar player and a really nice guy. I asked him to play on some of the songs and it brought a whole new life to the sessions. It was just incredible.

Berry came with him to at least one of our sessions. Over that week's time Duane and I became friendly and he told me about his new band, with Berry, Dickey, Butch, Jaimoe, and Gregg. He had a lot of energy and excitement about this.

The Allman Brothers Band's self-titled debut was released in November 1969, featuring five Gregg Allman originals, as well as Muddy Waters's "Trouble No More" and Spencer Davis's "Don't Want You No More." The latter was transformed from a light pop song into a hard-driving, organ-fueled instrumental, which opened the album and led directly into the pained majesty of Gregg's "It's Not My Cross to Bear." That song, which had heralded the singer's emergence as an original songwriter, now signaled his band's emergence as a powerfully original entity. The band had thrown down a gauntlet of musical precision and deep blues feeling, even if the production somehow tamped down the fire.

Though the group had been together less than six months and the members ranged in age from twenty-one (Oakley and Gregg Allman) to twenty-five (Betts), The Allman Brothers Band *sounds like the product of a veteran unit with a fully formed vision. They were perhaps the only group to pull off what every hippie with a guitar and a Muddy Waters album talked about in 1969: reinventing the blues in a manner both visionary and true to the original material. The entity's ability to keep their feet firmly planted on terra firma while blasting into outer space was unparalleled.*

All of this instrumental virtuosity was tied to a terrific batch of Gregg Allman compositions that captured the weary existentialism of the finest blues, expressing a fatalism profound enough to border on Southern Gothic. They were remarkably mature lyrical conceptions for such a young man, expertly executed in a minimalist, almost haiku style.

ALLMAN: Those songs on the first album came out of the long struggle of trying so hard and getting fucked by different land sharks in the business. Just the competition I experienced out in L.A. and being really frustrated but hanging on and not saying, "Fuck it," and going on to construction work or something.

JAIMOE: From the minute Gregory arrived in Jacksonville, we started working on these early songs, and he kept writing them, and we played them damn near every day. We very seldom "rehearsed"; rehearsal for us was just playing: "The song goes like this. Let's go." And we played it. No other shit, no talking, no messing around. We played the songs into shape. Those blues tunes that we copied, starting with "Trouble No More," they were just songs that were so good they couldn't be left off the album.

BETTS: Berry played a huge role in the band's arrangements. "Whipping Post" was a ballad when Gregg brought it to us; it was a real melancholy, slow minor blues, along the lines of "Dreams." Oakley came up with the heavy bass line that starts off the track, along with the 6/8-to-5/8 shifting time signature.

JAIMOE: "Whipping Post" sounded just like "Stormy Monday Blues." It would go into the 6/8 feel on the "sometimes I feel" section. Berry came up with that bassline that made you pay attention.

BETTS: Oakley called a halt to the rehearsal and said, "Let me work on this song tonight and let's get back to it tomorrow." By the next day, he had that intro worked out. When he played that riff for us, everyone went, "Yeah! That's it!" Oakley morphed a lot of those songs into something different.

DOUCETTE: Berry played a huge role in the songwriting. A lot of those feels that are at the core of the Allman Brothers' sound are Berry. He was huge within the band, and he was such a hip guy.

BETTS: A lot of the arrangements came about from jamming. For instance, we were all messing around with the theme from *2001: A Space Odyssey* and that morphed into "Dreams," which Gregg had written, but which didn't really have an arrangement yet.

JAIMOE: Gregg brought most of his songs pretty well done, but we really worked up "Whipping Post" and "Dreams," which is basically "My Favorite Things" with lyrics. I played the exact licks and fills on there that Jimmy Cobb played on Miles's "All Blues," which is something I would do all the time. I did a lot of copying, but only from the best.

ALLMAN: "Dreams" is the only song I ever wrote on a Hammond organ. It belonged to some dude out in California.

There's no songwriting process. I wish there was, but there are as many ways to write songs as there are songs. You have to feel comfortable. Once you get in a groove, you flow along with the tune, but it's finding that groove that's the hard part.

BETTS: For such young cats that band was really mature. I listen back to the early stuff now and it's hard to explain. Duane and Oakley had incredible leadership qualities, but it's really amazing that guys at twenty-two, twenty-three had that much seasoning and were such good players. One reason is that we weren't a garage band. We were a nightclub band. We had brought ourselves up in the professional world by actually playing in bars and that really gives you a lot more depth. We all had a lot of miles under our wheels when we first met despite our ages.

Duane had done that studio work, Gregg had been in L.A. and recorded. My first road gig came when I was sixteen playing in a band that traveled with "The World of Mirth" shows, to state fairs and such. We had a tent show called Teen Beat we put on in the midway. We sometimes did fifteen thirty-minute shows a day, playing Little Richard and Chuck Berry. I did splits and duckwalks and we would get on each other's shoulders and slide across the stage on our knees wearing kneepads hidden under our pants. All those gigs pay off.

DOUCETTE: This was a band of men. There weren't any kids in it, despite our young ages. We'd all worked. We'd all been on the road and taken responsibility—and most of us had either lost our fathers young or had absent fathers. These are things you have to understand.

SANDLIN: The first time I heard them live, they were really powerful—just incredible. I sat there amazed. They had the blues thing down and then it went off in so many directions. The music went on and on but it seemed like an instant. When I heard the record, I thought it was good, but not as good as they were live.

DOUCETTE: Everything was there to make the first record a great one—it has so much blood and guts and meat and bone—but it doesn't come through the speakers.

JAIMOE: I love the way the drums sound on the first album, panned hard right and hard left. You can hear both sets of drums as distinctively as Elizabeth Taylor and Richard Burton. They sound so natural, like they're in your living room.

TRUCKS: When Duane finally relented on the name, it was with the caveat that there be no pictures of just Duane and Gregg separate from the rest of us. Of course, they put a picture of Duane and Gregg on [the back of] our first album. Duane went nuclear when he saw that.

STEPHEN PALEY, *photographer who took the pictures on the debut album cover:* I had shot Duane a few times for Atlantic and got along with him really well, and the label hired me to shoot the cover for the first Allman Brothers Band album. I went down to Macon and hung out for about a week. I never liked a band more. I was one of them. I hung out with them, they got me girls, they gave me drugs. It was like being a rock star. I hung out with a lot of rock stars but no one ever did that to the same extent. There was just an ease to the whole thing. They really were the kindest, most fun band I ever worked with.

We spent a few days going all over Macon and shooting anywhere that looked photogenic: fields, old houses, railroad tracks, the cemetery. We shot a lot. They looked scary but they were sweethearts and they would do anything. I even went with Duane when he had oral surgery and shot him there—and, of course, they posed full-frontal naked! That wasn't my idea. I would not have had the guts to propose it. It was Phil Walden's idea. They trusted him and he said to do it, so they did. [*Rolling Stone* editor/publisher] Jann Wenner happened to be there, with Boz Scaggs, who he was producing. We were outside near a brook on Phil's brother's property and it just seemed like a natural thing to do.

TRUCKS: It was preplanned, because we had a bunch of soap bubbles, the idea being we'd put them in to generate bubbles to cover us up, but it was a pretty free-flowing stream so that didn't cut it. Luckily I had sliced my leg open the day before and had about thirteen stitches, which is why I'm standing up; I couldn't get that water in the cut, so I kind of positioned myself behind Oakley.

PALEY: Phil knew the band was special musically and I think he was trying to exploit every aspect of their image to draw attention. It's like being a street musician; you want to draw a crowd any way you can.

TRUCKS: After we took those pictures of everyone sitting down, Phil said, "Let's take some pictures of everyone standing up for posterity." And we all said, "Hell, no!" And he goes, "No one will ever see 'em." So we did it. The first time we played the Fillmore East [*December 26, 1969*], I'm walking around looking at everything and just feeling good and sort of amazed that here we are. I walk in the lobby and hanging up there is a double gatefold from *Screw* magazine of us standing up naked, full hanging and everything.

PALEY: That wasn't *Screw*. It was a broadsheet alternative newspaper that was the size of the *New York Times* and that picture was there full-size for all to see. It wasn't pornographic, though.

TRUCKS: The thing is all those guys had been sitting in that freezing water and I had been standing up, which worked to my advantage. Duane said the next day he went and visited Jerry Wexler at Atlantic and he had that picture sitting on his desk and said, "There's one thing for sure; you ain't the natural leader of this band."

JAIMOE: Everybody had their records that they listened to and we just shared them. I had no idea who the Grateful Dead or Rolling Stones were, though I had heard some of their songs on the jukebox. Butch turned me on to all that stuff. Dickey was into country and Chuck Berry. Duane, Gregory, Berry, and myself were the rhythm and bluesers—and to this day I consider Gregg an R and B singer.

BETTS: I always loved jazz—guitarist Howard Roberts, for instance— but once the Allman Brothers formed, Jaimoe really fired us up on it. He had us all listening to Miles Davis and John Coltrane and a lot of our guitar arrangements came from the way they played together.

JAIMOE: Thank God I figured out that music is music and there are no such things as jazz, rock and roll, country, and blues. I got caught up in that mess earlier. I wanted to be the world's greatest jazz drummer and didn't want to play rock and roll or funk. I used to say, "That shit's easy." Then I got a chance to do it and what a surprise: I couldn't play what needed to be played. That turned my head around and opened my mind. Everything has to be played right.

ALLMAN: The main initial jazz influence came from Jaimoe, who really got all of us into Coltrane together, which became a big influence. My brother loved jazz guitarists like Howard Roberts, Wes Montgomery, Tal Farlow, and Kenny Burrell. I brought the blues to the band, and what country you hear comes from Dickey. Butchie was more the technician; he taught drums. We all dug different stuff, and we all started listening to each other's music. What came out was a mixture of all of it and that's what you hear when you put on an Allman Brothers song.

JAIMOE: I'm absolutely certain that Duane had listened to Miles and Coltrane before he met me, but we did spin those a lot. His two favorite songs were Coltrane's version of "My Favorite Things" and Miles's "All Blues." Those two songs were the source of a lot of our modal jamming, without a lot of chord changes.

ALLMAN: Duane was all about two lead guitars. He loved players like Curtis Mayfield and wanted the bass, keyboards, and second guitar to form patterns behind the solo rather than just comping.

BETTS: Duane and I had an immense amount of respect for each other. We talked about being jealous of each other and how dangerous it was to think that way, that we had to fight that feeling when we were onstage. He'd say, "When I listen to you play, I have to try hard to keep the jealousy thing at bay and not try to outdo you when I play my solo. But I still want to play my best!" We'd laugh about what a thin line that was. We learned a lot from each other.

DOUCETTE: Dickey and Duane didn't hang out a lot, but the level of respect and musical love between them was profound. They were very tight and they had a lot of unspoken communication. They were both very smart, very intuitive guys, and what they wanted was to be the best they could be, not in relation to one another, but together.

HAMPTON: Dickey and Duane had a very close musical relationship, and Dickey is one of the top three or four musicologists I've ever spoken to. I've always been blown away by his knowledge of a wide range of music. He is a very humble, nice cat with a thirst for musical knowledge. He's always been able to talk about music he loves for hours.

PAYNE: Dickey's personality and ego were pretty powerful in themselves and I think he sometimes really objected to Duane being in the

spotlight, but he bit his tongue. I never saw any conflict or fighting between Dickey and Duane, though there was healthy competition there. I
remember hanging out with Duane and I'd say, "Let's go riding," and
he'd look over in the corner at Dickey practicing and say, "I think I'll
just stay here and work on things with Dickey."

BETTS: Duane and I used to laugh at each other all the time and say,
"You sure don't give me a break." It was the healthy kind of competition, where you push each other, but no one loses. Duane and I talked
about how scared we got whenever the other played a great solo and
then he said, "Well, this isn't a contest. We can make each other better
and do something deep."

RED DOG: Duane played guitar better than anybody out there—except
maybe Dickey Betts. Many nights Duane walked off stage and said to
me, "God damn, he ran me all over the stage tonight. He kicked my ass."
It's not that they were trying to outdo each other, but Dickey would
come up with off-the-wall shit and Duane would be like, "God damn!"
and have to keep up.

WARREN HAYNES: I discovered when I was just a kid that it was an
equal partnership, but a lot of guys didn't get that. Because of the
name and the fact that Duane did most of the talking between songs,
people assumed that he was the lead guitarist and Dickey was the
support. Many people attributed some of Dickey's great solos to
Duane.

BETTS: A lot of people assumed Duane was the lead player and I was
the rhythm guy because of the name of the band and because he was so
charismatic and I was more laidback. He would really get upset about
that and he went out of his way to make sure people understood we were
a twin-guitar band, saying, "This cat played that, not me. There's two

guitar players in this damn band!" We were both damn good, but I didn't believe in myself the way Duane did.

HAYNES: Dickey plays awesome straight, traditional blues, but he also has this Django Reinhardt–on-acid side of him that is very unique, and, of course, he has that major pentatonic, "Ramblin' Man"/"Blue Sky" side. All those sides of Dickey's musical personality played a big part in the Allman Brothers' sound. And most cats that can play blues as convincingly as Dickey cannot stretch out to that psychedelic thing like he can. He's very unique.

BETTS: My style is just a little too smooth and round to play the blues stuff straight, because I'm such a melody guy that even when I'm playing the blues, I go for melody first.

RED DOG: The way Dickey and Duane played, it was like . . . Fuck it. It was just so human, so emotional, like letting things out of you. It was like making love, caressing each other, but anger coming out at the same time. It was a little raunchy here, a little nasty there, a lot of love here. I thought Butchy and Jaimoe had the same thing going with the drums.

DOUCETTE: I knew Duane for a long time but had never heard Gregg sing until the first time I played with the Allman Brothers Band. Gregory starts playing that fucking organ and singing and I went, "Whoa. Now here's a guy who's in worse pain than I am." He pushed all that pain into his music and combined it with his artistry into something very special and unique.

McEUEN: The magic of Gregg Allman was and is an ability to sing anything like it's his. He can sing "Will the Circle Be Unbroken" like it was just written by him. Duane had the magical ability to play anything in a way that made you think, "Well, that can't be any better."

DOUCETTE: One time at the Fillmore East, Albert King came out to jam with us on a slow blues. He's up there in a lime green suit sucking on his pipe and doing his thing. Then Gregg starts singing and Albert damn near bit through his pipe. He's never heard this voice before and he's looking around, literally swiveling his head trying to figure out who's singing and he sees the skinny-ass blond behind the organ just killing it and couldn't believe it was him.

Though the debut album heralded the arrival of a new voice on the American music scene, few were listening.

WALDEN: The first album sold less than 35,000 copies when it was released.

ALLMAN: My brother and me did not get discouraged when it didn't go anywhere. Hell, we had already had two Hour Glass records eat dirt.

JAIMOE: We were just playing music and it was going great. We didn't think about how great it was going to sound in a month or what we would do next. I guess Duane did, but there were no other thoughts in my head except how great the music we were playing was. The whole world closed out.

TRUCKS: I did not have any doubts about the band. I don't think any of us expected to become truly successful. We had all been in bands before where that was all there was. We were trying to be rock stars and all we came out of it with was garbage. Then we started playing this music that was making us feel like this and that became so much more important than fame or fortune. We would just kind of drop a curtain in front of the stage and play for ourselves. We didn't give a damn if people liked it or not. We were not going to play "Louie Louie" just to get applause. We all had done that enough.

BETTS: We were just so naive. All we knew is that we had the best band that any of us had ever played in and were making the best music that we had ever made. That's what we went with. Everyone in the industry was saying that we'd never make it, we'd never do anything, that Phil Walden should move us to New York or L.A. and acclimate us to the industry, that we had to get the idea of how a rock 'n' roll band was supposed to present themselves.

TRUCKS: They thought a bunch of Southern guys just standing there playing extended musical jams was absurd. They wanted Gregg out from behind the organ, jumping around with a salami in his pants. They wanted us to act "like a rock band" and we just told them to fuck themselves. We were playing music for ourselves and for each other.

BETTS: Of course, none of us would do that, and thankfully, Walden was smart enough to see that would just ruin what we had. We just stayed in Macon and stayed on the road, playing gigs and getting tighter and better.

SCOTT BOYER, *guitarist in the band Cowboy*: Macon became known as a place to go if you were a musician in the South looking to get something going. It started because the Allmans were there and Capricorn was headquartered and it built on itself.

ALLMAN: Over the years, players from the South would find their way to New York or Los Angeles and break out of there. We elected to stay down South and do it from there rather than going where all the damn competition was. Everyone told us we'd fall by the wayside down there.

HAYNES: I grew up in North Carolina and it was a big deal for Southern musicians to feel like they could stay in the region and succeed, that they didn't have to move to the East or West Coast, which had been presumed. We all identified with and felt a connection to the music because it was made by people who looked like us, acted like us, and lived like we did. It was the first time the South was taken seriously as a place for great rock music to come from. It let us know that we could make it without changing, that it was cool to make rock music that sounded like it was from the South.

HAMPTON: The Allman Brothers transformed Macon from this sleepy little town into a very hip, wild, and crazy place filled with bikers and rockers. Every time you went down there, it was like mental illness in the streets: fights, bikes . . .

MAMA LOUISE: I started seeing them boys around town on their motorcycles, and Red Dog and Kim would pick me up and give me rides home after work. I always felt safe with them, especially Red Dog. He was a sweet man.

DOUBLE TROUBLE

Inside the revolutionary dual-lead-guitar approach of Duane Allman and Dickey Betts.

The Allman Brothers Band's first real musical breakthrough was the extensive use of guitar harmonies. This new concept in rock music was a natural outgrowth of having two lead guitarists, rather than one who primarily stuck to rhythm playing. Duane Allman's dynamic slide playing is revered, but he was a fully formed, well-rounded guitarist. Betts was also already a wide-ranging, distinct stylist by the time he and Allman joined forces, and he was almost certainly the driving force behind the duo's landmark harmony playing.

Though closely associated with guitar harmonies, the pair also had a wide range of complementary techniques, often forming intricate, interlocking patterns with each other and with the bassist, Berry Oakley, setting the stage for dramatic flights of improvised melodies. The precision with which the musicians landed together back on their riffs also elevated them above their peers.

WARREN HAYNES: Their guitar tandem came about naturally because Dickey was such a strong melodic player and Duane's ear was so good and he could play complementary harmony or counterpoint on the fly. Most of the dual-guitar stuff that they did was Dickey playing melody and Duane playing harmony.

DICKEY BETTS: From our first time playing together, Duane started picking up on things I played and offering a harmony, and we'd build whole jams off of that. We worked stuff out naturally because we were both lead players. We got those ideas from both jazz horn players like Miles Davis and John Coltrane and fiddle lines from western swing music. I listened to a lot of country and string [bluegrass] music growing up. I played mandolin, ukulele, and fiddle before I ever touched a guitar, which may be where a lot of the major keys I play come from.

HAYNES: Dickey had a deep western swing influence. He learned a lot of guitar from Dave Lyle, who had played with Roy Clark in Brenda Lee's band and the two of them had played a lot of harmony lines. That's where Dickey got the concept from and I don't think Duane had ever done anything like that before.

REESE WYNANS, *keyboardist in Second Coming, Betts and Oakley's pre-ABB group:* Dickey's whole thing from the first time I met him was harmonies. He would come up with these great melodies and he wanted to get harmonies going for them; he always wanted Rhino and me to follow him and play harmony parts. [Guitarist Larry "Rhino Reinhardt] Duane obviously got on the bus with that and took it to a new level. Having played with them in the earliest stages, it was no surprise at all that their pairing would work so well.

BETTS: It's very hard to go freestyle with two guitars. Most bands with two guitarists either have everything worked out or they stay out of each other's way because it's easy to sound like two cats fighting if you're not careful. It was real, real natural how Duane and I put our guitars together. Our system was not exactly technique. Duane would almost always wait for me, or sometimes Oakley, to come up with a melody and then he would join in on my riff with the harmony. Very seldom would Duane start the riff.

HAYNES: They worked out harmonies, but some of the stuff in Dickey's solos just came about in an impromptu way and you can tell when you hear Dickey play a melodic line and then the harmony comes in on top of it. That's why it has a few loose ends and unparalleled harmony parts; they were just winging it. Maybe all the notes weren't exactly parallel or perfect, but the vibe and feel were right on.

BETTS: A lot of Duane's harmony lines are not the correct notes you would choose if you sat down to write it out, but they always worked. Our band came around at a wonderful time for improv and we felt free to just play and work things out on the fly. I usually set the melody and if I played it twice then the third time he would be right on it with the harmony and it would sound great. We didn't usually sit down and figure out parts. Doing them on the fly gave it all a certain spark and sound.

HAYNES: The Allman Brothers Band is based on the fact that no one on stage can rest on his laurels; you have to bring it. That's where that fire comes from and it certainly emanates from the intensity of having two great lead players like Dickey and Duane throwing sparks off of each other. Jazz and blues musicians have been doing this for decades, but I think they really brought that sense that anyone onstage can inspire anyone else at any given time to rock music.

BETTS: Duane and I were very conscious of the snare-drum type approach to playing rhythm. It was a lot of counterpoint and interplay. I could set something with a push on the 2 and 4 and he would play on the beat. We were very aware of letting each person's downbeat appear in different spots so they didn't tangle up, because Berry was really busy, too. That generates a back-and-forth machine thing similar to playing snare drum with the right hand. It was all question and answer, anticipation and conclusion. You build up the anticipation with the first part of the phrase and answer it with the second. Duane was really more adept at that type of thing than I was, but we worked it out together.

DOUCETTE: I would play my solos then stand behind the line, behind Duane's and Dickey's amp—moving to whomever was playing rhythm guitar, because you could hear the leads fine from anywhere. I wish everyone could hear what I heard back there—and I would kill to have a cut of that stuff—because it was just spectacular. They were two wildly different rhythm players and they were so good, both just laying down beautiful rhythm parts.

HAYNES: Another cool thing about Dickey and Duane that stuck out to any guitar player was how identifiable each of their styles and sounds were; it was easy to tell them apart.

BETTS: The dream guitar sounds that we heard in our heads were opposite. He liked a spitfire, trebly sound with staccato phrasing and using the bridge pickup and my thing was more of a rounded-tone sound using the neck pickup.

Duane's melody came more from jazz and urban blues and my melodies came more from country blues with a strong element of string-music fiddle tunes. I had more looping phrasing and Duane was more cutting. We were almost totally opposite except we both knew the importance of phrasing. We didn't just ramble about.

One More Try

*I*N JANUARY *1970, Berry Oakley's wife, Linda, and his sister, Candace, rented a large Victorian house at 2321 Vineville Avenue while the band was on the road. They moved into the place in March, along with Duane, Donna, and Galadrielle. Others would move in and out over the next several years, as the communal home became widely known as the Big House.*

DOUCETTE: Candy Oakley, Linda Oakley, and Donna Allman made a huge, unbelievable difference in the band's life. We came back to the Big House and it was truly a home, which contained all the heart, feeling, and togetherness of the band. I had played in a lot of bands that had hangouts, but this was a different deal, made possible by those three women, and I was taken away by it and greatly admired it.

For their second album, the Allman Brothers worked for the first time with producer Tom Dowd, who had already recorded artists ranging from Ray Charles and John Coltrane to Cream. Due mostly to their hectic touring schedule, Idlewild South *was recorded in fits and starts in Macon, Miami, and New York, from February to July 1970.*

It included "Midnight Rider" and "Revival," which was Betts's first song-writing credit with the band. They also recorded Betts's masterful instrumental "In Memory of Elizabeth Reed" for the first time, opening up vast new terrain for the band to explore.

SANDLIN: I spent a whole lot of time with the Allman Brothers doing demos in the Capricorn studio for their second album. We recorded a version of "Statesboro Blues" and a first take on "In Memory of Elizabeth Reed." I thought it was phenomenal when Dickey brought that in; he introduced a whole new side to the Allman Brothers Band, a very unique instrumental approach which would, of course, become very important to their success.

BETTS: It's hard for me to even pinpoint where "Liz Reed" came from. It's jazz, but not really, and it was different than anything I had done before. The original version we recorded is awfully sparse compared to where we'd be taking it soon.

SANDLIN: I thought things were going well and I was overjoyed when they said they wanted me to produce their second album.

TOM DOWD, *producer of* Idlewild South, at Fillmore East, Eat a Peach: The first time I heard the Allman Brothers Band was in Macon. I was there to visit Capricorn and I walked by the rehearsal space and heard the most incredible sounds coming out. I got to Phil's office and asked him who in the hell was rehearsing in the studio. He said, "That's the Allman Brothers," and I said, "Get them the hell out of there and give them to me in the studio. They don't need to rehearse; they're ready to record."

SANDLIN: As it got closer, Phil said they wanted me to do it with Tom Dowd. This is very embarrassing to me, but Tom came to the Capricorn studio and I was acting like the co-producer, making suggestions, with

Tom looking at me oddly. When I realized that no one had told him about me co-producing, I couldn't even go into the studio because it was such an embarrassment, but that didn't last long, because they went down to Miami to record at Criteria, where Tom was more comfortable. He wasn't happy with the state of our studio—and he was right. It was still a work in progress.

ALLMAN: Tommy wanted us to go to Miami because that was his sandbox and where he knew how to play best.

BETTS: "Revival" was supposed to be an instrumental, and when I was writing the thing, I kind of got going and started singing, just screwing around, and the words came almost as an afterthought, but that was not typical. Usually, I'm definitely going to write an instrumental. You have to have an altogether different approach; an instrumental has to be real catchy and when you succeed it's very satisfying because you have transcended words and communicated with emotion. I don't really have a specific technique, but I put in hours of deliberation as to what note should follow each other in order to get the best phrase.

And I wrote this instrumental in Rose Hill for a woman I was involved with. I finished it and loved it but I didn't know what to call it and it couldn't have anything to do with her name, because it was all cloak and dagger, as she was Boz Scaggs's girlfriend. She was Hispanic and somewhat dark and mysterious—and she really used it to her advantage and played it to the hilt. I thought, "Well, where did the song come from?" And there was a grave right by "my spot" that said, "In Memory of Elizabeth Jones Reed, mother of . . ." and listed all of her children. The spot had provided me with so much peace and inspiration that I decided to name the song after her. Duane told some crazy shit about that graveyard. I don't wanna tell all—but that's the part that matters.

ALLMAN: "Midnight Rider" hit me like a damn sack of hoe handles. It was just there, crawling all over me. And about an hour and fifteen minutes later I had the rough draft down and before the sun set that day I was in the studio putting it on tape, bing-bang, just like that. They happen that way sometimes. Have you ever wondered where a thought comes from? Comes from nowhere. There's just something you see or hear or something you remember and it triggers a thought that will just hit you: "Pow!"

I couldn't find anybody in the band, so I went and found Twiggs Lyndon, put a bass in his hands, and said, "I want you to go right here," and I put his hands on the bass and showed him to play, "duhn duh-duhn duhn, duhn duh-duhn duhn." He did it over and over and he finally had it, and I said, "When I hold up my hand, by God, you stop!" And he says, "What do I play then?" And I said, "Just stop! Don't play nothing." Then I found Jaimoe and had him come in. So I had a twelve-string guitar and a bass and a drum and I cut me a demo of it and I just laid that on the band and bam that bad brother's done. We recorded it proper.

PAYNE: Phil bought a whole block that was falling down. Right next to the studio he had an old warehouse where we stored our equipment and had some practice sessions. Anyone could walk up there, kick down a board, and steal everything, so one of us roadies had to spend the night there every night the gear was in there.

I was on duty one night, in this little guard shack we had, and Gregg showed up in the middle of the night with this half-done song and he said he was having trouble with it. We were getting high and, honestly, he was starting to irritate me—because he was singing this song over and over and I got sick of hearing the band play the same shit over and over again until they got it right. So I just threw out the line, *"I've gone past the point of caring / some old bed I'll soon be sharing."*

Then we had it and Gregg loved the song and wanted to record it before it was gone, but we didn't have a key to the studio. We tried [studio musicians and managers] Paul Hornsby and Johnny Sandlin and they both told us to go to hell, come back in the morning.

SANDLIN: Something like that was not unusual. I remember several crazy nights with them waking me up at three in the morning and wanting to go in the studio to work and I never wanted to. I had worked all day and would be back in the morning and you never knew what they wanted to work on.

PAYNE: Gregg was intent on getting this on tape before he forgot it all. So we went back down there and just broke in; I smashed a window on the door and reached in to unlock it.

Then I was running around trying to figure out how to turn the board on and he was running around yelling into mics looking for a live one. I finally found what looked like a wall light switch hidden under the board, and boom, all these lights came on, microphones are live, and needles are jumping. We laid down one track with Gregg just playing an acoustic guitar and singing and he went back the next day and added some more. I would imagine that tape is somewhere.

JAIMOE: All I remember is Gregg came in one night hot to get the song down. Twiggs was playing bass, Gregory was playing guitar, and I played congas and we laid that down.

PAYNE: Afterwards, Gregg was leaving and I was going back on guard duty and he said, "You really helped me out with this song. If this thing does anything and it's a success, I'll cut you in and give you a percentage," and I laughed that off.

JAIMOE: We cut "Please Call Home" in New York, with [jazz producer] Joel Dorn. We did it in two takes. He said, "Play the song so we can get a feel," and we played it. I think I was playing with brushes and Joel suggested I try it with a mallet. We played it for a second time and Joel said, "Come on in [to the control room] and listen to it," and that was it. It was over.

BLUE SUEDE

A look inside Gregg's softer side—how he was influenced by acoustic singer-songwriters, including Jackson Browne, Tim Buckley, and Neil Young.

"A certain side of me has always viewed myself as a folksinger with a rock and roll band," says Gregg Allman. "I developed that perspective when I lived in Los Angeles and saw people like Tim Buckley, Stephen Stills, and Jackson Browne, who was my roommate for a while. All I had known was R and B and blues and these guys turned me on to a more folk-oriented approach and it's always stuck with me, even if a lot of Allman Brothers fans never realized it."

Gregg and Duane Allman moved to Los Angeles in the spring of 1967 with their band the Hour Glass, after Bill McEuen discovered the band, then called the Allman Joys, in a St. Louis club. McEuen managed his brother John's Nitty Gritty Dirt Band, whose debut was just being released on Liberty Records, which also signed the Hour Glass.

"Everything was cross-collateralized," Allman says, a financial arrangement which allowed them a small level of comfort, compared with other struggling musicians, including Jackson Browne, who had briefly been a member of the Dirt Band.

"Basically, our situation meant we had apartments," Allman says with a chuckle. "And that's why Jackson was crashing with me; he was from Long Beach and he was too proud to go home, and I really admired that. Jackson had been drifting around in this old broken-down Volkswagen, and he'd get a job every now and then in some shithouse coffee-folk place, where he might play for a tip jar or ten or twenty bucks.

"I really admired the way he picked guitar and wrote songs about stuff that I would think about and had gone through—stuff that hurts you. He already had different ways of saying things people were thinking and feeling, which is what I learned from him. It's knocking thirty-five words down to four and having 'em really mean something. That, to me, is being a poet. A real poet might read this and laugh but I think it's the art of saying something we all understand in a different way.

"Shakespeare said, 'A rose by any other name would be as sweet' and many people consider that profound; well, I think that people like Jackson Browne have said things just as profound. He really touched a soft side of me and I enjoyed every minute I ever spent with him, which inspired me to really get serious about songwriting."

Allman had been attempting to write songs for years. But exposure to Browne and other L.A. songwriters pushed his ambitions. Remarkably, the Eagles' Glenn Frey also credits Browne with inspiring his songwriting when the two had apartments atop each other. Allman's time in Southern California also helped him stretch his artistic potential on the acoustic guitar, an instrument he had played since he was a kid.

"I thought of an acoustic guitar as something you lightly strummed or picked the blues on, which I often heard my brother do," he says. "I didn't view it as something you could make art with until guys like Jackson, Buckley, and Neil Young showed me otherwise.

"Neil's 'Expecting to Fly' and 'Broken Arrow' inspired me more than I can say. Last time I saw Neil, I looked him right in the eye for his undivided attention and said, 'Man, are you ever gonna play those songs? God, they're good.' 'Expecting to Fly' is a piece of art like *The Lovers* or *The Kiss* or anything Rembrandt or Michelangelo have ever done. It is certainly just as potent to me as *Sgt. Pepper's Lonely Hearts Club Band*."

Allman says that his view of the acoustic guitar as a utilitarian tool reached back to his early days in Nashville, where the Allman brothers lived until moving to Daytona Beach, Florida, when Gregg was twelve and Duane thirteen. Nashville remained a second home, with the brothers returning every summer to stay with their grandmother.

"I had country music shoved down my throat and I couldn't stand it," he says. "At the time, it was String Bean and the Foggy Mountain Boys and all this crying-in-your-beer stuff and the Grand Ole Opry at the Ryman Auditorium had these horrible, uncomfortable pew seats just filled with rednecks. I'm sorry to speak ill of such a place, but it's the truth, and because of all that, the last thing I wanted to see was a Tennessee flattop box, which is what they called the Martin-style guitar down there."

With his view that acoustic guitars were tied to corny, old-fashioned music, Allman focused on his electric rhythm playing, not realizing that his songwriting might benefit from a nonamplified, resonant instrument.

"I was trying to write songs on an electric," he says. "But being on the road, I was often in hotel rooms and whatnot without an amp and the electric didn't sing to me. I didn't realize the deficiency but my brother did and I'll never forget what he did to get me my first real acoustic guitar. He traded his favorite road axe—a '56 Telecaster body with a '53 hogback Stratocaster neck with some kind of crazy booster on the side—for a Gibson J45. I couldn't believe he did that for me, because he loved that guitar, but he had seen legitimate signs of successful songwriting and he knew I needed a boost. And, sure enough, I commenced to just pouring out songs, though most of them were crap."

Allman says he wrote close to four hundred songs that he tossed aside before writing his first keeper in 1967: "Melissa." He did not begin to write consistently until he was immersed in California singer-songwriters and acoustic guitar playing, developing a distinctive style of open tunings with steel fingerpicks.

"I learned to Travis pick, which I found really interesting, and then I really developed my songwriting style," says Allman. "I learned so much and met so many wonderful people out there and it really broadened my musical horizons. I wrote 'Midnight Rider' and 'Come and Go Blues' by Travis picking in natural [open] G, and I don't think I ever would have written songs in that vein had I not gotten involved in a more serious way with the acoustic guitar. When I first got out to L.A., all I had known was R and B and blues and those guys' more folk approach really turned my head. Then I developed my style from combining these things together—folky songs with soulful vocals."

Though Allman lost touch with Browne, he remained enamored of his old friend's songs, recording "These Days" on his 1973 solo album *Laid Back*. A year earlier, Browne had made his album debut, which was packaged in a brown paper bag with the words "Saturate Before Using" across the top.

"I lost track of Jackson after my brother moved back down South [in 1968]," says Allman. "I moved in with some broad and he went his own way and got a girlfriend. I didn't know whatever happened to him. I didn't hear of him again until I was going by a record store in Macon one day and saw his name on a paper bag in the window and said, 'Jackson! I'm a son of a bitch.' I was so happy I went inside and bought one just as fast as I could. 'Cause if your friends won't buy 'em, who the hell will?"

In one magazine interview, Allman was asked who he would most like to record with. His surprising answer: Tim Buckley, the romantic folksinger and fingerpicking guitarist who had mesmerized Allman during a performance in

Los Angeles that Browne had dragged him to. Shortly after the interview appeared, Gregg answered his Macon phone.

"Someone I could barely understand on this bad line said, 'Could I speak to Gregg Allman?'" Gregg recalls. "I said, 'Who's calling?' And I thought he said 'Lord Buckley,' the comedian from back in the old hippie days. And it took me a minute to realize it was *Tim* Buckley, who was such a gentleman, such a wonderful person. That guy might have had a twenty-one-inch waist but he had a heart as big as Alaska and he could write down his thoughts in a beautiful way and pick this twelve-string acoustic with three steel Nationals on his fingers, and a Dobro thumb pick, which I also use. I got this from him and it gave my music a lot of life."

BETTS: Duane played the acoustic on "Revival" and "Midnight Rider" and everything else where you hear it. Getting a good acoustic sound in the studio can be tough, and Duane could do it much more easily and quickly than me at that point. Duane was a lot more studio savvy than the rest of us because of his experience at Muscle Shoals. He was really, really good in the studio.

ALLMAN: Even on the songs I wrote on acoustic like "Midnight Rider," I never played it on the records. We had enough guitarists.

For years, Duane didn't have a nice flattop [acoustic guitar], because he mostly played Dobros and National Steels, so he would rent an acoustic in the studio. But eventually he ended up with one of those old dark Martin D18s that looks almost like mahogany. He loved playing the steel guitars, and Dickey ended up with his favorite National—that's it on the cover of his solo album [*Highway Call*]. I wound up with two of his Nationals. I knew I wasn't going to play them properly and I knew I wasn't going to sell them either, so I gave one to Clapton and I gave one to Ronnie Wood.

The band also recorded a rearranged version of Muddy Waters's "Hoochie Coochie Man," featuring Oakley on his only studio lead vocal.

BETTS: That arrangement of "Hoochie Coochie Man" came right out of the Second Coming and was a really good example of what Berry and I were doing in that band.

Receipts show that the band stayed at the Chelsea Hotel in New York on April 26, 1970, in between gigs in Fallsburg and Stony Brook, N.Y., sharing rooms, mostly with a band member paired with someone from the crew. Room rates ranged from $13 to $22.50.

CHAPTER

Keep on Growing

*W*ITH THEIR SECOND *album done, the band returned to the road. One of Dowd's next clients was a hero of Dickey and Duane's— Eric Clapton, recording with Derek and the Dominos, his new band of American musicians formerly with his friends Delaney and Bonnie Bramlett. The band came to Miami to record their debut album with just a few songs written.*

DOWD: When I was working with the Allman Brothers on *Idlewild South*, I got a call from [Clapton manager] Robert Stigwood saying that Eric would like to record and asking if I could fit him in my schedule. Of course I said I'd be delighted. It became a lengthy conversation, which I normally would never have while I was working with someone. I put the phone down and apologized, saying to Duane, "You have to excuse me. That was Eric Clapton's manager. They want to come here and record."

He said, "You mean this guy?" and plays me an Eric solo note for note. I said, "That's the one," and he goes, "I got to meet that guy. Let me know when he's gonna be here. I'd love to come by and watch. Do you think that would be possible?" And I told him I was sure it would be fine, he should call me and we'd work it out.

ERIC CLAPTON, *guitarist, rock legend:* I was very aware of Duane. I had become aware of him when I heard Wilson Pickett's "Hey Jude." That break at the end just blew me away and I immediately made a call to Atlantic Records to find out who it was. It was one of the few times in my life where I had to know who that was—now!

We went to Miami just to record with Tom Dowd. It's where he was based, and he was raving about the studio and the musicians we could get if we needed anyone extra. Duane hadn't even been talked about at that point. That was much more coincidental.

DOWD: I was recording with Derek and the Dominos [at Criteria, on August 26, 1970], and Duane calls: "Is he there? We're gonna be in Miami tomorrow for a concert. Can I come meet him?" I said, "I'm sure you can. Hold on."

I grabbed Eric and said, "I have Duane Allman on the phone. His band is playing in the area tomorrow and he'd like to come meet you." And he goes, "You mean this guy?" And he plays Duane's solo off of Wilson Pickett's "Hey Jude" ' note for note. I said, "That's the guy." And he goes, "I've got to see him perform. We're going to that concert."

CLAPTON: When I heard they were playing nearby after we had been in the studio about a month, I immediately wanted to go.

DOWD: Now I knew the two of them personally and they were both low-key, beautiful human beings and wonderful musicians, so I thought, "This is gonna be fun." Sure enough, Saturday afternoon, we record for a few hours, and then head out to the limos Eric had waiting and go down to the Convention Center, where the Allman Brothers are playing. They snuck us in behind the photographer's barricade, sitting on the floor with our backs to the audience, right in front of the stage. Duane's in the middle of a solo, when he opens his eyes, looks down, sees Eric, and stops playing cold, in shock. Dickey starts playing to cover until Duane regains his equilibrium, and then he sees Eric and he freezes, too. That's how big Eric was to them.

BOBBY WHITLOCK, *Derek and the Dominos keyboardist:* They were playing on a flatbed behind an eighteen-wheeler that had hay bales around the front to keep the crowd back and we crowded up under the trailer and put our backs to the bales and were sitting there looking up at them. Duane was wearing it out and he looked down and saw us—saw *Eric* looking at him—and he just stopped playing. He always had his mouth open when he was getting down on it, but he didn't close it this time. Then Dickey was wondering what was going on and looked down and stopped playing, and I thought the whole band would stop, but they kept cranking and then the guitarists got back on it.

DOWD: After the show they met and hung out and all of a sudden I had half the Allman Brothers and all of Derek and the Dominos crammed into a limousine going back to Criteria, where they jammed until two or three the next afternoon. I kept the tape running the whole time. There's Duane playing Eric's guitar and Gregg playing Bobby Whitlock's organ and they were all in piggy heaven.

JAIMOE: Everyone was really grooving, but I wasn't all that knocked out by what Clapton was doing, or the whole scene, so I went out to the Winnebago, smoked some pot, and listened to Tony Williams's *Emergency!*

Many of these impromptu performances were eventually released on The Layla Sessions, *a twentieth-anniversary expanded box set, which included five jams totaling over 70 minutes.*

CLAPTON: Needless to say, Duane and me hit if off instantly—soul mates, instant soul mates.

WHITLOCK: This thing with Eric and Duane was such a natural. They had the same authority, and they dug from the same well: Robert Johnson, Elmore James, Sonny Boy Williamson, Bill Broonzy. I already knew Duane from working together with Delaney and Bonnie, so I wasn't surprised at all that they hit it off.

ALLMAN: That was a lot of fun and a lot of good music went down that night. I was glad to be there, man.

WHITLOCK: We had some drinks and other recreational relaxants and were just enjoying each other's company. But something deeper was happening right away with Eric and Duane, who were like two long-lost brothers. Those two guys started bouncing back and forth on each other and it was an amazing experience. Everyone else drifted away eventually, but Duane stayed all night.

DOWD: When it was over, they were all such good friends, then Eric said to Duane, "When are you coming back? We should record some."

CLAPTON: I just asked him if he'd like to come into the studio and play and help me out.

DOWD: The Brothers had to go back on the road, but Duane said he'd be back as soon as he could and a few days later he called and said, "I'll be there tomorrow."

DOUCETTE: Wexler called Phil and asked Duane to come back to Miami and he and I got into that Ford van and drove down. When we arrived we had about fourteen dollars, half a joint, and a wee bit of wine. Wexler goes, "You need anything?" I said, "We're broke, man, tapped." He reached into his pocket and pulled out a handful of hundreds and handed them to Duane, who eyeballed it and handed me about half.

This is close to midnight. He walks in there with his amp in one hand and his guitar in the other and all the guys are sitting around and they go, "Well, tomorrow we're going to get busy." And Duane goes "Tomorrow? I just drove fifteen hours in that piece of shit. Let's play some music." He plugged in and tuned up and everyone started getting up and going to his instrument.

WHITLOCK: He came and joined us at the Thunderbird Motel. He got a room right next to mine. One of the most amazing things I ever witnessed was in Eric's room there. The two of them were going back and forth hitting a Robert Johnson lick, then Elmore James and on and on. I knew I was witnessing something real special—these guys in front of me pulling all this from the deep well. I was in awe, because they were both in their early twenties and they were like two seventy-something old blues guys from the fields of Mississippi running it down.

DOWD: By then, the Dominos had recorded several songs and had arrangements set for others, but right away Duane started fitting in parts and the more he did that, the more songs started to radically change. Duane had unleashed this dynamic entity that was just ridiculous. They were feeding off each other like crazy and running on pure emotion.

WHITLOCK: We weren't really stagnant before Duane arrived. "I Looked Away," "Tell the Truth," and "Bell Bottom Blues" had been written and recorded. We had come up with "Keep on Growing" in a jam. Eric kept playing guitar parts and I ran out into the lobby with a yellow pad and wrote out the lyrics as fast as my fingers would move. So we had something, but we didn't have enough material for one album, much less a double album. We didn't have a plan and when

Duane came on the scene, everything exploded and things just started coming.

DOWD: I've never seen spontaneous inspiration happen at that rate and level. One of them would play something, and the other reacted instantaneously. Never once did either of them have to say, "Could you play that again, please?" It was like two hands in a glove. And they got tremendously off on playing with each other. That whole album is definitely equal parts Eric and Duane. The whole session was just so damn impromptu and fly-by-the-seat-of-your-pants brilliant. It was just a wonderful experience to witness such a meshing of musical minds, such telepathic sympathies.

WHITLOCK: We had two leaders then. We had Eric and Duane. Eric backed up and gave Duane a lot of latitude, a lot of room, so he could contribute up to his full potentiality, and Duane was full of fire and ideas. He'd just go, "Hey, how about we try 'Little Wing'?"—that was completely his idea and he came up with the intro by himself. He just started playing it.

Duane was very, very good in the studio. Working with the finest musicians and engineers on the planet really paid off for him. When he had the opportunity to be thrust into that environment, he absorbed what was right and righteous and then used it to killer advantage.

DOWD: It was never gonna happen again; if you didn't catch it, you blew it, so I had the tape rolling constantly. The spontaneity of that whole session was absolutely frightening.

WHITLOCK: Sam the Sham [*Domingo "Sam" Zamudio of "Wooly Bully" fame*] was in Studio B recording. I knew him from my childhood days and he suggested that we do "Nobody Knows You When You're Down and Out" and "Key to the Highway." Those were his ideas.

During the Layla *sessions, Duane also found time to join Zamudio to record three songs: "Me and Bobby McGee," "Relativity," and "Goin' Upstairs," all of which can be heard on* Skydog: The Duane Allman Retrospective.

WHITLOCK: We were just jamming and it turned into "Key to the Highway." The reason that song fades in is Tom Dowd was in the toilet and it was one of the few times during these sessions that tapes weren't rolling. He came running out of the can, screaming, "Push up the faders! Push up the faders!"

DOWD: There have been a lot of stories about how much drugs these guys did, but we started sessions every day at two, and everyone arrived clear-eyed and ready to work. As I dismissed people, they may have floated away, but it did not interfere with the album. Even in his wildest moments, Eric arrived at the studio on time with his instrument in tune, ready to play—and he would give absolute hell to anyone who didn't. Eric and Duane shared that. They didn't know each other from Adam before the sessions began, but they were both taskmasters. They didn't give a damn what anyone did on their own time, but when they were in the studio, it was *their* time, and you better be ready to go.

SANDLIN: No matter what else was happening with him or around him, Duane was completely serious about and dedicated to the music.

After about two weeks of recording, Duane returned to the Brothers, having missed a handful of shows. While this seems to have caused some dissension, everyone understood the importance to Duane of the "Clapton sessions." At the end of the sessions, Clapton asked Duane to join the Dominos.

WHITLOCK: We did talk to him about joining the band and coming with us on the road, but his loyalty was to his brother. He said, "I can't do that unless I bring Gregg along." I did not want another keyboardist and we all just knew that wasn't happening. He had his thing to do. Duane was a leader unto himself.

Of course, Duane did join us on stage twice, in Tampa and Syracuse. And, honestly, I didn't think he was as great on stage with us as he was in the studio. He was good in a structured environment. The Allman Brothers played the same thing last night that they played tonight. We weren't a structured band.

JAIMOE: Eric really wanted Duane in his band and we all knew that. We played at least a couple of shows without him, while he was doing those sessions and then went to play a couple of gigs with them. Growing up in Mississippi, I knew that one monkey don't stop no show, so I didn't really sweat it. I figured, "If that's what he's gonna do, that's what he's gonna do. I was playing music before the Allman Brothers or Percy Sledge and I'll be playing it after." But I know it was a concern with Butch and Dickey.

TRUCKS: Of course I was concerned. Eric asked him to join the band and Duane almost left. He very seriously considered it. I had a long talk with Duane one day when we were out fishing. I wasn't going to beg him but I said, "Duane, look, what we've got going—and it's yours. Are you ready to give this up to join someone else's thing? That's what you're gonna do, Duane, because it's Eric's band. Is that what you want to do?"

DOUCETTE: He said, "Man, they asked me to join," and he was pleased about it, but I don't think he came close to doing it. I think he liked being wanted, liked being asked. That made him feel good, and he genuinely liked Eric.

TRUCKS: Duane finally told Eric no. He felt that we were the best band in the whole world but at the same time, it's Eric Clapton for cripes sake.

And we hadn't gone anywhere yet. He had to make a decision: Am I going to stick with this music I love and I am building, or am I going to join Eric's band? It wasn't an easy decision, because he would be a rock star if he went with Eric, and he had spent a lot of his life with that as a goal. I don't know what the final determining factor was, but I'm just so glad he didn't go.

JAIMOE: When Duane got back, he figured out what I already knew: "Shit, Eric Clapton should be opening for us." That was the kind of attitude we all had and it was probably the best thing we had going for us. I just simply thought Duane had more going playing with us than with Eric. He had put together this band exactly how he wanted it and I think playing those dates with Eric helped him realize that. He was like, "I'm back. Will you let me back in the band?"

Dowd was left to mix the Layla *album on his own, sending cassettes of his work to Clapton to keep him up to date.*

DOWD: Eric called and said they wanted to come back to alter a part on one or two songs and remix one song. When they returned—with Duane—among the things they had in mind was adding a piano part to "Layla," and I couldn't understand where it went. The song was tight as a drum. I played them the cut, and they said it went on the end. I thought they were all stark raving mad, that we could never get everyone to match the brilliance of what they did the first time and make it fit.

Drummer Jim Gordon played the coda's piano part and is credited with writing it as well.

DOWD: When I set up, I expected Bobby Whitlock to play the piano, but Jim played it. I can't say whether or not he wrote it, but he had it mastered; that part was in the end of his fingers.

WHITLOCK: I did not want anything to do with the coda so Jim played the drums and came back and played the piano, but he's not a piano player, so there was no feel to it, and Tom asked me to put another piano on there. In the *Language of Music* movie [a documentary about Dowd's career], when Tom pulls the tracks to "Layla" up individually, there is a track labeled "support piano" and he says, "I forgot about that." That was me. Tom mixed it in to give the piano part more feel and life.

DOWD: Duane's guitar part on that coda is just absolutely intense and, of course, I was absolutely wrong about not being able to make the new part fit. We spliced it right in and it made the song. I knew immediately that we had something really, really special—as anyone would have.

WHITLOCK: To this day, I think adding the coda was a big mistake. When I was still with Delaney and Bonnie and Friends and living in the big house they had in L.A., they had a guesthouse up on top of the hill. I went up there and Jim, Rita Coolidge, and some other folks started messing around on this melody on the piano and asked me to join in . . . and I said, "Nah, that for sure ain't rock and roll." Well, they wrote this thing called "Time" which was later recorded by Rita's sister Priscilla—and that was the melody to the "Layla" coda!

It was Jim's brilliant idea to stick it at the end of "Layla" and I just did not think it belonged there. It was tainted goods, and it completely taints the integrity of this great song that Eric wrote himself from the heart. . . . I could hear how it would work, but I thought it was an ego trip on Jim's part and I was like, "What am I going to do when we play it live—walk over and play drums?" Of course, it became a moot point, because we only did it live once, with Duane in Tampa [on December 1, 1970], and it ended on a suspended note—no coda.

DOWD: When we walked out of those sessions, I told the band, "This is the best damn album I have done since *The Genius of Ray Charles*." And then the thing didn't sell for a year! We all knew how great it was—including everyone at Atlantic—but we couldn't get arrested with it. That was very hard to understand, and very disappointing.

The single and the album both failed to make much of an impression upon release, perhaps because Clapton's name was not prominently displayed and few knew that Derek and the Dominos was his band. "Layla" was rereleased on the 1972 compilation The History of Eric Clapton *and became a top 10 single in both the USA and the UK.*

DOWD: Suddenly, "Layla" was like the national anthem. And that seemed appropriate.

Living on the Open Road

WEEKS AFTER THE *final* Layla *sessions, the Allman Brothers' second album,* Idlewild South, *was released, less than a year after their debut. It was named after a cabin on a lake outside of Macon that the band rented for $165 a month and used as a rehearsal space and party pad. The name was a tribute to New York's Idlewild Airport, which was the original name of JFK, and referred to the high volume of visitors coming and going from the cabin. It was here that the band and crew had pledged allegiance to one another.*

PAYNE: Idlewild South is where the brotherhood came to pass. There was a pact made out there around a campfire—all for one and one for all. Gregg was playing acoustic guitar and singing "Will the Circle Be Unbroken" and the pact might as well have been made in blood. Everybody believed it 100 percent.

TRUCKS: Idlewild was just a really good place at the right time. There was enough room there to have a little privacy if you wanted it, or to just go out for a walk, or go fishing. It was a very old lake house that had been settling for years and I was sitting at my drums at about a 20-degree angle. Everything was crooked and it gave us a different perspective.

Idlewild South.

That's where we worked up most of the material on the second album, as well as other songs. "Hot 'Lanta" was written there one night. We had taken something strong and Gregg was sitting at his organ playing the opening lick and Dickey walked by behind him, sang the guitar riff, and picked up his Gibson and started playing it. Then we were all on our instruments and in a half an hour we had the whole damn thing worked out. Things like that happened out there all the time.

On the back of the album, among the credits, Mama Louise Hudson was thanked for her food with two simple words: "Vittles: Louise." Several members of the band proudly brought a copy in to H&H to show Hudson as soon as it was released.

MAMA LOUISE: I was real happy. I guess I did something good. I gave lots of people free plates when they was hungry. It was nice to get a thank-you like that.

I think it was around this time when Gregg and Red Dog came in and Red Dog said to Gregg, "Go ahead and ask her." And Gregg said, "How do you feel if we call you Mama Louise?"

I said, "I'd feel good." I knew that Gregg called his own mother "Mama A" and I always did feel like they was my sons.

Idlewild South sold only marginally better than its predecessor, though the band had a growing national reputation and the album included songs that would become staples of the band's repertoire—and eventually of rock radio.

ALLMAN: When the first record came out at number 200 with an anchor and dropped off the face of the earth, my brother and I did not get discouraged. But I thought *Idlewild South* was a much better record; I wrote some of my best stuff on that one and when that died on the vine, I thought, "Damn, maybe we were wrong about this group."

WALDEN: I doubted myself. It seemed like I had just been wrong and that they were never going to catch on. People just didn't grasp what the Allmans were all about—musically or any other way. But they kept touring, going across the country, establishing themselves city by city as the best live band around and building a base.

RED DOG: Every time we played someplace, when we came back, there was a bigger crowd, just from word of mouth; the band sold itself. The band sold the band. It just kept mushrooming like that.

ALLMAN: I felt pretty bad and it started dawning on me that the more we got around and got seen, it was worth ten times anything else we could do. The key was not to worry about the record sales, and trust that shit will take of itself. What we had to do was keep getting out there and letting people know that we're there.

Dickey Betts behind the lines, Tulane University, 1970.

DON LAW, *Boston promoter*: At the time, the most valuable piece of promotion available was word of mouth. That was true of everyone, but especially for a band as strong as the Allman Brothers. It was obvious to anyone who saw them that they were fantastic.

BETTS: Duane was bursting with energy; he was a force to be reckoned with. His drive and focus were incredible, as was his intense belief in himself and our band. He knew we were going to make it. We all knew we were a good band, but no one else had that supreme confidence. We were a progressive rock band and we used to sit and say, "This band is never going to make it because we're too fucking good."

TRUCKS: Our first few tours, it seemed like there'd be a few people really getting into it at every show and a bunch of others standing around going, "Huh?" We really didn't think we were going to take off. We just knew how good it was.

BETTS: Duane's confidence and enthusiasm were infectious. He helped us all believe in ourselves and that was an essential key to the [eventual] success of the Allman Brothers Band.

Duane was a natural leader, and if he got knocked down, you'd feel compelled to do everything you could to get him back up and going again. He and I talked a lot about that, and decided that would be the difference in our band as compared to every other band we'd ever been in: when someone falls, instead of talking about him or taking advantage of him, we'd pull him back up, but no one would be the leader. None of us would ever take that position in the Allman Brothers Band. Whenever we needed a leader, someone would step forward and lead. That's a Duane Allman quote. Of course, he'd also often say, "I'm not the leader of this band but if and when we need one, I'm a damn good one!" And he was.

PAYNE: Duane had this monstrous personality that was overbearing in any crowd. If you put him in the room with the President of the United States, he would have taken over the conversation in five minutes.

JAIMOE: If Duane had an idea in his head to do something, he would try doing it until he fell on his face. It's like the old saying, "If you're not part of the solution, you're the problem." No one would stand in Duane's way.

HAMPTON: Duane was the Douglas MacArthur of that band. He ran it like a general or an old-school football coach. It was his band and he let you know that you were in *his* band. Duane was never a dick. He was a wonderful, beautiful man, but it was Vince Lombardi stuff:

Jaimoe and Duane Allman at the Thunderbird Motel, Miami, 1970.

his way or the highway. And he would flip anybody's ear if they were out of line.

ODOM: Nothing was democratic with Phil Walden and Associates and nothing was democratic with the Allman Brothers Band. Duane was a natural-born leader. His philosophy was, "Get on my back. Follow me." And nobody ever questioned that. Any band that's going to be successful has got to have a leader: that was Duane.

RED DOG: There was no question that it was his band, even with Dickey, who was a pretty strong character in his own right. Everyone in that band would have followed Duane anywhere.

PAYNE: He was such a charismatic leader. If we ran into any kind of a roadblock, he would take it on head-on. He liked confrontation, not for confrontation's sake, but to solve a problem. He would take on any challenge, and get by it every time. He would negotiate anything with anyone.

RICK HALL: He would stand up to me, not in a mean way, but he was very tenacious. If I started opposing him—and I thought a lot of his ideas were crazy at first—he would put his arm around my neck and pull me close and get his way on anything we did. He wouldn't give in. My ankles bled all the time he was around, because he was always nibbling on them.

RED DOG: I would have followed Duane to the end of the earth. He instilled in you this confidence of his ability to lead. A situation would come up and Duane would make a decision and it would usually work out. And even when it didn't, we never really questioned the intent.

ALLMAN: He was always up to something; my brother never got bored. He either had his head in a book, his arm around a woman, or his arm around that guitar and it was singing to him.

TRUCKS: Duane read all kinds of things. He loved Tolkien and *Lord of the Rings*, of course; he named his daughter Galadrielle [after a *Rings* character]. He also loved T. S. Eliot, and I remember him reading some Frank Herbert and some philosophy. I turned him on to Rousseau and he absolutely loved it. He immediately understood and was drawn to the philosophy that we're all much happier in a natural state.

LINDA OAKLEY: Butch was the college boy and most of the other guys hadn't graduated high school, having dropped out to go on the road with bands, and he was always bringing books around. Everyone shared and passed them around and I also recall a lot of R. Crumb and Marvel comic books being read, with everyone having their favorite characters.

While Idlewild South *did not launch the band to glory, they continued their relentless touring schedule, winning new fans everywhere they performed.*

ALLMAN: We played [continuously] in 1970, traveling most of the off days. We were in a Ford Econoline van and then a Winnebago [nicknamed the Wind Bag].

ABB life on the road, early 1970.

PAYNE: That Ford van was famous for having walls so thin that ice would form on the inside during the winter, with all of us huddled in the back with the gear.

DOUCETTE: The band came to pick me up at my place in New York one day, in that beat-up Ford with no windows except the backdoor and the windshield. It had little, thin, striped mattresses up the wall and one guy would sit with his legs out, another guy on the other side with his legs out, and on down the line, with amps and guitars in there. Duane said, "Hop in man." . . . Later, I was like, "No offense, but if that's the transport for the band, I'll opt out." Duane started thinking and he was on the phone with Phil that night trying to get some non-embarrassing transport.

MAMA LOUISE: I remember the first time they brought that camper home. They were so happy. Red Dog came over and said, "Mama, you gotta come see this."

JONNY PODELL, *ABB booking agent:* I started booking the band in June 1969. Phil Walden said, "Get them dates. I don't care if it's Portland, Oregon, on Monday and Portland, Maine, on Tuesday." I tried to do a little better but that's what we did and they never complained.

Phil Walden (left) and Jonny Podell at a Capricorn picnic.

JON LANDAU: Jonny Podell was a fabulous booker. A crazy man, but a great, great agent.

PODELL: This was run like a machine, like a military unit. There were six in the band and management provided them with first five, then six crew, which was pretty unusual for the time and really quite extravagant.

ODOM: It got pretty hairy there for a while. We had a lot of money sunk into the band. When you're in the management business, you're in it to develop and that's what we were doing. When you have a band making $1,000–$2,000 a night, you can't reach out and take a 15 percent commission, but you can put it on the book and that's what we did. A lot of the money invested was just keeping them alive and on the road. In the course of a year, $100 here and $300 there adds up with a band and crew.

PAYNE: Getting the Winnebago was a real big deal, like, "Oh, happy day!" But it turned out to be not so great. The damn thing was a

27-footer, designed for a guy and his wife and two little kids to go fishing for a weekend, not to have ten guys and all their stuff living in it for months of coast-to-coast traveling. Technically, it could sleep ten people, but being on the road for two months we were just constantly stepping over each other's stuff and banging into one another.

ALLMAN: That kind of schedule puts a lot of wear and tear on your ass but we were sure getting better.

ODOM: That Winnebago kept them together. They needed it, and it was a big investment at the time.

RED DOG: I really think that kind of life led to a lot of the drug problems. It was tough. You had to have something to get you up and something to get you down. The coke would work: bingo, you're up! And the heroin would work: bingo, you're down! And there were always pills—blues, reds, yellows—to perk you up or calm you down.

PODELL: The business was just becoming somewhat professional and they were certainly one of the first to approach it from the management down as an investment, as a business. That was also reflected in the very nice Winnebago that Phil got them. It was a significant investment at the time for a band not yet making any money. For a bunch of six undisciplined hooligans road-crewed by six more undisciplined hooligans, they responded to the management and the booking in a very professional way. Obviously, in later years that began to unravel with the use and abuse of alcohol and drugs, but at the beginning, there was a true sense of brotherhood between those twelve guys and everyone working with and for them.

The touring helped the band slowly grow a fan base, but they were still struggling to make a living. Their 1970 tax returns show every band member with an income of $8,764.01, except for Gregg, who made over $5,000 more from royalty payments, and Duane, who made an additional $1,080, presumably from session work, including $300 he received for recording with Delaney and Bonnie in May 1970. Every band member was paid a per diem of $7.50 for every day on the road.

The grueling road trips and constant touring took a toll on the band and crew and may have played a part in what happened on April 30, 1970, at Aliotta's Lounge in Buffalo, New York. Payne and Mike Callahan arrived at the club to pack up the gear and collect the money for the previous night's performance. The band had been paid a $500 advance on a $1,000 guarantee but had left the club without receiving full and final payment, which the venue's owner, Angelo Aliotta, refused to make. He wanted them to play another night and refused to let them load out their gear. The band was planning on driving to Cincinnati to play a benefit for Ludlow Garage, one of their favorite venues.

JOHN LYNDON: Twiggs was very proud that he'd never not gotten paid. They had played until three a.m. and ended up leaving without the money. The booking agent said, "Forget it. We'll sue them and get it. Don't worry about it." Clearly, Twiggs was sleep deprived, eating speed to stay awake, and he didn't have any emotional resources left to deal with things.

DOUCETTE: Twiggs had road managed for Little Richard, Percy Sledge, and other guys on the chitlin' circuit—the toughest environments you can imagine—and he was very, very proud of the fact that he had always gotten paid. He treated that like Lou Gehrig's consecutive-games-played streak.

It's been widely believed that Aliotta's rationale for not paying the group was that they had been fifteen minutes late after driving all day from the previous evening's show in Stony Brook, Long Island, 450 miles away, but John Lyndon says this was not likely the case.

JOHN LYNDON: There's nothing in any of the notes I've read that being late was a justification for not paying the band. When they arrived, someone at the club actually told them, "We've got another band that's gonna open so y'all are not going on until ten or eleven. It's no problem that you're late."

The next day the band had a rare off day, but they were planning on playing the Ludlow Garage benefit, followed a day later by a show in Cleveland. In the morning, Aliotta again refused to pay the money owed when Payne and Callahan arrived to complete the load-out. They called Twiggs at the hotel.

RED DOG: It was a strange deal because the guy was messing with us from the start. It was, "I'll pay you . . . I ain't gonna pay you . . . I'll pay you." We left the club without being paid, which was not good, and the next morning the guy said on the phone, "Come over, Twiggs. I got the money." Before he left, Twiggs said to me, "If this guy says he ain't gonna pay us, I'm gonna off him." I said, "Don't talk like that," but I didn't take him seriously.

JOHN LYNDON: I never heard that Twiggs said that and it's not consistent with the notes in the investigation.

Duane was sleeping and Twiggs took his fishing knife. Maybe he took the knife for protection because he thought it might get rough down there. Then he meets with Aliotta, who's this fifty-five-year-old nice guy and he was trying to reconcile the difference. Then Twiggs gets in an argument and stabs this guy and he had no recollection of having done so.

PAYNE: Callahan and I were the only members of the troop there with Twiggs. We were on the stage and Twiggs went behind the bar and got in the man's nose. They started tussling and we thought Twiggs was just beating the hell out of him. We kind of took our time getting over there because we didn't know he had a fucking knife. Callahan jumped over the bar and I just went over to where it opened and as I got nearer I saw all the blood.

Twiggs was holding the knife out, saying, "Take this, son of a bitch." I was shocked and I grabbed the old man—he seemed old at the time—and stood him up. He had on a Navy-style tunic with all this blood spreading out on his lower right side. I pulled up his shirt and there were five little holes shaped like the five on a dice and the man was yelling in a weak voice, "Call the police. Call the police."

There were seven or eight people at the bar and someone did go call. Twiggs just walked over and sat down at a table. I went over and asked him if he stuck that man and he said, "I stuck him several times." I said, "You better run," and he said, "I ain't running no more." He just sat there and waited for the police to come.

JOHN LYNDON: He went to the police station and signed a confession.

RED DOG: We went to eat, opened the door, and Duane said, "I just got a call and Twiggs killed a guy," and someone said, "Oh, come on now." And Duane said, "No, man. He stabbed him."

He said he was going to do it and he did it. Twiggs did not bullshit. Obviously, some people could say that's premeditated murder, but I thought it was just one case where smack talking actually came to pass because of circumstances. I do not believe he set out to do this, but it freaked me out. Before he left, when I told him to calm down, he said, "Just make sure you get my camera equipment," and I couldn't even do that. I couldn't find it in all the commotion and I felt really terrible about that.

Lyndon was arrested, booked for first-degree murder, and held in jail. Callahan and Payne had to stay behind as material witnesses, while the rest of the crew and band managed to load up their gear and move on to Cleveland, skipping the Ludlow benefit.

CALLAHAN: It was some deep, bad serious bullshit. Me and Payne got left behind. We were told we can't leave town and we should assume another name when we checked into the hotel.

PAYNE: We had to load out. We were not going to leave our equipment unguarded and unprotected in that club. We just didn't want to leave our shit there and we insisted and they couldn't really come up with a reason that we couldn't do that. The cops were not happy about it, or about having to protect us while we worked. But first they cordoned everything off as a crime scene and took Callahan and me to the station to get our statements and the cops there were not shy about their feelings either. One came up to the guy interviewing me and said [about Twiggs], "We took that bastard's belt, but if you ask me, we should let him hang himself and save the state a whole lot of money."

They took us through all kinds of protective precautions—like they were hiding away John Gotti. They had five cars behind us and five ahead of us and drove us to another hotel, where we checked in under assumed names, as witnesses. They were paying for all this and Callahan decided to see how far he could push it, so he asked if we could stop by a liquor store for a little something, and the guy said, "Well, I don't see why not."

RED DOG: Twiggs loved that band so much that he killed a man over five hundred dollars. That was all it was, but it might as well have been five million to us at the time. It broke the law, obviously, but I think it abided by the code of the land: "I'm gonna have to do this to you because you are hurting my family."

One night we were driving on the Beltway around Washington, D.C., and I was lost in sadness. Duane was sitting up there with me, as he often did, and he asked me what was wrong. I said, "I'm thinking about Twiggs and where he is," and Duane said, "I didn't think you liked Twiggs." I said, "I love him. Just because we argue a lot, that don't mean nothing."

Twiggs educated me about gear. I had never known anything except the military and the hustle. I didn't know anything about music or equipment, and he taught me everything.

The group continued with their tour in Cleveland and called Willie Perkins, who was Lyndon's handpicked successor. After one more show, in Swarthmore, Pennsylvania, the band returned home to Georgia.

WILLIE PERKINS, *ABB road manager, 1970–76:* Twiggs was an old friend of mine and I had seen the band in the park in Atlanta and become converted. I thought they were the greatest thing I had ever seen and I asked Twiggs for a job and he said, "We don't have any money but the next time we have a slot, it's yours." He wanted to get out from being the road manager and move over to dealing with gear, and he knew that he could trust me. He gave the guys my number and said to call if anything ever happened to him.

ODOM: When Twiggs recommended somebody, Duane didn't hesitate or doubt.

PERKINS: Butch called me from Cleveland and said Twiggs was in jail and they needed me. They were on their way back to Macon. About a week later, they had a gig in Atlanta, at Georgia Tech, and I met them there. I got onto the Winnebago and Duane came and sat down in the lounge and said, "Man, we are a handful. We will sure enough drive you crazy." I knew that he was shooting straight and telling me the truth but I was in. I told him I needed two weeks to give notice and then I'd start.

I was a suit-and-tie-wearing auditor for the Trust Company of Georgia in Atlanta and everyone thought I was absolutely insane. My colleagues and friends and families could not understand what I was doing. They all said, "You are throwing away a promising career to go run around with a bunch of crazy hippies who make no money."

LINDA OAKLEY: I saw Willie go through such a transformation from a guy in a tie with neatly combed hair to a guy with eyes spinning around in his sockets from dealing with this group.

PERKINS: I tried to impose a little bit of business sense on them and started cutting down on expenses, doing things like sharing one hotel room so we could have a shower, but forcing everyone to sleep in the Winnebago. Guys went to Duane and complained I was too strict, that I was like a father, and he said, "Believe me, he'll be an asset to the band."

As Perkins quickly learned, the Allman Brothers Band was almost as well known for their beautiful, plentiful groupies as they were for their lengthy, high-quality shows.

PERKINS: I met with Phil Walden and he said, "You won't make much money, but you'll get more pussy than Frank Sinatra."

MAMA LOUISE: They had so many women. And Gregg was the lover boy. Oooh!

HAMPTON: I remember seeing them at American University real early and there were probably a hundred people there, all of them going nuts. Half of them were women in the front staring up lustfully.

RED DOG: One promoter from up North once said, "Someone in the Allman Brothers has slept with every woman in the South," because he was down there doing shows and anywhere he went, he'd meet all these women who told him they knew us, they had dated us, asked him to say hi to someone from the Allman Brothers Band. He said, "You guys must be fucking yourself to death." We attacked it all full blast. Wild music, wild women, wild times. We were living hard and fast.

LINDA OAKLEY: There were always a million girls hanging out backstage and we would go to shows and look at them and wonder who was doing whom. And they had their on-the-road parties, which were like marathon things, with everyone sharing everyone. Such fun, those bad boys were having. I knew about it and understood it, but it didn't really make it any easier. That's showbiz!

PERKINS: The girls would show up when the equipment truck did and blow their way through the crew. Then they had backstage passes when the band arrived. Later, back at the hotel, things would continue and the road crew would get the leftovers.

LINDA OAKLEY: Despite it all, we were real families and we had our own little lives: Donna, Duane and Galadrielle and me, Berry and Brittany and Kim and Candy at the Big House together. This was our Golden Age.

Even as the band settled into some form of domesticity in Macon, life on the road continued to be full-tilt, full-time. They danced on the edge of tragedy again in Nashville, where Duane and Gregg were born, following an October 30, 1970, concert at Vanderbilt University.

TRUCKS: Someone picked up a big piece of tar [opium] and we were pulling little balls off of it and eating it. We also found a club and jammed after our show. We finally made it back to our hotel and everyone scattered for the night. Red Dog, who was the official driver, hadn't participated in the evening's mind-altering delicacy and since the next show was only a few hours' drive away in Atlanta, he wanted to get everyone in the Windbag and drive while it was night with no traffic.

We started rounding up everyone and getting them ready to move. There was no answer in Duane's room on the phone, so we knocked on his door—no answer. We knew he had gone to his room so the first tingling of anxiety started. Someone got the hotel dude with the master key to open the door and Duane was fast asleep. We tried waking him up, then turned on the lights and the tinglings jumped through the roof. His lips and fingernails had a slight bluish tint.

PAYNE: Duane had turned blue and one of those Kools he smoked had burned down and blistered his fingers.

TRUCKS: An ambulance was called and we all jumped into the Windbag and followed it to the nearest hospital. The triage guy gave Duane a once-over, looked at us, and said something to the effect of "We'll do what we can but don't hold out too much hope. He's pretty far gone." Then they ran him in.

It was all a bit surreal. I had eaten some of the tar so my mind wasn't exactly clear. I will never forget, however, Berry looking up and on the verge of tears saying over and over, "Please just give him one more year." Someone finally came out and informed us that Duane had pulled out of it and that he would be just fine. We even made it to Emory University for the gig that night.

Duane and Donna soon separated. She and Galadrielle returned to St. Louis, after Duane signed an agreement acknowledging he was the baby's father. Duane had already been spending more time in Atlanta with his new girlfriend, Dixie Meadows; the couple was sharing an apartment on 10th Street with Doucette.

DOUCETTE: He was falling in love with Dixie and had to get out of the thing with Donna. We're sitting in Atlanta and he goes, "I got to tell Donna. This isn't fair." And I said, "Good." And he goes, "Come on. We're going." I said, "Going where?" And he goes, "Macon." That was the last place I wanted to go at 10 or 11:00 on a rare night off, but he said, "I got to tell Donna. I've got to clear this up."

I was sad, but I knew it had to be. He loved Donna and he loved his child, but things were moving fast, and not completely in the right direction.

LINDA OAKLEY: I was furious with Duane for the heartbreak he'd caused. Oddly enough, I found myself in a similar situation a year or so later.

As the band earned more money, they moved to incorporate. This forced Doucette, who played often with the band but valued his ability to come and go as he pleased, to directly address whether or not he would become an official member of the group.

DOUCETTE: Duane kept saying, "You're the seventh." He was trying to shoehorn me in there. Duane and I were great friends and we really liked playing together and hanging out together. The next thing I knew we were in a room and we're incorporating. I said, "What's this?" "You need to sign. We're incorporating." I said, "You don't need me here." And Duane said, "Man, I want you in the band." And I said, "No." And the look on Betts's face . . . he couldn't believe it.

BETTS: We offered Thom Doucette a job when we first started playing at the Fillmores, which I thought was a little nuts, honestly. Duane said, "Join the band" and Thom said, "Nah, I love to jam but if I was a member of the band I'd have to show up all the time and that would be a drag." I thought that was the coolest thing I had ever seen. Here's a band that has made it—we're playing at the Fillmore East!—and Thom Doucette says it would cramp his style to have a regular gig. How cool is that shit? He's the real deal.

DOUCETTE: I wouldn't trade playing in the Allman Brothers for anything, but they were complete. They didn't really need me, and I wasn't a joiner. Duane mentioned in a radio interview [with WPLJ New York's

Thom Doucette (left) and the Allman Brothers Band,
Skidmore College, Saratoga Springs, New York, May 15, 1971.

Dave Herman on December 9, 1970] that he wanted to add a seventh member and a lot of people thought he was referring to me, but I was already in the band—or I was and I had bowed out. I wanted my relationship with the band exactly how it was and I asked Duane if I could do that. I said, "Look, man. I'll show up, I'll play, you pay me, we'll laugh and have fun. I'll split." He laughed and said "Okay."

The guy he was talking about was Bobby Caldwell [drummer with the Johnny Winter Band]. But the only guy who liked him musically was Duane. No one else thought he had any place in the band.

TRUCKS: Bobby just played and played. Jaimoe and I sat there all night listening to one another, and Bobby just came in and barreled right through.

DOUCETTE: Bobby was a power drummer and Duane had a side that liked that. He gave everyone nicknames—he just started calling me The Ace—and he called Bobby "Fire." I said, "Duane, take Caldwell and a power bass—Oak can do it—and go make a record. Have a good time, then come back home."

In late January 1971, in San Francisco, the band and four crew members—Red Dog, Perkins, Callahan, and Payne—got matching mushroom tattoos on their legs. Pioneering tattoo artist Lyle Tuttle came to the band's hotel room following their show at the Fillmore West, where they played four nights with Hot Tuna and the Trinidad-Tripoli Steel Band, January 28–31.

JAIMOE: This guy came to our hotel and Duane said he was going to give us all mushroom tattoos. Duane went first. I'm watching this shit and thinking, "How can I get out of this?" But it seemed hopeless so I figured I'd try to deal with the pain. We had some hash, so I ate some, and then I drank some scotch and milk. I learned that from Phil Walden—the milk takes care of your health and the scotch takes care of your head. Duane jumped up, all three pounds of him, and said, "That don't hurt at all!" I was supposed to go next, but Berry jumped ahead of me and as I watched him, I thought, "Ain't no way you're getting out of this without getting a tattoo," so I drank the rest of the scotch.

Berry got done and then he put that thing on my leg and damn! He finished the outline and I jumped up and he said, "I ain't done. I got to color it in," and I said, "I'm done!" As much shit as I had in my system, that still hurt like crazy.

As the band became more popular and their nightly take finally began to top $5,000, they did not slow down their touring pace, or alter the insanity of their routing. The first two weeks of September 1971 provide a snapshot of the grueling schedule: the band played Montreal on September 3 and Miami the following night. They had five days off, during which they went into Criteria with Dowd and laid down the first tracks for "Blue Sky." They then played September 10 at the Central Theatre in Passaic, New Jersey, the following night in Clemson, South Carolina, and the night after that in Shippensburg, Pennsylvania. The *band then had three days off and played September 16 at the Warehouse in New Orleans, one of their favorite gigs.*

PERKINS: Don't ask me how we did it, because I don't know. My own naiveté probably helped me, because we just did what was asked, and made the gigs that were booked, but God! We used to call them dartboard tours because it seemed like someone had made the bookings by throwing darts at a map. We were zigzagging everywhere. We'd play

Tour manager Willie Perkins.

L.A. one night and Indiana the next. That Montreal–Miami back-to-back stands out in the memory bank.

ODOM: When you're on the road like that, your road crew is working eighteen to twenty hours a day. They're in the building at eight a.m. setting up and out at three a.m. It's a hell of a job to get things done and a lot of tension goes on. This road crew would make a jump from New York City to Clemson, South Carolina. They'd make dates under the most extreme conditions.

> **Red Dog letter to Twiggs in jail, 2-23-71:** *"We are flying to all gigs except for the truck, although we do fly the equipment when we have to. The Bag is broke down . . . I hope they fix her up."*

PERKINS: When we started flying commercial, it actually made it a lot harder. It was a nightmare logistically. Dickey was living in Love Valley, North Carolina, without a phone; Gregg might be in Florida; Jaimoe might be in Mississippi; Duane would be God knows where doing a session or whatever. I had to round everyone up, get them to the airport, get them on the plane, have rental cars waiting at the other end, and then do it all over again. They'd stay up all night and when they'd finally crash, it was time to go the airport. It would be quite a while before rock and roll bands figured out what country acts already knew—nice touring buses were the way to go.

DOUCETTE: We played a gig in Ohio, then were waiting for a puddle jumper airplane at a little sandwich shop in a podunk airport. These guys were messing with us, making fun of our long hair and flipping Dickey's hair. I'm watching him wondering what's going to happen because I had known Dickey for years, but he just sat there eating. Then the guy starts messing with Jaimoe and Dickey just puts his fork down and goes, "Come on." It was like a movie.

The other guy is standing next to Berry, who goes, "You're about to watch your buddy get his ass kicked." The guy looks at Berry like he's nuts but then bing, bing, bing, done. The guy's on the floor bleeding and Dickey's sitting back down. A cop shows up and starts in on us and the owner of the joint goes, "Nope. This is his party—the guy laying on the ground bleeding. You know him. He tried to push these boys around and they pushed back. Boys, your bill's on me." By then, our plane had arrived and we just left.

PERKINS: The gear could also be a nightmare. The band demanded to use their own equipment—they would not rent as most other bands did—so we had to get it there by hook or by crook.

JAIMOE: Use rental gear? Only if we really had to.

PERKINS: We drove the gear when we could, but sometimes we had to fly it, and then you had to worry about things like "Would Gregg's Hammond organ fit through the cargo hold door?" And when the roadies drove, that presented its own problems. I can remember many a night standing outside a venue waiting nervously to see that truck come around the bend—but it always appeared! Those guys never dropped the ball, despite everything. They did things that were physically impossible. These guys would be high as shit on LSD and breaking down a stage with perfect efficiency.

During the course of the year, the band's average guaranteed take doubled, from the $4,000 range to about $8,000, and they regularly made more than that, for instance, earning $13,000 for a September 26 gig in Houston. The band was still in significant debt to Walden Enterprises, which had been fronting them money since the beginning for living, touring, and recording expenses. Band members, their wives, and girlfriends, and the road crew all received advance checks from the band account, which also paid alimony and/or child support for Betts ($20 a month to Dale Betts, who had also been a member of Second Coming) and Duane ($100 per month to Donna).

CHAPTER

Live Alive

*T*HOUGH THEIR FIRST *two releases had caused barely a ripple in the marketplace, the band was drawing raves for their marathon live shows that combined the Grateful Dead's go-anywhere jam ethos with superior musical precision and a deep grounding in the blues. A live album was the obvious solution. To cut the record, the band played New York's Fillmore East for three nights—March 11, 12, and 13, 1971. They were paid $1,250 per show.*

The Allman Brothers Band had made their Fillmore East debut December 26–28, 1969, opening for Blood, Sweat and Tears for three nights. Promoter Bill Graham loved the band and promised them that he would have them back soon and often, paired with more appropriate acts, and he lived up to this vow.

On January 15–18, 1970, the ABB opened four shows for Buddy Guy and B.B. King at San Francisco's Fillmore West. They were back in New York on February 11 for three nights with the Grateful Dead. These shows were crucial in establishing the band and exposing them to a wider, sympathetic audience on both coasts.

TRUCKS: You can't put in words what those early Fillmore shows meant to us. The Fillmore West helped us get established in San Fran and it was cool—especially those shows with B.B. and Buddy—but the Fillmore East was it for us; the launching pad for everything that happened.

ALLMAN: We realized that we got a better sound live and that we were a *live* band. We were not intentionally trying to buck the system, but keeping each song down to 3:14 just didn't work for us. We were going to do what the hell we were going to do and that was to experiment on *and* offstage. And we realized that the audience was a big part of what we did, which couldn't be duplicated in a studio. A lightbulb finally went off; we needed to make a live album.

BETTS: There was no question about where to record a concert. New York crowds have always been great, but what made the Fillmore a special place was Bill Graham. He was the best promoter rock has ever had and you could feel his influence in every single little thing at the Fillmore. It was just special. The bands felt it and the crowd felt it and it lit all of us up. The Fillmore was the high-octane gig to play in New York—or anywhere, really.

ALLMAN: That was the place to record and we knew it. It was a great-sounding room with a great crowd. Bill Graham called a spade a spade and not necessarily in a loving way. Mr. Graham was a stern man, the most tell-it-like-it-is person I have ever met, and at first it was off-putting. But he was the fairest person, too, and after knowing him for a while, you realized that this guy, unlike most of the other fuckers out there, was on the straight and narrow.

PERKINS: The Fillmores were so professionally run, compared to anything else at the time. And he would gamble on acts, bringing in jazz and blues and the Trinidad/Tripoli String Band—and he had taken a chance on the Brothers, which everyone appreciated and remembered.

Bill Graham introducing the ABB.

DOWD: I got off a plane from Africa, where I had been working on the *Soul to Soul* movie [*capturing a huge R&B, jazz, and rock concert held in Ghana*], and called Atlantic to let them know I was back and Jerry Wexler said, "Thank God; we're recording the Allman Brothers live and the truck is already booked," so I stayed up in New York for a few days longer than I had planned.

It was a good truck, with a 16-track machine and a great, tough-as-nails staff who took care of business. They were all set to go. When I got there, I gave them a couple of suggestions and clued them in as to what to expect and how to employ the sixteen tracks, because we had two drummers and two lead guitar players, which was unusual, and it took some foresight to properly capture the dynamics.

Dowd was thrilled with what he was hearing until the band unexpectedly brought out sax player Rudolph "Juicy" Carter and another horn player, as well as Doucette.

DOWD: We were going along beautifully until the fourth or fifth number when one chap looked up and asked, "What do we do with the horns?" I laughed and said, "Don't be a smart ass," thinking he was joking, but three horn players had walked onstage. I was just hoping we could isolate them, so we could wipe them and use the songs, but they started playing and the horns were leaking all over everything, rendering the songs unusable.

ALLMAN: Juicy was playing baritone and would basically play along with the bass. Dowd was a perfectionist and the best one I ever met, but we didn't think it was that big of a deal.

We knew we were recording a lot of nights and probably just figured we'd get it the next night if it didn't work out. We wanted to give ourselves plenty of times to do it because we didn't want to go back and overdub anything, because then it wouldn't have been a real live album.

JAIMOE: Dowd started flipping out when he heard the horns, but that's something that could have worked. There's no way that it would have ruined anything that was going on. It wasn't distracting anyone, and it was so powerful.

BETTS: Dowd was going nuts, but we were just having fun and everyone was enjoying it. We didn't change our approach because we were recording. We never hired any of those guys. They'd just show up and sit in, and we all dug it.

PERKINS: The horn players would pop up and just sit in for a few songs. Those guys were friends of Jaimoe's—we just knew them as Tic and Juicy and everyone liked their playing. Nothing was rehearsed with them. They'd just get up and play. Them showing up at those Fillmore gigs was a surprise to me and I didn't think it was a good idea.

JAIMOE: Tic was a tenor player, Juicy played baritone and soprano—sometimes together, at the same time—and there was an alto player we called Fats, who was not at the Fillmore and didn't come around as much. We had played together in Percy Sledge's band and I knew them from Charlotte, North Carolina. Good guys and good musicians.

PERKINS: They often had some heroin with them and were welcomed for that as well.

JAIMOE: I don't know about that; if they showed up with a little something, it was probably because Duane or someone asked them to do so.

> *Gregg Allman, undated letter to Twiggs in jail: "Juice plays barry and soprano at once, Tick Tock plays the dogshit out of that tenor (and alto and flute) and Fats plays alto. . . . All we need now is two of the baddest trumpets we could find and commence to kick ass. Duane says if we can cut it payroll-wise, long about summertime we'd like to take them on full time."*

DOUCETTE: The plan was to bring on the horns full time. Shit, Duane would have liked to have sixteen pieces. Some of the guys thought it was weird for me to be there, but if Duane laid it down, it was down. If he said, "The Ace is playing," it was done. Duane had six different projects that he wanted to do and he just thought he could do it all at once on the same bandstand.

DOWD: I ran down at the break and grabbed Duane and said, "The horns have to go!" and he went, "But they're right on, man." And I said, "Duane, trust me, this isn't the time to try this out." He asked if the harp could stick around and I said, "Sure," because I knew it could be contained and wiped out if necessary.

PERKINS: Doucette had played with the band a lot so he was a lot more cohesive with what they were doing. Duane loved those guys, but he would also listen to reason and I don't think he put up any fight with Dowd.

DOWD: Every night after the show we would just grab some beers and sandwiches and head up to the Atlantic studios to go through the show. That way, the next night, they knew exactly what they had and which songs they didn't have to play again. They would craft the set list based on what we still needed to capture.

BETTS: You have to listen to it being played back to get a sense of whether or not it came together, and we loved having that opportunity. We just thought, "Hey this is cool . . . I didn't know I did that . . . That sounds pretty neat." We were just enjoying ourselves and the opportunity to listen to our performances. We didn't do a lot of that board tape stuff and we weren't real hung up on the recording industry anyhow. We just played and if they wanted to record it they could. We were young and headstrong: "We're gonna play. You do what you want."

ODOM: The band was obviously playing great but you also have to give a lot of credit to Tom Dowd. I've known two geniuses in my life: Duane Allman and Tom Dowd. Tom in the studio was like Duane on stage: totally charismatic and he knew how to get the best out of you. They both made everyone they worked with better.

ALLMAN: We sure didn't set out to be a "jam band" but those long jams just emanated from within the band, because we didn't want to just play three minutes and be over. And we definitely didn't want to play anybody else's songs like we had to do in California, unless it was an old blues song like "Trouble No More" that we would totally refurbish to our tastes. We were going to do our own tunes, which at first meant mine, and because of that there was a lot of instrumentals and long passages between the verses sometimes. Sometimes we had to keep playing to get wound up in search of spontaneity.

BETTS: We just felt like we could play all night and sometimes we did. We could really hit the note. There's not a single fix on there. All we did was edit some of the harmonica out, where there was a solo that maybe didn't fit. It wasn't doctored up, with guitar solos and singing redone in the studio, as on so many live albums. Everything you hear there is how we played it. We weren't puzzled about what we were playing. We were a rock band that loved jazz and blues. We really loved the Dead, Santana, the Airplane, Mike Finnigan, and all the blues and jazz greats.

ALLMAN: The Grateful Dead? Well, I never really thought so much of them.

TRUCKS: Jerry and Duane were friends. They really got along well and respected each other, and we all did. The Dead were definitely an influence on us—not huge but definitely in there.

JAIMOE: When I first heard the Grateful Dead, I thought, "What do these cats really want to do?" Then we played a gig with them and after we finished I had nowhere to go, so I got the conga drum and sat down on the stage behind the curtains and I just played along with the Dead and someone from their crew saw me and said, "Let him out on stage," and I went out there and got miked up. The minute I started playing with them it made a lot of sense. I had to be inside that music to understand it.

BETTS: I've actually had to try not to be influenced by Jerry Garcia, 'cause I love his playing so much. I've really tried not to let my peers influence me. When I was playing clubs, we played a lot of Cream stuff, and I learned Clapton's solos note for note. But there's a thin line between admiring your peers and letting them influence you, which gets real dangerous. That's when you have to go back and listen to Django and Blind Willie McTell, Robert Johnson and Leadbelly.

BOB WEIR, *Grateful Dead guitarist:* I understand that. I've actually done that myself with some people. Really, once you reach a certain amount of facility with your instrument you're going to find yourself playing what you just listened to. It comes out before you can think about it.

BETTS: I also like the Dead's philosophy, which is very similar to ours. We sound very different, because we're from different roots. They're from a folk music, jug band, and country thing. We're from an urban blues/jazz bag. We don't wait for it to happen; we make it happen. But we've always had a similar fan base and philosophy—keeping music honest and fun and trying to make it a transcendental experience for the audience.

WEIR: They were definitely more blues-oriented and we were more eclectic, with a jug band background and also some country, and we were also listening to a lot of modern classical music—just grabbing stuff from any and all idioms. But they used the same approach—improvising fairly heavily—and we were both looking to take a scene and run with it.

It was clear to me from the first time we played together that we were kindred spirits. We were both just starting to feel our oats. We felt like we were becoming a hot band and the Allmans definitely were real hot—they were tight, together, and they improvised very well together.

DOWD: The *Fillmore* album captured the band in all their glory. The Allmans have always had a perpetual swing sensation that is unique in rock. They swing like they're playing jazz when they play things that are tangential to the blues, and even when they play heavy rock. They're never vertical but always going forward, and it's always a groove. Fusion is a term that came later, but if you wanted to look at a fusion album, it would be *Fillmore East*. Here was a rock 'n' roll band playing blues in the jazz vernacular. And they tore the place up.

BETTS: There's nothing too complicated about what makes *Fillmore* a great album: that was a hell of a band and we just got a good recording that captured what we sounded like. I think it's one of the greatest musical projects that's ever been done in any genre. It's an absolutely honest representation of our band and of the times.

JAIMOE: *Fillmore* was both a particularly great performance and a typical night. That's what we did!

ALLMAN: You want to come out and get the audience in the palm of your hand right away: "One-two-three-four, bang! I gotcha!" That's what you gotta do. You can't be namby-pamby; you can't be milquetoast with the audience. There's a lot of good music out there. It's like what B.B. King did on *Live at the Regal* [1965], which is like one big long song, a giant medley. He never stopped. He just slammed it. The second big live record for me was James Brown, *Live At the Apollo* [1963] and that was the same thing. Those records are what got me into doing everything so meticulously—paying attention to arrangements, the order of the songs. The little things are important.

WALDEN: Atlantic/Atco rejected the idea of releasing a double live album. Jerry Wexler thought it was ridiculous to preserve all these jams. But we explained to them that the Allman Brothers were the people's band, that playing was what they were all about, not recording, that a phonograph record was confining to a group like this.

Walden won his fight to release At Fillmore East *as a double album "people-priced" for the cost of a single LP.*

ALLMAN: I still listen to *Fillmore*. Those licks that my brother plays are so fresh still and he has such a tone—and Oakley, too. That boy was one of a kind, just like Duane. Just the chance that we would all meet up and form a band is amazing—everything seemed to fall right into place and you can hear it on this record.

HAYNES: *At Fillmore East* was a dream come true for a young guitar player—a double record of guitar licks. You could go for a year without leaving your room, just running the needle back over and over saying, "How did they do that?" A lot of us wore multiple copies out, picking up and dropping needles trying to learn the licks.

ALLMAN: The release date came up real quick and everyone was wondering what to do for the cover. We wanted to come up with something cool because left to their own devices the people at Atlantic did horrible things. I mean, these were the people who superimposed a picture of Sam and Dave onto a turtle! [This was the cover of the soul duo's *Hold On I'm Coming* album.] We wanted to make sure that the cover was as meat and potatoes as the band and would do what the music would do. So someone said, "Let's just take a damn picture and make it look like we're standing in the alley with our gear waiting to go onstage."

BETTS: We took that in Macon. We were up at daylight out there to take the photo and we were all real grumpy. Jim Marshall, the photographer, wanted us out there then and we thought it was dumb—we figured it didn't make a damn bit of difference what the cover was or what time we took it.

This dude Duane knew came walking down the sidewalk and Duane jumped up and ran over and scored from this guy, then came back and sat down and we were all laughing, and that's the photo captured on the cover. If you look at Duane's hand, you can see him hiding something there. He had copped and sat down with a mischievous grin on his face.

ALLMAN: It was a collective decision, but my brother's idea to have the crew on the back of the cover. He wanted to do that because they were the unsung heroes. He really had a lot of respect for the people that make the shows possible, and set up the equipment just perfect every night. The crew always played a special role in our band and we were quite the tight family. Putting them in a damn picture was the least we could do.

PAYNE: They borrowed me out of the hospital for that photo. I had been shot off my motorcycle by a local cop and was in the hospital going through physical therapy every day, just to be able to bend my leg.

RED DOG: I would have given my life for any of them. If you had messed with Duane, Dickey, any of those guys, I would have said, "You're gonna have to kill this little dude first." I gave my disability check from being injured in Vietnam as a Marine to them—all the money I had in the world. I loved the band.

JAIMOE: How do you say thank you to a guy for giving up his disability check? He supported us at the beginning before we were making any money.

ALLMAN: We lived off the [government] disability checks of Red Dog and Twiggs. It was like, "Want a job? Great. You got any money?"

JOHN LYNDON: Twiggs was in the Navy but he was never injured and didn't get disability checks. He did often donate his own salary back to the band when they were first in Macon.

Twiggs was still in jail awaiting trial at the time of the photo shoot. An individual photo of him was superimposed on the wall above the crew.

PAYNE: We felt like we were part of the band. It was truly indeed more of a brotherhood than any kind of employee/employer relationship.

Everyone was equal. I heard through the grapevine that Duane put out a presidential law that the roadies would get paid before the band when money was tight—which was always in the first few years. He was just that kind of a guy.

RED DOG: The brotherhood was so strong. I can't talk for the musicians, though I truly believe that in Duane's heart it was just as strong as it was for us in the crew—especially Twiggs and me. I had only been back from Vietnam for less than a year when I met up with them, and I was pretty messed up from the heavy shit I did and saw over there. I lost a lot of friends. I couldn't hold a decent job. My marriage was breaking up. All that probably made me very open to this group of guys. They gave me a home.

PERKINS: Everyone, band and crew alike, got paid $90 a week. When I started, the band was advancing the road manager an extra $50 salary. I pointed that out and Duane said, "You deserve it!" And his iron-clad rule was, "If everyone can't get paid, the crew gets paid first." Once, on my birthday, he asked for a hundred-dollar advance. I said, "Are you sure? You've already taken a lot," and he said, "I'm sure." So I filled out the receipt, he signed it, I gave him a hundred, and he handed it to me and said, "Happy birthday. Make sure that goes to my account and not the band's."

JAIMOE: Duane truly appreciated everybody and understood that everybody was a piece of a puzzle. We all play together and every part is equally important and that goes for the bus driver, too. What you gonna do? Play all night and then drive the bus?

I remember one time Walden tried to get him to have a meeting and said he didn't need the rest of us in there, and Duane said, "Wait a minute, this is our band and there's nothing else to talk about. You can talk to all of us." They were trying to get it to be the Duane Allman Band and he said, "No. We're all equal in this band."

RED DOG: Duane would often bring us all into meetings and I'm sure Phil didn't quite understand what me and Kim and Callahan were doing in there. He wanted to talk to Duane and he had ten people in his office and was no doubt thinking, "Not only do I have talk to the other musicians, but I've got these road bums in here."

ALLMAN: They were part of the band, no doubt about it. We were always a little closer with them than the average band.

STEVE PARISH, *Grateful Dead crew member:* From the time we started running into each other at the Fillmore East we had a kindred spirit with the Allman Brothers and their crew—and a big part of it was that they were the only other group we came across where we saw a similar relationship and dynamic between the crew and the band members. We were very similar in the sense that we all hung out as equals. Most others we came across, there was a clear line and there was no doubt that the crew were employees.

PERKINS: The band was like a family, with a hierarchy, and Duane was the father.

JAIMOE: Berry was maybe like the big brother of the band. He was my man and the three of us had quite a bond going back to the time jamming in Muscle Shoals. He was a little bit more lenient than Duane. If someone started some shit, Duane wanted to knock him down. He couldn't have hurt a fly, but he'd go up against anyone who challenged him. Berry would be more like, "Let's work it out, bro."

DOUCETTE: Duane and Berry were so close. Their relationship was unbelievable. Duane would say, "It would be nice if we could do this . . . I was thinking we should get that . . ." and Berry would

Big Brother Berry Oakley.

just nod his head—and do it. Duane had the vision. Berry got it done.

RED DOG: I called Berry "the Deacon." He was a remarkable person also. He had a grip on things and was a great philosophizer, with a way of putting things that made sense to everyone. He helped keep things together in the rough days, always saying, "We'll weather this storm."

BETTS: Berry was also a huge personality. He was the social dynamics guy: he wanted our band to relate to the people honestly. He was always making sure that the merchandise was worth what they were charging, and he was always going in and arguing about not letting the ticket prices get too high, so that our people could still afford to come see us.

Berry Oakley, Alabama bust, 1971.

Just after the Fillmore photo shoot, the band was back on the road traveling from a gig in New Orleans to one at the University of Alabama, when they were arrested at a truckstop near the town of Jackson, on March 22, 1971. A police officer reported that he saw one member—Betts—behaving oddly, so he searched the car, where he found a pharmaceutical cornucopia. Every member of the band, along with Perkins, Joe Dan Petty, and Tuffy Phillips, was arrested and faced various charges, including possession of marijuana, heroin, and phencyclidine (PCP). They spent a night in jail before being released on $2,000 bail.

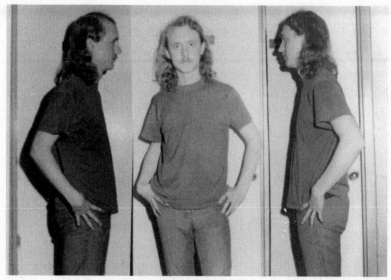

Butch Trucks, Alabama bust, 1971.

The charges hung over their head for months. The Buffalo defense attorney John Condon, who was retained to defend Lyndon, flew to Alabama to meet with the district attorney and assist in the case of State of Alabama v. the Members of the Allman Brothers Band.

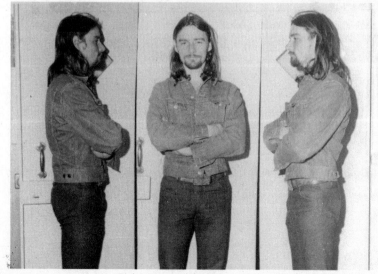

Dickey Betts, Alabama bust, 1971.

Condon traveled there in September 1971 and reported back in a letter to Walden that the DA found himself in a bind because the public wanted him to deal harshly with these hippie invaders, but he knew the case was flawed due to "the nature of the search." He also said the band gave the impression upon arrest that money was not a factor, and that the fact they had $4,000 cash on them influenced him to seek a $4,000 fine per man.

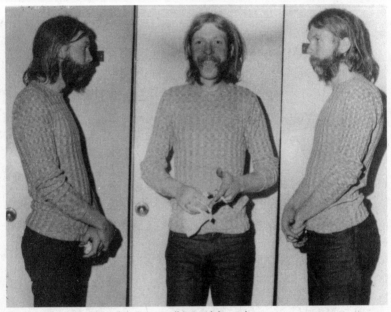

Brother Duane Allman, Alabama bust, 1971.

According to published reports, Condon eventually arranged for the charges against Petty and Perkins to be dropped; the others pled to drastically reduced charges of disturbing the peace and paid a combined total of about $4,000 in fines and court costs. Gregg would sometimes introduce the instrumental "Hot 'Lanta" by saying, "We dedicate this to the people of Jackson, Alabama." To which, Oakley would quip, "We met some of the nicest people down there."

Just three months after the band recorded their album at the Fillmore East, and less than two weeks before its release, Bill Graham decided to close his land-

Brother Gregg Allman, Alabama bust, 1971.

mark venue. He chose the Allman Brothers Band to headline three final nights,
billed with the J. Geils Band and Albert King, and to be the theater's final
performers, at an invitation-only performance on June 27, 1971, that also fea-
tured special guests Edgar Winter, Mountain, Country Joe McDonald, and the
Beach Boys.

PERKINS: Bill Graham never paid anyone top dollar at the Fillmore
and a lot of bands went off to other promoters as a result and Bill
would feel like they had turned their back on him. But we loved playing there. The guys hated most promoters, but they loved Bill.

ALLMAN: He closed the Fillmore with three nights and wanted us on all three, which I thought was the kindest gesture and coolest thing.

TRUCKS: The next-to-last night we played until the morning and we did things that we had never thought of before or since. Those are the moments that have always made this thing work, the reason we're still doing it and talking about it now.

ALLMAN: The second night we played up there for hours and hours, and walked out in the morning. The last night, everybody was already whipped from the night before. On one of the recordings we did, you can hear my brother saying, "It's awfully quiet in here." Everyone was burnt out.

TRUCKS: We were just dumbstruck when we found out that we were gonna close the Fillmore. Can you think of a bigger honor at that time? Jesus. Everyone wanted in on that gig. The Beach Boys showed up and unloaded all their stuff and said they'd have to play last, and Bill Graham said, "Well, just pack up your shit. I have my closing band." So the Beach Boys had to swallow their pride.

Bill was never one to talk much when he introduced bands—"Ladies and gentlemen, the Allman Brothers Band"—but that night he got up and read this speech about us and it was just incredible.

This is in part how Graham introduced the Allman Brothers Band for their— and the Fillmore East's—final set: "Last night, we had . . . them get on stage at about two-thirty, three o'clock and they walked out of here at seven o'clock in the morning and it's not just that they played quantity . . . I've never heard the kind of music that this group plays—the finest contemporary music. We're going to round it off with the best of them all, the Allman Brothers Band."

Graham's introduction can be heard in full on the 2014 box set, The 1971 Fillmore East Recordings.

CHAPTER

Push Push

A T FILLMORE EAST *featured just seven songs spread over four vinyl sides, capturing the Allmans in all their bluesy, sonic fury.* "You Don't Love Me" *and* "Whipping Post" *both filled whole album sides, while* "In Memory of Elizabeth Reed" *clocked in at 13 minutes. The album included Doucette on a number of songs, including* "Done Somebody Wrong" *and* "You Don't Love Me." *His solo was edited out of* "Stormy Monday" *and put back for later reissues, such as* The Fillmore Concerts.

The years of relentless touring, hard-driving rehearsals, and single-minded devotion had paid off: More than forty years after its release, At Fillmore East *still sounds completely fresh, totally inspired, and utterly original. It is the gold standard of blues-based rock and roll.*

Duane's constant faith seemed to be paying off with the album's strong initial sales—but things were far from calm within the band, or with Duane himself.

TRUCKS: Duane never stuck a needle in his arm, but he would snort heroin a lot. One night in the summer of '71 in San Francisco, Duane followed me to my hotel room and jumped in my face. He said, "I'm pissed off! When Dickey gets up to play, the rhythm section is pumping away and when I get up there you're laying back and not pushing at all." I looked him dead in the eye and said, "Duane, you're so fucked up on that smack that you're not giving us anything." He looked me in the eye and walked out the door. I think he knew I was telling him the truth and that's what he wanted to hear. He needed someone to tell him what he already knew, and it was one of the few times I had the balls to get in his face.

DOUCETTE: It was nuts. Everything was everywhere. The drugs never seemed to have a really bad effect on Duane's personality, but the drinking didn't work for him. I thought the booze affected the band a lot more than anything else we did. We were doing things, but the music was so far out in front of everything else.

JAIMOE: When Duane wasn't clearheaded to me, it certainly wasn't from doing heavy drugs. Duane did not need to drink alcohol—just like Gregory, he would become a different person. Drinking made them both somebody completely different. Duane could be so fucking nasty you wouldn't even want to admit you knew him. The other shit did not do anything like that to Duane. Doing smack may have slowed down his playing or made him not be able to control exactly what he wanted to be able to control, but he never did so much until he couldn't play and sound great. Duane moved five times faster than normal anyhow, so that stuff might have normalized him a bit.

PAYNE: Duane had two speeds: stop and wide open.

Duane's love of speed and his reckless motorcycle driving were no secret. As early as December 1969, Rolling Stone *ran a news item reporting on him being busted in Macon on eleven counts, including speeding (60 mph in a 25 zone), reckless driving, having no helmet, running two stop signs, an expired license tag, having no driver's license, and failure to obey an officer.*

DR. JOHN, *pianist, friend of Duane:* Duane was so special, man, a real sweetheart. He was out there past left field, but he was as sweet as they come. In some way, Duane knew he lived on the edge. I don't think he had a death wish, but he knew that he was pushing it—that his lifestyle wasn't necessarily compatible with life. I remember being in Miami with him and he got an Opel because that was supposed to be the car you couldn't turn over and he just wanted to prove that he could flip it.

PODELL: Duane Allman is the only person who ever intimidated me in my life. If he walked into a room, I became instantly speechless . . . which for me was extremely unusual. Bill Graham, one of the most intense men in the world, was my best friend. I dealt with every rock star and promoter you can think of, but only Duane impacted me in that way. I don't know why. It wasn't his words; he didn't say much, at least around me, but he had such a huge, huge presence.

HAMMOND: Yeah, Duane was out there—but we all were. These were heady, heavy times and bizarre behavior was somewhat the norm.

McEUEN: It was crazy times. I gave a guy a ride to Long Beach one day and said, "Hey, what have you got in the briefcase?" And he said, "Seventy-five thousand hits of acid." It was a big drug culture, but out in L.A., the Allmans also brought something that was a little different to people in that culture: Jack Daniel's. They went, "If we drink this and smoke that, wow." I'll never forget the time when Duane did that too much and couldn't hold his guitar at an Hour Glass session. But I'm sure that was because he was unhappy with the music. Duane was generally dedicated to playing his music and doing it as well as he could.

BOYER: He kept everyone in line. Duane wasn't that in line himself; he didn't miss out on anything, but he kept the focus on the music. It was the most important thing to him.

TRUCKS: Duane was strong, confident, and honest. He wanted to experience everything, good or bad, and when he realized that what he was doing was negative, then he would stop.

JAIMOE: Shit, we all were doing too much of everything. I did a lot of things, as much or more shit as anyone, but the music always came first. I wasn't going to be stopped by anything—no women, no drugs—which is why I was forty-two years old before my first child was born. What saved me was paradiddles [drum exercises] and push-ups. I was into bodybuilding and playing drums. I loved sports and being healthy and nothing came before the music. Anything that started to impact the music, I pulled back, and Duane was like that. There were times when he got to the point that he knew shit was getting in the way and he would pull back.

RED DOG: Duane was just very keen, very observant, especially about feelings. If you believe in ESP, he had it. He was very in tune with people and very mature. I was five years older than him and had done serious combat in Vietnam, but I never questioned him as someone to listen to and follow.

RICK HALL: I was thinking about today and he was thinking five years from now.

RED DOG: I was going through a hard time with the band at one point real early and was thinking of leaving because of some stuff Gregg had said to me. I did not discuss this with anyone, but Duane seemed to know what I was thinking. Me and him and Dickey were tripping on Coleman Hill in Macon, and we were down in these hedges, with a canopy of old-growth trees above us swaying together in the wind, and Duane said, "See that, Augie, no matter how hard the wind blows, it can't separate those trees." I looked up at them in the moonlight and nothing could replace the feeling of what he was saying without us ever directly addressing anything.

TRUCKS: When I first met Duane he was taking Black Beauties all the time until he realized it was messing with his music and he stopped. He'd go through these phases where he'd get really into something and push it too far; I saw Duane experiment with every drug there was but once he realized it was affecting his music, he would stop and he had the strength to do that.

JAIMOE: I just think about how great a band this was, how great the sound was, and it makes me think how great it could have been if we hadn't slowed ourselves down with all that shit. We'll never know.

DR. JOHN: We were there [in Miami] doing a session with Ronnie Hawkins and the three of us was havin' a drink with a hurricane comin' up and he said something like, "If I'm not here, could you look after my brother?" It wouldn't have been his style to be that direct 'cause he wasn't that clear about anything—but that was the gist of what he said. He knew he might not be around for real long and we both understood that's what he was saying. It was eerie, man.

PERKINS: Duane had told Phil, "Don't put all your money on me." He did not have a death wish, but he danced pretty close to the edge of the cliff and he knew it.

BETTS: Now that I look back after all these years, it was like he knew that he only had a certain amount of time to get things done.

In September 1971, Twiggs Lyndon went to trial for first-degree murder. He pled not guilty by reason of temporary insanity.

PERKINS: Phil called Atlantic, who put him in touch with Mr. John Condon, who was with the premier criminal defense firm in Buffalo.

ODOM: Someone at Atlantic Records—likely Jerry Wexler—turned Phil on to John Condon. He was a remarkable attorney. He said to me once, "I'm a defense attorney and I represent those that steal and those that don't." He was very good at his trade.

JOHN LYNDON: Mr. Condon decided that they needed to bring in Andrew Watson, who was a lawyer and a psychiatrist on the faculty of the University of Michigan Law and Medical Schools. They told him they would need him there for three or four days and Dr. Watson said that would not be possible for a year. Condon told Twiggs that it was his opinion that it was worth the wait to have Watson involved. Twiggs said he had no problem waiting and so they delayed the trial for a year.

The University of Michigan Law School biography for Andrew Watson, who died in 1998, includes this description: "Andrew S. Watson, M.D., was a pioneer in bringing together the fields of psychiatry and law, helping to establish an interdisciplinary approach . . . Watson brought his training as a psychiatrist to bear in legal cases, using psychiatry to explain both criminal behavior and the legal negotiation process."

Twiggs letter to Bunky Odom, 6-20-70: "I am still enjoying my rest here in jail, with no bail, leaving no trail and unable to sail. Blessed!"

Twiggs letter to Phil Walden, 1-22-71: "I still have my head well together . . . This jail time I'm doing is no problem at all. In fact, I dig it more than ever. The time really does go quickly and I have plenty to do."

JOHN LYNDON: Watson came up with the idea of tracing Twiggs's life from the moment he was born until the moment he killed Aliotta and establishing that Twiggs had no option but to commit the crime. He interviewed Twiggs along with two psychiatrists who were to testify for the state. At the end of the interview, they both agreed Twiggs had been temporarily insane, and the DA had to find other expert witnesses. Condon always gave Watson all the credit for the results, but he was obviously a brilliant lawyer as well.

"[Twiggs] was burned out from life on the road, and his whole existence was getting the band its fees," Condon told Dan Herbeck of the Buffalo News *in 1995. "And when Aliotta refused to pay what the band was owed, he snapped."*

JOHN LYNDON: The next thing [Condon] did was waive the jury trial in favor of having a judge decide the case. Condon said he thought the trial judge was a straight shooter and he knew that finding twelve unbiased jurors in the area was going to be very difficult.

PERKINS: John Condon and his team did a brilliant job. The key to the case was putting Berry on the stand. He could barely speak.

JOHN LYNDON: Twiggs said that Berry was nodding out as he was testifying so there would be a long pause between each question and Berry's answer. The district attorney was attempting to impeach Berry's testimony with his prior drug history and the cross-examination proceeded.

> **DA:** Mr. Oakley, have you taken LSD before?
> **Berry:** Yes.
> **DA:** Mr. Oakley, have you taken LSD on more than twenty-five occasions?
> **Berry:** Yes.
> **DA:** Mr. Oakley, have you taken LSD on more than fifty occasions?
> **Berry:** Yes.
> **DA:** Mr. Oakley, have you taken LSD on more than a hundred occasions?
> **Berry:** Oh, lots more than a hundred times.

Although Twiggs never used these words, the implication was that instead of impeaching Berry, Berry's testimony actually enhanced his credibility by his making no attempt to deny his drug history.

Twiggs also told me that the district attorney towards the end of cross-examination was getting more and more frustrated with Berry. He accused Berry of being under the influence of drugs, which Berry denied. The DA in an accusing manner told Berry that during his testimony he had repeatedly pulled pills from his pocket and taken them, and asked Berry to tell the court what those pills were.

Berry pulled out a roll of Tums and said, "Tums, for my tummy." The DA responded, "No more questions," and sat down.

Twiggs Lyndon was found not guilty due to temporary insanity, and sentenced to confinement in a mental hospital.

PERKINS: The judge concluded that life on the road with these guys was enough to make anyone insane.

CHAPTER

Sweet Lullaby

*A*T FILLMORE EAST *was released to critical and commercial acclaim on July 6, 1971. The record was certified gold on October 25.*

ALLMAN: All of a sudden, here comes fame and fortune. In a three- or four-week period, we went from rags to riches, from living on a three-dollar a day per diem to "Get anything you want, boys."

PERKINS: Phil and Capricorn had advanced the band over $150,000 over the years and they had finally paid it off. They were in zero territory and could start making some money. I remember Duane saying, "Boys, we're going to be farting through velvet underwear."

ALLMAN: You don't do it because you want to be rich and famous, but hell you get hungry working it out there. I don't think money ever even came up. It's not like we said, "I wonder if we'll ever be driving Cadillacs."

A couple of weeks before the gold certification, the band entered Miami's Criteria Studios with Dowd to work on their third studio album, which they had begun the previous month by laying down the initial tracks for "Blue Sky," Betts's sweet, country-tinged tune that would be his first vocal with the band.

DOWD: They only had a few songs ready to track and we never wrote in the studio. That was one way we saved money on studio time.

BETTS: I wrote "Blue Sky" for my then-wife Sandy Blue Sky, who was Native American, but once I got into the song I realized how nice it would be to keep the vernaculars—he and she—out and make it like you're thinking of the spirit, like I was giving thanks for a beautiful day. I think that made it broader and more relatable to anyone and everyone. That was a bad marriage but it led to a good song.

Dickey Betts at his wedding to Sandy Blue Sky.

TRUCKS: Dickey wanted Gregg to sing "Blue Sky" and Duane just got all over him. He said, "Man, this is your song and it sounds like you and you need to sing it." It was Dickey just starting to sprout his wings as a singer.

We were just starting to use sixteen tracks and did not yet have automated mix down, so Tom had eight tracks and I had eight tracks, and we were sitting there punching things in as we needed to. It was like a four-hand piano piece that Ravel would write. We were in sync and running through the song, when the studio door burst open and Stephen Stills [who was recording next door with Crosby, Stills and Nash] burst into the room, holding a tape. He ran over and hit fast-forward, completely losing our spot. Knowing we'd have to start over again, I leapt out of my chair and Duane ran across the room, tackled me, and said, "Don't kill him. He's crazy!" Duane dragged me outside and finally calmed me down.

The band worked on three songs—"Blue Sky," an instrumental track tentatively called "The Road to Calico," which would eventually have vocals added and become "Stand Back," and "Little Martha." The latter, a sweet, lilting Dobro duet, was the only composition ever credited to Duane Allman.

BETTS: Duane and I played acoustics together all the time backstage and in hotel rooms and buses. Duane usually had his Dobro, I had a Martin, and Berry had a Gibson Hummingbird. The three of us spent plenty of time sitting around playing blues—Duane loved Lightnin' Hopkins and we both loved Robert Johnson and Willie McTell. We also worked out things for our own songs. "Little Martha" was not at all typical of what he played—it sounded more like something I might do, really—but he had shown us pieces of it for years, so it wasn't a shock.

ALLMAN: My brother loved playing that kind of stuff, and I have to think there would have been more music coming out of him. He put "Little Martha" together piece by piece.

BETTS: The song is played in straight E. I played the low third and Duane played the higher third. He wrote that song for his girlfriend Dixie; she's "Martha."

*Betts's insistence on this title is at odds with what most others believe; that
"Little Martha" is named in honor of Martha Ellis, a twelve-year-old girl buried
in Rose Hill, with an eerie late-nineteenth-century statue atop her grave.*

TRUCKS: Until that time I had always been sort of the lead drummer
in the studio, but "Stand Back" was a perfect song for Jaimoe because
it was this funky R and B style he's so good at, and I said, "You play the
drums on this. I'm not even going to play." Jaimoe took the lead.

JAIMOE: "Lead drums?" I don't really call it that. What I was playing
fit the song more than the kind of feel that Butch plays. It was a simple
funk thing that fit what I was doing. There's a lot of things that maybe
he shouldn't have played on, but that kind of decision wasn't made.
There's always a positive and a negative to everything you do, so what's
the sense of even bringing this kind of stuff up? Well, it might be interesting for people listening to us to know these things, just like Miles
Davis or Elvis Presley, or anyone else people listen to and care about.

CHAPTER

11

Mean Old World

*W*ITH THREE SONGS *recorded in just about a week, the band took a break and returned to the road for a short run of shows, ending on October 17, 1971, at the Painters Mill Music Fair in Owings Mills, Maryland. The Allman Brothers sold 2,219 out of 2,500 available tickets and made $12,647.*

With many members of the band and crew struggling with heroin addiction, four of them flew to Buffalo and checked into the Linwood-Bryant Hospital for a week of rehab: Duane, Oakley, Payne, and Red Dog. A receipt shows the band's general bank account purchased five round-trip tickets on Eastern Airlines from Macon to Buffalo for $369. Gregg was supposed to go as well, and a receipt from the hospital shows that he was one of the people for whom a deposit was paid. He apparently changed his mind at the last minute.

JAIMOE: If one person did something, we all did. If I listened to Coltrane, everyone listened to Coltrane. When the drug thing started, everyone was doing it, and it really wasn't marijuana or wine. Certain things you better not get involved with—however strong you are, you better know what not to fool with, when to leave shit alone.

PERKINS: Duane had an aversion to needles. He would not use them and he always said, "There will be no needles in this band!" But there were needles in the band.

RED DOG: Duane came out to the camper one time and said to me, Payne, and Callahan, "Don't be shooting this stuff up." On the one hand, that was kind of hypocritical considering how fucked up he was. On the other hand, it was a big brother telling his little brothers to be careful: "This stuff can kill you. Just snort it and get off that way."

PERKINS: Almost everybody had a problem with heroin except me. We could have called it "Willie and ten junkies." I'm not sure about Butch, either; he definitely had the least issues with this.

TRUCKS: I never got into smack. I snorted it for three days at the Chelsea Hotel in New York. It was absolute bliss. Then I went back to Macon and suffered for about a week and I knew myself well enough to know that if I touched that stuff again I'd never get out. That's the last time I ever touched it. Everyone else started getting into it.

PERKINS: Dickey and Joe Dan decided to go cold turkey on their own, and went into the woods together and did it. Jaimoe was Jaimoe.

JAIMOE: When they all went up to Buffalo, I didn't go up there because I didn't think I needed to go. Simple as that.

RED DOG: Gregg was supposed to go but pulled out at the last minute. Me, him, Berry, and Kim, we had a habit. Nothing else you could call it. The other guys, I don't know, everyone was different. Butchie had the least issues.

PAYNE: Red Dog was never really a junkie, with the jones, the monkey on his back that drives you to go out hunting for the stuff, like some of us.

JAIMOE: Was Duane doing worse than normal? Yes and no. There's no simple answer to that.

PAYNE: I don't think Duane's drug addiction was getting worse at all. He was on a real positive upswing, moving away from using so much of anything that passed by him. The way he ended up there, to the best of my knowledge, is Delaney [Bramlett] came to town and [was] staying with Duane and . . . brought an ounce of coke with him. Duane was like a one-eyed cat in a seafood shop; he couldn't help himself, and that led to this trip.

LINDA OAKLEY: It was obvious to the girls at home that things were getting worse. Instead of coming home, relaxing, and having family down time, they'd come back and immediately start looking to score, waiting for the man. We used to get so excited for them to come home. We'd scrub up the kids and put them in their best clothes, and pretty up ourselves and then the kids would go to bed and we'd all disappear into our rooms for our little reunions. Then they just started coming back and only being focused on scoring and getting high again.

ODOM: They were in such bad shape that they were struggling even to do a forty-five-minute set. Duane recognized that and that was the reason to go to Buffalo and clean up.

PERKINS: They all needed help and everyone knew it.

LINDA OAKLEY: Duane just put his foot down and said, "This is what we need to do." When Berry was up in Buffalo testifying for Twiggs,

Duane came upstairs at the Big House into the room where Dixie and Candy and I were playing beauty parlor, putting pin curls in our hair.

We were embarrassed for him to see us like that, but he just said, "I know we've been treating you all really bad. It's not us, it's the dope and we're gonna quit. We haven't been fair to you, but we're gonna go up there and get clean. Condon found a place and I want you to know it's going to be different." And we took that seriously, because when Duane declared something, he meant it.

DOUCETTE: I had left the band in the middle of a tour, because my drug problem was getting out of control and I had to kick. I had been down in Florida for a few months when Duane called and said he's going up to New York to get squared up and I said, "Thank God for that. Take care of business, then get your ass down here and we'll go fishing." I was happy he was dealing with the problem.

PODELL: I was sitting with Duane on a bed in a hotel room in Buffalo as he was about to check into rehab and he said, "Podell, you know why I'm stopping this shit?" I gave a sarcastic "Why?" expecting some song and dance and unsure of where this was headed—because my real relationships were with the other guys, not so much Duane. But he looks right at me and says, "Because I'm not doing *it* anymore. It's doing me."

RED DOG: I cold turkeyed myself for six days before we went. I didn't really need to go to Buffalo, but where Duane went, I went.

PAYNE: That rehab was a joke. It was before real drug rehab existed, and it really was just a nuthouse, a psych ward.

RED DOG: It was a real nuthouse, with guys in white jackets and shock treatments going on behind some doors.

PAYNE: The ladies came up to visit us. Me and Berry busted out of there one night . . . and went and got some dope. Then we snuck back in. That gives you an idea of what it was like.

LINDA OAKLEY: Dixie, Candy, and I went to visit and support them. We missed them and they missed us. It was a conjugal visit. We went to the facility to see them and they were staying four to the room. I had Brittany with me and we had a nice little reunion. Then we went back to the hotel, and prepared to get some supper. There was a knock on the door. It was Duane, Berry, Kim, and Red Dog. They busted themselves out; to hear them tell it, they climbed out of the window. Every one of the guys had a lady there, except Red Dog, who had evidently had a little romance with a patient at the facility. More hotel rooms were secured and we were so happy to be together. Pretty exciting little adventure!

During this time, Twiggs Lyndon, post-trial, was serving his time in another Buffalo mental hospital.

RED DOG: They would take me out of there and drive me across town to the city sanitarium, where Twiggs was being held, so I could visit. I wasn't crazy or convicted, I was there for a drug thing but still they transported me in a special vehicle, with no door handles inside the screen cage. We get there, they take me out, escort me in, as soon as Twiggs and me are in there, they leave and I visit alone with Twiggs. Duane was supposed to go, too, but he didn't want to see Twiggs in there, like that, and I don't think Twiggs wanted to be seen by Duane. He was a very prideful person.

Duane checked us out of there and I was his excuse. They had put us all on methadone, and I was nodding off. The doctor was talking to Duane, who looked across at me and said, "Look at him. He quit before we came up here and he's nodding." That upset him and he was packing up minutes later.

LINDA OAKLEY: Hope springs eternal and I hoped they had turned the corner with this thing. Then Mr. and Mrs. Condon took us out to a very nice dinner. We were all kind of in a daze and the guys were on methadone. Candy was about to lose it because Kim was just showing his ass. We were sitting at a long table and Kim put these chairs together and just lay there with his arms folded across his chest, like he was laid out for his final viewing. Candy was trying to be sociable and show her gratitude to these people for all they had done for us. Perhaps because of the recent craziness, Kim wasn't cooperating.

JAIMOE: I guess they got a handle on whatever they went up there for, but it really didn't make nobody no saint.

During the visit, someone stopped at a liquor store, saving the $3.79 receipt for a bottle of J&B scotch so as to be reimbursed by the band's bank account. After checking out, everyone in the group returned to Macon, except for Duane and Dixie, who traveled to New York City.

ODOM: I went up to Buffalo and checked them out and Duane was clean. I do believe that Duane went to New York just to say "I'm clean" to anybody and everybody, and he wanted to visit his friend John Hammond Jr.

HAMMOND: He came over to my loft and we played acoustic guitars and had a blast for hours. I so wish I had taped it! He seemed to be in really good spirits, his head clear and excited to go on. Things were happening for them. The live album had come out and was a hit and they were playing bigger places. Their star was rising—which seemed exactly as it should be.

We talked about him perhaps producing an album for me. There were all these songs that I played in my show that I talked to him about recording and he said that he would like to be involved. There was nothing concrete, but he was talking business, what percent he would take and this and that. I was not a business guy like that, and he was very together about the band, his finances, dealing with the business end of things. He was a very bright guy who knew how talented he was and wasn't going to take himself lightly.

PERKINS: He was self-taught in business, as in everything else, and he learned quickly. I remember him coming back from the *Layla* sessions, walking into Phil's office and spreading fifteen hundred-dollar bills across the desk and saying, "Look what I got." I believe they had paid him union day rates and given him the fifteen hundred as a bonus. He was very proud of that, but Phil said, "That's great, but you should have gotten a lot more than that," and he worked it out for him to get royalties.

HAMMOND: We were both excited to work together again soon, but he had to get home, and I had a gig in Newfoundland, so I left and he left and we said we'd talk about this project soon.

PODELL: I was on a call when my secretary buzzed in and said, "Jonny, it's Duane Allman on line one." I ignored it, because Duane never called me like Gregg, Dickey, and Butch would. Five minutes later she called back, saying, "It's Duane Allman again, Jonny," and I ignored it again, thinking it's one of my friends, who used to call and say he was Elvis. She buzzed me again five minutes later and said, "Please pick up. It's Duane Allman again."

So I pick up, annoyed, and go, "Who is this?"

And there's that unmistakable voice: "*It's Duane Allman, motherfucker! I pay your rent.*"

My voice went up about ten notches in nervousness: "Duane, when did you get out?"

And he goes, "You know that friend of yours—does she have any downs?" He meant barbiturates, and I said, "No, she doesn't do that."

He had literally gotten out of rehab that day! I heard desperation in his voice, a desperation I would come to know all too well in future years. I was so sad and disappointed by that call, and my heart beats fast even talking about it forty-some years later.

PERKINS: I thought he was clear as a bell. He was clean from the heroin. He was doing lots of coke, like everyone else in the music business. But that really wasn't considered a problem at the time. My last recollection of talking to Duane is he was upbeat, positive, and ready to go. Things were just getting rolling.

McEUEN: I thought Duane had really cleaned up. I ran into him at the Atlanta airport that fall, and he said, "John McEuen, it's sure good to see you." He was just Mr. Nice Guy and seemed very upbeat and positive; it was like running into someone you knew from high school. He said, "I see you have your banjo there. Take it out and play a tune." I said, "Duane, we're in the airport," and he said, "Anyone in Georgia who doesn't want to hear a banjo doesn't belong in Georgia. Come on—take it out." So I sat there and played it for him for about ten minutes and he gave me an Allman Brothers T-shirt and we said good-bye.

After one day in New York, Allman joined the rest of the band in Macon, returning on the evening of October 28.

RED DOG: Duane visited me the night he got back to town, partly because he wanted to make sure I wasn't going to slide back into doing heroin, to make sure I was all right. He sat on my couch in my apartment, squeezing my arm and looking me right in the eye, and said, "You haven't done any, have you?" and I said, "No, man."

And I fired right back on him: "Hey, have you?"

And he said, "Me neither. I ain't looking back. Ain't no more beans for us. We're on our way now." He looked me right in the eye and said,

"This is a religion." He was aware of the spirit, though I don't recall ever directly talking about religion with him.

LINDA OAKLEY: Duane was so happy and full of positive energy. He was always like that unless he was just totally wasted. He was the leader, the great soul, and he kept saying, "We are on a mission and it's time for this thing to happen." He was moving forward, and that energized everyone else. Everyone fed off of that.

RED DOG: Everyone in the band felt it. It was coming after all those years of grinding. The band might have had instant stardom, but I wouldn't have traded nothing for the grinding it out, because we built something together.

On October 29, 1971, the day after returning to Macon, Duane called Doucette at his Florida home to check in on his old friend.

DOUCETTE: He sounded great. He jumped through the phone, with an urgency in his voice that shouted, "It's me. It's Duane! I'm back!"

He goes, "You doing all right?" and I said, "Man, never better. I'm grooving and the fish are running. This is it, baby." He said, "I'll be down tonight. I already booked a reservation. I'm gonna ride down to the office, get my mail and get some money. We'll go fishing and then we're going back to work." I wasn't so sure about going back to work with the band, but I was so happy to hear from him.

LINDA OAKLEY: It was my birthday. Berry and Brittany and I were outside carving jack-o'-lanterns when Duane and Dixie brought me this huge bouquet of flowers, and we were all so happy. All of our dreams seemed to be coming true. *Fillmore* was going to be their opus and they were about to become stars and all of our struggles would be done.

Duane Allman, 1946–1971.

After visiting for a while, Duane got on his Harley-Davidson Sportster, which had been modified with extended forks that made it harder to handle. He had also cut the helmet strap so the protective headgear could not be secured. Dixie Meadows and Candace Oakley trailed him in a car.

Coming up over a hill and dropping down, Allman saw a flatbed lumber truck blocking his way. Duane pushed his bike to the left to swerve around the truck, but realized he was not going to make it and dropped his bike to avoid a collision. He hit the ground hard, the bike landing atop him. Duane was alive and initially seemed OK, but he fell unconscious in the ambulance and had catastrophic head and chest injuries. He died in surgery three hours after the accident. The cause of death was listed as "severe injury of abdomen and head." It was two days shy of a year since Oakley prayed for Duane to recover from his OD in a Nashville hospital, begging God for one more year.

Duane was twenty-four years old.

Will the Circle Be Unbroken?

A s WORD OF *Duane's accident began to circulate around Macon,
many people began to drift toward the waiting room at the Medical
Center.*

SANDLIN: I was at my house when I got the call and went to the hospital. I was hoping it wasn't too bad and was planning on going in to see him. Guys were ending up in the emergency room from messing around with horses or bikes all the time.

I got there and everyone was standing around in the area where the emergency ambulances came in and I could sense the gravity of the situation. Then someone came out and told us he was dead. I went numb and don't remember anything else that day.

PAYNE: Earlier that day, I was heading up to Atlanta to pick up my bike at a custom shop and I stopped by Duane's new little house where he was living with Dixie to ask if he wanted me to pick up anything for his bike. He yelled at us for waking him up and we took off. When we got back, everyone was at the hospital. When I found out he had died,

I got pissed off, just angry at the world, at God. I was exploding with rage and I jumped on my bike, gunned it, and went straight up in the air and flipped over.

PODELL: I always felt he was a tough Southern motherfucker who wasn't scared of nothing and he had met his match. He wanted to stop but couldn't. He had met the devil and he knew the devil was stronger. It was a process of coming to grips: "I can't live with something being bigger than me." He had met his match and it was called heroin.

PERKINS: They had sent me off on a band-paid vacation to the Bahamas. I checked in and before I even went to dinner I got a phone call from Bunky Odom that Duane had an accident and then another call that he was dead and I started making plans to get back.

HAMMOND: I got a call in the middle of the night saying Duane had died and it was just unbelievable . . . literally something that could not be believed or grasped.

TRUCKS: It was just unacceptable that he was gone. Unfathomable. I walked around stunned for weeks.

ODOM: It was a complete shock. Phil was in Bimini and Willie was in the Bahamas. Carolyn Brown, Phil's assistant, got ahold of Phil and I called Willie Perkins and Geraldine [*Allman, Gregg and Duane's mother*] just to let them know that Duane had been in an accident and things did not look good and that I would get back to them as soon as I knew something. And then I had to make the next calls—the horrible ones—to Willie and Geraldine. I made those calls from the emergency room pay telephone, not from the office. I had to rise to the occasion. I had no choice.

DR. JOHN: When a guy like that is suddenly gone it's impossible to comprehend. I played at Duane's funeral and it was gut-wrenching.

LANDAU: *Rolling Stone* sent me down to cover the funeral and I flew on a private plane with Jerry Wexler, who delivered the eulogy, and Dr. John. It was all very somber.

SANDLIN: It's like everyone in the music business was there in this relatively small funeral home. The Brothers were set up and Duane's guitar was there on a stand with an empty seat. They played some songs with very serious faces but . . . man, it was tough. I just had my head in my hands.

RED DOG: I put a joint in Duane's pocket and Gregg put a silver dollar in there with him. I think someone put a Coricidin bottle in as well.

DR. JOHN: Years later, when I met Stevie [Ray Vaughan], one of the first things I thought was that he reminded me of Duane. They were both eccentric as hell and had the same kind of musical concepts—rooted in the past but totally open to the future. And they both came out of the old school, and took it deep, but were totally open to whatever came by. Today, guys are specialists, like doctors, but these guys weren't in that mode. They were totally into all music and it always came first—in a serious way—no matter what kind of drugging and drinking they were into.

WYNANS: Stevie and Duane were both incredible and I feel blessed to have been able to play with either, let alone both. They were both very dedicated to the music, deeply rooted but looking forward, not back. Stevie was probably more well-rounded in the blues but Duane would take more chances. You never knew where he was going to go and he just loved to jam. He was such a force and presence.

MAMA LOUISE: Duane was so nice. Everyone came in here at twelve or one to eat and he'd come back at three or four almost every day just to talk about life. He was so serious, just very serious about life. You'd forget how young he was when you talked to that guy. It really hurted me when he passed. It left a big hole in me.

ALLMAN: We didn't enjoy [our breakthrough with] *Fillmore* for long. A lot of the initial impact of the joy was absent because of the heavy tragedy that happened to my brother. We worked so hard, so long to get there, then, bam, he was gone. Right in the middle of a hell of a tragedy, the record went big, big, big.

The band was reeling, even as At Fillmore East *climbed into the top 20 of the album charts.*

LINDA OAKLEY: We were all in shock. It was like our guts had been torn out. When you grieve, you come together. There was so much love and support from so many people as we all grappled with and tried to overcome the loss of Duane. The guys needed to be together.

BETTS: We thought about breaking up and all forming our own bands. But the thought of just ending it and being alone was too depressing.

SANDLIN: You knew they would continue. They didn't know how to do anything else—none of us did. There's no stopping.

HAMPTON: They couldn't stop. The train was moving. No one was going to try and jump off.

LINDA OAKLEY: Duane was gone, but his spirit was so very much there. We all loved him so much.

TRUCKS: One of the last things Duane recorded, just before the *Eat a Peach* sessions, was Cowboy's "Please Be with Me" with Scott Boyer and Tommy Talton. A few weeks after he died, when I still hadn't really let loose or accepted it, I put on "Please Be with Me" and the dam burst and I started crying and crying, just racked with grief. I was sitting there listening to the song over and over and crying. To this day I can't hear it without getting choked up.

PAYNE: Me and B.O. would sit up in the music room at the Big House listening to Duane playing on *Layla* and cry like little girls. We played that album over and over, until the vinyl was almost see-through. And we just cried.

BOYER: Every musician in Macon was pretty down, just stunned. We couldn't believe Duane was gone. The guy was always friendly and he was such an incredible presence. He had so much energy that he just made things happen. He was always kicking everyone in the butt. It was inconceivable how someone that alive could be dead. He was a central figure for all of us, and, of course, he was *the* central figure for Gregg, who depended on Duane for a lot of things.

PAYNE: Duane was more of a father figure to Gregg. He was the only male in the house that Gregg had to look to for guidance and, given the strength of Duane's personality, that worked fine.

ALLMAN: He only and always called me "baby brah." Had we lived 'til he was ninety-one and I was ninety, I still would have been "baby brah."

PERKINS: It was big brother/little brother, but also father/son, and that was pretty clear to everyone who spent any real time with them. I never saw any conflict between Gregg and Duane last long.

BOYER: Duane was only a little more than a year older than Gregg but he was almost like a father. They were extremely close. Gregg was extremely tore up, which is only natural.

RED DOG: Gregg couldn't have loved Duane any more than I did—and that's not saying anything bad about Gregg or his feelings about his brother at all. It's just that we all loved him that much, and the whole band was like a family. Anyone's death would have been devastating.

LINDA OAKLEY: Berry's heart was so broken. There was just an empty spot, a chasm.

DOUCETTE: I was in complete shock, just dead. I didn't know if I ever wanted to play again.

HAMMOND: Duane was the force of that band. It was his philosophy, his concept that formed it and allowed it to progress. He set a standard for them that they lived up to.

PAYNE: The band had a meeting about continuing and it was clear they wanted to do so, but everyone was concerned about how. It was kind of a leaderless operation there for quite some time. The natural progression of things should have been that Gregg would take over as a leader, but that's not who he is. Dickey's personality and ego were pretty powerful, so he sort of took over, but in a different way.

DOUCETTE: I walked into the first rehearsal after Duane died and Berry and I shared a look of understanding: What was is over. It's gone. It very easily could have ended right there, but Betts pulled it out of the fire. A lot of people do not understand how really smart and connected Dickey is, because of his demons, which can take over.

The whole situation was just too weird. The reason I was there was Duane. I was his guy and he was mine. I loved everyone in the band like brothers, but there was some sorting out to be done and I didn't want to get in the middle of the Gregg/Dickey thing, which I saw developing.

Duane was not buried, remaining in cold storage at the mortuary. Duane had no will and was separated from Donna Allman, the mother of his heir, his daughter, Galadrielle, then just two years old. Duane was living with his girlfriend, Dixie Meadows, who signed his death certificate as "Mrs. D. Allman." The papers authorizing the release of Allman's body from the hospital morgue listed his final resting place as Riverside Cemetery. Gregg struggled to deal with the situation and make a decision.

PERKINS: The concept of common-law wife in Georgia was a bit legally vague and complicated and there were legal questions about who had the authority to make decisions for Duane's estate. In the meantime, his body remained at the funeral home. It got pretty embarrassing and there was a lot of discussion within the band, wondering what was going on. Nobody outside really seemed to notice.

LINDA OAKLEY: There was a lot of confusion initially about who Duane's wife was, but it was up to Gregg to decide about the burial. As I recall, his mother left it up to him and he told her he would take care of it, but he just couldn't deal with it. It was simply too much for him.

JAIMOE: If you're with a woman and she's living with you, then it is considered common-law wife and husband, whether you ever married or not. You don't have to go before God and ask for permission. The fact is, the only time I knew Duane to be married was with his first and only wife, whom I never met.

When Duane and I were living in that cabin in Alabama, one morning at seven some guy knocked on the door. I was sitting up writing letters to my grandfather or something and Duane came to the door in a pair of jeans, no shoes or shirt, and answers: "Can I help you?" And here's this guy in a suit saying he's selling insurance and Duane said, "Motherfucker, do you know what time it is?" He told him to get the fuck out of there and the guy left. Duane was all worked up and couldn't go back to sleep so he sat down with me and said, "You know what? You see that guy? I used to be like that. When I was seventeen I used to wear a suit with a skinny Beatles tie and go around selling stuff and I had a wife. I had a wife and a job and I tried that."

He never was divorced from that woman in terms of how society sees things. Then he was with Donna and fathered Galadrielle right in that cabin we were sitting in, and then he took it up with Dixie and she became his girlfriend, but I never heard him call either of them his wife.

Duane's legal wife, whom he married in Jacksonville, was named Patty Chandlee. They had a daughter together, who is deaf, and who has a child, Duane's grandson.

The band next door to the "hippie crash pad," Macon, Georgia, spring 1969.

Macon, spring 1969.

The band in Rose Hill Cemetery, Macon, spring 1969.

Duane Allman, Mercer
University, Macon,
summer 1969.

(PHOTO BY W. ROBERT JOHNSON)

Duane Allman at oral surgeon, Macon, August 1969.

(PHOTO BY STEPHEN PALEY)

The ABB's first free performance at
Piedmont Park, Atlanta, Georgia, May 11, 1969.

(PHOTO BY TWIGGS LYNDON)

Duane Allman, Piedmont Park, Atlanta, May 11, 1969.

(PHOTO BY TWIGGS LYNDON)

Jaimoe, Piedmont Park, Atlanta, May 11, 1969.

(PHOTO BY TWIGGS LYNDON)

Butch Trucks, Piedmont Park, Atlanta, May 11, 1969.

(PHOTO BY TWIGGS LYNDON)

Berry Oakley at Piedmont Park, Atlanta, summer 1969. Crew member Kim Payne is visible beneath Oakley.

(PHOTO BY TWIGGS LYNDON)

Whisky A-Go-Go, Sunset Strip, Hollywood, California, October 2, 1971.

Duane Allman, Santa
Monica Civic Center,
October 1971.

Butch Trucks, Whisky A-Go-Go,
October 2, 1971.

(PHOTO BY TONEMAN/
DON BUTLER ARCHIVES)

Gregg Allman, Whisky A-Go-
Go, October 2, 1971.

(PHOTO BY TONEMAN/
DON BUTLER ARCHIVES)

Berry Oakley, 1970.

Mama Louise Hudson and Twiggs
Lyndon, taken with timer.

Duane Allman, 1970.

The Wind Bag broken down and towed to a Sunoco, somewhere in the Southeast, 1970. From left: Jaimoe, Dickey Betts, Gregg Allman, Sunoco mechanic, Red Dog, Butch Trucks, and Duane Allman.

(PHOTO BY TWIGGS LYNDON)

Idlewild South sessions, Criteria Studios, 1970. Tom Dowd at the board, unknown engineer behind him.

(PHOTO COURTESY KIRK WEST COLLECTION)

Idlewild South sessions, Criteria Studios, 1970.

(PHOTO COURTESY KIRK WEST COLLECTION)

Duane Allman at WABC radio, New York, during an interview with DJ Dave Herman, December 7, 1970. "Take off your underwear, relax and let ol' Duane tell you how it is."

Berry and Linda Oakley at the H&H Restaurant, Macon, Georgia, April 1971.

Free, impromptu performance at Skidmore College, Saratoga Springs, New York, May 15, 1971.

Gregg Allman, Skidmore College, Saratoga Springs, May 15, 1971.

Duane Allman on stage,
Los Angeles, 1971.
(PHOTO BY STEPHEN PALEY)

Dickey Betts at City Park Stadium,
New Orleans, Louisiana, July 21, 1972.
(PHOTO BY SIDNEY SMITH,
WWW.SIDNEYSMITHPHOTOS.COM)

Five-man band publicity photo,
August 1972, taken at actor James
Arness's ranch, Southern California.
(PHOTO BY TWIGGS LYNDON)

Chuck Leavell, Lakeside Park,
Macon, Capricorn Picnic, fall 1974.
(PHOTO BY SIDNEY SMITH,
WWW.SIDNEYSMITHPHOTOS.COM)

Dickey Betts and Berry Oakley at the Warehouse, New Orleans, Louisiana, New Year's Eve 1971.

(PHOTO BY SIDNEY SMITH, WWW. SIDNEYSMITHPHOTOS.COM)

Five-man band, San Diego, August 1972.

(PHOTO BY TONEMAN/DON BUTLER ARCHIVES)

At the Warehouse, New Orleans, New Year's Eve 1972.

(PHOTO BY SIDNEY SMITH, WWW.SIDNEYSMITHPHOTOS.COM)

RFK Stadium, Washington D.C., June 1973—part of a two-day double-bill with the Grateful Dead. Twiggs Lyndon is to the left of the organ.

(PHOTO © JOHN GELLMAN, WWW.JGPHOTO.COM)

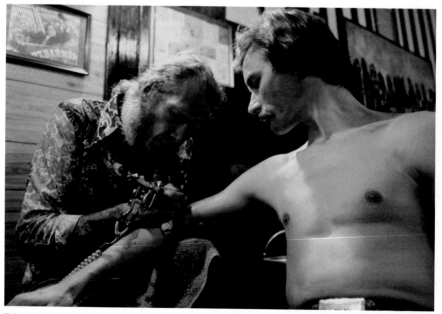

Dickey Betts with Lyle Tuttle in the latter's San Francisco tattoo parlor, 1973.

(PHOTO © NEAL PRESTON 2013)

Gregg Allman on the road, 1973.

Thom "Ace" Doucette and Gregg Allman outside Macon rehearsal space, 1974.
(PHOTO © GILBERT LEE, WWW.GILBERTLEE.COM)

Gregg Allman, Dickey Betts, and Lamar Williams in backstage rehearsal room, Boston, near the end of the first run.
(PHOTO © NEAL PRESTON 2013)

Ain't Wasting Time No More

*T*HE BAND TOOK *a short hiatus before regrouping, gravitating back to one another and immersion in their work. They committed to fulfilling previously scheduled dates in New York. Their first appearance without their leader was at C. W. Post College in Long Island on November 22, 1971; it was exactly three weeks after Duane's funeral.*

PERKINS: Everybody was ready to go back on the road, because we couldn't bear to sit around anymore. We got back out there so fast because I think everyone worried that if we didn't, we might never get back.

RED DOG: There was such sadness, and no one wanted to accept the truth. I thought we needed to go to work right then. I thought we needed to get out there and play. Sitting around, we'd probably go nuts. It's hard to put into words what it's like for someone you spend every day with to suddenly be gone, especially someone with a talent like that.

TRUCKS: We thought about quitting because how could we go on without Duane? But then we realized: how could we stop? We all had this thing in us and Duane put it there. He was the teacher and he gave something to us—his disciples—that we had to play out. We talked about taking six months off but we had to get back together after a few weeks because it was too lonely and depressing. We were all just devastated and the only way to deal with it was to play.

ODOM: We never doubted that they would continue. Never. How well it went was up to them. We can arrange things as best we can and set them up, but when they get on stage, they have to do it themselves.

PODELL: I was terrified of what would happen when the band walked onto the stage at CW Post. I just didn't know if they could do it—and truthfully, neither did they. They only knew like nine songs to play without Duane. The band was built around Skyman, the legendary Duane Allman. When you build a team around someone and they're suddenly gone, who's to say what will happen?

They stepped up. I called Phil, ecstatic about what they had done, and then I went home and asked my girlfriend to marry me—a week after explaining why I didn't think we should do that. That performance just changed my whole perspective on life. Everyone was pulling in the same direction and was riding high on what they had done.

Three days after the C. W. Post show, the band performed at Carnegie Hall, then did another two weeks of shows.

PERKINS: There were intensely mixed feelings at these shows. It was so painfully obvious that Duane wasn't there, which created such an empty feeling. You missed him so damn bad, but you also really wanted to prove that it was going to be OK, that there was still a reason to be out there, that the band could do it. There was a tremendous sense of pulling together.

ODOM: I can't imagine what Dickey went through. Here you've got Duane in Dickey's ear all night long and all of a sudden it's not there anymore. How do you fill those shoes? It was just horrible.

JAIMOE: I really can't remember anything about any of those shows. We just had to play and everyone played and you really didn't know what you missed more about Duane—being on stage with him or just life in general.

RED DOG: The day after we'd come back from being on tour, living on top of each other for weeks on end, we'd be home and I'd miss Duane and be banging on his door to say hello. Realizing I couldn't bang on that door hurt, man. It was stunning.

When the band returned to Miami in December to complete work on their fourth album, Twiggs Lyndon was with them, freed after serving 90 days in the psychiatric hospital.

A.J. LYNDON: I picked him up at the Atlanta airport, and he slid right back into it with the Allman Brothers Band.

Going forward, Twiggs would be the production manager, dealing with gear and logistics, while Perkins remained as road manager.

    The band recorded four more outstanding tracks with Dowd, including "Melissa," Betts's instrumental "Les Brers in A Minor," and "Ain't Wastin' Time No More," Gregg's defiant response to his brother's passing.

ALLMAN: I wrote "Ain't Wastin' Time No More" for my brother right away. It was the only thing I knew how to do right then.

TRUCKS: Of course, the music we recorded was all about Duane. Gregg wrote "Ain't Wastin' Time No More" and that was obviously

Five-man band promo shot, taken at actor James Arness's California ranch.

about how to deal with this tragedy, but I think "Les Brers in A Minor" is about Duane just as much. We did everything we could to try and fill the gap and "Les Brers" was Dickey's response—starting with the title, which is bad French for "less brothers."

BETTS: When I wrote "Les Brers" everyone kept saying they had heard it before, but no one could figure out where, including me. But it's in my solo on "Whipping Post" from one night. It was just a lick I was playing in there, and years later it showed up in a bootleg, which was kind of amazing. I mean, none of us knew where it came from until that tape surfaced years later. It just sounded familiar.

TRUCKS: We were all putting more into it, trying so hard to make it as good as it would have been with Duane. We knew our driving force, our soul, the guy that set us all on fire, wasn't there and we had to do something for him. That really gave everybody a lot of motivation. It was incredibly emotional.

BETTS: It was difficult to suddenly have to play slide and I put in some time to get my part down for "Ain't Wastin' Time No More." I've always enjoyed playing acoustic slide and would even often play it with Duane; when the two of us played acoustic blues I was often the one with the slide, but I never cared as much for playing electric slide.

The band also recorded "Melissa," a song Gregg had written in 1967—he says it was the first tune he ever considered a keeper after several hundred—but had never recorded.

ALLMAN: When we were finishing *Eat a Peach*, we needed some more songs and I knew my brother loved "Melissa." I had never really shown it to the band. I thought it was too soft for the Allman Brothers and was sort of saving it for a solo record I figured I'd eventually do.

The double album Eat a Peach *was completed with three live songs: "One Way Out" from the June 27, 1971, final concert at the Fillmore East, and two songs recorded during the March* At Fillmore East *performances: "Trouble No More"—the Muddy Waters track that had been the first song Gregg sang with the band—and the epic, 33-minute "Mountain Jam." The latter, which took up both sides of a vinyl album, had been an evolving staple of their performances almost since the beginning.*

DOWD: When we recorded *At Fillmore East*, we ended up with almost a whole other album's worth of good material, and we used [two] tracks on *Eat a Peach*. Again, there was no overdubbing.

ALLMAN: We always planned on having "Mountain Jam" on this album. That's why you hear the first notes of the song as "Whipping Post" ends on *At Fillmore East*.

TRUCKS: That "Mountain Jam" is only on there because it's the only version we had on multitrack tape and it was such a signature song of the band with Duane that we simply had to have it on a record. We played it many times so much better, but better a relatively mediocre version than nothing at all.

BETTS: That was probably the worst version of "Mountain Jam" we ever played. When we were recording live, we really were still focused on the crowd rather than the recording.

With recording done, the album had to be mixed. Dowd started the process, but the album had run over time and he had other commitments, so Sandlin was called to Miami.

SANDLIN: I think Tom had to work with Crosby, Stills and Nash. I went down to Miami the last day Tom was still working on it, and sat with him, and he showed me what he was doing and discussed some aspects of recording. As I mixed songs like "Blue Sky," I knew, of course, that I was listening to the last things that Duane ever played and there was just such a mix of beauty and sadness, knowing there's not going to be any more from him.

I was very proud of my work on *Eat a Peach* but really pissed because I did not receive credit, only a "special thanks." It was the first platinum record I'd ever worked on and it meant a lot to me, so that felt like a slap.

TRUCKS: After we were all done and the album was being finalized, I walked into Phil's office and they showed me the beautiful artwork, with this title on it: *The Kind We Grow in Dixie*. I said, "The artwork is incredible, but that title sucks!"

W. DAVID POWELL, *artist, partner in Wonder Graphics, which designed the* Eat a Peach *cover:* I saw a couple of old postcards in a drugstore in Athens, Georgia, which were part of a series called "The Kind We Grow in Dixie"; one had the peach on a truck and one had the watermelon on the rail car. I thought they were perfect for an Allman Brothers album so I pasted them up and bought cans of pink and baby-blue Krylon spray paint and created a matted area to make the cards on a twelve-by-twenty-four LP cover. I envisioned this as an early-morning-sky feel.

Then I hand-lettered the Allman Brothers name and photographed it with a little Kodak camera and had it developed at the drugstore, then cut the letters out and pasted them on the side of the truck, under the peach. Duane was still alive and the album had not been titled. We figured we'd go back and add that.

TRUCKS: Duane didn't like to give simple answers so when someone asked him about the revolution, he said, "There ain't no revolution. It's all evolution." Then he paused and said, "Every time I go South, I eat a peach for peace." That stuck out to me, so I told Phil, "Call this thing *Eat a Peach for Peace*," which they shortened to *Eat a Peach*.

It didn't occur to me until decades later that Duane's comment was a reference to T. S. Eliot's "The Love Song of J. Alfred Prufrock," though I knew Duane was a big fan. I was reading "Prufrock" and came across the reference to eating a peach and was blown away. The symbolism is obvious. Prufrock was totally anal and didn't want to do anything that would get messy and there's nothing messier than eating a peach. Duane would have loved that metaphor.

POWELL: The cover was kind of a new approach, a soft sell, because it did not say the name of the album—and the name of the band was just in tiny letters. We left that to a sticker on the shrink-wrap. When we showed it to someone at the label, he said, "They are so hot right now, we could sell it in a brown paper bag."

The double album opened up as a gatefold filled with another Wonder Graphics piece of art: an entire universe that seemed to promise some kind of psychedelic paradise. It told a story of happy, mystical brotherhood that was receding ever further into fantasy as the band grappled with the tragedy of Duane's death.

POWELL: That was really a cooperative venture between Jim and I, completed with almost no planning or discussion. We were working on a large piece of illustration board, on a one-to-one scale—it was the size of the actual spread—and we just started drawing, with Jim's work primarily on the left and mine on the right. This work was profoundly influenced by [Hieronymous] Bosch.

The whole thing was done over the course of one day while we were in Vero Beach, Florida. While one of us was drawing or painting, the other was out swimming in the ocean. We swapped off this way with virtually no conversation about the drawing, just fluid trade-offs.

DICK WOOLEY, *Capricorn vice president of promotion, 1972–76:* I had been the head of Atlantic Records promotion for the Southeast and Midwest and quit to take a break. I took my family to Europe and North Africa for six months, and when I came back I was looking for new opportunities and [Capricorn president and co-founder] Frank Fenter, whom I had worked with at Atlantic, invited me to a meeting with him and Phil Walden.

Over lunch, Frank and Phil did a dog-and-pony show pitching me on helping them grow the label and launch the new album by the ABB. They needed help because the buzz in the record business and on the street was that the ABB was finished as a band and would never survive without Duane. All I heard anywhere else in the biz was negative talk about the ABB's demise. I wanted time to think it over but then Johnny Sandlin played me some tracks from *Eat a Peach* and I took a flier and said yes—at half my usual salary. I was blown away and knew we had a winner. I was happy when radio programmers remembered me from Atlantic and took my calls. Some, I'm sure, picked up the phone out of morbid curiosity about Duane, but it did give me the opportunity to promote *Eat a Peach*.

To help promote the album, Wooley arranged to have the band's New Year's Eve appearance at New Orleans' Warehouse—one of their favorite venues and one of the last of the smaller halls they were still playing—to be live simulcast on radio. The Guy Lombardo Orchestra had played New Year's Eve since 1928, and there was a long tradition of broadcasting these shows nationally, first on radio and later on TV. Wooley sensed the time was right for a new kind of broadcast, a Rock and Roll New Year's Eve.

WOOLEY: I took a gamble and cobbled together a network of radio stations in the Southeast via Ma Bell phone lines. It was the first of its kind, and it got national attention and helped launch *Eat a Peach*.

The album was an instant classic and an immediate hit, peaking at number four on the album charts. As the band returned to the road, however, they all profoundly felt the absence of their guiding light.

WOOLEY: Everyone at the label kept up a good front, but I'm sure they had doubts. Dickey was the one who rallied the band members into action for tour support of the new album.

TRUCKS: We played gigs as a five-piece, but there was a big hole there. How could you not miss such a personality? But we were up there playing the music that he started. We were playing for him and that was the way to be closest to him. Duane had put this thing inside all of us and we couldn't walk away from it. We're musicians and musicians deal with their emotions by playing music.

CHUCK LEAVELL, *pianist, ABB member, 1972–76:* There was all kind of speculation amongst fans and other musicians around town about who was going to replace Duane and a lot of rumors flying around.

SIDNEY SMITH, *photographer:* There were a lot of rumors about who would be replacing Duane, including Eric Clapton. I asked Gregg about this and he said, "We have a guitarist who can play circles around Clapton. His name is Dickey Betts."

LEAVELL: I thought going on with no replacement was incredibly brave; it took a lot of gumption for the entire band, but especially for Dickey. Imagine the pressure on him. He was not known as a slide player but slide parts were so essential to those songs that they had to be played and I thought he did a really admirable job. He didn't necessarily play it like Duane would; he played it like Dickey.

BETTS: I completely lost my taste for playing electric slide after Duane died and I was forced to play his parts on "Statesboro Blues" and all these songs. That soured me on it. I always felt comfortable playing it before that but I totally lost my comfort zone once I had to play things in Duane's style. I couldn't find my own voice because I had to copy his licks, which I hated doing, and it really kind of spoiled electric slide playing for me.

The band resumed touring in earnest as a five-piece, with Gregg and sometimes Berry taking over Duane's job of introducing songs and Betts generally doing yeoman's work as the sole guitarist and primary soloist. They performed about ninety shows in the next year, including a West Coast tour that featured a special guest in their entourage.

MAMA LOUISE: Red Dog came in one day in '72 and said, "How would you feel about going to California?" I had a niece that Red Dog always liked because she had big legs, and when I said I didn't know about that traveling, he said she could come, too. And she did.

They said it was for cooking—that I'd be working for them—but when we got there, Dickey said, "No cooking for you, Mama. Have a good time." I looked over at Gregg with this beautiful woman and I said, "That's why y'all came out here."

On the way back from California, I was sitting on the plane with Red Dog and Joe Dan. A real proper white woman heard Red Dog call me "Mama Louise" and said, "Oh, is that your mama?" She didn't like it one bit. He said, "Yep. I call her Mama." She says, "Oh, is that so?" and looks at 'em with disgust. They were so mad they wanted to jump on her, but I told them to sit down and be quiet.

Finally making some money, the band fulfilled one of Oakley's communal dreams on May 3, 1972, when they closed the purchase of 432 acres in Juliette, Georgia, about 25 miles north of Macon. They paid $160,000 for the land in Jones and Jasper counties, which immediately became known as "the Farm" and became a group hangout.

At "the Farm" (from left) Kim Payne, Dickey Betts, Buffalo Evans, Tuffy Phillips. Dickey Betts's father is standing behind him.

SWEET MELISSA

*How one of rock's most beloved songs was
written and recorded.*

A teenaged Gregg Allman spent years struggling to find his musical voice, writing and rejecting songs. He says he tossed away more than three hundred.

"They were just 'I wanna swoon with you under the moon in June' or they were a few good licks that didn't really belong together," he says. "My brother and I were struggling with finding any sense of originality. Songwriting is not something you're born with."

Late in 1967, still struggling to write a keeper song, Allman found himself sitting in a room in Pensacola's Evergreen Motel, holding Duane's guitar, which was tuned to open E.

"I picked up the guitar and didn't know it was natural-tuned," Allman recalls. "I just started strumming it and hit these beautiful chords. It was just open strings, then an E shape first fret, then moved to the second fret. This is a great example of the way different tunings can open up different roads to you as a songwriter. The music immediately made me feel good and the words just started coming to me. I started singing but stumbled on the name."

Years later, Allman, relaxing in a dressing room at New York's Beacon Theatre following one of the Allman Brothers Band's landmark shows, starts singing a familiar melody: *"But back home he'll always run to sweet . . ."*

He stops and guffaws at the memory. "Nancy? Sweet . . . Stella? *What the fuck is her name?"*

Allman lets out a long, loud laugh before continuing: "I had the melody and the chords and the idea, but no name. That drove me nuts for about a week. Then I was in a grocery store late at night when a beautiful Spanish lady came in with a gorgeous little girl with black hair down her back, who took off running down the aisle, and the mother called out, 'Oh, Melissa, come back!'"

Allman leans back on the couch, lets his long blond hair out of a thick pony-tail, shakes it free, and looks up with a sparkle in his eyes decades later.

"When I heard her yell 'Melissa,' I knew I had it and I just sung out, *'But back home he'll always run to sweet Melissa.'* I wanted to hug that lady, but I just dropped my milk and ran home to my guitar and played it through and it was perfect. I just knew that was it.

"I made a little recording and played it for my brother and he said, 'It's pretty good—for a love song. It ain't rock and roll that makes me move my ass.' He could be tough that way. But we recorded a little version of it together."

That rough version was released on *One More Try*, a solo compilation heavy on outtakes and demos released in 1997 but quickly pulled from the market and now out of print.

"I had that song in my pocket for years and after a while my brother started telling me how much he liked it," Gregg says.

A year after writing the song, the brothers Allman recorded it as part of a Florida demo session with Butch Trucks's band the 31st of February. That version is thought to feature Duane's first recorded slide playing. The sessions were eventually released under the misleading title *Duane and Gregg Allman*.

When Liberty Records, who had the Allmans' band the Hour Glass under contract, demanded that Gregg return to Los Angeles to fulfill a contract, he did not have enough money to buy an airplane ticket. He says that he sold "Melissa" and "God Rest His Soul," which he wrote in tribute to Martin Luther King, Jr., to the producer Steve Alaimo for $250.

Recalls guitarist Scott Boyer, "Gregg came to me after Vanguard Records turned down the demos and asked what to do about needing money and having an offer to buy these songs so he could fly back. I didn't know what to do and told him so and he just went, 'Hell, I can always write another song.'"

Years later, while recording *Eat a Peach*, Allman Brothers manager Phil Walden arranged to buy back half the publishing rights for Gregg.

"I think Alaimo figured half of a song on an Allman Brothers album was better than 100 percent of nothing," notes Trucks.

Allman says he never brought the song to the Allman Brothers Band, in part because he no longer owned the rights and in part because he thought it too soft for the band. When Duane died, Gregg sang "Melissa" at his brother's funeral, and when the band reconvened to finish recording *Eat a Peach*, the song was an appropriate tribute to his fallen brother. While everyone recognized the song's appeal, it lacked an instrumental component as compelling as its chords, lyrics, and vocals.

"I knew it needed something and told Gregg I would come up with a lead line," recalls Dickey Betts. "I took a recording home and started playing around and I came up with that entire lead guitar portion that night, which was actually Gregg's birthday [December 8].

"I walked into the studio the next day and said, 'Happy Birthday, Gregg,' and laid that on him. Then we cut the song."

Allman has called Betts's melodic lead line on "Melissa" the "finest guitar work" he ever heard his longtime partner play. Four years after it was written, "Melissa" entered the rock pantheon, quickly becoming one of the Allmans' most beloved songs, used in movie soundtracks and commercials and forever a crowd favorite.

"I knew it was good but never could have guessed it would impact so many people for so many years," Allman says. "I've met a lot of Melissas named after the song."

PERKINS: At that point we had some money and we were going to make an investment. That property was the first major expenditure and Berry was the driving force behind the purchase. He wanted a place for the people. At one point it was going to be called ABBville and everyone was going to live there. No one thought about logistics like: How would everyone have their property deeded to them? How are we all going to build houses?

But when you walked down the main road into that place, it felt magical, like, "This is the place we need to be." Dickey built a beautiful rustic cabin and moved in—before that he was often going back to Florida or Love Valley when we came off tour. Butch had a trailer and grandiose plans to build a house and stables. Everybody else was also thinking about building a place.

LINDA OAKLEY: We had dreamed of getting this big piece of land where everyone could build a house and then it happened. I remember driving out there in our new cars. It was like, "Yes, it's all happening. Our dreams are coming true."

Drunken Hearted Boy

IN THE FALL of 1972, Gregg began recording his first solo album even as the ABB was recording a follow-up to Eat a Peach *in the same Capricorn Studios. Sandlin produced both projects, and brought the pianist Chuck Leavell in to play on the solo album, which became* Laid Back.

LEAVELL: I had toured with the Allman Brothers when I was playing with Dr. John and we opened a lot of shows. I loved the band and I would stay to hear them whenever I could and would often sit down and play my piano behind the curtain, playing along with the band and just finding my place. Apparently, the road crew heard me and thought it sounded good and told the guys in the band, but I'm not sure how much impact that made on anyone.

But I was around and Johnny [Sandlin] asked me to work on *Laid Back*. The Brothers were recording *Brothers and Sisters* at the same time, the sessions often overlapped, and we all hung around the studio an awful lot. Before I knew what was going on, I was working on that, too.

SANDLIN: I was recording Chuck for *Laid Back* and he was just an amazing player, one of the best I'd ever heard. He came to some All-man Brothers sessions and he just seemed to fit. It did not start out with a plan for him to audition for the band or anything.

LEAVELL: Things were pretty loose and I just found myself in the Allman Brothers. People were still grieving over Duane's death. It had been almost a year but the grieving process was still very much under way. I think perhaps these sessions offered the way forward.

SANDLIN: Chuck added another very strong voice, and another harmony instrument—and it wasn't replacing Duane. They did *not* want to replace Duane.

BETTS: Replacing Duane with another guitar player was out of the question.

LES DUDEK, *guitarist, played on "Jessica" and "Ramblin Man":* I originally came to Macon because the keyboard player in my Florida band was friends with Dickey and heard that he wasn't sure after Duane's death if the Allman Brothers would continue and he was looking for musicians to play with him. After a weekend spent jamming, I went home and Dickey called and asked me to come back to Macon. I started jamming with the guys all the time and everyone liked the way I played with Dickey and with the band.

TRUCKS: Les Dudek came to Macon, Georgia, within weeks of Duane's death and word got out that there was this guy walking around telling everyone that he was there to replace Duane. We went looking for this dude to kick his ass. Nobody was going to replace Duane and the very thought of it was infuriating to us.

SANDLIN: Les was a really good guitar player, but he really knew it. He just pissed me off from the start, going around town telling everyone, "I got the gig." If he had been the second coming of Duane he couldn't have impressed me. I didn't have anything to do with the discussions but I'm glad they did what they did.

DUDEK: Phil Walden told me he was going to make me a star and put me in the Allman Brothers but Dickey was clear from the start that he didn't want another guitarist and I told that to Phil: "You better talk to them before you offer me a job." Phil thought it would be natural to add another guitarist because orchestrated guitar harmonies were at the heart of the band's sound, and Dickey and I played very well together, but Dickey basically told me, "This is my band now and I want to pursue a different direction."

I thought a lot of it was Dickey being frustrated about having been in Duane's shadow and being determined to shine and not share that. In the meantime, I was there jamming all the time and Phil signed me up lock, stock, and barrel, as he liked to do: management, Capricorn Records, and publishing deals. I was twenty years old and didn't really understand what that all meant.

The sessions started strongly, as the band cut Gregg's "Wasted Words," with Betts laying down a hard-charging slide line, as well as "Ramblin' Man." The latter song was a left-field choice for the group, far more country-oriented than anything they had recorded before.

"Ramblin' Man" was not a brand-new song, however. Betts can be heard working through the song in embryonic form on The Gatlinburg Tapes, *a bootleg of the band jamming in April 1971 in Gatlinburg, Tennessee, during songwriting sessions for* Eat a Peach. *The chords and chorus are very similar to what emerged, though the lyrics refer to a "ramblin' country man." The tapes also include Betts working through the signature "Blue Sky" riff and the band learning that song.*

TRUCKS: During the *Brothers and Sisters* sessions, Dickey took over.

PERKINS: It's not like Dickey came in and said, "I'm taking over. I'm the boss. Do this and that." It wasn't overt; it was still supposedly a democracy but Dickey started doing more and more of the songwriting.

SANDLIN: Dickey is a much more prolific writer than Gregg is and he had the songs ready to go.

Dickey Betts and Berry Oakley, The Warehouse, New Orleans, December 31, 1971.

TRUCKS: While Duane was around, we were a blues-based band that added John Coltrane and Miles Davis to the mix. After Duane died, we started heading in a country direction because that was Dickey's background. We all thought "Ramblin' Man" was too country to even record. We knew it was a good song but it didn't sound like us. We went to the studio to do a demo to send to Merle Haggard or someone and then we got into that big long guitar jam, which kind of fit us, so we put it on the album and it became a hit. Then it more and more became Dickey's band.

LEAVELL: Dickey had a little more equal time in terms of songwriting and singing, but I don't think there was major tension between Gregg and Dickey or anyone else at this time. We were all pulling in the same direction, during what everyone recognized were challenging times.

SANDLIN: "Ramblin' Man" was obviously a different sound for them, but it worked. I never thought it was going to be a hit single. I thought it was crazy to even be released as a single because nothing else sounds remotely similar, with the possible exception of "Blue Sky," which had a similar, upbeat major-key bounce.

Dickey Betts, driving near the Juliette farm.

BETTS: I wrote "Ramblin' Man" in Berry Oakley's kitchen [at the Big House] at about four in the morning. Everyone had gone to bed but I was sitting up. Once I got started, I probably wrote that song in about twenty minutes but I'd been thinking about it for a year or two.

LEAVELL: It's definitely in the direction of country but that didn't bother me in the least. I thought it was a really catchy song. I dug the harmony bits and what Dickey did with the guitars, especially at the end. I don't think it was stone cold country and was proud to add some bounce with my piano and harmony vocals. I think our attitude was, "Let's take this thing and make it as great as we can," and of course it became the band's biggest hit. I don't think there's anything we can complain about.

DUDEK: I was in the control room when they were recording "Ramblin' Man" because Dickey and I had worked out harmony parts together and he was going to track them all. He kept coming in and asking my opinion about different takes and approaches and finally he just said, "Why don't you just come out and play?" And I did. We played it all live. I was standing where Duane would have stood with Berry just staring a hole through me and that was very intense and very heavy.

SANDLIN: Les played a lot of the harmony parts on "Ramblin' Man"—all those nice licks on the going-out part—and we knew when he and Dickey cut them that it was really good.

DUDEK: We played all those guitar harmonies and when we went back and listened to the track, the room was packed with the road crew and management people, and after we listened, it was just silent. You could hear a pin drop. Then Red Dog said, "That's the best I heard since Duane." We pretty much knew we had a hit, and that was a very nice feeling.

On November 2, 1972, after a few weeks in the studio, Leavell played his first gig with the band, at Long Island's Hofstra University.

LEAVELL: Berry was the coolest-looking guy and the most unique bass player I had ever played with. Rather than holding down the bottom end, he was very adventurous and constantly listening to the other instruments and popping out with great melodies. If he heard Dickey or Duane—or me—go to a certain scale or range, he was always there to support that improvisation. I could feel Berry following me if I started a melody, and it was just fantastic. He was not afraid to experiment, roam around and be adventurous, but he knew when to do that and when to go back and hold down the foundation. He also had the coolest bass sound; you could *feel* it inside. I'm just glad I got to play onstage with him.

Despite his strong playing on the two new studio songs, Oakley had been a shell of himself since Duane's death. Everyone around him was extremely worried about his escalating drinking and drug use.

SANDLIN: He was in an awful funk after Duane died.

LEAVELL: Berry seemed lost, but he was the first one to put his arm around me and say, "You're my new brother. What can I do to help you, to make you more comfortable?" He was so sweet; he was truly like a big brother. But everyone was very concerned about him because he was quite visibly suffering the loss of Duane and drinking very heavily. He was certainly going through some very, very tough times and I only wish that something could have occurred to ease his pain.

LINDA OAKLEY: He just felt like things weren't right no matter how much he, me, or anyone tried. He felt that it would never be the same and he started drinking too much and doing everything too much. It was never enough. This happened over time—it wasn't instantly after

Duane's death. I felt so helpless because it seemed like anything I did didn't matter because I couldn't bring Duane back, and it left an emptiness between us, too. It was like I reminded him of Duane and how things used to be, and would never be again.

PAYNE: Everything Berry had envisioned for everybody—including the crew, the women and children—was shattered on the day Duane died, and he didn't care after that.

PERKINS: It was not pretty to watch. It seemed like his soul had been sucked out of him.

PAYNE: He said over and over again, "I want to get high, be high, and stay high." That was his mantra for life and he'd be fucked up when he said it. It was a sad situation. Before Duane died, Berry was the most positive person you'd ever want to meet. He was all unicorns and rainbows, just someone who made you feel good. He did things, but he never got loaded, and all that turned 180 degrees after Duane's death.

RED DOG: Unfortunately, when Duane died we were heroin users and the combination of both [grief and drugs]—one being the crutch for the other—made it very hard to overcome. When Duane got killed, it was easy to hide in the drugs. Then the drugs consumed you and even if you wanted to fight back, the mountain was three times as high.

PAYNE: After a year, B.O. wasn't really showing any signs of pulling out of it. We lived together. I was probably closer to Berry than anybody else at the time and he was in really bad shape.

LINDA OAKLEY: Berry got involved with Julia Densmore, I think near the time of one of the first post-Duane shows. As months passed, I knew that this was something different than all the other women.

That's rock and roll. Berry needed someone to take care of him and I needed him to take care of me.

PAYNE: After Duane's death, he just lost all hope, lost his heart, his drive, his ambition, his direction. He was just lost and it was a sad thing to see. Hell, he probably didn't weigh 115 pounds, and it never got any better.

ODOM: Willie and I spent many, many hours talking to Berry after Duane's death and trying to break through, to no avail.

SANDLIN: Berry asked me if I would go on the road with them, saying, "You can play the rest of the night if I can't do it." I was honored, but that wasn't right. He was the one who created the parts and had to play them. But he knew he'd get too screwed up to play.

PAYNE: Joe Dan [*Petty, roadie and bassist who played in the band Grinderswitch*] had to take over for him several times. Once we played in Chicago, Berry's hometown, and all his relatives were there—grandma, grandpa, everyone—so they set up a special table by the stage and he fell right off the stage onto the table in the middle of a song. It was that bad.

There was loads of concern, and everybody was walking around looking at the situation and wondering what we were going to do about it, but not doing anything. I was very close to him, and we talked endlessly but never really about that. It's kind of strange to say that now, but that's how it was. His sister Candy was my old lady and even we didn't talk about that—and to her the sun rose and set on B.O.

PERKINS: We all talked with each other about how concerned we were, but people didn't know about intervention then. It was like watching a slow-motion train wreck.

LEAVELL: Berry was still troubled, dependent on certain addictions and experimenting pretty heavily with drugs and alcohol. I would like to think that there was the opportunity to come out of it, turn the corner and focus on music instead of escapism. But that's speculation. The facts are the facts and it was a very sad thing.

RED DOG: When Chuck was hired I thought that Oak was showing some signs of coming out of it. Chuck's presence gave him some new spark and life. Oak was pretty fucked up and a lot of people won't agree with me, but I honestly think he was on the edge of straightening out.

LEAVELL: Berry did gravitate towards me and went out of his way to make me feel comfortable. He seemed to be very excited to have me on board and to have some resolution about the band going forward. I think everybody felt a relief: "OK, there's another option to having another guitar player and it seems to work."

LINDA OAKLEY: I agree that things were looking up for Berry. He was always honest with me and didn't want to hurt me, but I wasn't surprised when he told me that Julia was pregnant. When I reminded him that he already had a daughter, he said, "This might be my son."

He was really excited, as difficult as it was for me. It kind of gave him a new love and new hope for a fresh start. And Berry felt some new musical life with Chuck and what was happening with the band. He had come out of the period where he would be so incoherent they had to have people sit in for him. I think he had turned the corner and I don't think he had a death wish. He was miserable with the business and he knew they were getting ripped off. He was talking to his dad about getting an attorney and was starting to look into the deals.

PAYNE: He may have put on a show to get someone off his back but I didn't see any signs of improvement and I was with him all the time. He was headed for a cliff and there was no stopping him.

On November 11, 1972, Oakley woke up filled with excitement; he was going to finally lead a giant jam session he had been talking about for several years: B.O.'s Jive Ass Review featuring the Rowdy Roadies and the Shady Ladies.

SANDLIN: He called me in the early afternoon and said, "Man, I'm having a jam session tonight. Why don't you come?" I asked him what time and said sure.

LINDA OAKLEY: He was out late jamming the night before, and he woke up early and was very happy. He said he had gotten this thing together that he had wanted to do for years, BOJAR, B.O.'s Jive Ass Revue, with the Rowdy Roadies and the Shady Ladies! He said it was finally happening and he was going to get all the musicians who were in town to come down to the club and they were going to have the big jam. It was my mission to go round up all the old ladies. Donna was in town to take care of getting Duane buried. She was going to drive me to see Linda Trucks, Joanie Callahan, Blue Sky, Little Judi . . . all the chicks, and get them to come down and practice our moves. We were going to be back-up singers and shake our maracas and our tail feathers. He was going out to spread the word. Berry told me I looked pretty before riding off on the bike.

PAYNE: We got on our bikes to go out to the Cowboy guys' house and tell them about the jam and Big Linda was not happy about it, because we were not straight when we left and we were involved in getting more and more not straight as the day went on.

LINDA OAKLEY: I don't recall knowing that, but I would have been neither happy nor surprised.

PAYNE: Nobody had a phone and if you wanted to get word to them, you had to go their house. He was so excited about that jam.

LEAVELL: He and Kim came out to Idlewild South, where I was living with Scott Boyer and a couple of other guys, to make sure we were going to show up at this jam. We all told him that we were going to come and he said if we wanted to rehearse, they'd be getting together at the Big House. It was very exciting, especially for me, because I was still new to the whole world and I loved playing with Berry so much.

PAYNE: We were riding home from Idlewild and he just rode smack into the side of a damn bus. I went back to him and he was lying there conscious, with just a little bit of blood trickling out of his nose. He otherwise looked fine and said he felt OK. I knew a cop would be arriving soon and I knew Berry had a bag of heroin on him, because we had been dipping into it all day, so I asked him where it was and he said, "It's in my hand," which made no sense. I kept asking and he kept saying that. I found it in his pocket and got it off of him and he started standing up, saying, "I want to go home." An ambulance had arrived and I tried to get him in there, but he refused. These two girls came riding by: "Hey, there's B.O. from the Allman Brothers." He said, "Hey there, give me a ride," and jumped in the car for a lift back to the Big House.

I got his motorcycle off the pavement, then I rode home and came in the back door. Big Linda was there, and she asked me what the hell happened. She wondered if he had gotten in a fight and been hit, saying, "He's upstairs talking crazy shit." I went running up there and he was in bad shape. He started turning blue. Chuck showed up and had a station wagon. We managed to drag him down and put him in there and, hell, he died forty-five minutes later in the hospital.

Oakley had fractured his skull in the crash, resulting in a brain hemorrhage. Like Duane, he was twenty-four years old. His son, Berry Duane Oakley, was born four months later.

DUDEK: Dickey, Joe Dan, and I were out at the farm getting ready to ride horses when Willie called and said Berry had been in an accident and was at the hospital. We jumped into my Cougar and hauled ass into town. We walked into the emergency room and a nurse came out and said, "Are you related to Mr. Oakley?" Dickey said, "Yeah, we're his brothers." And she said, "Well, I regret to tell you that he didn't make it. He is deceased."

SANDLIN: I got a call from another musician: "Did you hear about Berry?"

I said, "Yeah, I'm gonna go down there to the jam."

And he said, "No, man, it's not that."

And they told me what had happened and that he was in the hospital—that same hospital where we had all gathered for Duane a year earlier—and I went down there, and there we all were again.

PAYNE: Candace blamed me 110 percent for B.O.'s death and a lot of it *was* my fault. I should never have let him ride, but even today I don't know what I could have done to stop him. I guess everyone has a day in his or her life they wish they could redo and this is it for me. I think about it all the time. I wish I had never gotten on a bike with him, but there was no arguing. He'd have just said, "Well, fuck you," and gone without me.

But God, I've often wondered if I could have handled that whole thing differently. I could have wrestled him to the ground with one arm and tied him to a tree if he insisted on riding, but that's not a solution; what would happen the day after?

PERKINS: Kim carries that with him, but we all saw what was happening. Nobody would have wanted to be the one with him when it happened. I always felt like Berry died the same day Duane did. It just took him a year to go down.

LINDA OAKLEY: I never blamed Kim or anyone else. Berry wasn't a very experienced rider—I never got on the bike with him—and that bike was too big for his skinny ass. But everybody had a bike, so he wanted to have one to join his brothers burning up the road.

PAYNE: This doctor at the hospital talked to me a week or so later. I was feeling pretty guilty and down, what with his sister kicking me out and accusing me of having killed her brother. He said, "If there had been a neurosurgeon on the scene he couldn't have saved that man." He said he was a dead man the second he hit the bus. It was just a matter of time. He told me about an identical accident about two weeks

Berry Oakley, 1948–1972.

earlier on I-75 where a guy suffered the same injury. He said, "It wasn't your fault. You couldn't have done anything." That did make me feel a bit better, but I still don't feel good about letting him get on the bike in the first place.

LINDA OAKLEY: I always had this feeling that Berry wasn't going to live a long time and I think his mother did, too. This is why I stuck around. I would go away and then come back. I was losing my mind but I couldn't leave him because I had this fear that his time was coming. I know that sounds odd, but it was an ethereal sense, this haunted thing. Maybe he had it, too, but he was not looking for it. He did not have a death wish and he was so happy the day he died.

SANDLIN: It was like when Duane died; suddenly you're just going through the motions of daily life. I remember going to his memorial service at the Catholic church and it was just heartbreaking. Berry was such a great guy and a great bass player. He had a style that was totally his own. I've never heard anyone else play like him.

PERKINS: Berry was like Duane's lieutenant. He always seemed like second in command. It was a given that they would be buried together. Berry did not have a will either, but there was no question about who was in charge: Linda.

ODOM: It was horrible when Duane died and then Berry's death came along and made it worse. Just as Duane was the leader, Berry was the family man. But the Allman Brothers Band are survivors and somehow they have held it together. You have to respect that.

SANDLIN: I really didn't know how much more any of us could deal with.

RED DOG: It was like two kings had died.

Following Oakley's death, a decision was quickly reached that he and Duane would be buried side-by-side at Rose Hill Cemetery, where the band had spent so much time. Their final resting place is just around the corner and up a hill from that of Elizabeth Jones Reed, the Victorian mother whose name graces one of the band's greatest songs.

Their graves sit on a small bluff overlooking the river. Duane's headstone includes an epitaph taken from his journal entry of January 1, 1969: "I love being alive and I will be the best man I possibly can. I will take love where I find it and offer it to everyone who will take it . . . Seek knowledge from those wiser . . . and teach those who wish to learn from me."

Oakley's gravestone contains a Hindu proverb, selected by Linda: "Help thy brother's boat across, and Lo! Thine own has reached the shore."

LINDA OAKLEY: It was the hand of fate: Donna had come back to Macon to see that Duane was at last laid to rest. She was at the house with me when the thing happened with Berry. We later went together to Rose Hill and found this peaceful place in a valley; then to the mortuary where we chose tombstones of white marble. Donna

Duane Allman and Berry Oakley, brothers to the end.

THE BIG HOUSE

How a house became a home . . . and so much more.

The Big House, a three-story Grand Tudor at 2321 Vineville Avenue in Macon, Georgia, was the Allman Brothers Band's communal home from 1970 to 1973. "It was the band's logistical and spiritual center," says road manager Willie Perkins.

First and foremost, the Big House was a home, primarily to bassist Berry Oakley and his family: wife Linda, baby daughter Brittany, and sister Candace.

"A lot of us lived there at different times, but it always felt like Linda and Berry's house," says crew member Kim Payne. "Berry and Linda were a force for good, flower children who loved everybody and had extremely positive outlooks, and that was the vibe at the Big House in the beginning."

Linda and Candace Oakley saw a newspaper listing for 2321 Vineville in early 1970. "We had to get out of the little one-bedroom apartment where we were living," Linda recalls. "We were looking through the newspapers for a little house and we saw the listing and thought we'd just go look."

Linda, Candace, and Donna Roosmann Allman, Duane's "lady" and the mother of his baby Galadrielle, stopped by without an appointment. Standing in the yard, peering through the leaded windows, they began to fantasize about moving into this grand old home.

"We fell in love," Oakley says. "We were standing amidst the blooming wisteria peering in at the chandeliers and sweeping stairs and it felt like a fairyland. We wanted this house, so we called for an appointment, and dressed up in our finest clothes to meet the realty people."

The $225 rent was beyond the Oakleys' reach, almost $100 more than they had been paying for their loft above Butch Trucks's apartment. Then, Linda recalls, Donna had an idea: "She said, 'It's so big that there's room for all of us. I can talk to Duane and see if he wants to move in.'"

When Duane agreed, a communal house was born. The original tenants were Donna, Duane, and Galadrielle and the extended Oakley family, along with Gregg Allman, who was dating Candace.

"I went to Florida for a few days and got a call from Duane and Donna saying they had already moved in," Linda Oakley recalls. "Duane and the roadies were storming around; they broke into these loft rooms in the attic that we were not supposed to mess with and pulled out and set up a bunch of furniture stored up there, including a huge dining room table."

Shortly after moving in, Gregg and Candace split up and Kim Payne moved in. Many other band members and associates moved in and out, including Perkins, who stayed there when he first arrived in Macon in May 1970.

"When I arrived, [a guest] showed me around," says Perkins. "She opened the fridge and said, 'Here's the iced tea. The one with the silver tape around it has LSD in it. If you just want iced tea, have the other one. If you don't have anything you need to do for the next couple of days, drink the duct tape.' Right away, I knew this was not a normal household."

The Big House was also the scene of some significant heartbreak. On October 29, 1971, Duane had just dropped flowers off for Linda's birthday—a party was planned for that night—when he jumped on his motorcycle and never returned. Berry Oakley came back to the Big House following his own crash on November 11, 1972. He went from there to the hospital, where he died.

After Berry's funeral, Linda took Brittany to her parents' home in Florida to try and heal. When she returned in early January 1973, there was an eviction notice on the door. She moved out and the Big House became just another Macon house.

It turned into a boardinghouse with rooms for rent, then a new owner moved in and turned the ground floor into a hair salon, before eventually going into foreclosure. A family bought it from the bank in 1987 and lived there for six years until ABB "tour magician" Kirk West knocked on the door and said, "I want to buy your house."

West and his wife, Kirsten, moved into 2321 Vineville in July 1993 and the house became the Big House once again. West created a stealth museum, displaying his considerable memorabilia collection for pilgrims who began to show up from around the world.

In June 1994, Warren Haynes, Allen Woody, and Matt Abts moved into the Big House, set up their instruments and equipment in what had been the original band's music room, and rehearsed for eight days before heading out to do their first shows as Gov't Mule.

In 2009, the Allman Brothers Band Museum at the Big House was opened, filled with memorabilia from the band's forty-five years and re-creating the feel it had when it was the Oakleys' home.

wanted the thing from his diary to be inscribed and I drew a phoenix design for Duane and a ram's head for Berry and chose that proverb.

I used to come across all these little words of wisdom and I found that message and showed him. He just loved it because of the brothers thing. That's really how he lived his life. It was not an illusion. Sometimes I feel it was something I made up. Then I see some evidence in a photo or video or a letter and I realize, "This is for real. No one can take this away. I didn't imagine it." We all really loved each other.

Goin' Down the Road Feeling Bad

*J*UST A YEAR *after rallying together and moving on from Duane's death, the band found itself at another tragic crossroads. Berry died on November 11, 1972. On November 15, the group played at his memorial service at Hart's Mortuary, then once again had to make decisions about a cloudy future.*

LEAVELL: There was a meeting with Phil, which basically amounted to "What are we going to do?" The answer was immediate and unanimous: "Carry on. Let's arrange some auditions, get a new bass player, and keep moving." We didn't want to take a lot of time off and be dwelling on the negative. It was maybe a two-week period before we were back to work.

PODELL: It was exactly like when Duane died—no one knew if the band could pull it off again. But this time there was no doubt that they would try.

PAYNE: When Duane died, it was like, "We've got to go on. Duane wouldn't have it any other way." When Berry died, it felt like such a dirty deal, and the sense was "We're not going to let anyone or anything stop us." I had serious doubts about what would happen, as did everyone else, but there was never really a question about quitting.

Several bassists came to Macon to audition, including Lamar Williams, an old friend of Jaimoe's from Gulfport, Mississippi, two years removed from an Army stint in Vietnam.

JAIMOE: Lamar made his own picks, cutting them out of Clorox bottles, so what does he do? Cuts his freaking finger, man. He had to audition with a big cut on his finger and there were good players there; a guy came in from L.A. and another cat that used to be in a band with Gregg and some dude Dickey knew.

SANDLIN: Lamar came in and auditioned without Jaimoe being in the room because he didn't want any home cooking. And it was like Lamar had been waiting for the gig.

LEAVELL: We had auditioned three or four other bass players. Once Lamar came in, we all looked at each other and said, "This is the guy." He just got it. He had a good understanding of Berry's style as well as bringing his own unique style to the table and he was an easy guy to be with.

JAIMOE: After two songs, Butch asked Lamar, "Hey, man, have you ever played any of these songs?" and Lamar said, "No." Butch turned to everyone and asked if we could have a meeting. Lamar left and Butch said, "He doesn't even know these songs and he's playing them like he knows them inside and out. Let's get this audition stuff done and make this a rehearsal." That was the greatest thing I ever saw Butch do!

TRUCKS: His groove was just so rock solid that absolutely no one could miss it or deny it. It just felt too good to waste any more time.

Lamar Williams, 1973.

LEAVELL: Lamar slid right into the sessions and the band.

The band not only returned to work on the album, but to touring as well, appearing on December 9 at Ann Arbor's Crisler Arena, Williams's first gig with the Allman Brothers Band.

JAIMOE: Lamar was a hell of a bass player. I had missed playing with him so much; no other bass player ever felt right to me until I met Berry. Everyone else in between . . . just nope! I learned how to play the bass drum by listening to Lamar play. I had studied jazz drumming, not rhythm and blues, and there was nothing definitive about where to put the beat. Lamar explained that to me and he could play so much like [Motown bassist] James Jamerson it was ridiculous, and playing along with him as he did that, it hit me and I just understood how to make the bass drum work. Playing with him again felt like the most natural thing in the world.

LEAVELL: It was a feeling of brotherhood with two new brothers coming in. The band had been through these traumas and major changes and now they had a chance to be the Allman Brothers Band 2.0. There was a certain sense of freshness, with Lamar and me there.

PERKINS: When Lamar and Chuck came in, it seemed like it gave the band a kick in the butt musically.

Lamar Williams (left) and Chuck Leavell at the Farm.

BETTS: We did what we had to do—we were forced to bring new people into the band because two of our guys were killed. We added Chuck, and it changed the whole direction of the band—and you can hear it on "Jessica."

SANDLIN: "Jessica" was different but it worked. It was like, "The guy who was driving the bus is gone. Let's go down this different road." It's the happiest song I've ever heard. It still makes me smile every time I hear it. It gave Chuck a chance to stretch out and shine immediately.

LEAVELL: My attitude was to relax, play the best I could, and find the right places to contribute. No one could have replaced Duane and I think it was a good call not to have another guitarist come in, to take another direction. I wanted to make the most of it.

BETTS: I really need to have an image in my head before I can start writing an instrumental because otherwise it's too vague. I get an emotion or an idea I want to express and see what I can come up with. With "Jessica" I was experimenting, trying to write something that could be played with just two fingers on my fretting hand in honor of Django Reinhardt [*the Gypsy jazz guitar master who played with just two left fingers due to severe burns*].

Dickey Betts and his daughter, Jessica.

I came up with the main melody, but it was still just a bunch of notes going nowhere until I was sitting there and my baby daughter Jessica came crawling in smiling and I started playing along, trying to capture musically the way she looked bouncing around the room. And then the song came together. That's why I named it after her.

DUDEK: I co-wrote "Jessica" with Dickey. We had been jamming a lot and he called up and invited me and my girlfriend over to have some steaks with him and Blue Sky, and he told me to bring my acoustic guitar. I grabbed my Martin and while the ladies were in the kitchen, he said, "Let me show you this song I've been working on, but I'm stuck and haven't been able to finish." He had the opening rhythm for "Jessica" and the main verse riff. It sounded great but didn't go anywhere.

We played it for a while, then Dickey became frustrated and went in the kitchen to check on the steaks. I stayed with it. The verse section Dickey had was in the key of A. I felt the song needed a bridge, so I took it to G and came up with the bridge section. I yelled for Dickey to come back, and said, "Try this; after the verse section, go to the G chord and play this melody." So he did, and then he said, "Now what?" I said, "At the end of the phrase keep going up, up, up all the way to the top." Dickey said, "Then what?" I said, "Just stop, and start over again on the verse section and repeat."

And when we played it like that, Dickey lit up like a lightbulb he was so happy, because now we had the new section the song desperately needed. Dickey was so excited, we ran out and threw our guitars in the back of his pickup truck, because he wanted to go play it for everyone we could find in the band, to show them we finally had the instrumental song for the new record. We went by Jaimoe's house and played it for Jaimoe and Lamar that night and they loved it, but we couldn't find Gregg or Butch. I'll never forget, right when we got in Dickey's truck, it started to lightly, almost mystically, snow, as if it was Duane sending us a message: "Hey, you guys finally got that tune."

JAIMOE: It wouldn't surprise me if Les wrote that with Dickey because they were definitely playing together a lot and Dickey's songs often were kind of incomplete and worked up together. But I don't remember Dickey ever coming by my house. He's the only guy who never was there.

LEAVELL: We had put down three or four tracks before Dickey came into the studio with Les Dudek to play "Jessica" for us, so he could present the rhythm guitar and melody at the same time. He explained that he was paying tribute to Django and we could hear that. Earlier instrumentals were more serious in nature. This was more lighthearted and presented a challenge: How do we make this a little more intense and make it work as an Allman Brothers song? That presented a unique opportunity to make it special.

DUDEK: Dickey and I had worked out harmonies and I thought I'd be recording them with him, but the first day we started recording "Jessica," he said, "I know you wrote this song with me, but you already played all those harmonies on 'Ramblin' Man,' so if you play the harmonies on 'Jessica,' the critics might think you're gonna be in the band. So I want you to play the acoustic rhythm guitar part instead, and Chuck will play the harmonies on the piano." I was very disappointed, but there was nothing I could say about it, so I played the acoustic guitar part.

SANDLIN: Les played acoustic on "Jessica," which you can hear very clearly on the opening.

LEAVELL: I would not really agree that Les co-wrote it. I could say I co-wrote it, because I made a lot of suggestions, but I don't think that's fair. Dickey wrote the melody and he had the rhythm. Songwriting always has some gray areas, because if someone plays a particular riff does that mean it's part of the song or part of the arrangement? We all contributed to the arrangement of the piece, but it was Dickey's song.

DUDEK: Well, that's what Chuck saw, but he was not in the room when Dickey and I wrote the song. I agree that what we did in the studio was arrangements. It was all working out the solos and the links between them, and it took us about six days until we had it in a cohesive whole. That's arrangement—like what I did on "Ramblin' Man." That's not what I'm talking about; when I sat down with Dickey, he did not have a completed song, just the verse section, until I came up with the bridge. Dickey marched me right into Phil's office and told him I had co-written the song and should get some points. I didn't understand all that exactly at the time, but in retrospect, I should have got 50 percent. Because it wasn't a completed song until I gave him the bridge section, the part that goes to the G chord.

TRUCKS: I know Dickey came up with those melodies and I wasn't there, so I can't say what Les did or didn't do, but I take that with a grain of salt. Look at the track records of what else each has written. I do know that Dickey brought the song into the studio in pieces; he had some beautiful lines, but it really wasn't a song. He sat on the floor playing acoustic guitar and showing us these melodies, which we worked into a song. We spent a lot of time—several days—all putting together "Jessica."

JAIMOE: Dickey would often come in with an idea or a really nice melody and we'd all play our parts and make it into a song. I don't know how much you have to put in a song to have a credit, but that's not how we did things. Dickey always kept them.

TRUCKS: I think it could be a group credit almost, and if any one person would have a writing claim it would be Chuck Leavell, who added a tremendous amount to "Jessica."

BETTS: "Jessica" wouldn't be the same tune without Chuck, who is just a great, great player.

LEAVELL: We started working through it and then the next question was "How do we get from the piano solo to the guitar solo?" I came up with the transition phase that leads into Dickey's solo. We worked our way through the song and established the arrangement. One of the things I found really interesting was the three-part harmonies with the two keyboards and the guitar; it showed how the band could build on its legacy while changing.

TRUCKS: I've always said that Dickey Betts is one of the most lyrical guitar players in rock and roll. He plays beautiful melodies and always did, and a lot of those melodies ended up being the basis for a lot of those songs, like "Liz Reed" and "Jessica," but we worked those songs up together as well. The melodies are way superior and it's fair to say that no one but Dickey could have come up with them, but there's a hell of a lot more to a song than just a melody. I think Dickey was the first of us to really understand the value of songwriting credits.

LEAVELL: While Dickey was doing more songwriting, it's not at all true to say that Gregg was not musically involved in what was going on. He was very involved and "Jessica" was a great example, as we replaced the traditional Allman Brothers two-part guitar harmonies, with three-part harmonies, featuring two keyboards and one guitar. They were very difficult to work out—and he had to figure his parts out on a Hammond B3, which is not easy and points out a simple fact: Gregg is a great B3 player. He's not known for hot solos, but his use of the instrument is magnificent. He finds the right colors, knowing when to make them dark, when to brighten them up, and he exhibits excellent use of the Leslie [rotating speaker], with an innate sense of when to keep it slow and when to crank it up and add intensity.

JAIMOE: Gregory has been insecure about his musicianship over the years, but he is a very great organ player. What he plays, he plays very, very well, he's always in the groove and he sticks to things he knows— which does not stop you from growing. You can take something deeper and deeper and that's what he has always done with his organ playing.

BETTS: Writing a good instrumental takes months, which makes them totally unlike a solo, though people often think a song with no vocals is just a bunch of solos put together. It's a completely different process. Slow blues solos are just your heart coming out, but all the solos happen too fast to even think about. They're the closest thing to Zen that

I do. If I think about it, it's gone. It's ruined. If I'm stuck or I need a mental rest, I've got licks that I can hang there until I get my mind together to start something else, but it's mostly instantaneous and instinctive. It's like touching a hot stove; you don't think you're gonna jerk your hand back. You just do it.

The instrumentals, on the other hand, are very studied. It's called architecture, and for a good reason. It's much like somebody designing a building. It's meticulously constructed, and every aspect has its place. Writing a good one is very fulfilling, because you've transcended language and spoken to someone with a melody. My instrumentals try to create some of the basic feelings of human interaction, like anger and joy and love. Even instrumentals that are just for fun, like Freddie King's "Hideaway," talk to you.

Brothers and Sisters ends with another musical departure, the acoustic back-porch country blues "Pony Boy," where Betts displays his fluid, easy mastery of acoustic slide playing.

Dickey Betts at home, late 1973.

BETTS: "Pony Boy" has a real strong Robert Johnson influence where you strum the 2/4 in with the notes, building a rhythm even while you pick. And lyrically, Willie McTell inspires the humor. It's based on a true story about my uncle. When I was a kid, the family lore was he would take his horse out when he went drinking to avoid DUI charges and the horse knew just how to take him home.

That musical style is based on what used to be called "Black Bottom Blues." The term refers to the fertile black soil of the Mississippi Delta and "bottoms" is just a term country people have always used. Unfortunately, people misunderstood "Black Bottom" as having racial or minstrel show overtones, so it's fallen out of favor. But I've always enjoyed playing in that style and back in the early days of the Brothers we used to hang out with John Hammond Jr. quite a bit, and he taught us a lot about traditional country blues playing.

LEAVELL: Lamar played upright bass on "Pony Boy," which we wanted to be all acoustic.

SANDLIN: Butch played percussion by banging on a piece of plywood on the floor; there's no drum kit on there.

LEAVELL: I thought it was a neat touch to end with an acoustic song that helped balance things out, just as *Eat a Peach* had with "Little Martha." I thought then—and still do—that *Brothers and Sisters* had a really great balance, with the instrumental "Jessica," the deep blues of "Jelly Jelly," the countryish rock of "Ramblin' Man," and everything else.

ODOM: It was obvious there was a great album happening. Dickey did take the musical lead—not as a leader but as a musician, and there's a difference. In the studio, Dickey's influence on *Brothers and Sisters* was incredible. It was a very, very difficult situation, and Dickey just rose to the occasion.

The final track recorded for Brothers and Sisters *was the blues "Jelly Jelly," which was credited to Gregg though it features lyrics to Bobby Bland's song of the same name with a very different vocal melody and arrangement.*

SANDLIN: They needed one more song to finish the album and Gregg said he had something. He said he'd written new words to a blues based around this great arrangement they had of Ray Charles's "Outskirts of Town" [which the Brothers sometimes performed; a live version was captured on *Live at Ludlow Garage 1970*]. That was one of the earliest songs I ever heard the Brothers play and it was great. So we cut the track and Gregg kept not bringing in the rest of the words he supposedly had. He just didn't have the lyrics finished. Everyone was calling up, pushing me. Capricorn and Warner Brothers wanted that album. So finally, out of desperation, Gregg just sang the words to "Jelly Jelly," an old blues song, and some of the early presses actually listed "Early Morning Blues," the title of his new song.

LEAVELL: I didn't know any of the drama. I thought it was a classic Allman Brothers deep-blues-with-a-twist song and I loved recording it and was honored just to play a solo.

SANDLIN: As soon as he finished that vocal, people were waiting to take Gregg to rehab. He didn't pass Go before heading off to get help.

DUDEK: I went on the road with Boz Scaggs and then Steve Miller offered me a gig and I told him that I was tied up with Phil, but didn't know what was happening, and he said, "Go back to Macon and ask Phil if he intends to do something with you, and if not, ask for your release and move out here and join my band." He had his lawyer draw up a release and I got a cashier's check for the money I owed Phil that he had been advancing me for living expenses.

I parked myself in front of Phil's office for a week until he called me in and eventually I handed him the release and he signed it, very surprised and maybe offended that I came in there ready with a release and a check. And that also let me out of the publishing deal, which meant that there would be no cut going in for any credit I had on "Jessica" and since I had no written contract about that, I believe they just decided to leave me off. Years later, Dickey apologized about "the whole 'Jessica' thing" and said "they" told him he didn't have to pay me. Of course, I didn't accept that, but there was nothing I could do.

Demons

With Brothers and Sisters *in the can and being prepped for a late summer release, the Allman Brothers Band returned to the road. They were playing larger venues, making more money, and dealing with increasing drug problems, with less friendship and communication among the members.*

PERKINS: A combination of everything—drugs, money, the expanding size of it all—led to everyone feeling separate and distant.

PAYNE: We were going through an airport one time and these three suits had fallen in behind us. They were walking behind us making fun of Gregg, just saying the kind of things we would hear all the time like, "Look at that long blond hair . . . looks like a girl to me." We were ignoring them, but when we went to get in a cab, these three guys tried to take it. Gregg had already gotten in and one of them was trying to pull him out, and in the flash of an eye, Dickey was on them and all three of them were lying on the ground bleeding.

He and Gregg were not even getting along at the time. I'd hate to see what he would do to someone who messed with someone he loved.

RED DOG: Separation set in. I think management pushed Gregg a little bit away as the front man. Gregg and Dickey both had solo albums out or coming out . . . things just changed. And I watched money change everyone, including myself.

The feeling that the band was spiraling out of control came to a head on June 9 and 10, 1973, when the Allman Brothers played with the Grateful Dead at Washington's RFK Stadium on a co-headlining bill, with the Allmans opening the first show and closing the second.

Jaimoe and Dickey Betts, RFK Stadium, June 1973.

WOOLEY: Backstage, the Grateful Dead roadies dosed the food and drinks of as many people as they could with LSD. Bunky Odom warned us in advance so we didn't partake of anything. However the ABB road crew already had.

PAYNE: Any time you were around Owsley Stanley [Dead soundman and legendary acid creator who was known as Bear], you were in danger of being dosed, but I don't think we were that time. After our first few encounters with them, we were careful. We kept our hands over our beer cans, never left food or drinks unattended or consumed anything we hadn't opened. If you didn't take these precautions, you were likely to be dosed, which I was not fond of and I really think is a cruel thing to do—remember we were looking at driving six hundred miles after most gigs.

WEIR: That would have been a common practice in those days. Some of the folks with our crew, especially Bear, were evangelical about LSD and had no compunction about dosing people. All I can say is, I had to deal with that, too. I stopped taking LSD willingly in 1966 because as far as I was concerned, I had seen enough. I still got dosed numerous times, because a lot of those evangelicals did not think I had seen enough—that anyone possibly could see enough.

PAYNE: I remember the first time we played with the Dead, I was filling "Garg" afterwards—that was short for gargantuan, because it was a huge airline case filled with cables of all sorts. I opened it up and they were all moving and looked like snakes, which freaked me out because I have a fear of snakes.

PARISH: That was definitely something that people had to deal with around us, but I think by that time we were pretty careful with the bands we worked with, and there wasn't much of that kind of thing going on.

ODOM: It's always intense on stage and the road crew has to watch this and that, and I think Dick Wooley came on stage with some people and they didn't want him there. And Dick liked to fight himself, so when they got in an argument, things got out of control.

JAIMOE: The stage was really crowded and everyone there was specifically told not to come up without clearance from the tour manager.

PAYNE: I probably shouldn't have even been there. I had badly injured my foot in a bike crash about a month earlier and was limping around on painkillers. The stage was constructed on the field and it was not all that stable. The Dead had an entourage that must have been 300 people. We were playing and there were probably 150 people on stage, which was not designed to hold so many, and I could see the whole thing shaking and swaying. I was really worried about the thing falling.

I had already told Tuffy [Phillips, driver], "Nobody else gets on this stage," when he came over and said there was a guy who says he's with the label and wants to come up. So I hobbled over and there was this guy I had never seen before, with short hair wearing a suit and holding a briefcase. He said he was with the label and he was coming up and I just said, "No you're not," and punched him in the nose.

WOOLEY: I was in pretty good shape. I still competed in karate tournaments and was no pushover in any street fight.

JAIMOE: I think that Phil and Bunky were getting tired of the whole situation and since Wooley dabbled in martial arts, they were going to have him kick Tuffy's ass and Wooley fell for that. Tuffy told him to get the fuck off the stage and Dick Wooley got into this karate stance.

WOOLEY: When a dosed-up ABB driver blocked me from returning to my seat I looked to find the road manager and the driver sucker-punched me with a beer bottle. Stunned, I instinctively began punching and quickly got the better of the fight. But some cowardly ABB roadie saw this and began kicking me in the face with the heel of his boot.

PAYNE: He tumbled down the stairs. The Dead's security was Hell's Angels and when they looked up and saw it was me who hit him, they figured he was a bad guy and kicked the shit out of him.

PARISH: Not one Hell's Angel ever set foot in RFK Stadium as our security, though there certainly might have been a few stray Angels who were someone's friends. I don't know what happened because it was their business and we didn't get involved. We wouldn't have wanted them involved in our business and we returned the favor.

WOOLEY: Luckily, the Grateful Dead's roadies saw this and jumped in to separate the churning pile. I was bleeding from the kicks, but still swinging when a very large Grateful Dead roadie pulled me out of the pile using a police-type stranglehold. He picked me up and deposited me in the promoter's limo. So thank you, Big Grateful Dead Roadie.

A fuming Walden demanded that whoever was responsible for injuring Wooley be fired. Kim Payne, Mike Callahan, and Tuffy Phillips all lost their jobs.

JAIMOE: It was just, "Tuffy, Callahan, and Kim Payne have to go."

ODOM: Phil had to make a stand. After all, Dick Wooley worked for him, and it wasn't a good situation. The way a record company looks at it is simple: "We need these people. You need to be nice to them." Dick was very good at his job.

PERKINS: That was a culmination of everything falling apart. There was just a general malaise going on. It wasn't like anyone thought, "Everything's fine except for these three guys." They were a symptom of the problem—not the problem itself. On the other hand, the road crew had gotten pretty demanding, driving the promotions people crazy and controlling access to everything and everyone.

The word was Kim had saved Gregg from an OD just before. People said he saved the guy's life on Friday and got fired on Saturday.

PAYNE: I had saved his life from an OD, no doubt, but not the day before. We were back in Macon and I don't think anyone wanted to tell me I had been fired, so Dickey volunteered and he called me over to his house and told me I no longer had a job.

PERKINS: One of the most difficult things I've ever had to do was tell those guys about them losing their jobs and that it was a final decision—that they couldn't go back to the members of the band and try to get it back.

PAYNE: That kind of broke my heart. How do you fire a family member? It was a brotherhood from the minute we pledged it until the minute I was fired.

PERKINS: Well, you ain't gonna fire the band.

RED DOG: Drugs fucked up Kim and Callahan badly—especially Kim. It was more or less a domino thing—knock one down and they all go.

PAYNE: I can't doubt any of the charges against me because I was so full of drugs, between what the doctor prescribed for my foot and street drugs.

WOOLEY: In our organization everyone was out of control. Phil and Dickey were featured most in the local Macon paper. . . . Everyone back then was on a high, some could handle it, some couldn't. Everyone dealt with drugs in their own way, but it took its toll on everyone.

JAIMOE: Everything started to change one way or another. The message was "Look at all the dollars you're making now. Do you want to keep making them?" There were various ways of saying that to you, trying to make you realize so you will change your behavior. A lot of things started to change. One thing I can say is I still hold a lot of things I always felt and believed . . . I just do what I do and when I see things going on I don't like I just stay away from those kinds of people.

BRUCE HAMPTON: Jaimoe has never wavered. He's been the same forever.

WOOLEY: Being with Atlantic for many years, on the road with top talent like Eric Clapton, gave me the opportunity to observe how professional artist managers, artists, and crews acted and how they handled themselves both onstage and backstage.

I anticipated the same high standards at Capricorn because Twiggs Lyndon was a longtime friend and a backstage professional I'd worked with. Soon after settling in Macon I saw that Twiggs's influence over the ABB had waned and Duane was, of course, gone. Now leaderless and demoralized, the band was influenced mostly by the road crew that surrounded them. By industry standards the road crew was a cluster-fuck of drugged-out hangers-on that seemingly kept their job by keeping the ABB supplied with drugs and high most of the time. It was crazy and out of control.

CHAPTER 17

Mountain Jam

ON JULY 28, 1973, *the month after the debacle at RFK Stadium, the Allman Brothers Band and the Grateful Dead teamed up again, for what was then the largest rock concert ever, at Watkins Glen Speedway in New York's Finger Lakes region. The Allman Brothers were paid $117,500 for what their contract stipulated would be one 150-minute set beginning at 10 p.m.*

With three crew members suddenly gone and the largest gig in rock history fast approaching, the band needed some new employees. Among those quickly hired was Twiggs's kid brother A.J., then twenty-two years old.

A.J. LYNDON: When Twiggs called me, I was excited and my wife was not. She started crying, both because she didn't want me gone and because she knew what life was going to be like out there. I said no, and my mother told me I was foolish for not going on the road with the band. I signed on and my first two gigs were at Madison Square Garden.

PERKINS: Whenever we had a personnel change, it felt like, "We can't get along without that guy." But we never had a real problem. We never missed a beat.

A.J. LYNDON: After one of the New York nights, I came back and saw Dickey trashing his room and threatening his wife and he tried to beat me up, and I went to Twiggs and quit. I said I wasn't cut out for this work. Then Willie came and asked me to please stay through Watkins Glen because they needed all hands on deck.

Here's how things were in the rock and roll world in 1973: they taught me how to drive an eighteen-wheeler pulling a 45-foot trailer on the highway, with no special license, and my teacher sitting next to me drinking whiskey and snorting cocaine. Off to Watkins Glen!

RED DOG: We loved playing with the Dead, starting with the Fillmore shows. Duane loved sitting in with them—like, "We're gonna play all night!"

WEIR: We always loved playing with the Allman Brothers. We developed a close relationship with Duane that unfortunately never had the time to blossom because he was gone so soon. Over the years, I got closer with Dickey as well and have always enjoyed playing with him.

ODOM: Sam Cutler of the Grateful Dead and I put Watkins Glen together. I made twelve trips to San Francisco to meet with him and he came to Macon twice. It started with two dates we had booked together in Athens, Georgia, and Houston, which got canceled because of Berry's death. We wanted to work together more, kept talking and talking, and eventually decided to do three dates: the two at RFK and one at Watkins Glen.

PARISH: After the death of Duane we really tried to support them, to get them through that tough time. We scheduled some shows together and on the way to one in Houston, I crashed our truck and I was almost killed and our PA was all over the road and the whole thing was just a mess. I was lucky to be alive and we didn't know how we were going to

Jerry Garcia and Dickey Betts, Cow Palace, San Francisco, December 31, 1973.

make the show, but we were thinking, "At least we have the Allman Brothers there to pick up any slack." We got there and found out that Berry Oakley had died and they, of course, weren't coming. What a weird and horrible day.

WEIR: A joint show with the Allman Brothers was an opportunity to play to at least a partially new audience, which would always make it more of an adventure for us. We also looked forward to the cross-pollination; we would play with them, they would play with us, and that was always fun.

ODOM: We invited the Band to open Watkins Glen, which Sam and I decided on together, because we thought those three bands represented America. They were the three best American bands and they related to each other, the music related, they knew each other. It was just a great fit.

LEAVELL: It was very exciting to think about those three bands playing together. We knew it was going to be a big draw and the figure of 100,000 people was being thrown around in the weeks prior, which seemed incredible.

One hundred and fifty thousand tickets were sold for ten dollars each, but the crowd exploded to many times that number. The rest got in for free, though many people certainly never got within sight of the stage. The small country roads leading to the concert site became parking lots—first figuratively, then literally, as many drivers abandoned their vehicles and walked up to ten miles to the concert.

WEIR: It was hard to get in and out of that place. It got way, way bigger than we intended for it to get. We thought maybe if we're lucky we'd get 100,000 people; 60,000 to 70,000 would be nice and handle-able.

LEAVELL: We were staying in Horseheads, New York, in a small motel, and I remember being awoken by noise and commotion the day before, when we were supposed to have cars drive us up the road for soundchecking, then seeing this mass of people, like an exodus, out on the little highway. People were abandoning their vehicles in huge traffic jams and there was total confusion and mayhem.

PERKINS: When we first got there we were able to drive in and out of the site, but then the road became like Armageddon overnight. It was like there had been a nuclear attack and people had just abandoned their cars.

A.J. LYNDON: We were staying at a Holiday Inn thirteen miles away and cars were abandoned around there, that far away.

WEIR: As it turns out, the news reported there were 600,000 there and maybe two million people in the area and it was declared a disaster area. As disaster areas go, it was a pretty nice one, but people who were interested in going home, for instance, well, they couldn't. If they wanted to leave, it just wasn't possible. People had to be peeled away layer by layer.

PARISH: All the stuff like transportation just broke down. Amenities were impossible to maintain, fences were broken down. It became a serious security situation for the crowd, but the stage was secure. The Allman Brothers were a little more disorganized than us. We were hard at work building a tremendous PA system. Because of the crowds pouring in, the soundcheck day became a day of free music; it ended up being two days of music instead of one.

TRUCKS: The afternoon rehearsal ended up being my most powerful memory because in daylight you could see 600,000 people stretched out in front of you and . . . My God! Everyone should get up in front of 600,000 people some time in their life. It's sort of intimidating but also very, very inspiring.

LEAVELL: It became obvious that we weren't taking cars up there, so helicopters were summoned and as we got close, we asked the pilot to circle around so we could soak it in and it was absolutely stunning, exhilarating, and exciting to see this incredible mass of human beings. It was an ocean of bodies. We were all just really buzzed by the whole scene and situation.

A.J. LYNDON: We rode a helicopter there and we came over a hill and there was this sea of humanity and we all just went, "Oh, Jesus." It was like nothing anyone had ever seen or could even imagine, and someone asked the helicopter to circle around so we could take it all in.

ODOM: There were so damn many people. Cars were backed up forty or fifty miles, and people just got out and walked. There were a lot of problems but we got it done. We had the promoters fly Bill Graham in to be the stage manager, because both bands had total faith in Bill and that paid off.

PERKINS: We made it up there and found this little idyllic backstage that Bill Graham had set up, with palm trees and everyone having their own RV and everyone had a grand old time hanging out back there.

PARISH: We shared three days of hang time together. The guys were jamming on music together the whole time, mostly in the trailers set up in the back.

A.J. LYNDON: I was in one of the trailers and Dickey came into the room and asked others to leave. He sat down, apologized for his actions in New York and asked me to please stay with the crew. I was touched, and I knew it was a sign of how much he respected Twiggs. I never had any other problems with him.

LEAVELL: I was a fan of the Grateful Dead and was really excited about the opportunity to watch them and meet them.

WEIR: The music itself . . . well, typically for us, we didn't play our best show in front of our largest crowd. We got the short stick on who would open and who would close. As I recall, it was essentially determined by drawing cards out of a hat because it was impossible to rank the bands. It would have been nice to have the lights and we didn't get them because we played in daylight. I do remember the jam at the end was pretty spectacularly wiggy.

LEAVELL: It rained like hell and people didn't seem to mind. There's always something endearing about everyone getting wet and hanging tough that can bond everyone. I don't think we had the best show in the world, but it was just so exciting to be there. At the end, we had a long jam, and it was not exactly picture perfect—but there were interactions.

TRUCKS: One of the reasons that we had such a massive crowd is everyone was coming to hear the three best jam bands in the country jam together. But the jam was just ridiculous, because by the time we all got together everyone was fucked up—and fucked up on different drugs. The Band was all drunk as skunks and sloppy loose, the Dead were full of acid and wired in that far-out way, and we were all full of coke and cranked up. You put it all together and it was just garbage. While we were playing, we thought it was the greatest thing the world had ever heard, but then we listened to the playbacks and it was really horrible.

CHAPTER

Shine It On

*B*ROTHERS AND SISTERS *was released in August 1973, with
artwork that emphasized the band's family approach just as the title
did, with Butch's young son Vaylor pictured on the front and Oakley's daughter
Brittany on the back. The album opened up to an inside spread of the band and
their extended families and friends taken at the Juliette farm.*

Brothers and Sisters *became the band's first number one album and "Ramblin' Man" rose to second on the singles charts. Almost two years after their guiding light had been killed, the Allman Brothers were the most popular band in
the country.*

WOOLEY: Being the only one in daily contact with radio stations, I
saw the potential of "Ramblin' Man" first. Stations were reporting to
me that was the track they wanted to play as a single, so Frank, Phil,
and I just went with it.

*On September 10, 1973, Don Kirshner's Rock Concert show came to Macon to
tape the Allman Brothers Band and the Marshall Tucker Band at the Grand
Opera House. Billed as "Saturday Night in Macon," the show was being recorded*

for national TV just a month after the release of Brothers and Sisters *and was a major promotional event. Bill Graham was in town serving as the show's MC.*

SANDLIN: We set up to record, with a very nice truck from Nashville. It was a beautiful setting and seemed like a perfect thing. But Dickey was off from the start—supposedly someone dosed him. Gregg would say, "Now we're going to play a song off our new album," introducing "Ramblin' Man," and Dickey would kick off "You Don't Love Me" or something. That happened two or three times. Then in the middle of the show, Dickey put his guitar down and walked off stage.

JAIMOE: He put his guitar in his case, walked out of the theater, and started walking home—and I think he was living on the farm. He left us there on stage with no lead person. We basically had nothing but a rhythm section—two drums, two keyboards, and bass. That's fine if you play like that, but someone has to take over for what's absent.

PERKINS: Oh boy. That was another Nightmare on Elm Street. His equipment wasn't going right and Dickey just walked out the door, with Joe Dan running after him. Gregg was far from being on his game that night either.

LEAVELL: As I recall, Dickey was upset because the whole idea was for the cameras to come down and catch us as we are, the way we lived and played. There had been some direction from the Kirshner people that they wanted certain things certain ways, and Dickey got upset about it, feeling like they were supposed to be staying out of our way and recording it, not interfering with what we were doing. Did recreational items accelerate that? I don't know, but he flew off the handle and just left. We played a little bit without him, then took a break and waited. It was a very unusual and uncomfortable situation.

SANDLIN: Phil ran out and got him, stopped him walking down the street and eventually brought him back. It was awful. I was sitting there all ready to capture a great recording and they just didn't have a great performance in them.

LEAVELL: We were really upset. I guess Dickey had always been somewhat volatile and moody, but walking off the stage was a first for me. It was like, "Dude, what are you doing? We're all brothers here. If there's a problem, let's talk about it." At the end of the day, the important thing was to try and salvage the show and make it as good as it can be, but we were all looking at each other like, "What is this all about?" We were happy that he came back, but . . .

An obviously tense and unpleasant night may have clouded people's memories of this concert. The performance, while certainly not peak ABB, was stronger than most recall, though it featured only five live Allman Brothers songs, "Southbound" being the only track from Brothers and Sisters. *The Allmans segment of the TV show ended with the album version of "Ramblin' Man" playing over footage of an outdoor crowd that never shows the stage.*

PERKINS: I remember after the show Bill Graham and the director sitting on the stage discussing whether or not they had enough usable material for a show. They were not sure, so the decision was made to film Wet Willie down in the park and turn what was supposed to be an Allman Brothers concert into "Saturday Night in Macon."

SANDLIN: They were a great band, so even on a bad night they were good, but it was just sad—just like Gregg being whisked from the studio to rehab. There was often a sadness because they were so talented but they were their own worst enemy at times. I've thought about it a lot and I have no idea of just what happened or how it could have been different.

RED DOG: I still don't understand what happened, starting with Duane's death. I feel cheated, damn it. Somewhere, somehow . . . that wasn't supposed to happen. It was like giving a little kid candy and then taking it away. Somehow we ain't done something right and we're paying for it. Someone wasn't dealing from the top of the deck. We had something so good building and growing and then Duane and Berry were gone and everything got so hard. That's why a lot of us had to use drugs even more; for me, I always wanted something before I went to sleep so I didn't dream—because I knew they would be there.

As their tour grosses picked up radically, the Allman Brothers began to play arenas and stadiums almost solely. As travel became easier and the shows bigger, the brotherhood seemed ever more frayed and the drug use escalated.

TRUCKS: *Brothers and Sisters* took off and we became big rock stars and were the number one band in the country but the music became secondary to everything else and it felt hollow. Of course, having all these gorgeous women falling over us and everything else was fun. It was a big party, but the music and everything that had been all-important became secondary.

PERKINS: With Duane, and then for the first couple of years after he died, the band always seemed to play with one mind. Nobody got left behind. It was never rote and they were never on cruise control. That began to change.

RED DOG: When Duane was alive, everybody had their job. The band would sit down and discuss things and be on the same page, but Duane just knew what was happening. He knew what he wanted the band to sound like and where he wanted the band to go, and everyone understood their role and how to get there. They all wanted the same thing in the original band; they just sat down and played and what came out was what they wanted. I don't know who the leader was after that. It should have just been one person: Dickey.

JAIMOE: After Duane died, a lot changed. Everyone wanted to be Duane, but no one knew how to do shit except play music.

LEAVELL: There was no leader after Duane. As far as I can tell, Duane made a lot of decisions on behalf of the band. That changed and it became more of equal partners and there might have been some pull between Dickey and Gregg at times, but in terms of musical decisions, everyone seemed comfortable. It was more of a committee; the band as a whole made decisions.

DOUCETTE: With Duane around, the Dickey/Gregg rivalry was never an issue. Nothing was an issue. People respected Duane so much that there was no room for anything else. Duane laid it down and it was done, but that happened without him ever once saying, "This is my band." Never ever.

Back in Macon, Payne, now unemployed, began worrying more about receiving regular payments for his contribution to "Midnight Rider."

PAYNE: I was aware there were royalty checks coming in and before I got fired Gregg would sometimes just give me some cash for my assistance on "Midnight Rider." After that, I was a junkie with a five-hundred-dollar-a-week habit running around selling dope and hustling to survive and I wasn't seeing Gregg every day anymore. I knew that checks were quarterly and I knew when they were due and I'd have to chase Gregg down and twist his arm a little.

I wasn't signed up with a contract or nothing, and once it was way past time I should have gotten some money and I showed up at Jaimoe's house, where they were practicing. Gregg was sitting at the organ and when I asked for my money, he said, "I'll get back to you later." That was about the third time he blew me off, so I went outside, jumped on his custom chopper and went out and hid it. I told him when he got me straightened out with my money, he'd get his bike back. He went down to Phil's office, had a contract drawn that gave me five percent of the song, dropped it off to me, and said, "Now this is between you and BMI." I've been getting royalty checks ever since.

The Allman Brothers Band and the Grateful Dead never shared a bill again after Watkins Glen. Five months after the landmark concert, however, the Brothers played the Cow Palace in San Francisco on New Year's Eve, 1973, in a performance nationally broadcast on radio. The Dead were off that night, and Jerry Garcia and Bill Kreutzmann sat in for much of the second set and encore, with Kreutzmann taking over for Trucks, who was dosed and unable to continue playing.

The band's take continued to grow; by 1974, they were regularly making more than $100,000 in guarantees. On June 1, 1974, the Allman Brothers headlined the Georgia Jam at Atlanta Fulton County Stadium, which also featured Lynyrd Skynyrd, the Marshall Tucker Band, and Joe Dan Petty's Grinderswitch. The ABB cleared nearly $150,000 for that date. They continued to tour stadiums, including Denver's Mile High and Pittsburgh's Three Rivers, before crossing the Atlantic for the first time in July for shows in Amsterdam and London.

By the time of the stadium tour, the Allman Brothers were renting the Starship, a customized Boeing 720B made famous by Led Zeppelin and also used by the Rolling Stones, Deep Purple, Elton John, Peter Frampton, and others.

PERKINS: The Starship had a bar, a huge couch, a fake fireplace, and a bedroom, which Gregg always managed to get in. But the most decadent thing about that plane was just flying it around. In the middle of a fuel crisis so bad that people couldn't even get gas to come to the show, we were flying around on a big ol' Boeing airliner. "The people's band." I used to think about that and ponder what Berry Oakley would have thought if he were alive. It was expensive, man. I can remember making $50,000 bank transfers to the owners.

A guy Gregg used to know in L.A. was involved in that operation and he told Gregg and Butch about it, and I knew that once it was in their ears, there was no way we wouldn't be climbing on board. They tried to use it to go to Europe but it wasn't certified to do so.

ODOM: The main reason we had the Starship was we didn't have to put up with missing flights and all this nonsense. We could get to a gig and get back home. We tried to make it as easy as possible for them, because Willie was just being driven crazy trying to get everyone together. It was like moving the military.

PERKINS: When the Starship came to Macon to pick us up they couldn't shut it off because they didn't have the generator they used to crank it up. Sometimes that thing would be sitting out there idling for six hours until I could get Gregg on the plane. It was just ridiculous, but it sure solved our problem of getting everyone onto commercial flights.

ODOM: The band members were not getting along. They'd meet on the steps of the plane, get on, and go play a gig. That carried over to the studio.

PERKINS: There started to be tensions and issues and stresses in '73 and it was always a concern, but I thought they held it together and continued to mostly put on really good shows through the big stadium tour of 1974. That was the pinnacle commercially and also the last time that edition of the band was really on its game.

SOUTHERN MEN

The members of the Allman Brothers Band are the undisputed founders and kings of Southern rock. Too bad they hate the term.

Though the original members of the Allman Brothers Band have spent years trying to distance themselves from the term "Southern rock," they are the mountain stream from which this musical river flows. They started it all, a fact Dickey Betts acknowledges, even as he dodges the tag.

"We may have inspired the whole Southern rock thing, but I don't identify with it," says Betts. "I think it's limiting. I'd rather just be known as a progressive rock band from the South. I'm damned proud of who I am and where I'm from, but I hate the term 'Southern rock.' I think calling us that pigeonholed us and forced people to expect certain types of music from us that I don't think are fair."

The Allmans' breakthrough album, 1971's *At Fillmore East*, not only established them as rock's greatest live band, but also shored up a struggling Capricorn Records, leading the label to start signing more bands. Soon, albums were coming out of Macon at a furious pace, and the first great era of Southern rock was underway. And while they all shared a certain sensibility, the Capricorn acts were all considerably different: The Marshall Tucker Band, of Spartanburg, South Carolina, tempered their rock with country, blues, and jazz influences; Wet Willie, from Mobile, Alabama, mined Southern soul and kept the guitars relatively toned down. The second wave of Southern rock followed the massive commercial success of the Allman Brothers' 1973 *Brothers and Sisters* and Lynyrd Skynyrd's 1974 breakthrough with "Sweet Home Alabama." That song and Skynyrd's subsequent use of a giant Confederate flag stage backdrop helped establish the term "Southern rock." Record company A&R men were soon scrambling through Southern bars in search of the next big thing.

Among the groups who benefited were the Outlaws, Molly Hatchet, and Blackfoot. Charlie Daniels, a longtime presence on the Southern rock and country scenes, had his biggest hit in '79 with the fiddle-driven novelty tune "The Devil Went Down to Georgia."

"Southern rock became a parody of itself," says Warren Haynes. "I think the reason the original [Allman Brothers] members always had a problem with it is they look at it as someone coined the phrase so they would have a way to describe them and to lump a bunch of bands together and they wanted to be considered as their own entity.

"If the connotations that get conjured when you hear the term are positive, and especially if they are musical connotations, then I don't really have a problem with it. The problem I have is a lot of people associate it with rednecks and rebel flags and backward mentality. That has never been representative of the Allman Brothers Band."

CHAPTER

End of the Line

*T*HE TENSIONS AND *divisions within the band fully manifested themselves in early 1975 as they began to record their fifth studio album.* Win, Lose or Draw *was cut in noncohesive sessions from February to July, while Gregg was mostly living in Los Angeles and dating Cher, whom he married on June 30, 1975. Gregg and Cher's on-again, off-again relationship was big news, as he became more famous for being famous than for his music.*

ALLMAN: When we recorded *Win, Lose or Draw*, we were barely ever in the studio at the same time. I recorded most of my vocals from Los Angeles.

SANDLIN: I had to fly out to L.A. and cut a lot of Gregg's vocals at the Record Plant, because he wasn't around.

LEAVELL: Gregg was spending a lot of time in California and was not in Macon much. A lot of the music was recorded with him being absent, and there was definitely less interaction than there had been.

PERKINS: It was basically each person going in individually, or sitting around waiting for someone. All the issues that had been percolating became out in the open in the studio.

SANDLIN: That's probably the hardest record I've ever done, beginning simply with just getting everyone together. It was so weird. It wasn't fun at all. It was rough for me, and it was rough for them. Jaimoe and Chuck always seemed to enjoy playing, but the other guys seemed to be struggling just to put anything into it. It was just sad.

JAIMOE: We had so many rehearsals where the only three there were me, Lamar, and Chuck and we would just play and we started joking that we should start a band called We Three.

SANDLIN: We usually started sessions at nine p.m., except for the night that *Kung Fu* was on, because Dickey had to be in front of the TV for that. Weird stuff like that would happen all the time. There was the Gregg faction and the Dickey faction and you could just walk into the studio and feel all this tension. There might as well have been an electric sign warning you: "Things could get rough in here."

Sometimes you'd have two guys sitting there and sometimes you'd get everyone but one there, and it just doesn't work. Up to that point the band had recorded almost everything live—most of the guitar solos and all the rhythm tracks. This is not a band you cut one piece at a time, so we spent a lot of time waiting for someone to show up.

LEAVELL: Just think about everything that the band had gone through: the early days when it was very tough and they were traveling in a van, not making any money. All of a sudden you become successful, then go through the success, making good money, playing arenas and stadiums. Then you lose the leader of the band, grieve, pick it back up again—and lose another founding member. And pick it up again—and have even bigger success. By the time of the *Win, Lose or Draw* sessions everyone was exhausted. They were just tired. And when people get tired, other emotions can go along with it—anger, being upset. I just think the band had enough at that point.

The cover of Win, Lose or Draw *features the interior of an Old West saloon and is appropriately devoid of people. A poker table topped with half-empty whiskey bottles, cards, and chips sits front and center, surrounded by six empty chairs representing the then-current members. Two empty chairs lean against a small, empty table in the background representing Duane and Berry.*

TRUCKS: Twiggs designed the whole thing and there's no doubt he was honoring Duane with those empty chairs. The border features cut-outs of each of our profiles. Of course, Jaimoe and I are on the back—the drummers' lot.

SANDLIN: I never exactly understood that cover. I've heard a lot of interpretations and each one went deeper and deeper. All I know for sure is it's kind of alarming.

TRUCKS: The main problem with *Win, Lose or Draw* is simply that none of us were really into the music. Everyone was into getting fucked up and fucking. We were into being rock stars and the music became secondary. When we heard the finished music, we were all embarrassed.

SANDLIN: *Win, Lose or Draw* wasn't well received but I thought there were some really good cuts on it, especially "Can't Lose What You Never Had" and "High Falls." I wish we had been able to come up with a well-received album that could have helped them stay together, but it just wasn't happening.

PERKINS: Everyone kind of knew right away that *Win, Lose or Draw* was not up to what they had done, that it did not have any classics or that same spark of life. And it didn't do that well, and when we went on the road in support, we had some bad losers, shows where the promoters lost their ass. They didn't work from January '76 into the summer, and by that time the Gregg and Scooter Herring thing was going on.

Though the band was clearly drifting apart, the breaking point came when Gregg testified in the drug trial of the band's security man Scooter Herring. The testimony was regarded as a breach of brotherhood and many in and around the band labeled him a "snitch." He received well-publicized death threats and received law-enforcement protection. The derision grew when Herring was convicted on five counts of conspiracy to distribute cocaine and received a seventy-five-year prison sentence. Jerry Garcia reportedly called Gregg a snitch, fueling what became a permanent split between the Allman Brothers and the Grateful Dead.

    Allman had been threatened with prosecution himself if he did not testify and has always maintained that Herring told him to take the deal and offered to take the fall. The convictions were overturned on appeal and Herring pled guilty to a lesser charge in 1979, working out a deal with federal prosecutors, and was sentenced to thirty months in a federal penitentiary. He ended up serving fourteen months in jail and sixty days in a Macon halfway house. This news received a fraction of the attention accorded to Herring's conviction and initial sentence.

LEAVELL: Gregg was put in the unenviable position of having to testify. Let us remember that he was given immunity that forced him to testify or be jailed until he did so. That had to be an excruciating position to be in.

TRUCKS: We were told that Gregg just copped a plea and sold Scooter out and we found out several years later that Gregg was actually given immunity. We didn't bother talking to Gregg, because we didn't really talk to each other at that time. Gregg was out in L.A. with Cher, we weren't communicating, and we got our news from the newspapers, which made Gregg out to be a fake who just sold Scooter out and that's what we believed. We made our decisions based on that and I think everyone is sorry that was done and that all these comments were made without Gregg at least having a chance to tell us the truth.

He actually went to Scooter and said, "I don't give a shit if I go to jail. I ain't gonna sell you out . . ." And Scooter said, "No, the buck stops here. I did it and they're not offering you any other options."

LEAVELL: The outcome was very unfortunate not only for Scooter but for the band. It helped to sever the ties, but I think there was a lot of misunderstanding of what Gregg was facing.

TRUCKS: This whole damn thing was set off by a group of Republicans in central Georgia who wanted to take down Jimmy Carter and knew that Phil Walden was very involved in his campaign and that Phil was closely associated with Gregg, who was one of the most notorious druggies in the world.

Walden was active in Jimmy Carter's 1976 presidential campaign, helping the former Georgia governor raise money, in part by having his acts put on fundraising concerts. The Allman Brothers Band played a benefit at the Providence Civic Center on November 25, 1975, that was crucial to the campaign, raising much-needed funds for the upcoming Democratic primaries. "There is no question that the Allmans' benefit concert for me in Providence kept us in that race," Carter told People *magazine in September 1976.*

SANDLIN: When the band finally broke up, it seemed kind of inevitable. There just wasn't a lot of joy left in the music. There were a lot of other things blamed for the breakup, including the drug trials, but it just felt like it had to happen at that point.

TRUCKS: The bottom line is it was time for us to quit because all we were doing was destroying an incredible legacy.

JAIMOE: It had to end. We went through two deaths and the only thing that kept us from going crazy was the fact that we had something to do, something very intense to fill our time. If not, it could have really been a mess. What happened was, it just became a mess later on—and not as great a mess as it could have been. When you go through stuff like that, you need time to sit and think about things clearheaded and we never had that. We just plowed forward, which is what we had to do then . . . but it could only continue for so long.

Every one of us had things that just piled up, piled up, piled up. That trial was just the straw that broke the camel's back and it all fell on Gregg.

LEAVELL: We had a meeting, and Jaimoe, Lamar, and I definitely wanted to continue the band, but Dickey and Butch were adamant that they would not play with Gregg again. At that time it felt very much like a definitive breakup. There was no sense that the band would ever play together again and there were at least three of us who viewed it as very unfortunate. We would have preferred to go through a few meetings and say, "Can't we work this out?"

Butch and Dickey seemed very determined to sever the ties; they had very strong opinions about what Gregg was doing, and Gregg was going through his own very difficult times and may well have felt that it was time to move on as well. It became apparent there was not going to be a resolution.

JAIMOE: I actually wrote a letter to the *Macon Telegraph* saying I wasn't going to work with Gregory anymore, which was really just Gregory becoming the sacrificial lamb for all of us.

ODOM: Both Capricorn Records and Phil Walden and Associates desperately wanted and needed the Allman Brothers to stay together, but what are you going to do when you've got Dickey, Jaimoe, and Butch saying, "I'll never play with Gregg again"?

JAIMOE: It's easy to look back now and say it was obvious that splitting up for a while was something we needed to do and we just put it all on Gregg. It would be easy to say I regret writing that letter, but you can't try to get out of shit. If you did it, you did it. I did it.

BETTS: After Duane died, it was still very dynamic at first, but it just slowly slipped away and then we lost Berry and it was very hard to continue. I'm not weighing Duane's loss against Berry's loss—but losing two members was just so tough.

SANDLIN: Duane kept everybody together. When he said something everyone listened, and then there wasn't anyone to take that authority. You'd think Gregg would be the natural one, but that's not how he is. There's a lot of things Gregg doesn't want to be involved with.

WOOLEY: Dickey did his best to pull it all together, but he was not equipped to handle such responsibilities and Gregg was too far into the drug culture to organize anything but getting high twenty-four/seven. They are both great talents, but sadly missing a stabilizing compass to control a high-powered juggernaut like the ABB.

TRUCKS: The whole lifestyle had become so destructive that we were all killing ourselves. And it got to where we didn't like each other. We just couldn't keep it going. When we split up, we were the top-grossing band in the country and I was in debt. Phil Walden was the guy who ended up with all our money and when that all set in, it was just mind-blowing and depressing.

BETTS: The whole thing probably wouldn't have even lasted as long as it did if it weren't for Chuck Leavell. He was just such a strong player.

LEAVELL: I remember going into what was supposed to be a band meeting and just three of us showed up; the three who wanted to focus on the music and not worry about other things. At that meeting, we looked at each other, said, "This is reality; the Allman Brothers are no more. What do we want to do?" Obviously, what we did is form our own band—Sea Level—because we all loved playing together.

By the time the oddly named live album Wipe the Windows, Check the Oil, Dollar Gas *was released, the Allman Brothers Band was already broken up and Capricorn Records was foundering. The two-LP record, with nary a new song that had never been released before, met a lukewarm reception, seen as the last gasp of a dying band.*

JAIMOE: When that record came out, I said, "Why do we keep putting out these songs over and over?" A few years ago, a guy I know told me *Wipe the Windows* was really good. That got me to finally listen to the thing for the first time in years, and man, there's some unbelievable playing on it.

At the time, I felt like it was almost ripping people off to put out new versions of songs we had just done a few years earlier. I used to get annoyed with how many Coltrane and Miles records did that. It just didn't make sense to me. Now I get it.

LEAVELL: I think the fans felt, "Why would you attempt to redo the songs, some of which were on *At Fillmore East*?" I get that, because that was a landmark record, cut when the band was musically peaking. But when you go back and study *Wipe the Windows*, it's a lot better than it was given credit for. I'm very proud of it, actually.

JAIMOE: In Gregory's book [*My Cross to Bear*], he says that in this era you could tell what kind of drug was going down because of the way everyone played and that's exactly true and you can hear it on this album: if it was coke, it was edgy and fast. If it was jazzy and kind of groovy, it was codeine. I can listen to it and say, "That's a syrup song . . . That's a pot song." But that's a hell of a record and I'm glad we captured the Chuck and Lamar era. It didn't last all that long.

ORGANIZATION MAN

Twiggs Lyndon's wild life and eerie death.

In 1969 when Phil Walden heard about Duane Allman, the hot session guitarist burning up Muscle Shoals, he sent Twiggs Lyndon to investigate. A trusted employee who had worked as a road manager for many of Walden's soul acts,

Twiggs was already on the case thanks to his old friend, drummer Jai Johanny Johanson (Jaimoe).

"Twiggs and I worked together with Percy Sledge and pledged that we would bring each other onto any good gigs we found," recalls Jaimoe. "When I met Duane, he asked if I knew any other guys and I said, 'I know a great bassist [Lamar Williams], but he's in the Army. I've got a tour manager, though."

By the spring of 1969, Walden had signed Duane Allman and his band to management and recording contracts. When the Allman Brothers Band moved to Macon, Georgia, in May 1969, they moved into Twiggs's apartment, turning the one-bedroom flat into a den of iniquity known to all as the "Hippie Crash Pad."

Twiggs quickly became an indispensible part of the operation, overseeing gear procurement, rehearsal space, and transportation and becoming the road manager once the group started touring.

Twiggs's devotion to the ABB was returned. The band appreciated his attention to all details, including a carefully curated list of the age of legal consent for sexual activities in each state. A sharp-minded, creative tinkerer, Twiggs was also an obsessive-compulsive perfectionist with a violent temper that could flare up suddenly and unexpectedly. "He was kind and thoughtful and would do anything for a friend, but he also kept people on edge," says John Lyndon, the eldest of three surviving Lyndon brothers.

Willie Perkins, a longtime friend of Twiggs's who was his handpicked successor as ABB road manager adds, "I remember many times telling Twiggs that he was seeking perfection in an imperfect world. He could be driven bonkers by anything that wasn't exactly as he felt it should be."

On April 30, 1970, Lyndon stabbed club owner Angelo Aliotta to death in Buffalo, New York, in a dispute over $500 owed to the band. Lyndon was eventually found not guilty by reason of temporary insanity; his lawyer, John Condon, essentially argued that life on the road with the Allman Brothers had driven him crazy.

"Twiggs was a thin-line-between-insanity-and-genius kind of guy," says Jaimoe. "I loved him as much as I've ever loved anyone."

Lyndon's trial was delayed until September 1971, and he was still serving mandated time in a Buffalo mental hospital when Duane Allman was killed in a motorcycle accident on October 29. About a month later, Lyndon returned to Macon and promptly went to Miami where the Allman Brothers Band was finishing *Eat a Peach*. When the group resumed touring, Perkins remained the road manager and Lyndon became the production manager, overseeing logistical coordination and gear.

"They assigned Twiggs to me and I found him to be absolutely fascinating," says Chuck Leavell. "He was full of energy and he was a problem-solver with a superlogical common sense approach."

Lyndon relished fixing problems, such as building a case to cushion the transport of Leavell's Steinway grand piano, based around four VW shock absorbers, and devising a heating element that blew hot air above the keyboard to keep Leavell's hands warm for cold outdoor performances. Lyndon's perfectionism also sometimes led to conflict.

"Things could get testy," says Perkins. "When anything didn't precisely match the rider, something was one minute late, or the ice in the cooler wasn't to his liking, Twiggs would go through the roof and create some very tense situations."

After the Allman Brothers split up in 1976, Twiggs discovered the instrumental band the Dixie Dregs in Nashville, and helped get them signed to Capricorn Records. Lyndon had bought the ABB's smaller equipment truck, known as Black Hearted Woman, and was retrofitting it as a mini tour bus when he offered his and its services to the Dregs.

"He said, 'I'll be your road manager and show you how it's done,'" says guitarist Steve Morse. "He was an incredible asset and friend—super hardworking, loyal, and competent at everything he tackled."

Twiggs, a classic car aficionado, traded a 1939 Ford Opera coupé to Gregg Allman for Duane's 1959 darkburst Les Paul, determined to hold it for Duane's daughter, Galadrielle, until she was "old enough not to give it to the first guitar player she dated." He took the guitar on tour with the Dregs, using it for the one song he performed each night—the ABB's "Don't Want You No More."

When the Allman Brothers reunited in 1978, Twiggs joined them at Miami's Criteria Studios as they worked on *Enlightened Rogues*, but things soon turned ugly when Lyndon suggested to Betts that the band should re-sign with ex-manager Phil Walden.

"Dickey thought Twiggs was a Phil Walden man and when things got bad between the band and Phil, Dickey didn't want Twiggs around," Red Dog Campbell recalled in 1986. "It broke Twiggs's heart...I am certain that anything Twiggs did was because he thought that was the best thing for the band."

Lyndon returned to the road with the Dregs and in the midst of a tour on November 16, 1979, he met up with a group of skydivers in upstate New York to participate in a choreographed formation dive. He died when his chute did not properly deploy, leaving some to conclude that he had committed suicide. It was unthinkable to those who knew Twiggs that such a perfectionist would have made an error packing his chute. Twiggs had often discussed suicide, according to John Lyndon. And the name of the tiny town from which the plane had taken off was striking: Duanesburg.

Morse, who witnessed the death, rejects the notion that it was intentional.

"I watched Twiggs rehearse with the group for over an hour outside in bone-chilling temperatures, with him wearing only a lightweight jumpsuit better suited for Southern temperatures," says Morse. "He also kept a terrible diet, didn't sleep properly, and was running on coffee and other stimulants. The combination proved lethal.

"After the successful formation, they split apart. He was one of the last ones to get his chute out. The wind was strong, and his chute opened, but he appeared to be swinging back and forth, due to turbulence or a line being fouled. He cut away and tried to go to his reserve chute, then tumbled with no signs of movement. I'm absolutely convinced that he lost consciousness due to shock and hypothermia. If Twiggs had wanted to kill himself, he would have gone out in style, freefalling onto a target or something. He never would have limply tumbled over and disappeared into some trees as he did."

On April 2, 1990, Twiggs' brother Skoots Lyndon met Galadrielle Allman's mother, Donna, at Duane's Macon grave and presented her with the Les Paul, which Morse and the Lyndon family had safeguarded for eleven years. Galadrielle has since lent the guitar to the Rock and Roll Hall of Fame, where it remains on display.

Can't Spend What You Ain't Got

*F*OLLOWING THE BREAKUP, *Betts formed Great Southern, Gregg put together the Gregg Allman Band, and Jaimoe, Leavell, and Williams added guitarist Jimmy Nalls and became Sea Level. All three of these bands put out fairly strong albums in 1977. Still, the following year Allman and Walden approached Betts and broached the idea of a reunion.*

Their first joint appearance in almost three years was on August 16, 1978, in New York's Central Park, when Gregg, Butch, and Jaimoe came out and joined Great Southern for five songs. They quickly decided to reunite. When Williams and Leavell declined to leave Sea Level, the group added two Great Southern members: guitarist "Dangerous" Dan Toler and bassist David "Rook" Goldflies. The headline to a People *magazine article about the reunion summed up the public perception of the band:* "The Allman Brothers Band Finally Buries the Hatchet—and Not in One Another."

LEAVELL: Jaimoe had left our band, partly because of back problems, but Lamar and I were moving on with our career in Sea Level and were in the middle of doing an album when the possibility of doing an Allman Brothers record occurred. We were contacted and said, "Look, we don't think it's fair to throw the guys we just hired out in the cold. Let us finish this record, get three months to tour, and we'll come back." Well, they didn't want to do that. They wanted to start immediately and we had to make a decision—which was that it did not seem right.

PERKINS: Chuck and Lamar were invited to go back and it was pretty much an ultimatum. I don't think anyone expected them to say no.

LEAVELL: I would have liked to be a part of it, but I have no regrets. I was with the band during a very difficult and very productive period. I'm very proud of it and I'll always consider myself an Allman Brother.

DAVID "ROOK" GOLDFLIES, *ABB bassist, 1978–82:* We, the other guys in the band, didn't know the reunion was going to happen in Central Park until just before. Those guys came out and the crowd went bonkers and it hit us all for the first time just what we were part of. You can understand something intellectually but not fully get it until you experience it, and that was the case here. It was very exciting.

JAIMOE: We were a little rusty—maybe a lot rusty—and we were playing with some different guys, but it felt good to be together.

Eight days later, the reformed Allman Brothers Band made a surprise appearance at the annual Capricorn picnic, performing four songs. They then returned to Miami's Criteria Studio to work with Dowd on what became Enlightened Rogues, *a term Duane used to describe the band. The album was released six months after the Central Park show, and the band promptly returned to the road.*

The band had renegotiated their deal with Capricorn Records, but many questions about royalties lingered. An audit was undertaken and Dickey Betts filed suit against Walden, alleging nonpayment of record and publishing royal-ties. Betts's lawyer Steve Massarsky was managing the group.

DOWD: We tried very hard to reach the classic sound on *Enlightened Rogues*. We worked our fingers to the bone, but it was laborious.

TRUCKS: That band just didn't work. The chemistry wasn't there. The only reason the first album was half successful was that Tom Dowd produced it and worked so hard.

BETTS: Some of the groups we had around that time just could not measure up to the original band. We did not have a slide guitarist, so I had to do it. Not only did I not enjoy this, but it altered the sound of the band, which needs to have my sound and the slide working to-gether. Even when we had some great players, there was a pull, a tension—the unity was lacking. We used to say it was like having two trios on stage.

GOLDFLIES: What I saw many times, especially towards the begin-ning, was a real effort from both Gregg and Dickey to be really gracious to each other. I sensed there was a real effort to make it work. They tried to make it happen.

I think the "two trios" thing became more apparent towards the end of this stint. Then it did often feel like there was a Gregg band and a Dickey band onstage at the same time. Danny Toler, a wonderful guy and guitarist, came in as Dickey's right-hand man and ended up being Gregg's guy. I was considered "Dickey's guy" and I never really got in Gregg's boat.

In his book, Gregg said that I played too many notes. But I never once remember Gregg asking me to play any specific way. I would have loved some feedback from a musician of his caliber! Conversely, Dickey and I spoke all the time about music and he was like, "Jazz it up . . . rip

"Dangerous" Dan Toler, 1986.

it out." I was playing the way Dickey wanted me to, and he was very patient and gracious with his time, showing me what he wanted. We spent a lot of time on buses and in hotel rooms playing together and working things out. It became a mentor/mentee relationship.

JAIMOE: I'd like to say I was optimistic heading into this reunion. Since this band began, I've been excited to go back on the road after a break. It might fade very quickly at times, but the initial excitement is always there—but it wasn't then. Sometimes I'd be walking off stage and see Rook or one of the guys and it was almost like I had forgotten they were there. It was like seeing your neighbor pull into his driveway and thinking, "Oh, that guy still lives here?" It's not a good way for a band to operate.

There's a lot of things I've learned in life and it's not gonna be that you don't know what you need to do. We would have known if we would have been looking.

Capricorn Records was teetering by the time Enlightened Rogues *was released, and filed for bankruptcy in October 1979. By that time, Betts had won a substantial arbitration settlement, and the rest of the Allman Brothers' members were next in line, likely to be followed by a litany of other Capricorn artists.*

"It went down like a greased safe," says Dick Wooley, who had left the label in 1976.

Massarsky steered the Allman Brothers Band to Clive Davis's Arista Records, which had put out two Great Southern albums. Arista also signed the Grateful Dead and the label pushed both bands to modernize their sounds.

For their Arista debut, the Allman Brothers started working with Nashville songwriters Mike Lawler and Johnny Cobb in search of a hit. The duo ended up producing the album and Lawler was soon a member of the touring band, playing keyboards and eventually coming center stage to play keytar solos that most fans consider the band's nadir.

MIKE LAWLER, *keyboardist/producer:* I was writing songs in Nashville with my partner Johnny Cobb for Acuff/Rose Publishers and I got to know Dickey when he recorded one of my songs for a solo album that never came out. I got him onto the Grand Ole Opry, where he played "Ramblin' Man" with the Opry band, and he was thrilled about that and bam, we became best friends. He asked me to fly down to Florida to write together for the next Allman Brothers album. Then Johnny and I started hanging around and would often play keyboards with the Brothers when they were rehearsing and doing preproduction.

Butch walked in one day and said, "We have a problem; Tom Dowd is caught up with Rod Stewart and isn't going to be available for a while." Johnny said, "Why don't we produce you?" And Dickey went, "Great idea!" And just like that, I was producing the Allman Brothers, a few years from being the biggest band in the country, at age twenty-four. I couldn't believe it and frankly they all should have said no!

We rented this studio on [Georgia's] Lookout Mountain, to keep everybody out of trouble, out of the way of the city and various bad influences. We were living in a giant old mansion on the mountain.

TRUCKS: That drum ensemble in the middle of "From the Madness of the West" is the only piece of music that was ever put down in written form by the Allman Brothers Band. I wrote that damn thing, but look at the record and see who gets credit for the song: Dickey Betts alone. I should have known better and understood publishing by that point and I really don't have any excuse.

Butch Trucks, 1979.

JAIMOE: "From the Madness of the West" is the only time we did real drum arranging. Butch sat down and wrote out about a sixteen-bar drum solo and we played it together along with a session percussionist. That's really the only time we did that. We were trying to create a stereo effect. Every other song we've ever recorded we just listened to and started playing and our parts fell into place.

LAWLER: As a guy making a living playing on people's records, I felt like they hated to record. It just wasn't high on their agenda. They wanted to play live. We were getting started and they came in and said, "Hey, guess where we're going? We just booked a bunch of dates. We got a good offer. We'll be back when that's done." And I went, "Well, what am I gonna do? I blocked out this time." And they went, "Come with us and play!" They had this Fender Rhodes they were dragging around since Chuck was in the band, and Gregg wasn't really playing it. So I played that run and just like that, I was in the Allman Brothers Band.

PODELL: Drugs and alcohol got really bad for all of us in the late '70s and people got nuts. This is what happens with substance abuse, and all of us were in deep. There was real disgusting, horrible things being said behind people's backs. It was like tribal feuds in Afghanistan. You could feel the drug influence transforming this band of beautiful hippies who just wanted to play music: jealousies, resentments, rivalries . . . most of it directed at management, but sometimes at one another.

LAWLER: It's hard to talk about the Allman Brothers and not discuss drugs. Their entire story is altered by that stuff. It just is. With those guys at that time it was a crapshoot just about every night. You showed up for the gig having no idea what might go down.

GOLDFLIES: I saw some excesses that were pretty creative. It was like living inside a Hunter S. Thompson story. It's no news flash that the Allman Brothers were part of a drug culture. We all got caught up in it to some extent, but I always felt like an amateur compared to those guys. And, yes, any situation becomes less stable when you add a lot of chemical stuff.

LAWLER: One night, during "Blue Sky," Gregg got up from his organ, crouched down, walked all the way behind the amps and back line, came out by my keyboards, and jumped into the audience—because a security guard was hassling the guy holding his dope. He gives the guy his laminate, goes down the foyer, all the way back behind the stage, and sits back down at his organ—all before the song was over. He was back for the final flourish and the band just played right through.

Another time, Dickey disappeared with some guys for a few days, then resurfaced at a gig. Dickey had been up for days and had amphetamine psychosis. He came out there, karate kicked his SG because he couldn't get it in tune, ran off, then came back and started screaming, "I'm having a nervous breakdown."

These are extreme examples of the type of thing that would happen a lot. You just didn't know. You'd invite your parents or somebody to a gig and be scared to shit of what might go down.

GOLDFLIES: Dickey was a gem when he was straight—a super-intelligent, artistic guy who would sit at his house and paint beautiful pictures. There was a lot of good there and the bad wasn't a deal killer and mostly came about through alcohol.

LAWLER: Butch seemed to hold it together, and Jaimoe was always a lovely man who was just out of it sometimes. I love him, but I once saw him nod out over a bowl of black walnut ice cream and cut his eye on a walnut. The real unpredictability came from Gregg and Dickey. Would Gregg make the gig? Would Dickey get mad and hit someone?

GOLDFLIES: Dickey was a powerful force in that band. His guitar playing was so absolutely melodic and beautiful—like Jascha Heifetz beautiful. His improvisations were excellent. They went places and they made sense. I watched him take 100,000 people on a ride with his solos.

Dickey Betts and David "Rook" Goldflies.

Bonnie Bramlett, who had appeared on Enlightened Rogues *and toured with the band from April 1979 through mid-1980, was also to be featured on the first Arista album, even singing lead vocals on one song. Lawler says he went to sessions one morning and found out she was gone.*

LAWLER: Their egos were on fucking Mars. I came into the studio ready to record Bonnie and she was nowhere to be seen, so I ask where she is and someone says, "Hell, she left the mountain. She was in her bed and Gregg came in with his wife and said it was his bed and they got into an argument and she left."

I thought, "What the fuck is wrong with all these people?" They were playing big concerts, riding around in limousines, first-class everything. When they signed to Arista, they figured they were going to just take right back off and be stars.

TRUCKS: Clive Davis destroyed any hope that we had that we could make the thing work again. He wanted us to be a Southern American version of Led Zeppelin and brought in outside producers and it just kept getting worse.

LAWLER: I wasn't alone in fucking up the worst part of their career but I have to take some credit or blame. But as much as I loved the Allman Brothers, we all knew that Southern rock was on its way out.

Mike Lawler, 1981.

JAIMOE: People wanted the band to go in the direction where all the money was. It was like, "You're supposed to be the biggest band in America, so write some songs like this." It's not really that big a deal to do that, but what's the cost?

BETTS: When the music trend started turning away from blues-oriented rock towards more simple, synthesizer-based, dance music arrangements, the record company started to dictate what type of record we could make, and we got caught up in that whole thing.

Eric Clapton has a way of being a chameleon, of finding songs that keep him in the forefront and surviving through times when the kind of music he loves to play isn't popular. The Allman Brothers Band was never able to do that. We either sounded like our band or we didn't. We never really had anything special when we were not able to do the instrumental jams and improvisation, which were taken away from us for a while. We were even asked not to mention Southern rock in interviews or to wear hats on stage.

LAWLER: Anything that we played or did that sounded like traditional Allman Brothers, it would be, "Oh man, they just sound like the same old Allman Brothers. What's new with that?" Clive Davis wanted them to have a newer sound—and most other bands of their era were trying to do the same thing. One thing people did not know in 1980 was that the baby boomers would have all the power a few years later and would say, "We want the Allman Brothers and the Doobie Brothers and the Grateful Dead to be just like they were and we're fucking rich and we can get anything that we want." I didn't know that in the late '70s/early '80s— and neither did anyone else. All those bands were trying to modernize. Anything we did that didn't sound like the good old Allman Brothers was applauded.

RED DOG: The band got so far apart from one another. It was like a big canyon opened up. It just got out of hand and broke my heart. I was irritable and frustrated because I saw it falling apart and couldn't do nothing about it. That was driving me up the wall.

Red Dog himself would soon be fired after getting into a fight and punching his roommate—Rook Goldflies.

RED DOG: That fight with Rook was the end, but sometimes the new guys on the crew thought I was ego-tripping. Even if I was, I had earned that right to stick my little chest out because I hustled and busted my ass and gave my heart and everything I had to be in that position. I was even lucky to be hired back, probably. Maybe I was a bad memory for some of them—seeing me brought back too much. Even when I knew it was over, I wouldn't leave. Butch had to come tell me.

Any illusion that the brotherhood had not been strained to the point of breaking by this time was shattered by the band's decision to fire Jaimoe and replace him with Toler's brother Frankie, who had been a member of Betts's Great Southern. The key issue, Jaimoe says today, was his insistence on having his then-wife and manager Candace Oakley, Berry's sister, handle all of his business affairs.

JAIMOE: Dickey didn't fire me, as has been said. The band fired me because they said that Candace was gonna break up the band. She was doing pretty much what I asked her to—I play the drums and you take care of the business—and they didn't like that. So I get this call one day from Butch, who said, "Jaimoe, we're not thinking alike, like we used to. You need to get Candy out of your business or we're gonna break up the band." That's what he said, not that they're gonna fire me. So they started right away with bullshit, because I knew the band was not going to break up, because when people are making money they will keep doing whatever they need to. But when he said, "It's either her or us," I said, "Well, it's been great working with you" and hung up the phone.

TRUCKS: I had many conversations with Jaimoe and said, "Go to New York and get yourself the meanest, nastiest lawyer you can get and we'll deal with him but we can't deal with your wife."

What finally triggered it is we had a European tour and at the last minute Candy said, "Jaimoe's not going." That put us in a terrible position. It's something I've always hated—hated it then, hate it now—but we really had no choice. We couldn't function as is, so in order to continue functioning, we had no choice but to do so without Jaimoe.

JAIMOE: There was a gig in New Orleans at the Saenger Theater and I get this call from the road manager and he told Candy not to let me miss that gig. It was a setup for me not to show because I would have broken my contract. So I got on an airplane, went to New Orleans, and when they were coming out of baggage claim, walking along having a good time, I said, "Hey, fellas, how you doing?" Frankie Toler was so uncomfortable. He said, "Jaimoe, I got hired to play this gig. I don't know what's going on . . ." And I said, "You were hired to do something, go do it. It's not about you."

GOLDFLIES: Frankie was a very good drummer, so musically we were OK in that transition, but there's no doubt that something bigger was lost with Jaimoe gone. I sometimes felt like I could feel Duane onstage with us. There was this thing that would happen with Gregg, Dickey, Jaimoe, and Butch. They would do stuff all together that wasn't rehearsed or talked about and it was an echo of Duane. They had all shared something very intense, something that was a bond that no matter how much I played with them I would remain outside of, because I had not shared it. They did real musical things that were very subtle, just a way of playing together that was really remarkable to witness. Musically speaking, when they were on, it was as good as it gets— even during this era no one really likes now. But without Jaimoe, a piece of that chemistry and vibe was gone.

Frankie Toler.

JAIMOE: That whole thing hurt me, but I was kind of a tough character. My father got killed when I was seven years old and that instilled in me something about just hanging in there and doing what you need to do. I remember telling my mother, who was crying, "Don't worry. I'll take care of you." And I did that until the day she died.

Allman Brothers' mothers: Mrs. Allman (left) and Mrs. Johnson.

LAWLER: I feel like I got blamed for trying to take them in a place where they didn't need to go. Well, I was only twenty-five and sort of going with the program and bringing what was wanted. I believe now that I could have made a record that I'm not ashamed to put on today.

Before recording their second Arista album, Brothers of the Road, *the band changed managers, hiring the promoter John Scher after Massarsky eased himself out, reportedly saying, "It's a million-dollar headache and a quarter-million-dollar job." Bert Holman, who would become the band's manager a decade later, worked for Scher running day-to-day ABB operations.*

JOHN SCHER, *manager, 1981–82:* I didn't feel like it was more hassle than it was worth at all, and Steve said he wanted out, but remained very much in the loop as Dickey's attorney. This was an extraordinary band. They were trendsetters. They created a style of music that was uniquely American and I think they were still capable of being very good. During my time managing them, there were issues with Dickey that could get a little scary, but he was generally good and he was reliable when you needed him to be. Gregg was often barely functioning.

One time, we had a meeting with Clive Davis about the next record, in the middle of the afternoon. They were staying at a hotel in New Jersey and I met them there to go to New York. Dickey and Butch were dressed, ready to go, but nobody could find Gregg. We kept calling his room and knocking on the door, and then calling everyone we could think of who he might be with or who might know where he is. We're still in New Jersey at the time the meeting is supposed to start and I'm on the phone with Clive's assistant, saying something came up and we're late.

We finally got hotel security to let us into his room in case there was a clue there, and Gregg was passed out on the bed, completely fucked up. Butch and Dickey pulled him up, threw him in the shower, and we filled him up with coffee and within an hour, we were on the way. We go into Clive's office and start talking about the record and Gregg has a little bit of a cough and Clive asks, "Are you sick?"

He goes, "Yeah, I got this really bad cough." He saw that he got Clive's attention and he really starts coughing a lot and Clive says, "You want me to get you a doctor? I've got a great guy." Now it's probably six at night and Gregg says, "Nah, I just need my cough medicine refilled." He pulls out a bottle from his pocket—something with codeine—and Clive says, "Well, you need to see my doctor if he's going to write a prescription," but Gregg is going, "No, no, this is what I need." And Clive goes, "Let me see what I can do."

He calls his doctor, hands the phone to Gregg, they go back and forth, and the guy says he'll call it in, and Clive gets back on the phone and tells him what drugstore and it's all done. Suddenly, Gregg asks, "Clive, what size refill did he get?"

He says, "I'm not sure."

So they call the pharmacy and it was just a couple of ounces to get him through until he sees a doctor, which did not please Gregg at all. He tried to get Clive to call the pharmacy back and get more. As the manager I was so embarrassed. I just wanted to get the hell out of there.

LAWLER: They got a name producer, John Ryan, who had hits with Styx and the Doobie Brothers and tried to really go there, and he took them even further away from their roots. That album did not even have an instrumental and the single was [the light, poppy] "Straight from the Heart."

GOLDFLIES: "Straight from the Heart" was an odd little tune and it was an odd decision to record it, much less release it as a single. The Allman Brothers swung, playing a lot of triplets with Butch's great shuffle feel, and suddenly we were playing straight eights and everyone felt weird. Their rhythmic feel had swing and polyrhythms—rock with jazz and cool country overtones—and when we played the straight beats on a song like "Straight from the Heart," it felt lifeless. We all tried to make it come alive, but it was an experiment that failed.

LAWLER: They were trying to get a hit: Dickey co-wrote "Straight from the Heart" with Cobb for a reason. He allowed it to happen; it's not like the two of us came in and dictated to the Allman Brothers Band what they should do and how they should sound.

GOLDFLIES: There were a lot of forces at work: the label, management, the people in the band and their own desire to have a hit. Looking back, that obviously wasn't the best thing to do. The band was kind of countercultural the whole time, and attempting to become cultural was a little death, but they got swept up in the prevailing moods.

Gregg Allman, 1986.

(PHOTO BY KIRK WEST)

Dickey Betts, 1990.

Butch Trucks, 1990.

(PHOTO BY KIRK WEST)

Jaimoe, 1990.

(PHOTO BY KIRK WEST)

Warren Haynes, 1990.

(PHOTO BY KIRK WEST)

Allen Woody, 1990.

(PHOTO BY KIRK WEST)

Rolling Stone photo shoot, Bradenton, Florida, April 1990.

(PHOTO BY KIRK WEST)

VH1 video shoot, Bradenton, April 1990.

(PHOTO BY KIRK WEST)

Gregg Allman passing
through the Black Hills of
South Dakota, August 1990.
(PHOTO BY KIRK WEST)

Haynes and Betts, 1990.
(PHOTO BY KIRK WEST)

Dickey Betts, Boston, 1991. Gibson
photo shoot.
(PHOTO BY KIRK WEST)

Memphis, 1991. Outtake from *Shades of Two Worlds* album cover shoot.

(PHOTO BY KIRK WEST)

Band with Bill Graham, Telluride, Colorado, June 1991.

(PHOTO © KEN FRIEDMAN 2013)

Warren Haynes, Dickey Betts, and Allen Woody, 1990.

(PHOTO BY KIRK WEST)

Derek Trucks and Dickey Betts, Atlanta, Georgia, 1991.

(PHOTO BY RICK DIAMOND)

Backstage band photo, Laguna Seca, California, July 1993.

(PHOTO © KEN FRIEDMAN 2013)

Polaroid collage from *Guitar World* cover shoot, March 1994.

(PHOTO © DANNY CLINCH)

Beacon Theatre, New York City, 1994.
(PHOTO BY KIRK WEST)

Marc Quinones, 1995.
(PHOTO BY KIRK WEST)

Oteil Burbridge, 2000.
(PHOTO BY KIRK WEST)

Three drummers, 2002.
(PHOTO BY KIRK WEST)

Derek Trucks, 2000.
(PHOTO BY KIRK WEST)

Warren Haynes and Gregg Allman, Uptown Theatre, Kansas City, Missouri,
September 20, 2005.
(PHOTO BY KIRK WEST)

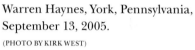

Warren Haynes, York, Pennsylvania, September 13, 2005.
(PHOTO BY KIRK WEST)

Derek Trucks, Council Bluffs, Iowa, September 17, 2005.
(PHOTO BY KIRK WEST)

The drum circle, Kansas City, Missouri, September 20, 2005.
(PHOTO BY KIRK WEST)

Warren Haynes, Derek Trucks, and Eric Clapton,
Beacon Theatre, March 2009.

(PHOTO BY KIRK WEST)

Gregg Allman on stage
during a soundcheck at
the 40th anniversary run,
Beacon Theatre, March
2009.

(PHOTO BY KIRK WEST)

ALLMAN: Arista tried to throw us into doing something that we weren't. The whole music scene of the '80s just wasn't conducive to our music at all. We cut two albums and . . . it was very frustrating. Embarrassing, really. All that led us to go on a big hiatus. We backed out before it got too bad.

TRUCKS: We compromised and tried to write hit songs and wound up with the two worst records we ever did. They were a huge embarrassment. It just wasn't fun. We didn't like the music we were making.

SCHER: I tried to get Chuck Leavell, who I thought was a great creative force, back in the band, but Gregg would hear nothing of it. Those kinds of things got them at loggerheads, along with the drugs, personal lives, marriages, who got along with what wife. Butch and his wife were actually moderating forces, but I thought the biggest problem was that Dickey and Gregg had different advisers giving them bad advice, especially Gregg.

His lawyer was adamant that Gregg would not accept Chuck as a member of the band. He would intimate that Gregg would have a major problem with Chuck being brought in, saying things like, "What are you going to do if Gregg leaves, call it the Brothers Band?" I thought he had a lot to do with the tensions that existed.

BERT HOLMAN, *who assisted Scher in day-to-day management and has been the ABB manager since '91*: There were lingering business issues with Chuck related to Capricorn royalties, which became an issue within the band because of the manner in which Chuck handled it. I think at the time Dickey, Butch, and Gregg were on the same page about not playing with Chuck. That would obviously change.

SCHER: Jaimoe was not in the band. He would have been a very steadying hand because he was not only a great drummer but was and is a great guy. To this day I don't have an explanation for why he wasn't, but rarely does a spouse representing a husband or wife work well in a band setting, which should be a democratic process, where everyone can speak his mind. It was a shame and definitely did not help the overall situation.

The band found themselves banging heads with Arista as they discussed ideas for a third album on the label. Davis did not have approval rights on material, but he did have final say on producers and rejected everyone the band suggested, including Tom Dowd and Johnny Sandlin.

BETTS: We broke up in '82 because we decided we better just back out or we would ruin what was left of the band's image. In some ways it was easier for Gregg and me to go out with our own bands because that didn't have the same weight of expectations. We could do things a little differently—get good players and play without people comparing us to the history of the Allman Brothers Band. And doing that with the support of our great, hard-core fans allowed us to keep our tools sharp and to get great new players, so we were ready when the time was right to try the Allman Brothers again.

SCHER: The best thing I did for the band was getting their royalties from Polygram bumped from 6 percent—which continued the original deal with Capricorn—to 12 percent. It really should have gone to 18 percent, but that wasn't in the cards and 6 percent was unconscionable, though horrible contracts and royalty rates were not uncommon in early rock and roll. I don't think what Phil did was really different than what Jerry Wexler, Ahmet Ertegun, and other music entrepreneurs did at the time; if they could get away with a small royalty, they did.

Even one person [Walden] being their manager, record company, and publisher is not that weird in the context of the times. They were a generation after guys like Fats Domino, Chuck Berry, and Little Richard were completely screwed—they had some protection. But Phil was a very smart guy—smart enough to know that he had to raise their royalties after they started selling millions of records. Unquestionably, he should have done so, and the minute Polygram got the masters, they should have upped the royalties, but there's a lot of greed in the record business. It went on way, way too long.

The band's final performance was on Saturday Night Live, *on January 23, 1982. They played a double-time version of "Southbound" and the appropriately titled "Leavin'," which seemed likely to be the last song the group would ever play together.*

SCHER: Gregg's lawyer was convinced that he could do just as well as a solo act, which is why he pushed everything so hard. And he was totally wrong.

PERKINS: Gregg called me in '83 and asked me to come help him get his solo career back up and running. I eventually took over managing him along with Alex Hodges. The first time I went to see Gregg, he was playing a dive bar in Jacksonville and I couldn't believe where he was. He was playing and singing great, but commercially he had fallen so far. It was a tough time for this kind of music. Southern rock was a bad word, and everyone was suddenly in vastly changed circumstances.

He wanted a record deal and the gigs were not great. He was basically playing clubs and it was a grind, but Gregg was cool with it, because he'd rather be gigging on a dime than not gigging. He likes to play and used to tell me he wanted to be like B.B. King and keep playing until an advanced age and, "I want to play every gig like it's my last one." He worked hard.

ALLMAN: It wasn't quite like starting over, but it sure was close, after all those years. That was the age of electronic music and disco and there wasn't much of a calling for us or what we did. It was hard. It really was, for all of us.

BETTS: We were trying to survive the disco thing by playing in beer joints. Remember that group BHLT [Betts, Hall, Leavell, and Trucks]? It sounded like a deli sandwich but it was a pretty good band. But it died; nobody would even let us record an album.

SCHER: When the band split up, Gregg went his way, and we got Jimmy Hall from Wet Willie, and got Chuck back with Dickey and Butch and that [BHLT] was a really good band. But Dickey and Butch were still signed to Arista and Clive did not want to do a record and it kind of drifted apart.

CHAPTER

It Was Twenty Years Ago Today

*T*HE MEMBERS OF *the Allman Brothers Band toured with different groups throughout the '80s, most of them needing to stay on the road to pay their bills. In 1986, Betts and Allman mounted a joint tour in which Betts opened, Allman and his band performed, and then the pair joined forces for a set. The Allman Brothers Band also performed together twice in 1986, at Charlie Daniels's Volunteer Jam and Bill Graham's Crack Down on Crack benefit at Madison Square Garden.*

PERKINS: Things started to look up a little bit. The joint tour was successful and, after having no record company interest—and I mean no interest from nobody—Epic suddenly called after hearing the "I'm No Angel" demo. We knew as soon as we heard that song what Gregg could do with it; it was autobiographical, though he had not written it.

MICHAEL CAPLAN, *Epic Records A&R:* I found Gregg's four-song demo cassette in my bosses' garbage and picked it up. I was new in A&R and looking for my first project and I was a longtime, serious Allman Brothers Band fan. This was the height of the record industry with CD money rolling in and most label higher-ups were only interested in potential megahits. The Allman Brothers were not sexy. I listened to that demo and the first song was "I'm No Angel," which I thought was great. So I got in touch with Willie Perkins and Alex Hodges and signed Gregg to Epic.

PERKINS: I thought the Allman Brothers reunions for the Volunteer Jam and the Crack thing in New York went well, but Gregg was also busy working on *I'm No Angel* and the timing didn't seem right to try a full-fledged reunion. I actually tried to beg off the crack show because I didn't think Gregg would do well. He was drinking heavily and I just thought, "How am I even going to get him to this thing?" We were in Florida recording and he was barely coherent.

But he got up there and did his job perfectly. He could play through that stuff remarkably well. Offstage, it was sometimes a different story, but Gregg very rarely embarrassed himself onstage regardless of his condition.

Gregg's first solo album in a decade, I'm No Angel, *was released in February 1987 and was a surprise hit. The title track garnered heavy airplay and rose to the top of Billboard's Album Rock Tracks chart.*

Gregg Allman and Dickey Betts, joint solo tour, 1986.

CAPLAN: Once we got it rolling with Gregg, I thought, "Let's get Dickey." I knew the way they had always worked and figured they would eventually make up and want to play together again. So I signed Dickey, who was just putting this great band together with Warren, Johnny Neel, and Matt Abts, and we started working on *Pattern Disruptive*. We did it at Butch Trucks's studio in Tallahassee and Butch hadn't been playing and we got him to guest. I told Dickey that he should do an instrumental and he was like, "No one does that anymore," and then recorded one ["Duane's Tune"].

I enjoyed working on these records, but I was just waiting for the natural thing to happen.

Allman's second Epic album, 1988's Just Before the Bullets Fly, *fell flat despite a strong title track written by Warren Haynes, then in the Dickey Betts Band and soon to be a major figure in the revival of the Allman Brothers. The following year, Betts's* Pattern Disruptive *also failed to make a mark.*

A new radio format—classic rock—had given the Allman Brothers' catalogue songs renewed prominence. The four-album Dreams *career retrospective box set also shined a light on their legacy and the band was celebrating their twentieth anniversary; the time was ripe for a reunion.*

BETTS: Classic rock stations really brought the Allman Brothers back, and Stevie Ray Vaughan opened the whole thing up. He just would not be denied and kept making those traditional urban blues records. He just shoved blues down people's throats and they got to likin' it. He kicked the door open. I remember how beautiful it made me feel to hear him on the radio. And I think that a lot of other people felt the same way and were more ready for us to reappear.

ALLMAN: Disco went out and good old blues came back around. If you notice, the blues always seem to come back eventually, because that's the basis for good, honest rock and roll.

Jonny Podell, who had booked the band since the beginning and was recently back on his feet after his own bouts with drug and alcohol addiction, saw an opportunity.

PODELL: I was representing the Dickey Betts Band, ICM was booking the Gregg Allman Band, and I thought, "Wait a second; I know everyone and have everyone's trust and respect and this had been the greatest band in America." I got everyone together and came up with a manager that I thought everyone could agree to: Danny Goldberg.

DANNY GOLDBERG, *manager, 1989–91:* Johnny Podell called me up and said, "You are the guy to help get the Allman Brothers back together again." He thought Dickey would trust me because I was managing the music career of his friend Don Johnson, who was at the apex of his *Miami Vice* fame, and Gregg would like me because I knew some people in the movie business.

PODELL: Gregg always had that little love of Hollywood. I knew it would be appealing. I had my own admitted agenda—I knew we could do great business and it seemed crazy not to do a twentieth-anniversary tour.

Jaimoe was back behind his kit when the group reformed.

JAIMOE: I knew that the best route to express myself musically was through the Allman Brothers Band, the best door to reach the people I need to reach is through the Allman Brothers Band, and the best door to make the money and live the way I want to live is through the Allman Brothers Band. I'm no dummy about any of that.

GOLDBERG: Obviously, the key to the whole thing was Gregg and Dickey and whether they could exist together, so I met with each of them before I even spoke to Butch or Jaimoe. They both had been touring solo and had not been doing remotely as well as they could together, so they had financial incentives to do it and it became clear pretty quickly that they were ready and able to work together again and the band came together pretty quickly after a few meetings.

In June 1989, the band took to the road for a twentieth-anniversary tour, featuring guitarist Warren Haynes and pianist Johnny Neel, both from the Betts Band, and bassist Allen Woody, who was hired after open auditions held at Trucks's Florida studio.

The first Beacon show, September 27, 1989.

BETTS: The Who were touring, and the Stones were getting ready to hit the road. Epic wanted us to get back together because everyone else was doing it—but it wasn't that simple. We had to go slow, to see if the music was up to snuff and whether we really wanted to do it.

ALLMAN: We knew we had to tour before we recorded, to make sure it was there.

BETTS: The release of *Dreams* [a 4-CD box set summing up the band's career] really worked out well for us, because we were in a Catch-22. We did not want to record without touring first, but it was hard to tour without a record to support and generate some interest. The box set took care of that for us, and allowed us to go out on a twentieth-anniversary tour.

PODELL: I approached that with the beginner's mind: the possibilities are endless. I was hopeful, because there was a tremendous legacy to build on, but there were also drug problems and personality conflicts that I knew were going to be challenges. They had a great band together but who knew how long it would last?

CAPLAN: I wasn't thinking short-term, but who would have thought it would turn into the longest-lasting incarnation of the band? We all knew it was volatile and not to look too far down the road.

TRUCKS: We weren't sure we'd even get through the first tour. We all had agreed that if the band wasn't solid and we weren't a good representation and couldn't live up to our legacy, then we weren't going to keep doing it. But we started playing good music and doing those old, classic songs proud. Then I figured maybe we could get a three-to-five-year run in.

GOLDBERG: The music was good and they were making money from the start. And one of the greatest things about working with them was they had this great crew that was thrilled to be back on the road with them. This guy Red Dog came up to me and said, "Thank you for giving me my life back. I was dead and now I'm alive again."

JOHNNY NEEL, *keyboards, 1989–91:* I did one tour with Gregg's band and then he told me that the Allman Brothers were re-forming and he wanted me to go with them. He was kind of emphatic about it. He really wanted me to be in the band, but I'm not sure about everyone else.

TRUCKS: We had open auditions for bass at my studio in Tallahassee. Allen Woody just came in and kicked butt.

ALLMAN: I hated having to have open auditions after all those years, but it became clear fast that Allen was the guy.

ALLEN WOODY, *bassist, 1989–97:* I had listened to the band for fifteen years and thought I knew what made it tick, but I had no idea what my role would be. The day I auditioned there were ten bass players. I played last, because I wanted to see if I could pick up anything I was doing wrong. What I figured out was that the other bassists honed in on one or the other of the drummers and tried to catch a pocket with him, but to make the rhythm section work, it has to be every man for himself.

HAYNES: Everyone else who auditioned walked in with one bass and plugged into the rig on stage. Woody brought a boatload of instruments and his own SVT [amp] rig. When he walked in and put all these basses on stands and plugged in that rig, some people thought that it was kind of over the top. Everyone was scratching his head about all those basses because the Allman Brothers were generally a group where someone played one bass all night, but Woody was bound and determined to bring his personality with him and part of that was, "I'm over the top. I'm a gear freak instrument collector and I have all these great basses to choose from." And in hindsight, him having his SVT there was probably a plus, because it gave a hint of his tone and approach, which were both totally unique.

Woody was hired, but once the group hit the road, the original members quickly began to worry about his playing.

BETTS: Allen was a little shaky on his feet when he started with us.

TRUCKS: The first month or so on the road, Allen was struggling and we were starting to have doubts. He had some rough nights. Jaimoe finally sat him down and said, "Remember how you played when you auditioned for this band? Well, you better start playing like that again."

And he did. I think once he got the job he was a little nervous about being in the Allman Brothers and someone had to get it through to him to relax and play. There's no room for doubt up there.

JAIMOE: He was confused, because he had Gregg telling him one thing and Dickey telling him something else—and not in as nice a fashion as Gregg. Between trying to please Dickey and please himself, he was going crazy.

He was a much better bass player than what he was playing in the Allman Brothers Band and I just told him that: "You played your ass off in auditions and rehearsals and you're not doing it on the gigs. Just go ahead and play—don't be bothered by this, that, and the other. This is your gig." We'd go to these jams and he was just killing it and I'd say, "That's how you have to play *on your gig*!"

HAYNES: Woody was going crazy because everyone was telling him what to play and giving him different directions. Dickey wanted him to come from the Berry Oakley tradition of the bass being part of the guitar line, while Gregg favors a more in-the-pocket R and B approach. Johnny Neel played a lot and was always telling Woody what to play to stay out of his way. And I was guilty myself of telling him what I thought he should be doing.

JAIMOE: There's no formula to this. You listen to the songs and play what's right, and when it comes time to jam, you get a little more hyper. It doesn't mean you don't play the way you feel. It's just that you have to make adjustments and play to the song.

NEEL: It's hard when one guy says one thing and another says something else. I wouldn't want to be in that spot. Playing piano, I could fade in and out, pick my spots and just do my thing. Being the bass player is probably the hardest job in any band and in the Allman Brothers it's even harder, because of the tremendous, unique legacy of

Berry Oakley and how important that was to Dickey, especially. Berry had such a distinct style. You either got it or you didn't. There wasn't no in-between.

JAIMOE: Betts was a dictator, man. He was always trying to tell the bass player what and how to play, and that's not something that you do, unless it really, really needs to be done. You're supposed to be a good musician and figure that out. Allen was a good musician.

BETTS: There was an immense amount of material for him to learn and he was going through a learning process, but then he settled down and found his home.

HAYNES: Woody and I had this talk and I remember saying, "Look, you're the man. They hired you for a reason. Forget all of us. Follow your gut and go for it." And once he did that, everyone loved him.

WOODY: It was a lot to take in. The third gig I played with the Allman Brothers I was scared shitless and started feeling a little lost so I turned to look back and saw Jaimoe walking around his drums, adjusting cymbal stands in the middle of a song in front of twenty thousand people.

NEEL: Rolling down the highway with two drummers, two guitar players, and a bass player is a good feeling. That two-drummer thing Butch and Jaimoe create is incredible. It was like riding a big old stallion.

Johnny Neel, 1990.

WOODY: Butch and Jaimoe listen to each other all night and they

never contradict what the other guy is playing. They really complement each other and I realized I couldn't reinforce either of them too
much; I had to go somewhere down the middle, catching the groove
they create together. You have to hear them as one drummer. Typically, Butch is the timekeeper and Jaimoe sits there waiting for a hole
to erupt.

MATT ABTS, *Gov't Mule drummer:* Butch is a great, very unique drummer. I've heard countless drummers sit in with the Allman Brothers,
including myself, and no one can replicate exactly what he does. That
is testament to his creativity and being an equal part of the ABB chemistry. Butch in a different context might not be the same, but inside
the ABB, he is indispensable.

Jaimoe is like an encyclopedia of drumming going back to the jazz
era. He just has such a history of the drums and you can hear it in his
playing. He is the consummate listener with huge ears to play around
what Butch does. What they have going on together is very, very unique.

HAYNES: The reason that Woody brought all those basses to the audition is he was always looking to express different sides of his personality. Eventually I realized he was really a guitar player and guitar players
do that: we switch sounds a lot, pick a different instrument and approach to match the song, whereas bass players, especially in the old
school, stayed consistent. While this may have seemed odd at first,
I think it had a lot to do with his style fitting in with the Allman
Brothers—because Berry Oakley was also a guitarist and his style was
very aggressive, not focused on playing in the pocket.

Woody was psyched once he joined the band to utilize a wide array
of sounds—and some of these sounds maybe weren't welcomed with
open arms. Woody always talked about how Berry liked to roughen up
the edges of whatever was being done, to turn country or blues songs
into rock and roll.

NEEL: You have to bounce around a little bit and figure out who to listen to when you're just a guy they hired to play and not a full member of a band. It's a funny place to be and it could be hard to read anyone's mood on any given day. I think anyone would say that in any job where you're a junior staff dealing with four executive vice presidents. You never knew what was going to happen. There's a lot of history between them boys and that's about all I got to say about that.

JAIMOE: Gregory's biggest problem was he had run his own show and now he was back being one of four partners and he had to adjust to that. And Gregory don't listen to music like the rest of us do, so he had gotten used to different arrangements and he would say, "That's not the way it goes." And Dickey pretty quickly got back to his bullying ways. The only thing I was paying attention to is that I was sitting at my drums playing music with the people I had played it with the most.

GOLDBERG: Each of these four guys had their own quirks. Jaimoe was the easiest. He didn't want to get involved in the business. He just wanted to come play. Butch was generally a very positive force. It really was just about keeping Dickey and Gregg happy and together.

Dickey was the strongest willed, very forceful and very much the leader. In that moment, Gregg was basically just the singer. He's obviously the signature voice in a very profound way and his name is Allman, but he was not the major creative force that Dickey was. Dickey said to me once that he wished he hadn't agreed that the band be called the Allman Brothers, that he felt cursed and marginalized by that. He felt that he had written a lot of music and been integral to the band but because his name was not Allman, he would never have the clout, and that bothered him. And he certainly had a point.

PERKINS: I was with Gregg through the 1989 twentieth-anniversary tour. After that, we spent a day shopping for houses with him in Nashville. While I was out with him, a fax came into our office saying that Strike Force would not be retained, a very personal way of telling us that we would not be representing Gregg anymore. We were so resentful and frustrated, because we had spent years building him back up and just as it was paying off, he jumped ship and we were out.

GOLDBERG: With very rare exceptions like Van Halen, lead singers are a band's most famous member and signature. The difference was the Allman Brothers were a guitar band and Dickey was a major guitar force and songwriter. And Dickey was a very brilliant guy in ways that were often underappreciated. He's very knowledgeable about all sorts of things: jazz, blues, classical music, art, the worldly news of the moment.

Gregg is obviously very smart, especially about the band's career. But he was disengaged. He was not in his healthiest period. I'd love to know him the way he is today, judging by what I've seen and my brief, friendly interactions in recent years. The Gregg that was then was pretty inward, in his own world most of the time. He always sang great, but he was not that engaged. Butch also had ideas about what the band should do, but Dickey was primarily driving things.

CAPLAN: Dickey was the bandleader. Period. He was the guy to deal with and he was capable of really being great, but also capable of getting really mean and physical. People were scared of him, especially when he was drinking. Gregg sometimes struggled in the studio to get his vocals done. It could be a painstakingly slow process.

CHAPTER

Revival

*T*HE GROUP RETURNED *to the studio with Dowd and produced 1990's* Seven Turns, *a strong recording that made it clear that this reunion would be different than the '80s efforts. The album kicked off with the slide hook and guitar harmonies of "Good Clean Fun," establishing that Haynes and Betts were resurrecting the classic ABB sound and approach. Allman was in good voice, and Betts stepped up, writing or co-writing seven of the nine songs, including the title track, which was inspired by the Navajo concept that each person faces seven crucial decisions in life.*

ALLMAN: I felt like *Seven Turns* was timeless; it sounded like it could have come out in '69, and one big factor in [that] was Tom Dowd. He's very much like an eighth member of the band. He's like a father to me: teacher, father, guru—take your pick. He was real supportive of us and was always real supportive of me with the drug thing. He helped me get through some tough times. He came out for most of the whole tour we did before recording *Seven Turns* and knew where we were and that made it real easy to get where we needed to be.

Dickey Betts with his Navajo spiritual mentor, Stewart Etsitty.

BETTS: Tom worked with Ray Charles when he was just starting out and he carried that kind of experience with him and offered so much. He played a huge role in helping us make a worthy comeback album.

HAYNES: Tom was probably special when he started out, but he's recorded with everyone from Cream to John Coltrane, from Aretha Franklin to Lynyrd Skynyrd. He'll hint around at something and make you think it was your idea.

BETTS: Tommy is so easygoing in his approach that when you finish an album with him you wonder what the hell he contributed. That's because he makes you feel that you did everything yourself. He [was] really a genius psychologist, capable of getting you to pull things out of yourself that you didn't even know were there.

WOODY: Tom can pull you up way above your potential. He pulls things out of you and deceives you into thinking you did it yourself.

BETTS: I've learned a lot by studying Tommy Dowd for many years, though I have a more assertive way of doing it. People definitely know when I've made a suggestion or told them to play a certain part.

ALLMAN: Aside from all these great qualities, it's just wonderful to work with someone when you know each other so well. You have to be able to communicate with the producer and vice versa. A lot of times you don't even have to talk; you just make signs. Like, if you want to start at the top, you just put your hand on your head. You have to stay in the same frequency all day and that's so much smoother with someone you've known for a long time like Tom or Johnny Sandlin.

BETTS: *Seven Turns* was a tough album, because we knew that the critics would use it to determine whether or not we should have remained broken up. We were under pressure to show that we belonged back together. We never doubted it, but the album simply had to prove that.

ALLMAN: To me, there wasn't a lot of pressure on *Seven Turns*. It was more of an adventure: let's see what a few years away from each other did for us. And it was good. We needed a break from each other and came out swinging.

BETTS: I think all the expected things you're used to hearing on an Allman Brothers record are there: the instrumental ("True Gravity"), the slide and guitar harmonies on "Good Clean Fun," which is the first song Gregg and I ever co-wrote, and then "Seven Turns," which is a nice light color to the heavier blues, similar to what we've done before with my songs like "Blue Sky" and "Ramblin' Man."

HAYNES: Dickey, Johnny Neel, and I were working out the three-part harmony stuff for "Seven Turns" in the studio hallway and Gregg was in the lounge shooting pool. As we rehearsed the "Somebody's calling your name" part, I heard Gregg answer it. I don't even know if he did it on purpose. It wasn't like he said, "Hey, check this out . . ." He was just singing along to what he heard us doing as he shot pool. And I said, "Hey, listen to that. This is what we need." It was all very coincidental and it became one of the pinnacles of the tune, when Gregg comes in on the answer vocal at the end of the song.

BETTS: One reason that group worked better than some of the others was Warren and Allen knew what we were after. They had studied us for years and understood where they fit into the band. And Warren was the first guitarist who came along since Duane who could really stand on his own and play off of me, which is the basis of our whole style. He's a great player and he has his own style, so he was not pulled into constantly trying to sound like Duane, though he was plagued with that comparison from day one.

TRUCKS: Warren and Woody really reenergized us and helped us get back to being the Allman Brothers Band.

HAYNES: I had listened to the Allman Brothers since I was nine years old and I studied that music hard. But once I joined the band, some of the things that they were doing became obvious to me in a way that I could never have figured out as a listener.

WOODY: I felt that the music was like a sacred trust and it couldn't be violated. I had complete respect for the history and legacy.

HAYNES: As much as Dickey loves to improvise, he was also very studied about the guitar parts, especially when I first started playing with him. We would sit in hotel rooms or backstage working out harmony parts and he would be very specific about nailing things. He was always open to my thoughts, but wanted to be precise about things like how long to hold the notes out, when to cut them off, that the length of a sustained note be in sync, as well as where to start the vibrato and when to not have vibrato and things of that nature. He had tremendous attention to detail.

BETTS: We made changes we had to make in earlier versions of the band, but it was a little too much in the end. It wasn't by any means all bad, but the band headed off the path of what the original players had envisioned from the first day. With Warren and Woody, we got back on that path. A big part of that was Warren being such a strong slide player. In between Duane and him, we didn't have another slide guitarist so I played slide, which . . . removed the sound of my guitar, and to sound like the Allman Brothers Band you need the Dickey Betts guitar and a slide guitar together.

JAIMOE: Warren gave us a lot of fire and energy. He is a master guitarist, with a range of talents. He's a master songwriter, vocalist, and bandleader, and all of that impacts one another.

ALLMAN: From the start, Woody and Warren were full-on Allman Brothers—much more so than some people in earlier incarnations. And that made a big difference, as did the fact that Warren and Johnny Neel had been in Dickey's band and really understood what we were doing and the material.

HAYNES: The fact that Dickey and I had played together for almost three years played a huge role in the band sounding so good from the start, because that relationship is central to the Allman Brothers. At the beginning I was constantly drawing the line about how much of Duane's influence to show. It was always left up to me how much of it to insert.

WOODY: There are a few songs where I play virtually the same exact thing Berry played—for instance "Midnight Rider" because a lot of his bass lines actually matched the voicings that Gregg played on acoustic guitar. And I couldn't change the beginning of "Whipping Post" or they'd tie me to a whipping log. But in everything else I just try to capture Berry's spirit. In any case, my playing has always been very similar to his, because he was such a big influence.

HAYNES: I've listened to Dickey all my life, so I understood what he wanted. When I first started with him, he would look at me when he was playing one of his great melodic riffs in a way that said, "I'm going to repeat this and I want you to play it with me." The third time through, I would jump on it and play the harmony. That was Duane's role when they played together, but my mission was always to interject my own personality. At times, maybe that required going against the grain a little bit and trying to forget how classic songs were played and try to take it somewhere else while sounding natural. That is a hard thing to do.

BETTS: Warren was never really replacing a legend. A legend was killed over twenty years earlier, and that was the end of that. Nobody's gonna replace Duane. We were just going on to the next day. And after those guys came on we returned to the sound that we always had in our heads.

HAYNES: They definitely allowed me the creative freedom to interject my own personality into the music. They've always said, "Play like you. That's what we hired you to do." Not a lot of bands could or would do that. The Allman Brothers were very open-minded about that from the beginning, because the music was built on the foundation of two guitar players working equally together. If you don't have that, the music suffers.

WOODY: A big part of the Allman Brothers music is a jazz approach to rock and blues, which seems to be a dying art. Not many bands get up there and just jam anymore, but we are not looking to play things the same way every night. Our approach to jazz is a lot different than—and I hate this word—fusion. For instance, I play these descending lines at the end of "Kind of Bird" that are like bebop played through a Marshall.

BETTS: Jazz has become this sacred temple. And there's some people getting away with a hell of a lot on that account. I'm no musical genius, but I have ears. And if I can't understand it, it's probably 'cause it ain't worth a shit. But a lot of people think, "Well, that's over my head." You should be able to understand jazz unless you're so down and out that your mind don't work. You don't have to know what and why they're doing, but you should be able to follow it. It's just like art. If you look at a painting and say, "God, that's a piece of shit," it probably is—at least to you. And it very well may be that the guy's fooling you.

HAYNES: While we were recording *Seven Turns* in Miami, we had a night off and Butch said, "Hey, man, we ought to go out and hear my nephew play. He's amazing."

Somebody said, "Cool. How old is he?"

And Butch goes, "Oh, he's ten," and interest immediately waned and turned into snickers. But Woody said, "No, man, I've heard this kid. He is amazing. We should go check this out. You're not going to believe it until you see him." So me, Woody, and Butch grabbed Gregg and headed down there.

ALLMAN: I didn't know anything. Butch said, "Come on, guys, I want to show you something in South Beach." So we go down there and it's just starting to get dark and there's all these beautiful girls with nothin' on—I loved it down there, man. We're walking up to this nightclub on the strip and there's these two boys throwing a ball back and forth and Butch walks up to one of them and says, "Gregory, this is Derek. Derek, this is Gregg." He looked up at me—a cute little kid—and smiled and I guess we shook hands. I still didn't know what we were doing there.

Derek Trucks, 1991.

We walk in and the club has a stage behind the bar, with the band standing up there like a go-go dancer might. They had a keyboard and a place for two guitars, bass, and drums. Much to my surprise the little kid from the street who Butch had introduced us to gets up, picks up a Gibson that I swear was bigger than him, and just starts burning. He played only slide and he wailed. And that's the first time I met Derek Trucks. That was him playing catch and he had to go outside the club when he wasn't playing due to his age.

BUTCH TRUCKS: Derek's my brother's kid but I really can't explain him. He blew my mind and I needed to show the other guys; there was no point in trying to explain. He started out listening to Duane and at that point that style was all he could do, but I mean he nailed it.

ALLMAN: Warren looks over at me and says, "Why don't we have him step down and we'll play?" I said, "Is the kid making you sweat, man?" Ha-ha!

HAYNES: I don't remember that but what I know is we got up there and played some songs and there was what Woody would call a little TV tray keyboard, a little synthesizer thing that Gregg would normally not be caught dead playing, but he liked the idea of us all playing together so he got over it. We were all having fun and Gregg would turn to his left, look at Derek, and just shake his head and wonder and smile. Derek was really small. The SG was bigger than him.

DEREK TRUCKS: I was a kid so it's all pretty blurry to me, but I certainly remember how thrilling it was playing with them all for the first time. Even more exciting was what happened after—there was a hotel pool in the back and I was out there with Gregg and Red Dog and they gave me one of Duane's Coricidin bottles. He was my musical hero and that was a musical relic holy grail.

ALLMAN: I think starting with slide was a great way to approach it, because it's hard for little fingers to fret. He was about the same age that I was when I started playing. By the way, he was a real whiz kid at school and everything, with incredible grades. He's quite an intelligent customer.

DEREK TRUCKS: I kind of did everything backwards. I started with slide; at nine or ten that felt more natural because my fingers were so small. Ever since, I've been trying to work my way up to being a regular player.

HAYNES: Derek is just amazing and always has been. From the time he was a kid, he was fearless—he would play anything you called out, with no idea what it was.

BUTCH TRUCKS: By the time Derek was fourteen or fifteen he had already gone past the Duane licks and was headed to new places.

As the band continued their comeback, preparing to record a follow-up to Seven Turns, *they let their contract with Goldberg and Gold Mountain lapse and set out on their own. Gold Mountain would soon be managing Nirvana.*

GOLDBERG: When our initial contract ran out in 1991, they told me that they had decided to move on. You always hope to continue these things, but I had sort of accomplished the purpose I had in their life, helping them get up and running again, and I could understand going forward why they would want to do what they did and it worked out pretty well for them. It wasn't a big drama, and working with the All-man Brothers is still one of the things I'm most psyched about when I look at my career. The music was amazing, they were making money, and they were very professional.

PODELL: Bert Holman was the road manager and when the band decided they wanted to "manage themselves" they designated Bert to be in the position. It was very important that they be "self-managed," but it quickly became obvious that Bert was the manager.

HOLMAN: They wanted to manage themselves with me as the manager. I'm an employee; they are not signed to my management company. We

Memphis, 1991, during the *Shades of Two Worlds* sessions.

created a very unique situation where I'm an equity participant. The goal, as created by [lawyer and ex-ABB manager] Steve Massarsky, was to create a situation where there's an incentive for me to help them make more money and at the same time it's costing them less than a traditional manager.

MARCH MADNESS

How the Allmans at the Beacon became a Manhattan tradition.

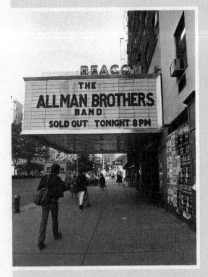

The newly reformed Allman Brothers Band made their first appearance at New York's Beacon Theatre in 1989, when they played four September shows as part of a run of theaters that included Boston's Orpheum, Philadelphia's Tower, and Fort Lauderdale's Sunrise.

"The band was just back together, had come off a successful summer tour, and wanted to do a series of shows to help reestablish themselves in some key markets and to make some decent money," says booking agent Jonny Podell. "I put two shows up and quickly went to four. I thought it was a pretty safe bet: the return of the Allman Brothers to Manhattan. The drama had been played out in *Rolling Stone* and everywhere else. It was like putting a toe in the water."

The next run of ABB Beacon shows came in 1992. Wanting to record a live album, the band had captured a four-show run at the Macon City Auditorium, December 28–31, 1991, which did not go well. They would have to try again.

"We were looking to book a few shows in theaters in strong markets, where we knew the crowd would be good and we could feed off the energy, and where we could settle in for a few days to get comfortable and get a good recording," recalls Allman Brothers Band manager Bert Holman. "Boston and New York were the obvious places to try this."

The band sold out two shows at Boston's Orpheum, added appearances in Poughkeepsie and Wilkes-Barre in between, and put two Beacon shows up for sale, with the idea of announcing two or three more if and when the first ones sold out. When tickets went on sale in January, the band was in Japan for a nine-show tour. It was less than two months before the first Beacon dates, which were scheduled for a Tuesday and Wednesday, with a tentative plan to announce weekend dates if those sold.

"I woke up in Japan and checked my messages and Jonny had been trying to get hold of me," says Holman. "This was, of course, pre-Blackberry and instant access. I called him and he said, 'We're putting Tuesday and Wednesday up for sale!' I said, 'You mean, Friday and Saturday' and he said, 'No, I put those up, along with Sunday, and they sold out in an hour. We're into the next week!'"

The 1992 Beacon run ended up being ten shows, starting on March 10. The first song they played was "Statesboro Blues," featuring their old jamming buddy Thom Doucette on harmonica. The number of sold-out shows astounded everyone, including the band.

"We thought doing five would be incredible," says Holman. "Ten was not even on our radar. At the time, no one was doing these long stands in the States, but they were popular in England, and it seemed like a great concept."

Adds Podell, "I heard about Eric Clapton playing for a month at the Royal Albert Hall in London and I thought that was the coolest thing, that he would do that rather than playing two nights at Wembley."

The group ended up recording *An Evening with the Allman Brothers Band, First Set*, at the Beacon and Orpheum shows. They were just getting started. The Allman Brothers Band did not play the Beacon in '93, but returned for eight shows in '94. They moved to Radio City Music Hall for six shows in '95, before returning to the Beacon in '96, when they sold out thirteen shows and firmly established themselves as a New York rite of spring. They peaked with nineteen shows in March 1999.

"The Beacon has become something very special," says Allman. "We will be back there for as long as we can."

The group took 2008 off as Allman underwent treatment for hepatitis before returning to the Beacon the next year with a guest-star-laden fifteen-show fortieth-anniversary celebration. They were forced out of their home in 2010, heading uptown to the United Palace Theater when MSG, newly managing the Beacon, absurdly booked Cirque de Soleil in March. The Brothers returned to the Beacon in 2011 and have sold out more than 222 consecutive shows there as of this writing.

"This whole amazing thing happened because we needed a place to record some shows," Holman says. "No one could have anticipated it becoming such an institution, including any of us."

Second Set

*J*OHNNY NEEL LEFT *the band in 1990 and percussionist Marc Quiñones joined the following year. The Brothers followed* Seven Turns *with* Shades of Two Worlds *in 1991. It was a strong, diverse album that seemed to indicate that the Allman Brothers were truly back.*

MARC QUIÑONES, *percussionist, ABB member since 1991:* I was a member of Spyro Gyra, and Butch and his wife came to a show in Tallahassee. Afterwards, the manager says, "Butch Trucks from the Allman Brothers wants to meet you." I'm like, "I don't know who he is or they are, but OK."

He comes in and goes, in front of the whole band, "Man, my wife and I couldn't stop watching you. You were the fucking show. You're exactly what we've been looking for for years and we're going to steal you!"

I'm a Puerto Rican from the Bronx who didn't grow up listening to rock and roll and I'm thinking, "I don't even know who this dude is." We exchanged numbers and a few months later he called and invited me to

Memphis to "play on a couple of tracks." That was my introduction to the Allman Brothers. I see Jaimoe sitting on a cooler and think he might be one of the roadies. I see Allen Woody and think he's Charles Manson's brother—some crazy dude. I record a few tracks and go home—just another session. They liked it and asked me to go on the road for a run and see how it worked. I've been there ever since.

BETTS: I was real pleased with *Seven Turns*, but thank goodness we moved ahead a little bit. *Shades* is much more open musically. We were more used to each other, and we got rid of the second keyboardist, which was important. The band had headed off the path of what the original players had envisioned from the first day. And with [*Shades of Two Worlds*] we returned to the sound that we've always had in our heads.

Chuck Leavell and Johnny Neel are probably the best blues pianists around, but the band with them was never true to the original members' vision, which we had before we even started the band. I think this band sounds like what we would've sounded like if we had the original players together—if we'd stayed together, which I think we would've. Sure, we'd have broken up from time to time. You have to, for God's sake. Even the Dead break up. They just have enough sense not to talk about it. But this was the first time I felt that way—that we sounded like we would have—since Duane died.

NEEL: I was disappointed that they did not want me to continue when my contract ran out, but I wasn't quite playing like they wanted me to play. I think I was experimenting a little bit too much. I was hardheaded and wanted to make my mark, do my own thing. I thought I was bringing something to the table that they didn't have, but they didn't want that. I think I made some mistakes.

BETTS: It was kind of frightening for Gregg to see Johnny go because he hadn't been stuck out there having to shoulder everything for a long time. But he plays great blues piano. It's not complex, but it's exciting. He's not expected to be a virtuoso; he's the singer and the piano is mostly coloring—and it fits in great with the guitars.

NEEL: I know that Gregg was the one who really wanted me in the band in the first place.

BETTS: Warren was also really coming into his own.

HAYNES: I had been trying my whole life to establish my own voice as a guitar player. I never wanted it to be obvious to a listener exactly where I was coming from; you want to spread your influences out enough so that you can hear a little bit of this and a little bit of that but it still sounds like you. Then suddenly I was in the Allman Brothers and had to struggle with hitting those notes. It was a challenge to do that and retain and develop my own personality, but being in the Allman Brothers taught me a lot. Being on stage with people who have had their own voice for a long time kind of puts it front and center what that means—in search of the elusive original tone.

I played with Dickey Betts for eleven years, so of course my playing leaned more towards that school. If I had spent those years playing with Mitch Mitchell and Noel Redding, I'd probably play more like Hendrix—but I still wanted my own personality in there at all times. I would try to forget how I listened to a song originally and the way they first played it and take it to another place, while still making it sound natural and not forced, which is hard to do. I do feel like I got much better at it after a few years; it helped to write more original music together.

BETTS: It takes a lot of time to get up to the level where you can really improvise together. Warren co-wrote these last two instrumentals "True Gravity" [from *Seven Turns*] and "Kind of Bird" [from *Shades*] with me. That's something I'd never done before; I could collaborate on [songs with] lyrics, but I wrote instrumentals strictly on my own because I never wanted to give anyone a chance to mess with my babies. But I really enjoyed writing these two with Warren.

HAYNES: "Kind of Bird" is such a complicated song, and writing it with Dickey was such a fun challenge. We would work during the day composing and that night we would rehearse whatever we had written, then write another section the next day. That went on throughout two weeks.

BETTS: Duane and I used to play "Come On in My Kitchen" all the time and we made up that arrangement. Robert Johnson's original version doesn't move off the one chord much, so we put the chords for "Key to the Highway" to it and I made up a vocal melody. Duane recorded a similar version with Delaney and Bonnie [*on 1971's* Motel Shot].

Going from Robert Johnson–style acoustic, dirt-road blues on "Come On in My Kitchen" right through the urban blues things into an abstract, lyrical thing like "Nobody Knows" and a Charlie Parker tribute, "Kind of Bird"—that covers a hell of a lot of ground, a giant spectrum. It is shades of two worlds: from real life to the imaginary world. I think that is also implied by the cover, with the real down-to-earth picture on the front and the very mystical thing on the back.

During the recording sessions, Dowd suggested that while the group had a strong set of songs, they lacked a single track that would become the album's centerpiece. "Write something like 'Whipping Post,'" he suggested.

Betts returned with the mystical "Nobody Knows," written for Gregg to sing. The song became a point of contention, ratcheting up tensions between Betts and Allman. Gregg objected to the song's similarity to "Whipping Post," the relatively wordy lyrics, and Betts's insistence on telling him how to sing it. When Dowd finally told the song's composer, after repeated interruptions, to quit telling the singer how to phrase the lyrics, Betts stormed out of the studio. Despite these creative differences, the final version of the song became a centerpiece of the album and subsequent shows.

Dickey Betts, Tom Dowd, and Greg Allman during the *Seven Turns* sessions.

The band toured hard behind Shades *and released the live* An Evening With the Allman Brothers Band, First Set *in 1992. Once again, things were less calm than they may have appeared to fans seeing consistently strong performances by a band with a fairly ambitious touring schedule. The Allman Brothers Band played sixty-eight shows in 1990, eighty-seven in '91, and seventy-seven in '92, but there was growing tension during the '93 summer tour and on July 31 Betts was arrested at a Saratoga Springs, New York, hotel the morning after a show at the Saratoga Performing Arts Center when he shoved two police officers responding to a call from his wife saying he was drunk and abusive.*

The Saratoga show had been part of the HORDE Festival, also featuring Widespread Panic, Blues Traveler, and Col. Bruce Hampton and the Aquarium Rescue Unit, and the same bill would be repeating the next night in Stowe, Vermont. The Allman Brothers did not know whether or not Betts would be joining them there.

HOLMAN: Jonny Podell happened to be there and I immediately pulled together some cash and gave it to him along with a tour bus and told him to go bail Dickey out while the rest of us went on to the gig in Stowe. He paid the bail, but Dickey insisted on being driven to the airport, where he got on a plane to Sarasota. This was before cell phones and Jonny could not get ahold of us. We arrived at four or five and were going on at nine and we did not know whether or not Dickey was going to make it until Jonny pulled up in an empty bus at about seven. We were talking about the alternatives and possibilities and Warren was going around seeing who was there and could help us out.

HAYNES: My solo band was on the bill and playing at about noon. We drove overnight to Stowe and were staying in a bed-and-breakfast. We got there and crashed at about seven a.m., and an hour later there was banging on my door and someone saying I had an emergency phone call from Bert Holman. There was no phone in our little bungalow and I had to walk all the way up this hill to the main house to talk to Bert, who said Dickey was in jail and probably wouldn't be there. I had to start thinking about what to do—and my solo band was due on stage in just hours.

KIRK WEST, *ABB "Tour Magician" and logistical coordinator, 1989–2009:* I had traveled with Warren and we were there trying to figure out who could help out, but Warren was going on before most of the bands had arrived, so there was no one to talk to yet. There was a lot of scrambling going on, trying to figure out what the hell was going on and what we were going to do about it.

Amid the scramble, Haynes managed to not only perform his own set, but to sit in with Widespread Panic for two songs. That night, Aquarium Rescue Unit guitarist Jimmy Herring subbed for Betts and the band was also joined by Blues Traveler harmonica player John Popper for seven songs and Warren Haynes

Band keyboardist Danny Louis for two. While these guest musicians helped to plug a gaping musical hole, they were all going their separate ways with the HORDE tour, and the Allman Brothers had a gig the next night at the Great Woods Amphitheater in Mansfield, Massachusetts. They started looking for a replacement, for what was originally presumed to be a single gig. Herring was continuing his tour with the ARU and was not available.

HAYNES: I said that we should bring in Chuck Leavell. I said that the fans love Chuck, he's a big part of the history, he sounds great, he's contributed so much to the band's music through the years, and he knows all the material. Bert and Jonny [Podell] were concerned that there needed to be two guitar players on stage, which I disagreed with.

They were saying, "This is a guitar band. People want to hear the two guitars." I was assuming we were talking about one night and I thought, "No, the best way to get through this show is gonna be with Chuck Leavell. We'll have a blast. People will love it." There was concern about people demanding refunds, but I figured that while people would surely be disappointed that Dickey wasn't there, in that situation you stay to see what happens, because what happens is probably going to be really cool. Worst-case scenario is it's going to be one to remember. When it became obvious they wanted another guitarist, I said, "Well, let's get Jack Pearson."

Pearson, a Nashville-based friend of Haynes, had a run of festival dates booked and did not want to break his commitments, particularly with no guarantee that the Allmans gig would go on for more than one or two shows. The search for a sub continued.

DAVID GRISSOM, *Austin, Texas, guitarist:* I was out playing gigs with John Mellencamp and was on my way home. I called my wife from O'Hare and she said, "Someone from the Allman Brothers called and they want to know if you can come out and play some gigs." Um, yeah! This was all pre-cell-phone-in-every-pocket, so I called and left a message for Bert, then got on a plane, and by the time I got back home they had already gotten someone else.

HAYNES: I called Jack, but he couldn't make it, then I called David and couldn't reach him, and the decision was made—not by me—to bring Zakk Wylde in.

HOLMAN: By the time Grissom called back, we had gotten ahold of Zakk and I think he was literally on the red-eye to Boston to join us. We told David, "We've got this covered, but we're going to put you on deck."

Zakk Wylde had been playing with Ozzy Osbourne since 1987 and was known to be a fan of Southern rock, performing Allman Brothers and Lynyrd Skynyrd covers with a band dubbed Lynyrd Skynhead. He also had some connections to the Allman Brothers: Jonny Podell booked him, and Michael Caplan worked with Ozzy at Epic.

ZAKK WYLDE, *Ozzy Osbourne guitarist, 1987–95:* I was in the studio recording with Ozzy when I got a call from the Allmans' manager, who knew that I was a big fan. He called at six and said that Dickey couldn't make the next night's show, and that they'd like me to sit in but I'd have to fly out that night—at eleven on the red-eye. I grabbed my guitar and headed for the airport. I was pumped.

WEST: It was clear this was a bad idea before he ever walked on stage—from the moment he got there. He had a rebel flag Les Paul with Budweiser bottle caps nailed into it, and the target Les Paul and he looked wrong and acted wrong for the Allman Brothers.

WYLDE: I got there at seven in the morning, listened to the tape they had for me, and jammed a couple tunes. Warren and I went through some stuff before the show, but no one told me much about what we would do. We just had a soundcheck/rehearsal, which was hilarious. Butch Trucks asked if I knew how to play "Dreams" and I said, "What, that Molly Hatchet song?" And they all cracked up. Gregg said, "Brother Zakk, keep talking like that and we're gonna have to send you home."

HAYNES: We had a long soundcheck to rehearse. He had been given a list of songs to learn, and part of their selling point convincing us to bring Zakk in was that he played in an Allman Brothers cover band in his spare time and knew all the material. For me, who the other guitarist on stage is going to be is a sensitive topic, especially in the Allman Brothers. Zakk is great at what he does, but I don't think until he got there he understood what makes that music click—and maybe he still doesn't.

HOLMAN: Zakk loved the music, but the problem is, he had never really seen the band play. He thought they were Lynyrd Skynyrd. He's a nice-enough guy and he plays well, but he was not really attuned to what we do and wasn't ready to listen to what anybody else was playing. His idea was "Everybody vamp and I'll solo."

WEST: He was out there with his Ronnie Van Zant hat on running all over stage, fanning Warren with a towel and trying to put his hat on Warren's head. He was very excited and had no clue how the Allman Brothers Band behaved onstage.

HAYNES: It's not something that's obvious—how to take a jazzy improvisational approach to what most people would consider rock music. In order for us to play our best, we have to listen to each other like a jazz band does and most rock musicians are not geared for that.

WYLDE: They were way fuckin' cool, man. But it was hysterical, 'cause when we played "Dreams" I must have soloed for twenty minutes. I'd died and gone to heaven and I wasn't going to stop. I was just jamming. But I almost gave Butch a coronary, 'cause every time we got to where the band was repeating the same lick, preparing to come out of the jam, I'd just keep soloing. I came over to Butch in between songs and he goes, "Zakk, fuck, man! Calm down a little bit, brother." And I go, "But this is my favorite band." And he goes, "Yeah, it's mine, too, but just fuckin' relax!"

We even did an acoustic set; we did "Melissa" and "Midnight Rider." Warren was really helpful. I spent a lot of time standing next to him, staring at his hands and saying, "Dude! What the fuck?" Warren's a killer guitar player, which made it a lot easier on me. I had the time of my life. It was just awesome.

While Wylde enjoyed himself and allowed the band to fulfill their gig, the Allman Brothers were not amused by his antics, which included spitting mouthfuls of beer in the air and standing atop his front stage monitor—normal behavior in his world, which did not translate to theirs.

CAPLAN: I worked with Ozzy and made the connection to Zakk, who said he knew all the music and was very excited to do it. I was at the show watching him jumping off the amps and thinking, "Boy, am I in trouble."

HOLMAN: Everybody said, "This ain't working. Thank you very much."

WEST: That was one of the biggest mistakes in Allman Brothers history. There were guys in the parking lot at Great Woods who could have played a better Allman Brothers show than Zakk Wylde. It was an embarrassment, but it was just one night. Zakk's behavior was no more obscene than the behavior that got him on that stage in the first place, but clearly we were going to have to try something different.

GRISSOM: I was back in Austin in a music store trying out some guitars and I got paged. My wife was on the phone and said the Allman

Brothers had called back. She said, "It didn't work out last night and they want to know if you can be on a plane in two hours." I didn't even know where my guitars were, because they hadn't arrived back from tour.

I got a guitar and my reverb unit, put it in an Anvil case, and flew out to D.C. They picked me up at the curb at midnight in the tour bus. The next day we had an hour or so rehearsal at soundcheck, then played a full gig to a sold-out Merriweather Post Pavilion. And that was the last rehearsal or soundcheck we had.

HOLMAN: We basically dropped Zakk off at the airport and picked Grissom up.

HAYNES: David is a great player, he's a sweetheart of a guy and he's a quick study. He kind of saved the day, really, because we had no idea how long this was going to last.

GRISSOM: It was like a fantasy experience. When I was sixteen, I'd jam with two drummers and play a lot of those tunes, and to be standing up there next to Gregg playing "Dreams" was surreal. I played about ten shows, and it was a total joy from the minute I got there until the minute I left. I felt the joy of music flooding back into me. It was such a different experience from my other big rock tours. There was so little drama or pretense and so little instruction or pressure to play someone else's licks. The only ones who said anything to me were Warren and Woody, who basically said, "You can stretch out longer if you want."

We'd all amble out, make sure we were in tune, and just let 'er rip. I felt like I had played a jazz gig, but in front of a giant, totally appreciative crowd. Having a crowd that size really listening to every note was phenomenal. The audience is such a huge part of the deal with that band. I was sad to come back to my real life, but I returned with a renewed sense of purpose and love of music, and a keener understanding of why I do this.

WEST: We went through a few days of literally not knowing where Betts was and then he surfaced and Grissom settled in and everyone relaxed. The music was good, the tension was gone, and the shows were fun.

Following Grissom's nine shows, the band finished the tour with Pearson playing nine more.

JACK PEARSON, *sub guitarist, 1993; ABB member, 1997–99:* I had learned Duane's and Dickey's parts when I was a kid and I knew every note they played on *At Fillmore East* and *Eat a Peach* by heart, so I was ready to go. I flew to Dallas with no rehearsals. Warren and I spent a little time in a hotel room and I just said, "Which part are you playing?" and then I played the other one. We just went out and played. Gregg liked it and said, "Hey, man, come play with me and come out to my house and write." I went to his place and we wrote "Sailin' 'Cross the Devil's Sea."

"Sailin'" would appear on the ABB's next album, 1994's Where It All Begins. *Pearson also joined Gregg Allman and Friends, playing with Gregg's solo band for most of the next three years and appearing on his 1997 album* Searching for Simplicity. *Betts, meanwhile, returned to the Allman Brothers Band in November 1993, seemingly refreshed.*

BETTS: I got on about a three-year drunk there. The first two years was a lot of fun, and the last year got to be a living hell. But then—at least I was intoxicated. The other guys had to put up with it sober.

After Betts's return, Allman's own struggles with drugs and alcohol worsened. The pair seemed to be locked in a strange, destructive dynamic in which if one went up, the other went down.

QUIÑONES: It was like a roller coaster with those two. When one was raging, the other was kind of cool. They were never really fucked up together. It was one or the other, which was kind of strange.

CAPLAN: Gregg and Dickey had this weird dynamic. I always felt like they were Clark Kent and Superman, but you never knew who was which.

HAYNES: It was difficult on the rest of us.

WEST: When Gregg was absolutely insane, Betts would have it reasonably together and vice versa. From a show perspective, it was better when Dickey had his shit together, because you could roll Gregg down in the mix and he'd sit in the dark and usually be able to sing halfway decently. But when Betts was feeling his oats, he was the loudest guy onstage. It was very hard to ignore Dickey when he was fucked up, and it created some bad scenes and a lot of tension.

QUIÑONES: Dickey could really lash out and be unpredictable and violent. Gregg is more passive-aggressive, and when he was in bad shape, he was more like the passive drunk. Nobody was scared of him.

HAYNES: I was becoming the person that Dickey could talk to when he couldn't talk to Gregg, and that Gregg could to talk when he couldn't talk to Dickey. I was like, "push me, pull you," trying to be neutral, trying on a moment-by-moment basis to keep the peace and also figure out what was best for the band musically and creatively. It was a tough spot to be in. It was very frustrating and it made me feel more and more like maybe I'm doing the wrong thing, maybe I need to be concentrating on my own stuff.

CAPLAN: They looked to Warren more and more to do things—because he did them.

WEST: Dickey and Gregg talked very little to each other. There were very few band meetings. When things had to get done, Bert would make the rounds, one by one, saying, "Here's what we need to decide. What do you think?" And when it was a musical decision or question, they often would go through Warren. He was always in the middle.

Warren has always held the entity of the Allman Brothers Band in extremely high regard, as did Woody. They thought it was their responsibility to hold it up and take it further. They took that seriously and it was not always an easy job.

Even as Haynes was becoming ever more indispensible to the band, he was tiring of the stress and uncertainty. He considered leaving when Tales of Ordinary Madness, *his first solo album, was released in 1993. He stayed and the Warren Haynes Band opened for the ABB for much of the '93 Summer Tour—the one that was shaken by Betts's sudden departure and the scramble to find replacements. Haynes was performing double duty through many of these shows, opening with his own band before taking the stage again with the headliners, bearing much of the responsibility for keeping the Allman Brothers Band on track.*

HAYNES: When I joined the band in '89 I was in the middle of starting to pursue my solo career, which I had put on the back burner to join the Dickey Betts Band a couple of years earlier. Things were starting to come to fruition for me and I had a lot of opportunities that I didn't want to pass up, but I also had this amazing opportunity to be in the Allman Brothers.

The more the communication would break down and the overall vibe and positive aspect of the band, especially the original members, would start to deteriorate, the more it would push me to concentrate on my own music. I would almost take it as a sign that that's what I should be doing. As the vibes got more and more negative, I would wonder what I was doing there.

Despite his misgivings, Haynes stuck with the band, Betts returned, and the band reached another period of relative stability, returning to the studio to cut their third post-reunion album, which became 1994's Where It All Begins, *recorded live on a soundstage at Burt Reynolds's Florida ranch.*

HAYNES: Dickey and I mentioned to each other a bunch of times over the years how nice it would be to record without headphones, because your guitar never sounds like your guitar through headphones or small speakers. So you play to the tone of the amp and trust that they'll make it sound good later. On *Where It All Begins,* we just set up our live gear and played. It was a big pleasure to play without headphones on.

BETTS: Our playing together is just so different live. There's an eye contact and body language thing we do with one another. For instance, often when I'm playing rhythm, my rhythms turn into kind of sympathetic chord solos. And I'll be watching his body language much like a boxer would watch for the counterpunch. I can kind of see where he's going and react to it. You can't do that kind of thing in a studio setting, even if you're playing all of your parts more or less "live."

HAYNES: We always recorded with everyone tracking live, but on *WIAB* we set up like we were on stage, with monitors, lights, and everybody in the same room, and I think we were able to re-create more what we did on stage because that's how we were seeing and hearing things. I think any time you can record like that, whatever you lose from a technical standpoint, you more than make up for in music and feel.

BETTS: I actually wrote "No One to Run With" ten years earlier with a hometown friend of mine named John Prestia. It was during the '80s when no one would give us the time of day. Having that song return from the grave points out how much things [had] changed in the music business.

HAYNES: We were ahead of schedule, which was rare. We basically recorded everything slated and had more time booked. Dickey went home and Gregg said, "Why don't we do your song 'Soulshine'?" I knew Gregg had heard it, but the suggestion came out of the blue. I never really thought of it as an Allman Brothers song until I heard Gregg sing it. We recorded it and left space for Dickey's parts and sent the tracks to him to finish. I left him a lot of space to fill but he played very little.

Maybe because it was the one song on the album we didn't play everything together live, I never was really satisfied with how that version of "Soulshine" turned out. It sounds too sparse.

TRUCKS: Warren brought in "Rockin' Horse," originally intended for Gregg to sing, and I think we cut a version of it, but Gregg didn't want to sing those lyrics. Warren's response was, "OK. I'll sing it," and we cut it, but Dickey refused to finish the song. He wanted another one of his songs on it, and said, "We're doing 'Mean Woman Blues' instead." "Rockin' Horse" was a much stronger tune.

HAYNES: I somewhat like my playing on *Seven Turns*, and somewhat more on *Shades of Two Worlds*, but when I listen back, I know that I've learned a lot since then. I like my playing on the live records and on *Where It All Begins* much more. I feel like we were really starting to come into our own with our own sound and approach.

A lot of that was settling on a tone that blends in with what you've heard all your life without stealing anyone's tone, because the last thing I want to do is cop Duane's sound. That's his tone and it's very distinct. I faced the same challenge when playing with Phil [Lesh] and the Dead and dealing with Jerry Garcia's legacy.

BETTS: I don't think I'd be nearly as good a guitar player today if I hadn't been working with Warren. When I wanted to get Warren in the band, everybody thought I was crazy. All the business people said, "Are you sure you want him in the band? He . . . you know . . . I mean . . ." They wouldn't quite say it, so I asked, "Are you afraid he's going to blow me away?" And they said, "Well, he's awfully good. Are you sure you want to deal with that?" And I said, "I don't want to get some fucking lackey in the band." If I had somebody in the band that I couldn't get anything out of, we might as well not have another guitarist. Warren drives me to play things that I wouldn't otherwise. And hopefully I do the same thing for him.

Warren Haynes and Dickey Betts at the first Beacon show, September 27, 1989.

HAYNES: It's cool, because there's a healthy thing that goes on onstage where all seven of us at any given point are capable of kicking one another's ass, which makes all of us play better. And that's the way it should be.

In a larger band, you have the comfort of being able to lay out and it still feels great. We all do it. That's part of the beauty of a big band. It can be a trio, a quartet, a quintet, a sextet, or a septet at any given moment depending on who's doing what. And I think that's wonderful.

JAIMOE: If you're playing something that's not adding anything to the music, it don't need to be there. If you can't hear an instrument then it's distracting to the music.

BETTS: I feel that I've been given a gift, which is a knack—maybe genetic—to play music. I don't take it for granted and I'm very grateful for it, but I always knew that this was what I wanted to do. When people asked what I was going to be when I grew up, before I was in first grade, I would say, "I'm gonna be a guitar player on the radio." But along with that gift comes an obsessed kid who plays six hours a day. You have to do that in order to really apply yourself and discover what talent you might have.

HAYNES: I think most people who come this far share that. Before I could get a guitar in tune, I knew that's what I wanted to do for the rest of my life. And it really is an obsession. We all go through phases where we play for hours upon hours every day and you just don't want to put it down. You're never going to get there unless you apply yourself that way.

I knew I was going to play guitar for the rest of my life, whether I did it professionally or not. It's a release that I'm very grateful to have in my life. And even if, God forbid, I fixed computers for a living, I would still go home and play guitar. I always know that if I'm in a shitty mood I can pick up my guitar and feel better. And sitting in your bedroom playing does the same thing for your soul as playing to ten thousand people.

BETTS: I always knew that I'd play my guitar all my life—but I never knew I could make a life out of it. And I never dreamed that we would be accepted the way we are. You have to be just truly grateful for that. I mean, saying you knew you were going to be a guitar player is one thing, but to be accepted the way the Allman Brothers Band has and be blessed with such a long career—we seem to have the longevity of an elephant—is just something you could never anticipate. It's really more than I ever dreamed could happen. You have to be grateful every day when you get up that people still want to come pay money to hear you play guitar. And that keeps me going when I'm not feeling that strong at a concert. I look out there and say, "They paid money to come hear me."

Blues giant Albert King and Dickey Betts, Memphis, 1991.

We've always tried to remain a band of the people in terms of the way we dress and the way we conduct ourselves. And that's worked out well for us. The Dead are the same way. People come to hear you play and for the feelin' that they get from the band, not for how we look, thank God. I would feel really stupid trying to dance around and look like a young man, but that was never what we were about anyhow.

Playing music the way we approach it, there's gonna be good nights and bad nights and that's all there is to it. And what we do on a good night is something that you just cannot rehearse. We could rehearse for twelve weeks like the Stones did before they did the Steel Wheels tour. But five days of playing means more than five years of rehearsing for us.

HAYNES: We always sound like shit at rehearsal unless someone we want to impress comes walking in. But you can't really rehearse for these lengthy shows. We rarely play under three hours, and sometimes we go as long as four or four and a half.

BETTS: We put in our contract that we're gonna play two and a half hours or we ain't playing. So we never play less than two and a half hours. Ticket prices being what they are, you want to give those people their money's worth. And, besides, that's the only time it's any fun for us on the road. The dead time just kills you, but when we finally get on stage, the fun begins.

ALLMAN: I think somebody somewhere marked us for playing three hours or more every night and it can be overkill. Three hours is too long. I mean, it's very, very few nights, especially at the age of fifty and up, that you are into it enough to play for three hours. I don't know why we do this. The crowd gets you going and keeps you up—they keep pulling that energy out of you, but afterwards, you need a goddamn walker to get back to the bus. You are totally exhausted, man.

BETTS: It very difficult to go out there and try to play the same song different. And if we don't do that we feel like we've failed. I feel like hell if I go out there and I just don't have it. That usually happens if I didn't eat properly and I suddenly feel weak or tired. You have to take care of yourself on the road, especially when you're not doin' drugs to overcome that. No matter what you ate during the day, you can do a nose full of cocaine, and have plenty of energy for the show. Well, that works short term, but, of course, long term is a different story.

Riding through the turmoil, the Allman Brothers Band continued to tour with greater frequency. In 1994, they played 91 dates, the most since they performed 127 times in 1971. No one was more surprised by the band's ongoing resurgence than the members.

HAYNES: The Allman Brothers was a year-by-year thing. There was no indication that it was capable of staying together for years to come. We all looked at it as each tour could be the last one, and there was no reason to think otherwise. I'm sure each member of the band was thinking about his own future and what was best for themselves, because it was always fifty-fifty if next year was going to happen.

CAPLAN: There were a lot of people making their living off that band. It's not unique to them, either. This happens often with groups—they need to play dates to make their payroll.

HAYNES: I personally felt many times that taking a year off here or there would have helped the band creatively and maybe even been the right thing to do in a business sense. I think things might have played out differently if we had done that, but a lot of people worried that if we took some time apart we might never get back together. A lot of the gigs happened because people wanted to pursue the opportunity while the band was hot and sounding great, knowing that we might turn around and it would all go away.

HOLMAN: This is just what they do. If they had taken a break, Gregg would have gone and played bars. Warren wanted to take a break because he had other ambitions, but the band wanted to perform.

In 1994, the Allman Brothers Band cemented their legacy as one of the fore-fathers of the jam band universe, headlining the burgeoning HORDE Festival, performing most of the thirty-three shows with Blues Traveler, Sheryl Crow, the Black Crowes, and the Dave Matthews Band. The Allmans seemed to be solidifying their bond with older fans while also reaching out to a new generation.

BETTS: We started seeing more young people at our shows around the time we did the HORDE tour. What's really nice to see is it's the first time I can remember a situation where there's no generation gap. I like watching the kids and also the guys my age unbuttoning their shirts. As a human being, you can have fun and be innocent no matter what your age. You're not making a fool out of yourself by having fun. So many people get to a certain age and they think they have to be reserved all the time. Well, when you come to our show, it's your chance to just get loose and have fun for a while.

HAYNES: The one thing that was really frustrating to me through those years was that we had a pretty limited repertoire. That became more obvious when we started having younger crowds drawn in by HORDE and other things and especially after Jerry [Garcia] died [in August 1995] and Deadheads started coming to our shows more. They would like what they heard, but then come back again and hear more or less the same show and that was not acceptable. Kirk West started really pointing this out to us, and Woody and I began trying to get the guys to expand the set lists.

BUTCH TRUCKS: This was a massive issue. It was boring to play the same sets night after night. The bottom line is Dickey insisted we put a set together at the start of the run and play it every night because he had a hard time remembering songs. I started going online on the ABB forum and talking to people and picked up how upset people were with us playing the same damn set every night. So many people would come to multiple shows and as much as they liked it, it got boring seeing the same show. I started really hounding everyone, "We got to do something," and finally Dickey caved in and we had an A set and a B set and then we got up to three sets. People at the Beacon looking to buy tickets would try to figure out which night we'd be playing which set so they could see different shows.

JAIMOE: Playing the same sets wasn't a big issue for me. We did that a lot with Duane, too, but there was a big difference; we may have been playing the same songs but we weren't trying to play them the same. We weren't playing an album to promote it. It's not really what you play, it's how you play it, and I felt like when we were in that stage of playing those rotating set lists, we were playing things too crystal clear and clean, without enough fire and passion. What I try to do is find the groove in anything we do; to block out everything else and play the groove. It's no different than a drum kit, where you have eight pieces but may only need the snare and tom for a particular song.

During the Beacon run in 1996, years of tension between Betts and Allman came to a head and almost caused the cancellation of a performance, an incident that could have had much larger implications than a single missed show.

HOLMAN: We were sitting in the Beacon and Gregg wasn't there and no one knew what was going on and Dickey went, "I'm getting out of here before there's a riot. When Gregg's ready to play, somebody call me and I'll come back." And he walked out. So there we were with no Dickey or Gregg at the Beacon. We decided that Jonny would go after them and I would stay at the Beacon and try to keep things calm.

PODELL: Bert and I look at each other and I go, "What are we gonna do?" And Bert goes, "What do you mean *we*? I'm going to stay here and hold down the fort. Go do your thing."

WEST: The whole structure was they'd show up at the last minute—ten minutes before they'd be on stage—and Gregg and Dickey both always wanted to be the last one there. So it took a while until most of us realized there was an issue. Then we started scrambling.

PODELL: I am a pretty cool customer, not easily intimidated, but I was shitting bricks as I walked into the hotel. It was eight o'clock, the crowd was filling up at the Beacon, and there's no show as I go walking into the valley of death. I'm Jewish, but I kept saying, "I will see no evil, fear no evil." I was thinking, "Dude, you are walking into the Philistines. What am I going to do with Dickey?" His reputation for violence was well known for many years—though never directed at me. And what would I do with Gregg? He was a full-blown alcoholic, fighting the urge to drink every minute of his life and not winning the battle at that moment.

I go to Dickey first. I walk in and the Betts posture in times like this—and I bailed him out of jail a few times—is he would sit profile to you, giving you the side of his face, unwilling to acknowledge you, with the cowboy hat very deep over his eyes.

He goes, "What do you want?"

I go, "Dickey, come on. We've got to do a show." I had an amazing relationship with Dickey and convinced him to come back and he goes, defiantly, "Fine. Who are you riding back with?" That was an "Oh shit" moment, but I said, "I have to go with Gregg . . . you're a big boy. Go."

Now I go to Gregg's room and say, "Get dressed, dude. We're going back to the Beacon and I am not fucking with you. Come get in this cab with me. There's a full house. If this show don't play, the whole run's over." And I wasn't being macho. I could talk to Gregg like this because we have always been very close and I have never felt threatened by him. He goes, "Fine, but I got to have a drink." I said, "OK. One drink at the bar." Then the fun begins. He has a quick shot, then tries to take another one. I knock it down and that continues on and on. We finally get in the cab.

HOLMAN: I was back at the Beacon trying to keep [promoter] Ron Delsener calm and telling him the show would go on. At the same time, we were trying to get the [equipment] trucks there to load out because if they didn't play, the Beacon run was over. Every night, it's a possibility that it could be the last time they ever play and we were certainly staring into that abyss. We were half packing up the gear. The crowd was pretty restless.

WEST: In those days there were an awful lot of standing-room tickets sold and many, many people coming in the back door. There could be a few hundred people in there without seats and things could get un-ruly real fast.

PODELL: It was extremely dramatic, because we all knew what was on the line—it wasn't just a show. The whole credibility with the history of drugs, animosity, breakups—the whole Allman Brothers soap opera—was being played out and how it would end would determine their fu-ture. It was potentially not only Beacon-ending, but career-ending.

WEST: Podell could talk straight to them, and say, "This is what's go-ing to happen to your career." They would listen to Podell. They re-spected him as someone who knew them from the start and who was sober, too. You're going to listen to somebody who's been there and he told them exactly what time it was. He made the point that if they don't do this, it's the end of the line.

HAYNES: After the word started spreading that the show might not happen, we were all thinking, "This could be it."

BUTCH TRUCKS: We were upstairs in our dressing rooms and had reached a point where we decided we're probably going to have to can-cel the show—and the rest of the Beacon. I'm sitting there thinking, "This is it. This is how it finally ends." We had thirty cops out in the lobby just in case.

HAYNES: There was nothing to do but sit and wait and see what happened, but those folks were quite confident it would work out.

PODELL: I remember Delsener saying we have to start giving money back and I said, "Dude, do not. This show is going to play." I was all bluster. I really didn't know what was going to happen. I was totally bluffing. I just knew that if you give the money back, you are totally out of control.

BUTCH TRUCKS: Just as we're about to make an announcement, Jonny called and said, "Gregg had a few drinks and we're on the way."

WEST: Jonny Podell earned every penny he ever made from the Allman Brothers Band that night.

Gregg Allman and Dickey Betts in the *Late Show with David Letterman* dressing room celebrating their induction into the Rock and Roll Hall of Fame, January, 1995.

This incident was more than a year after the band's January 1995 induction into the Rock and Roll Hall of Fame, which Allman remembers primarily for what he didn't do: speak coherently. A drunk, bloated Gregg, looking exposed with his beard shaved off, took the podium after Betts gave a humorous, moving speech thanking Bill Graham, Tom Dowd, Steve Massarsky, Jonny Podell, and Bert Holman. Looking down at the notes in his hand, Allman paused and muttered a thank-you to "the greatest friend, brother, guitar player, and inspiration I've ever known, my brother Duane. He was always the first to face the fire."

ALLMAN: I could barely stand up. I meant to say something about my mother and something about Bill Graham. I meant to say a lot of stuff and I was too gone to say any of it. All day I tried to be really cool about it but you just cannot. Afterwards we played and I started feeling a little better so that night wasn't a total loss, but I watched it on TV and I was mortified, and that's what it took for me to get serious about cleaning up.

BETTS: Substance abuse is an occupational hazard of being a musician. It's like working in an industrial waste factory. That shit is around, and it's so easy to get—and it's so easy to get your energy where it should be anyway, but it ain't. And you can go for three hours and feel like a king, but it doesn't work in the long run. And, man, I've been there.

The morning after the Hall of Fame induction ceremony, Allman got into a limo at his New York hotel and went to a Pennsylvania rehab facility. The stay got him over his acute illness, but his next, more significant step came the following year at his California home. With the support of his sixth wife, Stacey Fountain Allman, Gregg made a determined attempt to get sober, and was soon proclaiming that he had quit everything, including cigarettes.

"I hired a private nurse to come in to my house and it was rough . . . but I sure needed it," Allman recalled in 1997. "There's no way I can even explain it. It's like having a five-hundred-pound weight lifted off me, or like I was blind in

one eye and now I can see out of both. I can see better, taste better, smell better—
all five of my senses are waking up and I'm appreciating them all.

"There's a whole lot of stuff that I used to take for granted that I don't any-
more, and one of them is being alive. I've come so close that . . . That life of being
wasted day in and day out all pretty much seems like a dream, or something that
happened to someone else."

Though Gregg's road to sobriety would prove to be more winding and com-
plicated, there was immediately a marked change in his appearance and on-
stage demeanor following this '96 cleansing. Allman was in notably better
condition for most of the next decade.

CHAPTER

Stand Back

*A*s *ALLMAN STRUGGLED with sobriety, tensions with the band continued to simmer, boiling over on a late summer 1996 West Coast tour. On September 1, the band traveled from Las Vegas to San Francisco, where they had an off day followed by a performance at the Fillmore West that was a fund-raiser for the Bill Graham Foundation. (Graham died in a helicopter crash on October 25, 1991.)*

QUIÑONES: After a very long ride, Dickey wakes up and goes, "Where are we?" Bert says, "About an hour from San Francisco." And Dickey goes nuts: "I need to go to Pebble Beach. I have a tee time there. I pay for this bus. Turn it around!" So we all grumble but have to go back down to Monterey to drop Dickey off to play golf. Then we drive back to San Francisco and enjoy a day off before the next night's benefit gig at the Fillmore.

WEST: Dickey loved Bill Graham and even thanked him in his Rock and Roll Hall of Fame induction speech, but he did not show up for this gig and everyone was embarrassed and furious at him. He arrived in San Francisco from Pebble Beach the night before in a limo with some new friends he had picked up and was a total mess and then he vanished again.

QUIÑONES: We had to play without him again and this time we had no idea where he was. When he disappeared before, we knew he was sick, arrested, whatever. Now there's no rhyme or reason and Bert is calling the airport and anyone he can think of; we're putting out the search party for Dickey Betts.

WEST: No one knew where he was and the next gig was in Idaho, and we get on the buses and start heading there.

QUIÑONES: Eventually, Bert got Dickey's wife on the phone and asked if she had heard from Dickey and she goes, "Oh, he's here sleeping in bed." And we were like, "What the fuck?" He went home to Sarasota without telling anybody.

WEST: They got ahold of Derek, put him on a plane, and he flew out there to play for Dickey.

QUIÑONES: He went home and we figured he's staying home and Butch had Derek on the way to sub for Dickey. Butch was so angry. He called back Dickey's wife, who refused to wake Dickey up, and Butch was yelling, "Wake that motherfucker up! I've got a few things to tell him. How dare he leave us in the middle of a run!"

Then, at some point, Dickey calls Bert and says, "I'm coming back out and we're going to have a band meeting." So in a day and a half Dickey flies home to Florida and back to the West Coast.

WEST: After this long drive from San Francisco, like twenty-four hours, we get to the place in Idaho and Dickey shows up.

QUIÑONES: We're all in a normal double-bed room in the hotel that Bert had booked for this meeting and here comes Dickey Betts. He walks in with his hat pulled down so you can't even see his eyes and sits down in the corner chair next to Butch. He looks around the room and says, "If you guys think this is a fucking intervention, you are highly mistaken."

And we're like, "Dude, you called the fucking meeting."

He looks over at Butch and goes, "You got something you want to say to me?"

And he goes, "No, I don't." He said later he figured if he said anything else, it would be another broken nose.

Dickey goes, "Does anyone else have anything they want to say?" I raise my hand and he's like, "What?"

I go, "I just want to know why you fucking left us without any notice."

And he goes, "I'm not gonna fucking answer that!" So I'm thinking, "This is going to be very productive."

Then Butch goes, "As a matter of fact, I do have something to say." He starts to say that he was pissed off that Dickey would leave just like that and Dickey interrupts him and says, "No, you listen to me! You owe everything you have to me, Dickey Betts, motherfucker! That Jaguar you were driving in 1974 was because of me."

And I'm thinking, "Nineteen seventy-four? This is some pent-up anger." He starts throwing all this shit in Butch's face.

BUTCH TRUCKS: All I remember is a half-hour drunken tirade that didn't make much sense but boiled down to "Butch Trucks owes me every penny he's ever made."

QUIÑONES: He ends that tirade by walking to the middle of the room and saying, "Fuck you! Fuck you!"—pointing to every one of us and giving us the fuck-you. Then he goes, "I fucking quit this band. If you want Dickey Betts to play in the Allman Brothers Band, you're going to have to pay me forty thousand a show." Then he storms out.

We're all dumbfounded, looking at each other like, "Wow. What just happened? What do we do now?"

Butch goes, "Derek's on the way already. Let's just finish this run and show the motherfucker this is not the Dickey Betts Band. He's been holding us hostage for years. Fuck him."

I'm going, "I think this is a bad idea. We should fold up the tent, go home, and assess the damage." But they're like, "I don't think so."

WEST: It was an unworkable situation. Derek couldn't play with Dickey sitting on a bus and no one would play with Dickey, because they were so pissed, even before that meeting.

BUTCH TRUCKS: Ever since Duane died, anytime anyone challenged anything Dickey said, he'd either threaten to beat you up or threaten to quit. If I heard it once, I heard it a million times.

QUIÑONES: We're still sitting in the room trying to figure this out, and there's a knock on the door. "It's Dickey! Open the fucking door!"

BUTCH TRUCKS: Bert opened the door, Dickey came in, went, "Where's that son of a bitch?" and came charging right at me.

QUIÑONES: Allen Woody was sitting on one bed and I was sitting on the other. Woody gets up to block him and Dickey goes, "Woody, get out of my fucking way!"

And Woody goes, "No, I'm not going to do that."

And Dickey cocks his arm back and punches Woody in the face. Woody was stunned. He was an intimidating figure but he was the sweetest guy that I knew. I never before saw a violent bone in Woody's body, but the last thing he expected was to be punched in the face by one of his idols. He grabs Dickey by the throat and cocks his arm and I jump up and grab Dickey in this armlock from behind, telling Woody not to do it, it's not worth it, and Woody's holding him by the neck, screaming, "I was your fucking friend!" over and over. Dickey's yelling at me to let him go and I'm going, "No, I can't do that. This is not going to go down like this. The only way I'm letting you go is if you walk out of this room."

I turn him around and inch him toward the door and he leaves. That moment for me was like, "What the fuck am I involved in here?" I grew up with relatives who drank and did hard drugs, so joining the band was like being back home, except with some crazy white guys. I thought I understood all that, but hearing the anger behind this old history was stunning. I couldn't understand how these guys could make such fucking great music and be in that place personally. Gregg stayed out of the whole fray. It was almost like he wasn't there. And I think he and Dickey went down to the bar and had a drink together, if you can believe that.

BUTCH TRUCKS: They didn't go to the bar together. Gregg went to the bar and started drinking and Dickey joined him and said, "You and me are the Allman Brothers, so fuck everyone else. Let's go out and tour." Gregg was thinking, "Yeah, right," but saying, "Yeah, yeah, yeah . . ." Gregg is not known for his confrontational abilities and never has been.

WEST: The gig was canceled at show time, along with the next two, in Portland and Seattle. The next morning I was rounding up people to get on the bus and go to two different airports to fly home, and Dickey was milling around the lobby. Warren got on the bus, managing to do an end-around and not see Dickey.

QUIÑONES: When Dickey showed up in the lobby, he called me over and goes, "Quiñones, I'm sorry about what happened yesterday. That was a little crazy." I got along great with Dickey. He never messed with me and we respected each other, so I tried to give him some loving guidance: "Look, maybe you should take this time to try and get some help and clean up." And he goes, "Fuck you, man! Don't you ever talk to me like I'm a child!" So I just got on the bus.

WEST: Woody comes strolling through the lobby and I send him onto the bus. I was at the back of the bus when Dickey comes around the corner and stops Woody at the door, which is standing wide open. Dickey reaches out, touches Woody's shoulder, and grabs his hand to shake in a seeming gesture of friendship.

While standing very close, making direct eye contact and holding tight to Woody's hand, with his other hand he reaches into his back pocket, opens a knife, and holds it behind his back as he keeps Woody there while he's talking to him. Apparently it goes well enough and Dickey closes the knife and slips it back into his pocket. It was a very scary thing to witness.

JAIMOE: After Woody stood up to Dickey, Dickey was deeply intimidated by him and became determined to get him out of the band. We all knew that getting Woody out without Warren was going to be impossible.

WEST: Woody always played too loud and there was off-and-on complaining about that throughout his tenure, and it was used as an excuse, but everyone knew what was really happening.

In interviews at the time both Betts and Allman referred to the band getting too loud—a persistent Allman complaint often directed at Betts as well. Woody and Haynes remained with the ABB for a pair of private parties over the winter and for the thirteen-show Beacon run in March 1997. During these shows, however, it became clear to band insiders that a break was imminent. Shortly after, Haynes and Woody announced they were leaving to focus on Gov't Mule, the power trio they had formed in 1994 with drummer Matt Abts.

BUTCH TRUCKS: It became obvious that Woody and Dickey could not be in the same band together, and we knew that Warren was sticking with Woody. I will always regret that I went and met with Warren at his apartment in New York and told him what was going down. I said, "If I was you, I would focus on Gov't Mule and resign from the Allman Brothers because Dickey is not going to work with Allen anymore." That was the point where we should have said, "Fuck it, enough of this guy. It's time to try it without him."

HAYNES: I don't know how much he knew that Woody and I had been contemplating leaving the Allman Brothers for a long while at that point, but one of the things I remember Butch saying is he wished he had built himself a back door. He was basically saying, "I wish I had a Gov't Mule" and I think that's part of what led to him forming Frogwings [a band with Derek Trucks, Jimmy Herring, and Oteil Burbridge].

BUTCH TRUCKS: Gregg wasn't there to help; he was still in such bad shape that I couldn't even have a real talk with him about things like that and Jaimoe just wanted to play music, so it was me and only me having to make all these difficult decisions. I wish I had not had that talk, but I have a wife and kids and I was doing everything I could to hold the damn thing together.

QUIÑONES: Warren and Woody had already started having conflicts with scheduling and whatnot with the Mule, and after that shit went down, I think they just collectively decided it was time to focus on the Mule.

MATT ABTS: It got really intense with Woody and Dickey . . . It got to the point where Dickey was maybe going to fire Allen and no one knew what was going to happen. It was very comforting to them that they had Gov't Mule to turn their attention to, and very exciting to me that they were willing to say, "OK, we're out of there." We had a record out that we thought had wings and they were like, "We don't need these guys. We can fly." Regardless of the situation, splitting the Allman Brothers was a ballsy thing to do.

HAYNES: There was so much negativity in the Allman Brothers camp and so much positivity in the Gov't Mule camp that it became more and more untenable to stick with the status quo.

ABTS: They had been talking for a while about how stagnant the Allmans were and how they were growing frustrated.

HAYNES: The Allman Brothers weren't rehearsing, we couldn't work up new material, people weren't talking to each other . . . and Gov't Mule was at the opposite end of everything. We were bursting with ideas, dying to work out songs, to rehearse, perform, record as much as possible. Things had escalated in the Allman Brothers to a point where we knew it was time to make a change, which we had been talking about for at least a year, maybe two, but had been procrastinating.

It's not an easy decision to leave an institution like the Allman Brothers behind. On one hand, yes, it can fall apart at any moment and we're going to be wondering what's next—which in our case was cool because we were building a back door. On the other hand, if it was something that could be salvaged and get back on the right track and continue to make great, legendary, timeless music, then you want to be a part of that—especially if it could coexist with what you're doing. That's where we were for a couple of years but as things changed and the negativity got more intense in the Allman Brothers camp, we said, "We have a lot of faith in what we're doing and now is the time to give it one hundred percent."

Guitarist Jack Pearson, who had played in Gregg's solo band and filled in for Betts for those nine shows in '93, was hired to take Haynes's place. While that was an easy, natural fit, the Aquarium Rescue Unit's Oteil Burbridge was such an outside choice to replace Woody that even he was surprised to get the call.

BUTCH TRUCKS: Dickey asked me if I thought Derek was ready and I said no. I really had not played with him yet and while I knew his slide playing was more than ready, I was not sure about the whole package.

OTEIL BURBRIDGE, *ABB bassist since 1997:* I got a call to go down to Dickey's house in Florida to play with him for a few days. I went out and bought all their records, but I barely knew where to start. I listened to everything to get a feel, knew that I could learn it all and figured I'd just pick up the songs as we went, which was, of course, a big mistake. If I had been savvier and smarter, I would have figured out which tunes Dickey wrote and learned all of those parts.

Jack [Pearson] was also there at Dickey's house. He played an acoustic blues and when he finished, Dickey just got up and walked out of the room. He came back and handed him one of Duane's glass slides [an original Duane Coricidin bottle]. Just like that, he was in.

PEARSON: I played a Blind Willie Johnson song—on Duane's Dobro, the one he recorded "Little Martha" on. Dickey and I had played a lot of electric guitar together, and then he said, "I want to hear how you can play slide," and went and got me the Dobro. We had a good time. Obviously, receiving Duane's slide was a very special moment.

ALLMAN: After he played with him, Dickey said, "Either we hire him or I ask him for lessons." That's [how] we all felt.

TRUCKS: Jack is a great rhythm player. From the get-go, he played great comps behind Dickey's solos and innately understood when to play with us [the drums], when to play with the organ, and when to play counterpoint to Dickey or the bass line. That happened immediately, and with every gig, he established his solo voice more and more. He concentrated on learning and even improving the song first and establishing his identity second, which I think is appropriate.

BURBRIDGE: Jack had the gig, but I handled the whole thing poorly. I had my six-string, which Dickey didn't like, and I had not learned enough songs properly, arrogantly thinking I could just pick them up. So Dickey would for instance say, "Let's play 'Jessica,'" and I'd go, "OK. Show me how that goes." And we did that for a few songs and he was rightfully annoyed and he said, "Don't you know any of these songs? How did you grow up in Birmingham (where I lived) and not learn some of these?" And I was like, "I'm from D.C.!"

Dickey was taken aback, and was thinking that he could get a guy who had these songs in his fingers. I lost the sure gig and Dickey wanted to bring in other guys and have us all audition. I hadn't even touched a four-string in ten years, and I hadn't played with a pick in nearly as long. But in between playing with Dickey and this audition, I listened more and more to the albums, focusing on Berry's parts, and also on Lamar Williams and Allen Woody's, for the material from their era, and realized that to nail those parts, I had to play what they were playing.

God bless Joe Dan Petty [*Dickey's guitar tech and a longtime crew member who was also the bassist in the band Grinderswitch*]. He took me to buy a Mexican Fender Jazz bass that I used in the tryouts; it was $185! He not only altered the course of my life by reintroducing me to the four string—I didn't even own one at the time—but he showed me some crucial fingerings that Berry used, for instance on "Leave My Blues at Home." Unless you finger it that way, it will never feel the same. What a gift.

WEST: Everyone knew that Oteil was a hell of a player. They had done the HORDE tour and seen him up close and he was playing all over

Atlanta, but there was some concern if he was the right fit. They flew him and two other bassists down to Sarasota. I was driving them all to the tryouts and Oteil was pretty nervous. Joe Dan knew that Oteil had the chops and the spirit and he wanted him to get the gig and just took him under his wing to help him any way he could.

BURBRIDGE: Playing with this band is a real challenge, because you have two drummers, plus a percussionist, as well as two guitarists and Gregg's organ. There's so much going on in the music that you really have to work to find something to lock down on.

PEARSON: It was pretty easy for me to fit in and settle down, having played with the band before and worked with Gregg a bunch. Basically, I knew all the songs and understood the dynamics.

BURBRIDGE: I was so nervous, I could barely sleep or eat, but everyone was really helpful. Tom Dowd helped me figure out how to lock in, and when to follow whom. I found that the key was to treat the drummers as one entity because they gel so well. Joe Dan also pro-

Jack Pearson, 1998.

vided insight into how Dickey felt about the role of bass guitar in this band, how Berry felt about his role and approach, and a bunch of other things. Jaimoe was a great help, too, for instance, making the connection for me between Miles Davis's "All Blues" and "Dreams." But really everyone in and connected to the band has helped me to understand the music. Butch, Gregg, Dickey, Marc, Warren, Jack Pearson, Jimmy Herring, Chuck Leavell, Ace Man

Tom Dowd. . . . And others like Joe Dan, Red Dog, Bert Holman, Kirk West, Chank, Babuna, and many others.

The more of the story you learn from the cats who were actually there, the better off you are. Living history is the best. They told me things like not to panic if Dickey came and got right in my face, which he likes to do. Usually, he's just saying, "Time to come with me."

PEARSON: They really let me play whatever I wanted from the get-go, which is so wonderful and rare. Usually a musician has to choose between playing the big pop gig and the small, express-yourself gig. This is a very rare situation where it's both at once.

BURBRIDGE: There was no doubt that they could have hired someone else to replicate the classic sound perfectly. I, of course, had the obligation to learn the history and replicate the right feel and sometimes the precise sounds, but bringing in a guy like me or Marc Quiñones—guys coming from very different places, with no rooting in Southern rock—shows that they also wanted to go somewhere different. We didn't even own any ABB records! Regardless of musical background, these pulses and grooves are something we have in common and if we're listening we can make music together naturally. You have to open your ears and your heart to the music.

As Pearson and Burbridge settled in, the band adopted a slightly quieter, more in-the-pocket style.

PEARSON: We actually worked on getting the parts closer to the originals at our first rehearsals. They had changed through the years and I thought Duane's harmonies were great, so I wanted to play those. It was cool and a lot of fun getting the original sound back—Butch, Red Dog, and Joe Dan all talked about this and Dickey seemed to enjoy it.

JAIMOE: Oteil drove me crazy for a while. Like Woody and Rook, he had a hard time figuring out the role of the bass in this band. He may be a better musician than I am in some terms, but there's some things that he don't know and like everyone else after Berry, he had to figure out how to play in a way that made Gregg and Dickey both happy. It didn't seem that hard for Lamar, but everyone else has struggled to a degree. The thing is, Gregg is not wrong about what he's saying and Dickey is not wrong. You should be able to do both; it's like playing in the studio and the gig—two different approaches.

BURBRIDGE: You give them each what they want in their songs. Of course both of them wanted opposite things on different days so it's like surfing. Each wave is different and you take them as they come. You're required to stretch out as a bassist with these people, but it's got to be straightforward, too, like a big king-size bed that's comfortable for everyone to lie down on.

PEARSON: One of my favorite things was when Butch and I would look at each other and lock into a good rhythm and Dickey would just take off. There was something about locking up together and getting into that groove that was very exciting and special. Duane and Dickey were great rhythm players, too, which was a very important part of the band's sound.

It was an honor to be in the Allman Brothers Band and I took the gig very seriously and tried to do the best I could. The original band is still one of my favorite bands of all time. I wore those records out learning how to play what they did. I tried to play in honor of Duane, and also play like myself. Sometimes it was tricky—and not always in the way you might think. There were a few songs where I'd get up there and be soloing and I'd think, "Ooh, I have to back off because my Dickey Betts influence is coming out." Dickey was a real hero of mine and it could be odd to be playing next to him and start playing like him. I would quickly change approaches.

ABB, 1997-99, with Jack Pearson and Oteil Burbridge.

This lineup was not captured on any official recordings, despite playing some very strong live shows. Pearson, who struggled with tinnitus, was drawn into an ongoing battle about stage volume, which Allman and Betts had long waged. It came to a head during the 1999 Beacon run.

BUTCH TRUCKS: Jack seemed really unhappy and was struggling with his ears. He said, "I could be playing sessions in Nashville right now," and I said, "Why yes, you could." He had bad tinnitus and our stage volume had just gotten so loud, with Dickey turning up, that it was a nightly battle for him.

PEARSON: Dickey was playing through two or three hopped-up 100-watt Marshall heads. There was talk about him switching to 50-watt heads, but that never happened and it became very hard for me to get a good sound—or a sound that I could even hear onstage. Everyone else was struggling to be heard and to hear each other over Dickey's volume, which he basically wanted loud enough so he could feel it. I would get bigger and bigger gear and I still couldn't hear it properly. I was having pain from the damage.

Gregg was setting up as far away from the guitar amps as he could; I would have to walk ten or fifteen feet to talk to him. He couldn't handle the volume and Dickey didn't want any Plexiglas on stage. I was wearing the highest-end, custom-made plugs you can get and it still was not enough. I had a couple of meetings with Dickey, where he said, "I don't know how much longer I can take it either, Jack, but I'm not turning down."

I was seeing an audiologist, who told me that playing with them was causing me damage and it was getting irreparable. It was like, "Do I stay in this band I love being in, or protect the hearing I have left?" I was in tears. It was not an easy decision to leave that band, but I was worried about having to stop playing in the middle of a long summer tour and I tried to do the right thing. My ears were so messed up that I barely played at all for the next two years. It was an honor to be in that band, and I wish it could have lasted longer.

BUTCH TRUCKS: We knew we had to do something—and I knew what we had to do. Not long after I had said Derek wasn't ready in '97, I formed the band Frogwings with him and Oteil and Jimmy Herring, and after playing a bunch of shows I realized how wrong I was. He was more than ready, so we called him up.

Butch's nephew celebrated his twentieth birthday by joining the Allman Brothers Band for their thirtieth-anniversary tour. He was younger than any of the original members were when the band formed.

DEREK TRUCKS: It was an honor to be part of such a great institution from the start. When I first got the gig, I was just trying to maintain the spirit of the whole thing while hopefully bringing some fire to it, hoping to hold up my end while also expressing my own voice. I spent more time practicing after I got that call than ever. I usually listen to music for eight or ten hours a day, and just play for a few, because I'd rather hear the masters play than myself. But I spent a lot of time woodshedding, playing along with tapes and being awed by the level of musicianship—and the number of songs I had to learn. But I wasn't intimidated. I was excited about playing with Dickey. I had listened to him forever, and knew it would be a trip playing off of him and behind him. I was looking forward to learning a lot from a master.

I listened to tapes of everything, but for the classic material I went to the source, which is Duane. I don't want to do an interpretation of an interpretation. I love what Warren and Jack and Dan Toler did, but I knew that I had to put my stamp on it. One of the hallmarks of the band is everybody gets their own voice. They don't dictate what you play, but you have to hit the milestones and that's good—I always need some forced discipline. That first tour was sink or swim. I wasn't too worried and it's nice to be forced to play things that you don't normally do. I think it made me grow. Being thrown into a situation like that, with a legendary band, large crowds, and so many people with distinct, strong sounds and identities forced me to reach beyond what I would normally do.

BURBRIDGE: Derek was my friend and when I heard he was coming on board, I was a little apprehensive, truthfully. I didn't think it was the healthiest environment for a young person.

DEREK TRUCKS: No one warned me of exactly what I was walking into, but as young as I was, I had been on the road almost ten years and had an idea of what happens out there. I had an innate sense of when to stay out of the way and when to mix it up. If it's not my fight, I'm not gonna mix it up. It wasn't really that stressful to me. It was like people-watching in New York City—you see crazy things and just observe. The Allman Brothers were an amazing opportunity but it wasn't my ship to steer.

BURBRIDGE: It was tense in the band back then and I had only been in it for a couple of years. I still didn't really understand what I had gotten myself into, and I was also going through a hard time personally. In some ways I thought Derek knew them better than I did since he was related, but he was still very young. He proved to be one of the most mature of all of us.

HAYNES: Derek is so mature—and even when he was a kid, he was far more mature than most people I've worked with that are twenty or thirty years older than he is. He plays music for all the right reasons and is an extremely selfless musician. He plays for the music and he has so much reverence for the music and the people playing it. I've played with him in so many different situations, and whenever there is a new person, a guest, or he's sitting in with a legend of some sort, at the beginning he'll take it all in and you'll think, "Oh, Derek is laying back too much." But he's just settling in, letting everybody get their groove and getting his own groove and waiting until the right time to explode—and explode is what he does.

DAVID GRISSOM: When I played those shows with the band in '93 Derek sat in one night and his guitar was bigger than him. I thought to myself, "This is the Allman Brothers Band. It is not right to have a little kid up here just because he's related to someone." Then he played like three notes and I said, "You're kidding me." I was astounded. Obviously, he's grown by leaps and bounds, but he was damn good at that young age.

DEREK TRUCKS: I've always had mixed emotions about people talking about how much I sound like Duane. Obviously, the fact anyone would say that is a great compliment—especially when I was just starting out—but you don't want to get lumped in one bag, or with one person. Your first influence stays with you, especially when you listen too hard and don't let it go through. I actually never tried to sit down and copy licks. I would just listen and play.

ALLMAN: Duane was his mentor—Derek's posthumous teacher, if you will—and you can sure hear him in there. But Derek's in there, also—and always has been, from the first time I heard him. He's got his own style.

BETTS: I think Derek sometimes tries too hard not to sound like Duane and I wish he would just go ahead and play. But he has truly got his own voice and original playing style.

DEREK TRUCKS: I went through a phase of rebelling and stopped listening to all guitar players from about fifteen to nineteen. I got tired of hearing people yelling for "One Way Out" or "Statesboro Blues." I wasn't in the Allman Brothers; that wasn't my music, wasn't what I did, and I found the best way to establish yourself is to fully take a left turn. Of course, you run a lot of people off, but it makes you a better musician. It adds another layer to what you do. It's easy to give people what they want when you know the handful of tricks that will make people clap. It's much harder to stay inspired.

BUTCH TRUCKS: I think Derek is what Duane may have become if he had more time. Remember, Duane was twenty-four when he died and had only been playing slide for a few years.

KICKIN' ASS

The story of Gov't Mule.

Allen Woody, Matt Abts, Warren Haynes, Macon, Georgia, 1994.

Gov't Mule was an idea before it was a band, born in countless conversations between Allen Woody and Warren Haynes on long-distance bus rides from one Allman Brothers gig to another. The two younger Brothers would sit up all night listening to music and talking about the kind of group they would like to form.

"We were listening to a lot of Led Zeppelin, Jimi Hendrix, Cream, and Free, caught up in the musical freedom they displayed," says Haynes. "That sparse use of space seemed like a complete one-eighty from playing your role in a seven-piece band like the Allman Brothers, so naturally that's the approach we were drawn to for what we imagined would be a fun side project. Woody and I had gotten much closer as friends and musical cohorts and doing something together seemed like the next natural step."

Haynes played with drummer Matt Abts in the Dickey Betts Band from

1986 to 1989 and they had stayed in touch. "Warren called out of the blue, very excited about putting a band together," recalls Abts. "He and Allen were very intent on a power trio." On the Allman Brothers' next visit to Los Angeles, where Abts lived, Warren and Woody joined the drummer at a Sunday-night jam session that confirmed the trio's potential.

"Warren and I had played together for about five years by then and I loved it," Allen Woody said in 1997. "Then, the first time I played with Matt, I thought, 'This is it. This is the drummer I'm supposed to play with.'"

The band didn't have a name until Woody, Warren, and Jaimoe watched a James Brown show from the side of the stage. "Apparently, Jaimoe kept saying, 'That's a government mule,'" Abts says. "When Allen realized he was referring to James Brown's wife's behind, he thought it was the funniest thing he had ever heard and our band had a name; Gov't Mule was named after James Brown's wife's booty."

The Mule debuted at the Palomino, a North Hollywood club, on May 12, 1994. "I think we only knew six songs," Abts says. "We were basically just jamming, and a lot of friends joined us for a second set."

A month later, the trio went to Macon, Georgia, moved into the Big House, then the home of Kirk and Kirsten West, and spent a week jamming and writing music in the same room where the original Allman Brothers Band had rehearsed. They emerged with a cache of songs, then played three shows in three nights, and Gov't Mule was born in earnest.

"We didn't have aspirations of being a full-time band or going beyond one experimental record," says Haynes. "We wanted to have fun and fill a void that we felt existed: an experimental power trio. The audiences were small, the ticket prices were low, and we were having fun and not putting pressure on ourselves. That led to a certain looseness."

In October 1995, Gov't Mule released their self-titled debut and hit the road, touring incessantly around Allman Brothers runs. The group's sound both tightened and expanded; their shows were high-volume, high-intensity three-way musical conversations that could roam from a capella Delta blues to ear-splitting covers of Black Sabbath. In March '97, as they finished work on their excellent, ambitious second album, *Dose*, Haynes and Woody announced they were leaving the Brothers to focus on Gov't Mule.

"There was so much tension within the Allman Brothers and Warren and Woody had the balls to walk away and say, 'Let's put our energy into Gov't Mule and be happy,'" says Abts. "It was so much fun—and we were so happy. For a couple of years, we were having the times of our lives, a band of brothers making music that we loved."

Adds Haynes, "We were best friends getting ever closer and tighter. It was a really magical period for the band and the music. We were playing together almost every night, we were getting to know each other personally and professionally quite well, and it was just a lot of fun."

That camaraderie began to crack in 2000. There were growing tensions throughout the summer tour in support of their third studio album, *Life Before Insanity.*

"Allen was having a real hard time," Abts says. "His life was spinning out of control. We basically had an intervention and said, 'You have to straighten up or we can't play with you.' We were going to take a break, which no one wanted to do, because things were tight, but it just had to be. Allen was going into rehab in September and of course he never made it there."

Woody died in his sleep in a New York hotel room on August 26, 2000, and Abts and Haynes had no real idea what they would do next.

"It was not clear if we could or should continue the band," says Haynes.

Says Abts, "We spoke with people from a lot of bands which had lost members—Metallica, the Dead, and, of course, Gregg and the other Allman Brothers. We were soaking up advice, and everyone said, 'Keep the band together. You have to continue. You never forget, but life doesn't end.'"

Haynes and Abts launched an acoustic Smile at Half Mast tour that included nine shows opening for Ben Harper, with Woody's rig set up onstage as a haunting reminder. "It was comforting to do that," says Abts. "It was an important part of the grieving process."

Haynes and Abts next began recording *The Deep End,* which became two separate CD releases, featuring guest bassists, ranging from the Who's John Entwistle to Phish's Mike Gordon.

"It started because we were joking that to replace Woody we'd need Chris Squire on one song and Flea on another, and then we decided to try and record a song with each of them," says Haynes. "Almost everyone we called said yes."

After touring with a rotating cast of bassists and keyboardists anchored by Oteil Burbridge, Widespread Panic's Dave Schools, and Chuck Leavell, the group added bassist Andy Hess and keyboardist Danny Louis as permanent members. "We knew we could never be a trio again," says Abts. "We had to move on without trying to re-create what we had with Woody."

In 2008, Jorgen Carlsson replaced Hess and the band has kept on keeping on. In 2014, the band, which formed to record "one experimental album" celebrated its twentieth anniversary.

DEREK TRUCKS: No one's ever taken slide guitar all the way, which is why I was drawn to it. Duane was heading there, but he never had a chance to fulfill his destiny; he only played slide for about three years! He had everything that the earlier guys, the blues masters, had, and then he took it somewhere else. I want to see where slide guitar can go, and it's a great vehicle for expression, because of the way it can mimic the human voice, wavering on one note and playing melodies on one string. My voice really doesn't work, so I use my guitar instead.

WEST: Derek was special to both Dickey and Gregg from the start. He wasn't just another guitarist; they saw Duane in him.

ALLMAN: Where does Derek come from? I don't know, man, but if you believe in reincarnation . . . I mean, sometimes I look over there [at Derek] and see my brother and . . . well, I can't explain it, but I enjoy it.

JOHN HAMMOND JR.: People sometimes talk about Duane being reincarnated in Derek and there's something to that. Derek is phenomenal and he has that same sort of easygoing yet very intense style.

Lay Your Burden Down

*O*N *JANUARY 8, 2000, Joe Dan Petty, an Allman Brothers road crew member since 1970 and one of Dickey Betts's oldest and dearest friends, died in a private plane crash. Petty was remembered with a memorial service at Macon's Grand Opera House, featuring a stirring performance by the Allman Brothers Band, joined by Haynes for the first time in three years and Leavell, who had not played with the group in over a decade.*

HAYNES: Woody and I both loved Joe Dan, who was a wonderful, sweet guy. It took someone like that to bring together some people who had not even spoken in many years. It was an emotional and special day.

WEST: After the memorial concert, everyone came back to the Big House, which was my home then, and it was very meaningful to everyone to all be together there. I remember looking out and seeing Dickey, Butch, Chuck, Bonnie Bramlett, and Leroy Parnell sitting together on the sunporch, gathered around a table and talking for hours. Everyone was so sad about Joe Dan but so happy to be together, especially in the Big House.

A few days later, while he was still in Macon comforting Petty's widow, Judi, Betts learned that his spiritual mentor, the Navajo medicine man Stewart Etsitty, had also passed away. Betts was still heavily grieving both losses when the band arrived at the Beacon for thirteen March shows.

WEST: Joe Dan and Dickey were close friends since they were kids and the comfort zone that Joe Dan created for him onstage was gigantic. He also had his way of making a point with Dickey that other people who just tuned and handed him a guitar did not have and could not have. Losing Joe Dan hit him hard and losing Stewart so soon after knocked him off balance.

The Beacon performances were shaky, as can be heard on the CD Peakin' at the Beacon, *a curious release that captured what was probably the band's worst run ever at the theater. Things degenerated considerably in a month, however, and an eight-show spring tour of the Southeast that started on April 28 at the New Orleans Jazz and Heritage Festival was erratic and tension-filled.*

WEST: The spring tour was a fiasco from the first night and it just got ridiculous and it was consistently bad. It was a horrible situation. Red Dog was getting ready to quit. He was going around telling everybody good-bye in Nashville. We went from there to Memphis to Atlanta. Those shows were embarrassing to the legacy of the Allman Brothers. There was so much anger coming from everybody.

BURBRIDGE: I had never worked in a situation where it was impossible to even get through a whole song without it going completely off the tracks. The crowds still cheered. I was bewildered. Rock and roll, celebrity, all that was new to me. It seemed like a surreal movie.

WEST: The last show of the run was at a festival in Atlanta, so it was a big, cheering crowd; "Yay, the Allman Brothers!" But I thought, "This band's breaking up right here." I felt like I was standing on the side of the stage of the last show of the Allman Brothers Band.

BURBRIDGE: It had probably been that bad in the past, maybe worse at times, but when it's the umpteenth time and you can see it coming a mile away because you've lived through the cycle so many times before, then it's harder to swallow.

BUTCH TRUCKS: It wasn't that the gigs were that bad. It's that he was starting to go down that slope again and I wasn't going with him this time.

WEST: It was still light when we finished and I watched Butch and Dickey walk off the stage ten feet apart and the anger and hostility between them was so strong that you could feel it. I was certain it was the end of this thing, and it was all within spitting distance of Piedmont Park, where they had really begun.

BUTCH TRUCKS: When I walked off that stage, I looked at my wife and said, "That's the last time I'm gonna play with that motherfucker," and I meant exactly what I said. I figured that's the end of the Allman Brothers Band.

DEREK TRUCKS: The year I was in the band with Dickey there was obviously a lot of other stuff going on, a lot of internal tensions that had nothing to do with my arrival and that I tried to steer clear of. There was never weirdness in my own relationship with Dickey. He was always very good to me, dating back to when I was ten years old and sitting in with the band.

When they all returned home, Allman, Trucks, and Jaimoe sent a letter to Betts, the fourth partner in the Allman Brothers Band, informing him that they were going to tour without him that summer.

ALLMAN: I just knew that either I was leaving or he was leaving. Honestly, my first thought was I was leaving. I was getting ready to walk because I could not stand the situation anymore. I even wrote a letter of resignation.

BUTCH TRUCKS: I came close to quitting several times. The bottom line is, as bad as Dickey was fucking up and as difficult as some of the situations were, we were still making a lot of money. Had that been the case in 1982 we probably would have kept going then, too. We all needed the income, sad to say. We try to be as aesthetic as we can be and as true to our roots as we can be, but we've got to feed our families. Now it just reached a point where something had to give. And I was ready to quit before I spoke with Gregg.

ALLMAN: I spoke with Butchie and he was thinking the same thing, and we just realized that was crazy. He asked me, "Are you through? Have you done all you can with the Brothers? Have you had enough?"

I said, "To tell you the truth, no. I feel like he has spoiled something really good that belongs to all of us. He's destroying it." Butch said, "He doesn't have to destroy it. Why should we leave if he's in the wrong? Hell, let's get rid of him." And I said, "Let me sleep on that." The next morning, I said, "Please, just let me write the letter," and he wisely said, "Let's get together and do it." I was just really fed up. I had written this real stinger of a letter and I'm glad I didn't send it.

BUTCH TRUCKS: Both Gregg and I were ready to say, "That's it. Let's walk away." But Jaimoe said, "I'm not going to do that. I'll agree that he has to get help. I'll say we will tour without him this summer but the only way to leave the Allman Brothers Band is to die or quit; you can't get fired." We wrote Dickey a letter and said we would not tour with him that summer, but dates were already booked and we were going to honor them with someone else and we hoped he would get some help.

JAIMOE: I said you can't get fired and I meant it. I thought Dickey would take some time to clean up or whatever and come back to the band after we played some shows without him. He'd done that before and come back basically fine until the cycle started up again.

ALLMAN: We did not fire Dickey. We laid him off for the summer tour. We made this decision for a simple reason: the music was suffering. It had ceased to be a band—everything had to be based around what Dickey was playing.

BUTCH TRUCKS: Dickey's volume was so high that no one on stage could hear anything else. There was nothing to do but react to Dickey's playing, or have a train wreck.

HOLMAN: Everyone was out of sorts at the end of that tour, and the stage volume and how that impacted everything was a major sore spot. The other guys felt that Dickey was so loud that [they] had to follow what he did. I spoke to Dickey and said, "There are real issues with the volume on stage. They want you to use fifty-watt Marshalls." And he said, "I'll talk to Gregg. Don't worry about it."

BETTS: I called Gregg and he said, "I don't owe you an explanation. Listen to the fucking tapes [of the spring tour]," and hung up. A lot of things have been said about our relationship over the years, but we were actually the closest guys in the band.

TRUCKS: He responded by hiring a lawyer and suing us and then we sat there in arbitration for weeks and after all the stuff that was said, there's no way we can work together again. Once he filed against us, I spoke to Jaimoe, who said, "Well, I guess he quit."

JAIMOE: In reality, Dickey quit the band.

ALLMAN: I don't see playing with Dickey again unless something really major happened . . . No, I just don't. No.

HOLMAN: Dickey had the potential to come back. If he had come to a self-realization and stopped drinking, I really think that Gregg and Jaimoe would have done it. Instead, he filed arbitration. We had a meeting with a facilitator, which had the potential to be the start of reconciliation, but Dickey made a statement and then walked out. The band wanted it to be the five of us having a meeting, but he came with two lawyers so the band had to bring lawyers to protect themselves.

When that didn't turn out to be constructive, we were on a different path. It's like going to couples therapy. You either put your marriage back together or it enables you to get divorced, which is what happened. The other three guys said, "You know what, this is not going in a positive direction." Then the band entered into a very, very lengthy arbitration.

ALLMAN: After so many years of drinking and abusing drugs, I finally cleaned up and I didn't want to waste one minute of time for the rest of my life. God, I had wasted enough time! I was finally sober. That monkey was off my back. I even quit cigarettes and I quit it all at once. I realized I was on death's doorstep and I was thankful to God that I had woken up before all the innings of the game were over. And I wasn't gonna put up with nothing—not another minute of bullying or negativity mixed with music. I'd quit music first and I don't think I'm ever gonna quit music.

BETTS: I knew that there was tension that had to snap but I had no idea that it was all on me. I thought I was doing pretty good. I thought something would snap that I would have to take care of, like I had so many times before. I had no idea that I would be snapped out of the picture. I thought it was cruel and impersonal.

ALLMAN: Having a band is like having a relationship with a woman. If you've ever been in a real bad relationship, you know how little by little you learn to live with somebody who's absolutely dragging you down and your whole environment is kind of twisted and you don't even realize it until it's stopped. It's definitely hard to maintain a band for so many years for many, many reasons. It's a give-and-take thing, so similar to a marriage or relationship. It has to maintain a balance or everyone suffers.

BETTS: I'm just real disappointed in the way this all went down, but I'm not going to bad-mouth anybody in print. No matter how nasty those guys can get, I won't do that to them. But I think the band broke up in 2000 and I think it's just been a copy band ever since. If you enjoy going to see Derek and Warren play my and Duane's stuff, that's fine. You don't have to feel guilty . . . I'm trying to be a gentleman, but all I can say is they still play my songs, but if you come hear my band, you will not hear "Melissa."

ALLMAN: I don't think anything could have kept us all together at that point. There comes a place where there's just a line and we were already way past crossing that line.

HOLMAN: They didn't really ask me. I caught wind of what was going on and I couldn't stop it. They had made up their minds. They had had enough. The train was off the tracks.

PODELL: They didn't consult me, maybe because they knew I would have tried to talk them out of it. After the whole thing went down, I went and visited Dickey because I'm not a fair-weather friend. I thought the whole thing was a mistake and wished I had had a chance to try to help them work through it.

BURBRIDGE: I wasn't surprised at all when I heard what the partners were doing. The band was going to break up.

Manager Bert Holman (center) with Dickey Betts and Gregg Allman.

ALLMAN: You can say, "Look who's talking about drinking problems," and that's fair. I had the alcoholism real bad, but at least I showed up for gigs and I didn't take my problems on stage with me and torment everyone else with them. Somehow I kept eking it out.

BUTCH TRUCKS: Yes, Gregg struggled with alcohol for years, but when he had problems, he tended to get real quiet and almost shrink away. When Dickey drank, he got louder and more difficult to deal with . . . just very mean.

HOLMAN: Dickey felt he had more power and say because in his mind he had held the whole band together and had stepped up when no else could or did. The problem is, to be a leader you have to lead by attraction, and Dickey was leading by intimidation. His implication was "If you don't do this, I'll quit, and are you gonna let him lead it? You gonna play with this drunk?"

The reality is none of them are good leaders. Dickey was the best of the bunch, but his personal issues got to be too much and undermined his ability to lead. He's a very charismatic, committed, passionate guy, but he's not willing to embrace what other people have to say. He'd bully them into doing things his own way rather than making everyone feel a part of it, which is what I think Duane did.

JAIMOE: When Butch and Gregg told me what they were thinking, I was surprised and then I wasn't at all, because Dickey has always been unpredictable and difficult since day one. We'd be playing somewhere or rehearsing and he didn't feel right or didn't like what he was playing and he'd pack up his guitar and just go walking, or sit and listen to the band, and Duane would say, "What's the matter, hoss? Why you not feeling good?" Duane could deal with him, but for so many years without him . . .

PAYNE: From the very beginning, Dickey could get very introverted and not even speak to anybody for days. He was very moody. He could be a wonderful, sensitive guy or he could be brooding and silent—or angry and scary.

JAIMOE: When Duane was there, it was one thing, but without him it was something else.

PERKINS: I never saw a mean streak in Dickey until Duane was gone. Around the time of *Brothers and Sisters* he started to be hard to handle and have a tempestuous relationship with Gregg.

HOLMAN: Duane had charisma and vision and he didn't put people in conflict. He made decisions that were popular. They all emotionally agreed with what he wanted to do. We try to make decisions in the Allman Brothers that are unanimous and not have situations where you have to say, "You were outvoted." They try to do things by consensus and if someone feels really strongly, they can often turn the consensus around.

BETTS: It was a real family for so long and we took care of brother Gregg, we took care of brother Butch. And, yeah, they took care of me. We always tried to avoid a competition thing. If one guy was down, the rest of the guys didn't try to run him into the stage; they tried to carry him. We'd look at each other and say, "I'm flying with one wing tonight," and carry each other in those situations. That's the way this band always tried to be. Unfortunately, at certain times drinking and drugs and crooked managers and thievery and other things have caused us to lose sight of that. But that was our essential thing. And I think it kept us playing the way we did for so long.

Then after thirty years with our two big brothers gone, it finally flew apart, and it's kind of OK. You see, what's so complicated about the band is we had three bandleaders, three visionaries: Duane Allman, Berry Oakley, and me. And we had a very gifted singer/songwriter who didn't quite see the whole picture: Gregg. The fact that the band carried on for another twenty-five years after Duane's and Berry's deaths is amazing. It's sad that I happened to be in the position of being the one that it came down on, but I think they had to execute somebody to carry on.

PODELL: At one point I told the whole band, "You know, your income is very possibly going to be reduced by 25 percent or more." No one argued with me, but Gregg said, "I don't care. Every day, when it's time to go to the gig, I get agita. I get tense. It's no longer fun. If you're telling me I have to make less, so be it. I'll vote for serenity." That was a very valuable lesson for me. And Gregg coming up with that? Out of the mouths of babes . . .

BURBRIDGE: Quality of life is important. Time is as important as money at a certain point in your life. Maybe more important. The partners didn't want to spend any more of their time in preventable turmoil and disability.

ALLMAN: The Brothers can be so lead-weight, so draining. Bands have their psychodramas, and for all those years we had four people trying to drive one truck, and it could get really fucking frustrating. But it's something inside me. It's just part of my skin, part of my metabolism. It's part of my nervous system, and I dearly love it. It's like, I can't be me without you.

CHAPTER

Walk On Gilded Splinters

*G*UITARIST *JIMMY HERRING joined the band for the 37-date 2000 summer tour, which kicked off on June 16 in Virginia Beach and continued through September. Herring had played with Burbridge in the Aquarium Rescue Unit and is close friends with Derek Trucks. It was jarring to see the Allman Brothers Band with the three young friends on the front line—and without Betts, who had for so long been the center-stage focus. The music, however, was strong from the start.*

HOLMAN: It was a risk and an unknown. We realized pretty quickly we would be OK musically, but it was a challenge keeping it together on a business level. There were questions about the viability, and certainly some big Dickey fans who were very vocal about it.

QUIÑONES: A lot of the press was really negative and a lot of fans were saying they wouldn't come out because the Allman Brothers are not the Allman Brothers without Dickey Betts. I really did not know what would happen.

Jimmy Herring.

HOLMAN: Derek was still very young and didn't have the maturity to take a leadership role.

DEREK TRUCKS: When I first heard what they were doing, I thought, "Here's this Rock and Roll Hall of Fame band, one of the legendary rock institutions, and I am the only guitarist in the band." I was like, "You guys have an inflated sense of confidence that I can do this, but let's go!"

PODELL: For me, it was like when Duane died—I just really did not know if it was going to work. I had some real doubts, but I work for the band and do my best. Just like thirty years before, I put everything I knew into play, positioned it, and hoped for the best. And then I prayed.

DEREK TRUCKS: When Jimmy's name came up, I knew it would be musically great, but does that make it the Allman Brothers? Even I didn't know.

JIMMY HERRING, *guitarist, 2000 summer tour:* It was a great honor to even get the call. The Allman Brothers were the reason I started playing guitar. I got on a plane and listened to Allman Brothers songs all the way there. Just because you've played all those songs doesn't mean you really know them. I took the obligation to do them right very seriously.

BUTCH TRUCKS: Jimmy Herring really was great, but he was never comfortable being known as "the guy who replaced Dickey Betts."

HERRING: It was bittersweet and bizarre. I was really excited to be a part of that great band and to play with Derek, who is one of my best friends and favorite players. But this wonderful opportunity happened at someone else's expense and I don't want to benefit from someone else's demise, especially someone I revere as much as Dickey. I stepped into Dickey's place and I'm a huge Dickey fan. I felt real strange about being there without him. It was such a mix of emotions. You can feel the history and it makes you want to do your best. Gregg is an icon—my idea of the perfect rock star—and then you have the incredible rhythm section. It's a machine that is just a pleasure to play with.

ALLMAN: Man, Jimmy Herring is a great player and he got us through that summer beautifully.

HERRING: Being up there with my friends Derek and Oteil balanced out my star-struck feelings about playing with Gregg. The amazing thing is he never told me what to play. He actually said, "I don't want you to be hung up playing what you think the Allman Brothers is. Just play what your heart tells you."

WEST: We anticipated it being musically spectacular, but we all knew there could be some issues. For one thing, Jimmy doesn't sing and Gregg had never not had another singer in the band. He's not going to sing every song, so it had to be a much more instrumental show, and you just knew those boys wouldn't be able to help themselves, that they'd get out there in a hurry.

BURBRIDGE: It was totally impossible to contain our "out" impulses. Hey, you are who you are. It got us in trouble with Gregg once.

DEREK TRUCKS: We would take it off the rails from time to time. One night we just couldn't help ourselves and we took "Mountain Jam" to Mars, which is what Red Dog was always urging us to do. He'd say, "The original band took the song out! It was different every night. You can't play the record." But after the show, we get on the bus, Gregg walks on and goes, "OK, who's the fucking Phish fan? That was too much." And he goes to the back of the bus with all of us looking at each other a bit stunned. After about ten minutes, he came back up and apologized. He said, "I used to go 'round and 'round with my brother on that same stuff. You play whatever you want. You guys are a part of this."

BURBRIDGE: Gregg said, "It's your band, too. You guys do your thing." He confessed that Duane used to love to go out like that, too.

DEREK TRUCKS: My take on this was Duane from thirty-five years ago whipped his ass again. He did not have to apologize to us, that's for sure.

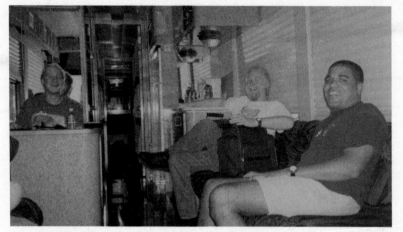

"The Allman Rescue Unit," 2000: Derek Trucks, Jimmy Herring,
Oteil Burbridge, on the bus.

BURBRIDGE: Duane loved Col. Bruce Hampton, who was my and
Jimmy's professor of out. Duane was responsible for the Hampton
Grease Band getting a record deal with Phil Walden, who then sold it
to Clive Davis at Columbia Records, supposedly for $300,000! Funny
how things come to pass over a long period of time.

BUTCH TRUCKS: We knew Jimmy was not entirely comfortable so
no one was surprised when he told us he was moving on.

HOLMAN: I think Jimmy felt very emotionally guilty about replacing
someone who was very much alive. He was hoping that Dickey would
get it together and come back.

*After months of testimony, Dickey Betts received a cash award, the details of
which are subject to a confidentiality agreement. The arbitrator also ruled that
the band could continue to perform without Betts, who remained a partner/
shareholder in the Allman Brothers Band merchandising and existing recording
partnership, which was never really in dispute.*

Now out of the Allman Brothers Band, the guitarist soldiered on. Within a year, he had released Let's Get Together, *an album of new material with a new band. It included several songs the Allman Brothers had played live over the previous few years, including the instrumentals "Rave On" and "One Stop BeBop." The Allman Brothers had not released a studio album in seven years.*

BETTS: I'm not mad at anyone and I'm not carrying any kind of grudge. I'm not happy with what happened or the way things went down, but I'm also not bitter because I'm moving on. I'm just going with the changes that happened beyond my control and some great things have come about as a result. I have seven new original compositions on this album. A few are tunes we were working on with the Allman Brothers but were never completed or recorded for one reason or another, in some cases because no one else really showed any enthusiasm to work them up. But I wrote four in the three months before recording. I really got energized and came up with some great new material.

While we don't like things to change, they do anyway. We want things to stay more or less how they are and that's not the natural way of the world. You just have to be grateful for having thirty years with a band that accomplished all the things the Allman Brothers did and now it's over and it's time to change. I didn't change it myself, but I'm just going with what is naturally happening.

I briefly considered just retiring when this thing with the Brothers came about, but I'm not ready for it. I have too much music left. I've got a lot more to say before I put my guitar down. The Allman Brothers operation was so well oiled that there wasn't much you had to worry about; I just showed up for the gigs. That's good in some ways but it has its downside. You get a little cushy and tend to be less creative than you are when you really have to do it yourself. I had to build something new from the ground up. Special things happen when you find yourself needing a knockout punch in the fifteenth round. That's when you have to dig down deep and see what you've got. That's when you can surprise yourself.

CHAPTER

One More Ride

HE ALLMAN BROTHERS Band had performed twenty-seven shows with Herring on August 26, 2000, when Allen Woody, who had been struggling with substance abuse problems and was scheduled to enter rehab in a few weeks, died in his sleep in a New York hotel room.

Though he had been out of the band for over three years, it felt like an exclamation point on the fact that an era of the Allman Brothers was over. Betts was home, Woody was dead, and no one knew what would happen next.

Haynes was grieving his best friend and musical collaborator, unsure of what his next move would be. Scheduled to fly to California to rehearse for ten days with Phil Lesh for an upcoming tour at the time of Woody's death, Haynes contemplated backing out.

"Phil was one of the first people to call me after Woody's death," Haynes says. "He said, 'I know what it means to lose someone whose musical connection is too profound for anyone else to ever understand.' Unfortunately, a lot of people in this business understand that. I knew I had to get out there and play music.

"I flew to rehearsal right from Woody's funeral and I didn't know if I would be able to rise to the occasion. But for the first time since Allen died, I was able *to momentarily forget some of the negative feelings, which is a huge part of the healing process."*

Allen Woody, 1955–2000.

While rehearsing with Lesh, Haynes began lining up a tribute for his late friend to benefit Woody's daughter, Savannah. "One for Woody" took place just over a month after the bassist's death at New York's Roseland Ballroom and featured the Allman Brothers Band and the Black Crowes and a final set featuring Gov't Mule's surviving core of Haynes and Abts joined by an endless stream of guests, including Phil Lesh, the blues great Little Milton, Widespread Panic's Dave Schools, and Mountain's Leslie West. Haynes was on stage for over six hours.

With Derek Trucks unavailable, Haynes and Herring played with the Allman Brothers Band; it was just the fourth time Haynes had appeared with the band since leaving three years earlier. When Herring accepted an offer to tour the next year with Lesh, the Allman Brothers Band again had just one guitarist. Haynes agreed to return for their annual March run at New York's Beacon Theatre, billed as a special guest, along with Chuck Leavell.

HAYNES: No one knew what I was going to do, including me. I had some concerns about coming back to the Allmans but Gregg's phone call asking me to play at the Beacon was a saving grace. I needed to stop wallowing in my misery over Woody's death and plunge into something. It's human nature to want to wallow in the mire of your own depression, so you have to pull yourself out of it.

At the time, I'd sometimes be feeling fine and suddenly a darkness would descend upon me. I was regularly having dreams where Woody came to me and was not dead. He was very much alive and it felt more real than any dream you've ever had. I told Gregg about that, and without missing a beat, he said, "Those will never go away."

BUTCH TRUCKS: Warren was the guy we needed. I'm not sure we would have continued at all if Warren hadn't taken the job. I simply can't imagine who else could have done this gig.

HAYNES: I agreed to play some shows and see if the vibe and the music were good.

QUIÑONES: The band needed Warren and Warren needed the band. He was mentally and emotionally in limbo after Woody's death and didn't know what was going to happen. He had needed a break from the Allman Brothers, and it was four years and now he needed a breath of fresh air from the Mule.

HAYNES: It was my first time with the band in four years and it was very comfortable. I took on a different role than people were used to seeing me with the Allman Brothers, playing with Derek instead of Dickey. It was very strange to play in the Allman Brothers without Dickey and I knew it would be. Dickey's sound is a big part of what we all grew up loving, so it is definitely strange for it to be absent.

I wouldn't have done the shows if I thought I was holding up him playing in the band, but I spoke to Dickey and also the other guys about the situation, and it was pretty obvious that no one wanted to resolve it. That being the case, I just did the best I could.

Haynes's return was a success in the eyes of all concerned: himself, the rest of the band, and the fans who filled the theater. When the Allman Brothers Band kicked off their summer tour on June 15, 2001, in Alabama, Haynes was on stage, no longer a "special guest," once again a key member, helping to revive an American institution for the second time.

Warren Haynes: Has guitar, will travel.

DEREK TRUCKS: It took Warren getting back into the fold for it to make sense again without Dickey. He had logged so much time with

Gregg and Dickey that he had total legitimacy and, of course, knew and understood the music from the inside as well as anyone.

QUIÑONES: After Warren left, we went through all these guitarists and none of them were Warren Haynes. He brings things to the table that no one else does, including his singing and his overall understanding of the band and ability to pull it all together. It was so great to have him back.

ALLMAN: It was such a kick to play with Warren again. I love his guitar playing and it's also great for me to have a second lead singer—and he's great to sing harmony with, either part, lead or harmony. He phrases quite a bit like me, so it's just really a pleasure.

DEREK TRUCKS: Warren and I playing together without Dickey is an entirely different beast. First of all, because we were both playing the same role—the "Duane" role opposite Dickey—for so long, we both had to relearn the Allman Brothers catalogue so that we could switch parts with each performance. I had never played the nonslide parts to songs like "Statesboro Blues" and "Done Somebody Wrong," and learning the catalogue both ways has deepened my understanding of everything. And the fact that no one is playing Dickey's role means we both have to establish our own voices to a greater extent.

HAYNES: It's a little strange because when I left the band, Jack Pearson and then Derek inherited the parts that I used to play, whether they were Duane's parts from the old days or my parts from the latter-day records. Derek and I played the same parts, so one of us was going to have to learn the other parts—Dickey's parts. To be fair, we decided to split it up. And since Derek and I are both slide players, we decided the best thing to do would be to split the slide duties up as well, even to the point where one night I played slide on a given song and the next night Derek did. We did that a lot at those first shows, and it was a good thing. It was a lot of fun and it allowed us to take a different approach every night, which allowed things to be more open-ended.

Instead of it being automatic, I really had to think about what to play. That is challenging, but it's always good to keep yourself fresh.

DEREK TRUCKS: Before, we were both tipping our hats to Duane and then putting our own thing on top of that. Now we just have to play ourselves while keeping in mind that it's the Allman Brothers Band. When you know music so well and have lived with it and listened to it as much as Warren and I have, you can re-create the feel without playing the same notes.

Derek Trucks playing with Warren Haynes.

HAYNES: The band has certainly undergone a strange transformation. This particular unit plays great together and probably listens more intently than any band I've ever been in, which makes it easy to go someplace different every night. And that is the goal: to take this venerable institution someplace new without ever losing touch with the four-decade tradition that makes the Allman Brothers Band something really special.

DEREK TRUCKS: It's just an underlying respect for the history and legacy of the band, which Warren and I share. You want to make music that can stand on its own, and you want to be able to listen to it in twenty years and be proud. It's a big obligation to make music as the Allman Brothers and both of us want to make sure that the name is back in a very positive way. You don't want to be the guy who let it slip! And there's a responsibility to being in the group in bigger ways, as well. You don't want to be the guy who played a part in ending this great institution.

JAIMOE: It's funny to hear people say, "Listen to what Derek is playing compared to what Warren is playing." Same way I've always felt about people comparing me and Butch. It's about the big picture, the whole picture. Can Derek play all of that and also direct a band? No. I don't count songs off. That don't mean I'm not playing. Everyone has his role and that's what makes a band.

PEARSON: Jaimoe is one of my all-time favorite drummers. I can tell his playing in three notes. He always sounds like him no matter what drums he plays.

Jaimoe loosening up.

ALLMAN: Warren is a master. As great as he is, he serves the song, and he has a knack for pulling everyone together because he is about the group, which is not always the case with lead guitarists. He doesn't put a fill in every phrase, or play just to hear himself; everything he does says something and has a purpose.

HAYNES: The direction of your solo changes as soon as someone plays something different than expected. If Oteil or Jaimoe play a riff or Derek plays a rhythm figure in a hole I left, then my response changes the direction I was previously headed. To open yourself to the music reaching its full potential you cannot have a predetermined solo that you play regardless of what anybody else does.

DEREK TRUCKS: It's the nature of improvising. For me, it's different with this lineup because there is a whole new level of comfort among the three guys up front. With Dickey in the band, it was follow the leader. Now it really is three guys tossing ideas back and forth.

HAYNES: The example I always use is the Miles Davis Quintet with Wayne Shorter, Herbie Hancock, Tony Williams, and Ron Carter. No matter who's soloing, as soon as they take a breath, someone plays something really cool in the hole and that changes everything. The next thing that came from the soloist would be based upon what that person played in the pause. It wouldn't be preconceived; it would be responding. We're trying to open ourselves in the same way, knowing it may be a little less Allman Brothers–ish at times. But that's cool, because we're here to grow.

DEREK TRUCKS: A lot of time that leads to it being more of a band solo than a soloist front because everyone is both following the stream and directing it.

HAYNES: And that's the best it can be. A great band solo is better than a great individual solo.

LEAVELL: So often in bands everyone is focused on playing their parts. In the Allman Brothers, everyone has always been listening to each other and focused on the big picture. I think that listening is one of the really powerful things about the Allman Brothers. Whether it's a drum roll, a guitar lick, or a phrase that Gregg sings, everyone is looking to complement one another and make the whole better and bigger. It's a very different approach than worrying about your own part and playing it properly.

JAIMOE: This band is the greatest one since Duane and Berry, and why shouldn't it be? Everyone knows the tradition and everyone has his own personality—which is the only thing that makes any music different from any other.

Duane would come up with stuff in his head and just start playing spontaneously on the bandstand, which was one of the great things

The Allman Brothers Band frontline since 2001: Warren Haynes, Derek Trucks, and Oteil Burbridge, during 2007 Beacon rehearsals.

that the Allman Brothers were built on. At a recent gig, Warren went right into a new song in the middle of a solo and man it was beautiful. I was so happy. After the gig, I told Warren, "You see what you just did out there? That's what the band was built on. If you heard something in your head, you played it! And it built from there." That's the only sort of thing that can save this band from not just going out and playing gigs but playing with some sort of meaning. It's ideas that Derek or Warren or Oteil come up with.

HAYNES: You spend your whole life trying to become proficient on your instrument, then you get back to chasing that childlike wonderment you had before you even knew what you were doing. For a lot of my life, it was all about trying to have the ability to play what was in your head. Now it's sometimes more about "Do I want to play that or do I want to play something different?" Or do I want to pause and listen to what someone else is playing and let that push me into a new direction?

Hands down: Gregg and his keyboard.

YOUNGER BROTHER

Derek Trucks has grown up in public and on stage.

It's easy to imagine that Derek Trucks was born with supernatural guitar powers. He was touring when he was ten, recording with blues great Junior Wells at fourteen, sitting in with Bob Dylan and Buddy Guy by fifteen and a full-fledged member of the Allman Brothers at nineteen. His uncle Butch was a founding member of the ABB, and Gregg Allman is among those who have wondered if Duane Allman was reincarnated as Derek—who was named after Derek and the Dominos.

Susan Tedeschi and Derek Trucks

But all of that overlooks the commitment to perfecting his craft that Trucks has always shown, his thirst for musical knowledge and eagerness to listen to and adapt a wide range of influences, from Delta blues to Indian classical music.

"You've got to log the hours to master the instrument," Trucks says. "You've got to put the time and energy in no matter how good you are. To make something have any worth, there has to be some sacrifice."

Though his parents, Chris and Debbie, named their sons Derek and Duane after their favorite guitarists, Derek insists that nothing was ever forced on them.

"This music was always around my house and I knew that my uncle played in the Allman Brothers and it was somewhat sacred but no one made a huge deal out of it," he says. "I heard a lot of somewhat mythical stories, but it was the music that really drew me in; nothing else struck me the same way. I got into listening to and playing Duane's stuff before I was ever around the band."

An early teacher suggested that Derek learn to play slide first, a highly unusual approach. He never adapted his unorthodox style, still always playing tuned to open E and never using a pick, instead favoring a unique, self-taught right-hand technique that is difficult to describe and even harder to imitate.

Trucks started playing at eight and began performing the next year, at first billed as Derek and the Dominators and backed by older, barroom veterans. He moved remarkably quickly through the trained-monkey phase so common in kid performers, sitting in with the Allman Brothers Band for the first time at eleven. He was a little kid with a Braves hat dwarfed by his red Gibson SG and wowing hard-core fans with his quivering Duane licks. Trucks quickly added other, far-reaching influences, notably "sacred steel" gospel music, deep Delta blues, and Indian classical music, which can be heard in his masterly microtonal playing that can make each note sound like an entire universe.

"One of the things I love about playing slide is you can hold a note and very subtly bend it. There are very few instruments where you can do that," says Trucks. "When you stay on one string, you can really emulate a human voice."

Trucks was nineteen when Uncle Butch called and asked if the nephew was ready to become a Brother.

"It sounds strange to people, but I never imagined myself in the band," Trucks says. "Getting the call was crazy and overwhelming and exciting. From the start I took being a part of that band very seriously."

Six years later, Eric Clapton called and asked Trucks to "do some recording."

"That was just like the Allman Brothers call but it was a level crazier, because there was no family connection," says Trucks. "It was just a musical connection. I've been fortunate enough to have that experience with several of my heroes. You put it out there and play this music and you get a call from Herbie Hancock or B.B. King or Junior Wells asking you to play. It's very humbling. Eric calling out of the blue was a pinch-myself moment."

Trucks appeared on Clapton and J. J. Cale's 2006 recording *The Road to Escondido*, then joined the guitarist's band for a yearlong world tour.

"My whole family came to London for the Royal Albert Hall shows and Eric invited all of us out to his country estate," Trucks says. "Watching my dad, the roofer from Jacksonville—the guy who named his son after Derek and the Dominos—sip tea with Eric, I was astounded. I was thinking, 'This is one crazy life we're leading . . .'"

In 2009, Trucks broke up his long-standing solo band and formed a new group, the Tedeschi Trucks Band, with his wife, singer Susan Tedeschi. They are seeking to craft a new path forward, not just musically but personally, struggling with a rock and roll variation of finding work/family balance.

"Guys like Duane Allman and Jimi Hendrix provided a great template for how to be musically successful but not necessarily personally successful," says Trucks, who has two children. "They sadly died young and did not get to incorporate their great music into a full adult life. I want to make great music and also have a strong marriage and family."

Before joining the Allman Brothers Band, Trucks was exploring more Indian and jazz music and went through an extended phase of listening primarily to horn and harmonica players, avoiding guitarists and rock and roll. Then he became a core member of one of rock's most storied bands, and toured the world with another rock icon. The experiences have altered his vision of music and what it can and should accomplish.

"I think playing in the Allman Brothers has probably kept my own music grounded and prevented me from taking a hard left," Trucks says. "I want to make music that's challenging but also the kind that I sit back and listen to. I don't want it to just be for musicians. I don't want to look up at a show and only see guitar nerds with notebooks out there. It's nice when you see all of humanity. I'd like to see the occasional woman.

"I'm all about going on a musical trip and taking it as deep as you can take it. Music is supposed to become a part of your life in a major way. The Allman Brothers have done that and are fully ingrained into many American lives. At the end of the day, that's the highest compliment. That's the goal."

DEREK TRUCKS: Playing with Oteil is just awesome and amazing because he is so rare: an incredibly technical player who puts the groove first and never, ever loses that focus because it's so deep in his soul. He can do Michael-Jordan-of-the-bass moves without leaving the pocket. That can't help but inspire all of us to play differently. I can't even describe how much fun it is to play with him. If you don't enjoy listening to Oteil, you must be listening sideways.

HAYNES: Gregg is playing his organ more aggressively and singing great and it's an absolute pleasure to work with him like this. I'm really pleased about that. Also, the stage volume for the band has gone down and you can hear the organ and vocals better, which makes it even more apparent. A lot of what he used to do was drowned out.

PEARSON: Gregg plays some funky rhythm on that organ and I always thought it was a shame how low in the mix it often was and how overlooked his playing was by so many fans. I loved being on stage with that sound next to me.

ALLMAN: My voice has been real good to me, man, the way I punished it.

Hittin' the Note

*I*N *MARCH, 2003, the Allman Brothers released* Hittin' the Note, *their first album of new material in nine years and the only one to feature Haynes and Trucks together—and not to feature Betts, whose impact on the band could still be heard loud and clear.*

The ABB in Gregg's Georgia backyard, 2003.

HAYNES: It was really different to record an Allman Brothers album without Dickey, and playing in this band without him has led me to alter my style quite a bit. His playing is marked by a very clean tone and beautiful melodic sense, so I tended towards a nastier approach playing with him. The melodic thing and the clean-versus-dirty tone contrast both have to be there to sound like the Allman Brothers, so I've taken some of those things on myself. To go too far against the grain just wouldn't be right . . . which is why you hear those ascending lines on songs like "Firing Line" and "The High Cost of Low Living."

DEREK TRUCKS: "The Dickey lick."

HAYNES: If Gov't Mule was recording the song we probably wouldn't put that lick in there. It's there because it's an Allman Brothers riff, and you need things like that to keep the thread going from 1969 until now—though I must say that Gregg wanted it out. He said, "We've been doing that shit for thirty years. Can we take that lick out?"

DEREK TRUCKS: A lick like that is the band's sound. The rhythm section and Gregg's organ sound lend themselves to certain guitar lines and you play them almost without realizing it. When you're playing a tune, you think, "This is what the Allman Brothers would do." You just happen to be in them.

HAYNES: There are just simply different rules in the Allman Brothers Band. I remember one time during my first years with the band, we were working up the solo section of a new song and Gregg asked why there had to be a guitar solo. Dickey responded, "Because this is the Allman Brothers." And he was right. Most bands don't need a guitar solo in every song, but I don't think there's ever been an Allman Brothers song without one. Even "Midnight Rider" has that short, memorable solo.

DEREK TRUCKS: I was really happy that we got this new batch of material. It's impossible not to fall into ruts if you're playing the same stuff every night. Any time you add to the active catalogue it makes the tunes you've been playing over and over fresher, and we want every song to be different every night and to have the spark and excitement of improvising.

JAIMOE: Bringing in new songs is gonna trigger something, whether or not they are as intense as "Whipping Post." I always bug Warren and Gregory about this; when are they gonna write some new songs? It makes such a difference.

ALLMAN: The only thing about adding new songs is I get real self-conscious with the crowd. After all these years, I still get stage fright. I start sweating when I get out of the bath and it doesn't go away until I'm maybe halfway through the first verse of the first song. Then it's just over and gone, man. I think if I didn't have it, something would go fiercely wrong. It's a pretty ridiculous syndrome at this point, but I guess it's just meant to be.

I've just learned to accept it, and the only time it returns after the very beginning of a show is when we introduce a newer song. At times like that, you just roll your eyes back in your head and sing for the gods and the people just happen to be there. That's not an original line by the way. Some old blues guy told me that a long time ago. The truth is, the people give you the energy to deal with your doubts.

HAYNES: New material allows you to relax and it changes your perspective about the whole night. Bands that thrive on improvisation stagnate without realizing it if they get bogged down in the same material. Writing all of these songs and doing the record is the best thing that's happened to the band in a long time. That's also why I like to have us work up a bunch of "new" old tunes that haven't been done in a long time as well as blues and jazz covers.

"Rockin' Horse" started out as an Allman Brothers song, but it didn't make it onto *Where It All Begins* and then the band started splintering, so Woody and I decided to cut it on the Gov't Mule debut. I brought it back to the Allman Brothers, intentionally making it very different on *Hittin' the Note*. And the song keeps evolving live.

ALLMAN: I haven't found that many people I really enjoy writing with. It's real easy with Warren, a pleasure. He came down to my house and we worked on a bunch of these tunes together.

Warren Haynes and Gregg Allman, rehearsal at the Beacon, New York, 2009.

HAYNES: Our process varies greatly from song to song, but it's generally different than most people would expect. The most interesting process was "Old Before My Time." Gregg wrote most of the music on acoustic guitar; he is a really cool fingerpicker. I sat there listening and going, "That's great, but try going to a C." We ended up with this nice piece of music and I had a lot of good lyrics, but no real theme or starting point. Gregg went to bed that night and I sat there with my notebook trying to put the words together. I sat at his piano—I'm a terrible

piano player but I like to mess around—and something he had written at breakfast was sitting there: "There is a long, hard road that follows far behind me and it's so cold I'm about to die. Chasing a dream
around the world has made me old before my time." Wow. That inspired me to write the rest of the tune, pulling together all these un-
focused ideas.

Gregg co-wrote five of the tunes on *Hittin' the Note*, which is the
most he's written in a long time. I think he feels more confident right
now about where he is as a person, as a singer, as a writer, and as a musician. My relationship with Gregg has solidified more and more through
the years, partially because when you're friends that's what happens
and partially because he's in a much better place. When Gregg got
sober, it made the opportunity for personal relationships to flourish
much better.

ALLMAN: It was hard to feel comfortable as a singer for a long time. I
just started to realize that I had a voice that you can distinguish who it
was in the last ten years or less. I've always been real critical of my
voice. I started singing because my brother told me to; when we were
just starting, we needed a singer in our little band and it wasn't going
to be him. I would get so pumped up and nervous when we hit the stage
that I sang sharp, which sounds way worse than singing flat, and that
feeling of horror never totally left me. I finally learned to keep my heart
rate down and not get too excited. I sometimes close my eyes and pre-
tend I'm sitting under a big ol' magnolia tree singing to myself—
anything to just relax.

You have to be comfortable within your own skin and your own
singing. I have to go with the gut feeling, and for a long time that told
me I was nothing special. It's not that I thought I was a bad singer, but
I would hear some Ray Charles, some Otis Redding, some Little Milton. We all learn from someone and it's all fathers and sons—but I did
not hear an original style.

For decades, I could not listen back to anything we recorded, because I just heard flaws and mistakes. Recently, I've been going back and doing the YouTube thing and some of the live things are incredible. I can finally appreciate that a little.

PEARSON: Gregg is a great musician. He knows a lot more than what he carries on stage.

ALLMAN: People think I was born with my voice, that I just opened my mouth and it came out, but I went to great lengths to develop it. I devoted my whole life to it because I really, really wanted to learn how to sing. I think the only musical talent you can be blessed with or cursed without is the ability to carry a tune. You gotta work for everything else.

I listened and tried to learn. Ray Charles was the first one that just really blew my dress up. He is the first one that rung my bell, and he was a big, big influence, both on my singing and my playing, once I started to figure out keyboards.

HAYNES: Gregg is a minimalist, the ultimate example of trying to do the most with the least. One of the first things I learned from Gregg is a lyric has to be able to be sung properly. He's really taught me that it doesn't matter how a lyric looks on paper. He'll often say, "That don't sing right."

DEREK TRUCKS: He likes to breathe when he sings.

PEARSON: I learned a lot about singing from being with Gregg. The way Gregg breathes as he sings is incredible. I learned so much playing acoustic with him in a hotel room and having him sit on a bed two feet from me, singing. The first time it was just him and me, and hearing him sing like that was just remarkable.

HAYNES: And his phrasing, of course, is impeccable and all about finding out how beautiful you can make it and still have it be simple.

ALLMAN: Singing is just like guitar playing—the phrasing means as much as the sound of the licks or the tonal quality. The phrasing in your voice has to, in some way, really relate to the music, and I put a lot of work into that.

HAYNES: A lot of people will try to be tricky and clever, but Gregg is completely clued in to the truth that whether it's your instrument or your voice, the goal is to speak from your heart and clutter it up as little as possible. I'm still working on that.

DEREK TRUCKS: That belief is at the heart of the Allman Brothers' music, not just the singing. A lot of Duane's best solos are very simple ideas perfectly executed—just cut right to the chase and nail it.

HAYNES: That's why it's easier for me to play more simply and fit it in better in the Allman Brothers than anywhere else—because I am surrounded by people who have made an art form out of it. Whenever Gregg hears a guitarist overplaying, he says, "That cat sounds like he's getting paid by the note." You hear it about a hundred times and you start to think, "Less notes is better."

DEREK TRUCKS: Playing with three drummers and Oteil creates such a huge rhythm pocket that you can do anything you want in there. But at first I was just trying to stay on top of learning the tunes right and having the right feel and being respectful to the music. When you step into an institution that's been around for thirty years, you want to make sure you're not stepping on anyone's toes. Now that I really understand the parameters, I know when and how much I can break them.

BUTCH TRUCKS: I still have no idea what Derek is going to do. Every time he plays something it's a surprise and it's astounding what that says about his musical depth. He just blows me away. I've played with a lot of really great guitar players, and after a while you start to know what they're going to do; they get predictable. Derek is still not predictable.

Family Matters: Derek Trucks and Butch Trucks.

ALLMAN: I still really like to play acoustic guitar, though me and electric guitars have parted ways. It's like having a dragon on a leash. Those things scare me. You can't make up for talent and chops with volume, I will guarantee you that. I understand about tone and all that, and I understand that a really good guitar player adds a hell of a lot to a group. It's just that guitar players are so crazy, man.

The Road Goes on Forever

*I*N 2008, THE *band skipped their annual Beacon run as Gregg Allman underwent twenty-four weeks of Interferon treatment for hepatitis C. The band played their Wanee Festival in April without him, with a host of guests helping round out the "Wanee Family Band." Allman returned to the stage in August for an abbreviated summer tour.*

The following year, the band turned their fifteen Beacon appearances into a celebration of their fortieth anniversary. Every night except one—March 26, the actual anniversary of the band's first rehearsal—featured special guests, including Eric Clapton, Billy Gibbons, Scott Boyer, Levon Helm, Taj Mahal, Boz Scaggs, Buddy Guy, the Grateful Dead's Bob Weir and Phil Lesh, Phish's Trey Anastasio and Page McConnell, Jimmy Herring, Johnny Winter, and Sheryl Crow. Dickey Betts was invited to return for three songs one night and seriously considered the offer, but never actually responded. The run took the band's growing habit of welcoming special guests to the Beacon stage to its logical conclusion.

HAYNES: I think the tradition of having series of guests at the Beacon just happened organically. Since I lived in New York, I probably knew more people and that played a part in who came. In the beginning, there were only certain people that we felt comfortable bringing on stage and then the band grew more and more open to having other people join us. We've all been of the mind-set that there's a certain type of musician that can come up and add to rather than subtract from the Allman Brothers sound. There has to be a trust factor that things will elevate—or at least stay the same. Everyone would be very wary of making the wrong decision.

As that became easier to do and we began to have more and more people sit in, then of course the task became "If so and so is going to play, what is the song that they would add the most to?"

I enjoy the challenge of figuring out who's going to play what and I think I've gotten better at it through the years as that opportunity has been presented to me, and I think it's a way of presenting music that not only the audience might never see or hear again, but also creating music that goes to another dimension that it couldn't have gone to without that happening. All that takes place only if you have a stage full of open-minded musicians who have no qualms about going into uncharted territory. Gregg has become more and more open to having guests and I think I've earned his trust about who I might invite. At first I think it pushed him out of his comfort zone a little bit.

ALLMAN: We love the Beacon and have always had fun there, but that [2009 run] was the most fun I've ever had in that building. It was a combination of the great New York crowd and all the incredible guests. At first, part of me doubted that we would find enough worthy people to guest every night, but it was fantastic. We planned on just having people my brother played with, but it's been a while now and that list was getting thin, so we expanded it.

DOUCETTE: That whole thing was amazing, because it was exactly what Duane wanted. He and I talked years ago about how cool it would be to play an extended run in one place and have guests come join the band. That was premature, of course, because the band was just jumping off, but he just loved playing with people. If Duane was here, he would have absolutely eaten this up. He would have loved the idea of people like Eric Clapton and Billy Gibbons coming to play with his band. Unfortunately, Duane died just on the downstroke of the diving board, as the band was about to launch.

HAYNES: It was some of the most fun any of us have ever had playing music. The whole run felt surreal, and even stopping to think about it never burst the bubble and allowed the music to deflate, which can happen. There was something really incredible happening that had to do with the right combination of the audience and the band creating something that neither on its own can create. Plus, we had the incentive of what we were trying to do: pay homage to Duane and the fact that the band had survived so long and hopefully lived up to his initial vision. Everyone connected on that thought process and no one's ego interrupted it. Everyone stayed part of this tapestry and it was just incredible.

ALLMAN: The whole thing was one of the highlights of our career. Usually we're running out of steam by the end of the Beacon runs, which can be pretty grueling. This time, we were getting sad as the end approached. We wanted it to keep going.

BILLY GIBBONS, *ZZ Top guitarist:* One thing that struck me when I joined the Brothers at the Beacon was a need to commend Warren's skill as a bandleader. He holds down the front line as kind of the musical director, keeping a keen eye on arrangements and on maintaining a good balance. He's looked up to with respect by all of the Brothers. Warren is studious and serious about the music but he doesn't let that get in the way of having a good time.

HAMMOND: It was tremendously fun to be there and play with those guys and it made me pause and appreciate how amazing it is that they have held this thing together for so many years and come out the other side sounding this good. There were several times I thought the whole thing would fall apart, including when they let Dickey Betts go—I couldn't imagine the band without him, but there they are. Derek and Warren are so strong in their own ways that it just works. And being on stage with them as your backing band is just phenomenal.

BUDDY GUY, *blues guitarist*: Those guys were a lot of fun to play with. Gregg's one of them guys who've been keeping the blues alive and in the spotlight all along.

ALLMAN: I called Mr. Dixon "Willie." I met Muddy Waters and called him "Mr. Morganfield" and he said, "Call me Muddy." How much is that worth? It's an honor beyond anything. I am so grateful for that. I met Jimmy Reed, and the great Albert Collins played one of his last gigs ever with the Allman Brothers. That guy looked like he'd kill you in a minute but he was the sweetest man in the world. Buddy Guy and Junior Wells, Johnny and Edgar Winter, KoKo Taylor, Bo Diddley,

Gregg Allman and B. B. King at the Apollo Theater, Harlem, New York City.

Bobby Bland: I look up to every one of them and always will. And don't forget John Lee Hooker, who called me every birthday to say happy birthday and that he loves me. I loved that old man.

GUY: Nobody told me that they had three drummers, in addition to the two guitarists. I didn't even know what to do so I just sang and waited for my solo. Those guys were holding it down.

ALLMAN: The one guy who of course my brother had a real thing with and had never played with the Brothers was Clapton, and it was just real good to have him there. That was a long time coming and really fun and meaningful.

Derek Trucks, who spent a year touring the world with Clapton in 2006–07, facilitated the British guitarist's appearance.

DEREK TRUCKS: I had mentioned it to him a few times, but the band wrote a letter—it was really important that it come from them—and I just made sure it got delivered. It was a group effort that basically said, "This is the Allman Brothers Band and we are paying tribute to Duane to celebrate our fortieth anniversary. Please join us."

BUTCH TRUCKS: We've been trying to jam with Eric for years but have never been in the same place at the same time. Eric is a big fan of the Allman Brothers, and when Duane died, probably his three best friends outside of our band were Eric Clapton, John Hammond, and Delaney Bramlett. Eric and John were at the Beacon and Delaney had sadly died a few months earlier. That's why it was so important to us to have Eric there.

HAYNES: It was a really big deal to the Allman Brothers Band because that had never happened, which is pretty incredible given the history between Duane and Eric. We were so honored to have him there and the fact it turned into seven or eight songs, going well beyond what we originally agreed upon, was icing on the cake. He was great to work with, he played great, and everyone was on his best behavior because we all knew what a special moment it was.

We were all very impressed with Eric's desire to learn Allman Brothers songs rather than just get up and jam and not just choose ones that would make it easy on everybody. We were hoping for the opportunity to play some of the centerpieces, like "Dreams" and "Liz Reed," and Eric was more than game. "Little Wing" was an afterthought and the coolest part of the rehearsal. Everything went very smoothly and when we had basically played through all the songs we agreed upon, Eric looked around and said, "Is there anything else we should think about? What about 'Little Wing'?" Our group reaction was, "Well, we've never played it, but sure." We started working it up from scratch and I thought it was one of the highlights.

Clapton's "Little Wing" suggestion was particularly profound since it was Duane Allman's idea to record it on Layla. *Clapton and Haynes sang harmony*

Eric Clapton with the Allman Brothers Band, March 19, 2009, Beacon Theatre, New York City.

vocals on the song. On Thursday, March 19, 2009, Clapton joined the band for six songs: "Key to the Highway," trading vocal verses with Gregg, "Dreams," "Little Wing," and a trio of Derek and the Dominos' songs: "Why Does Love Got to Be So Sad?", "Anyday," and "Layla." The next night, he also played on "Stormy Monday" and "In Memory of Elizabeth Reed."

ALLMAN: He took a private jet in from New Zealand or someplace to be with us and then took it back to resume his tour. When he was here with us, he just gave it all. That was special, man.

DEREK TRUCKS: I knew he would come prepared but I was still a little taken aback by how much energy he had put into it. He had only hung with Gregg once or twice and obviously Duane was very important to him. He told me that the time he went and saw the Allman Brothers in Miami he was blown away by them—what they looked like, how they sounded. It was a part of his life that he had never put away and he came loaded for bear.

HAYNES: Eric Clapton was my first guitar influence, along with Johnny Winter and Jimi Hendrix, so it was a very big personal moment for me as well. I sometimes forget how much I learned from him in my formative years, but it certainly came back those nights! And on top of that I sang a duet with him on "Little Wing." I was just emotionally ecstatic.

DEREK TRUCKS: Afterwards, when we were hugging, Eric whispered in my ear, saying something like, "I haven't played like that since 1969."

I think it's really incredible that a band could have a fortieth anniversary and have it be a musical highlight. I can't think of anyone else who has or could pull that off.

BOYER: There's a phrase called courting the muse, and that's something you have to do if you want to be an artist or real musician. You can't just run through the motions. Gregg is still doing that. He loves to play.

ALLMAN: I'm proud to say that I have a lot of good music to live up to so I can't get out there and do it halfway. I'm one of the fans, too. In fact, I'm the biggest critic and I've got to be satisfied with it before it's right.

DEREK TRUCKS: It amazes me how, despite all the drama, at the end of the day what's right for the band trumps all. That's what keeps this thing driving and that's what's different about it. Everyone is free to voice their ideas and opinions and have them considered. It's very much a band in that way. I've been a part of major tours and I've never seen a situation where a band that's been together this long will let everyone have their say. If something's working and it's musically happening, they follow it, regardless of whose idea it was. Every one of us has made suggestions that ended up being followed. We all chime in, and not just about our individual parts. It's always about "What are we trying to say here, and what's the best way of saying it?"

BUTCH TRUCKS: That spontaneity is still there—the feeling that anyone can come up with anything at any time to lead us in a different direction—and that's the reason we are here almost forty-five years later. It's still flowing. We still come up with things that surprise one another. You know what it feels like and you want to get there; it's better than sex!

LEAVELL: Eventually we all grow up and the most important thing to all of us is the music. It has to be or we wouldn't still be doing this. At the end of the day, the music prevails and I'm very happy that this is the case.

JAIMOE: The fact is, you perform better with people you've performed with the longest. You do learn something when you have been around each other for so long, whether it's criminal or something great. That's just the truth of the matter.

BURBRIDGE: It's like: How do you understand a wife better after so many years? You become aware of nuance. It's the same with a band: singular and group nuance becomes more defined. You can tell better what mood an individual is in. What the group spirit is. You need to talk, too! People are not mind readers, even if they *think* they're great at it. So many small things that all matter when you are trying to make up something new, on the spot, collectively, in front of thousands of people, every night. It's quite a dance. Fortunately, I love to dance.

LEAVELL: We've seen a lot of fallen soldiers through the years—Duane, Berry, Lamar, and many, many others. You look back at them and they are reminders of how lucky we are to be here, and to make this music. It makes it even more exciting to do it, to carry on, to take care of yourself physically, emotionally, mentally . . .

JOHNNY NEEL: People come and go but the Allman Brothers endure. Dickey's out, Warren left and came back . . . it's more than a band. It's an institution and it's like a big ol' animal, an organism that can regenerate itself.

GIBBONS: Derek and Warren hold down a serious dedication to re-creating something that hasn't been done since, and it's remarkable how their talents have preserved what we've come to know and love about the Allman Brothers sound. They are younger guys who have devoted their musical careers to something very, very special. They are re-creating a really fantastic form of music that is indelibly emblazoned and that resonates with most brains. And as soon as you walk on the stage with them, you feel it.

QUIÑONES: I'm proud to be part of this legacy. I've been with the band for half their life now and have come to realize what an important role the Allman Brothers have played in American music. I feel honored and blessed to be a part of this history, and it blows me away when I meet people and realize just how much this music has touched them, what it's done for them over the years.

ALLMAN: The drummers are back there behind me and I'm on the line. One night at the Beacon, I looked down and realized I was the only one left on the front line. I guess it makes me appreciate the whole thing even more, really. It's hard to stick together, and that's probably why a lot of other good bands don't last this long. My brother, Woody, Oakley . . . they can't be replaced because they were all unique individuals, but it doesn't mean the whole shebang has got to fold. We still have music left to play.

The Allman Brothers Band, 2009.

DEREK TRUCKS: I don't know if the ABB could withstand any more major personnel changes. If it's going to remain legit, it has to be this lineup. Beyond that, it would be tough to keep it going and I think everyone is of the same mind-set that this lineup is the way it's going to go out, whenever that time comes.

I think the chemistry between Warren and I has really grown over the past five or six years. It's a pretty simple thing. The attitude is right and it's never combative. We're pushing each other on. There's always a sense of trying to make shit happen, trading riffs, pushing each other. You want to make music, push it forward. And while we are not competitive, you don't want to be second. Warren has that in him, and I have it in me. It was that way with Dickey and Duane; good players make each other better. As long as you're moving forward, then it's right.

Gregg had a liver transplant in June 2010, just months after appearing quite strong at eight shows at New York's United Palace Theater, where they played that year instead of the Beacon Theatre.

ALLMAN: Most people are two steps from the coroner when they finally get a transplant, so naturally they feel refreshed when they come out the other side, with fresh, clean blood running through them. Phil Lesh [who had a liver transplant in 1998] called me before the surgery and said that when I was done I would feel like a new man, but the thing is I still felt pretty good, though I was drinking those five-hour energy drinks right and left and getting B-twelve shots two or three times a week to keep my energy up.

I had to sleep all day in order to play at night, but I'm not much of a day person anyhow, so that wasn't that unusual. But they told me I wouldn't be able to do that routine for more than two or three years before I'd start going down into a very slow, painful death that would take about two and a half years. I needed the operation as soon as I could have it.

When I found out there was a match, I was really excited. I had no idea what I was in for. When I first woke up, it was the worst pain I ever dreamt of, much less had. I didn't even think about that going in there and they don't even let you know anything about that because if they did, a lot of people would say "No thanks" and they would die. The first four days, the pain is just unbelievable. They have this thing to spread your rib cage. It's like building a battleship in a bottle so they take this big forceps thing and stretch your rib cage and when you wake up, Ooohhh God! The pain right across the middle of your back all the way around is just unbearable. But within weeks I started to feel very clearheaded and healthy. Of course, this was a godsend, and it makes you real humble and stop and feel appreciative.

As Allman recuperated in his Savannah, Georgia, home with the help of long-time friend Chank Middleton and housekeeper Judy Lariscy, he began itching to get back on stage.

ALLMAN: As I began to recover and feel better, I was laid up for 120 days and that was the longest I've gone without performing by far. I've been doing this since I was sixteen and, man, did I miss it. What I missed was getting out there and making it work. What I miss ends at the front of the stage. I just love to play, man, and am seriously devoted to that music. Plus, I've got a lot of gypsy in my blood and I don't mind traveling for as long as I can possibly do it. Just being home that long was real strange and I didn't really like it.

Allman returned to the stage with the Allman Brothers Band on November 10, 2010, at Philadelphia's Tower Theater, the start of a nine-show tour of North-eastern theaters. He appeared remarkably vigorous but suffered some health set-backs over the ensuing eighteen months. When Gregg missed the final show and a half of the 2012 Beacon run and appeared greatly weakened at the Wanee Fest a month later, Haynes was once again sent scrambling to round up appropriate guest stars and many fans started to write the obituary of the Allman Brothers Band. Perhaps they should have known better, given the long history, but the concern extended to the band itself.

QUIÑONES: We really thought that we lost Gregg for good musically. It was really, really scary to watch him on stage; we had never seen him like that. And Butch also had some health problems, which led to me playing a lot of drums in his place, so for a while we had two-thirds of the original band in precarious situations. Me, Derek, Warren, and Oteil were looking at each other on stage with a lot of concern and we had a lot of dinner meetings, discussing what to do, how to get the band back on track. There were some moments that we thought it was the end of the line for the Allman Brothers Band.

BUTCH TRUCKS: I have glaucoma and it got to where I had 20 percent vision in my right eye. I needed surgery but couldn't have it before the tour, so the ophthalmologist put me on this medication to take the pressure off the eyeball but it led to a lot of other issues. It stops your body from producing sodium and I was getting worn out mentally and physically. My mother died of Alzheimer's and Derek was old enough to see that, and when he looked at me, that's what he was seeing in my eyes and it understandably freaked him out and scared me, too. I went straight to New York for an MRI and they said there's nothing wrong and took me off the medication and I got back on my game.

QUIÑONES: It sometimes seemed like we were more concerned about the legacy of this band than the original members were. We didn't want to go out on stage sounding like that and for people to start bagging the band. After working so hard for this unit to sound so good, we didn't want to go out like that. When the guy forgets lyrics for songs he's been singing for forty years, we've got a problem, man. We got together towards the end of the run and went to talk to Gregg in his hotel room.

BUTCH TRUCKS: When Gregg forgot the first line to "Statesboro Blues" we knew we had a serious issue. We had a meeting at the end of the tour to flat-out tell him, "Pull it together—do whatever you have to do or there's not going to be any more Allman Brothers tours." And he kind of pulled the rug out of our meeting by saying he knew what the problem was and what the meeting was about before we could say a word.

QUIÑONES: Before we could say anything, Gregg said, "Guys, I know. I've decided to go into rehab at the end of this run." And that's what it takes—for the addict to say, "I need help." It has to be their choice, their decision, so when he said that, we were really, really happy and surprised.

He came back the following March [2013] for the Beacon in unbelievable shape. The first day of Beacon rehearsal, we rehearsed an hour and a half straight, which had never happened in the twenty-two years I've been in this band. We used to go to Sarasota for three weeks and if we got three good rehearsals in, it was a lot.

HAYNES: We had about a week to rehearse and we packed a lot more into each session than we normally would. We got a lot more accomplished and it was a pleasant scene. Everyone was psyched that everyone individually was in good shape. Gregg and Butch were doing way better, which was a big relief, and the music really benefited.

Gregg's condition and the band's extra rehearsal time were evident throughout the 2013 Beacon run, as they introduced two new Haynes-penned songs as well as several ambitious new covers and some ABB songs that had fallen off their set lists. Gregg sang and played stronger than he had since at least 2009.

BUTCH TRUCKS: The last three nights I had to tape my snare drum down because I was hitting it so hard it was bouncing up to my crotch. I was having more fun than I've ever had in my life. That was the best run ever, made all the sweeter by the difficulties of the previous year.

HAYNES: I think we played a higher level than we have at least since the fortieth anniversary. It was a very satisfying run.

Less than a month later, the Allman Brothers band headlined the first night of Eric Clapton's Crossroads Festival at Madison Square Garden, a two-night orgy of guitar greats, including Jeff Beck, Buddy Guy, B.B. King, Keith Richards, Vince Gill, and many others.

Over the past few years, the band has toured less, with most members working with various other bands: Derek in the Tedeschi Trucks Band; Haynes in Gov't Mule and his self-named band; Allman in Gregg Allman and Friends; Jaimoe in his Jassz Band.

ALLMAN: Now I got my own band and I've got the Brothers and I like them both. The big-amp thing in the Brothers is one thing and my thing is different and to get total fulfillment in music I need both. And I think the reason that I like them both so much is that they're both there, if that makes any sense. You understand?

JAIMOE: I think everyone having other bands is great. When you go off for four or five months and play with other people in other contexts, you bring different ideas and influences back with you, and you play different things. You really grow. Combine that with an ability to communicate, which we have, and you can get something great. The band becomes more able to go in all these different directions.

DEREK TRUCKS: So many of us having our own bands is one of the things that's kept it fresh over the last decade. Everyone is doing his own thing and when you get back it's like an old comfortable sweater that you're happy to put on. It's like, "This is home." But you also bring fresh energy and ideas back. Everyone goes through changes; you don't play the same year to year, and we all welcome these changes that subtly alter the dynamics of the whole band. For instance, Warren and I always do a dance, where we have to respond to the other guy playing with more or less volume or aggression or an altered tone. You can counterbalance it, or match it.

HAYNES: Every time you play in new musical situations, it's a new learning experience and it can alter your approach to everything else.

Working in all these different situations, you cannot help but learn from them. I think it is important for me to always try to do something that I have not tried before.

QUIÑONES: The scheduling allows time for everyone to be apart and it works well whether guys are playing in their own bands or not. Once we stop playing in September we don't really come together until February. That allows you to bring new air into the lungs and get ready to do the next shows and come back really excited to see one another and make some music.

DEREK TRUCKS: I'm not an actor; if I'm not inspired, I can't do it well. If I'm not fully into the idea, people can tell, and just about everyone in this band is the same.

HAYNES: I think the Allman Brothers both individually and collectively have found ourselves in a place where we just want to shake it up and not do what is expected of us—not go out night after night and play the hits, or the most popular staples in the repertoire. When I rejoined the band, Gregg asked if I would make the set lists. It takes a lot of energy and focus, but I enjoy it. We keep a log of all the set lists and when we're touring, I look back to see what we played the last time we were there and possibly the time before that. I want to make sure the majority of the songs are different. The right combination makes for a great Allman Brothers show.

BUTCH TRUCKS: Warren is basically our onstage leader, and we actually had some issues with him for a while because when he came back we spoke about him needing to put the set list together and Warren took it a step or two too far—he thought it meant I wanted him to take the leadership of the whole band, and we had to have a couple of conversations. But Warren is absolutely an integral part of the band and this thing is unimaginable without him.

Warren Haynes, guitarist and much more.

QUIÑONES: Warren has taken on the unofficial role of musical director. Someone has to put this thing together, to tell people what to listen to in order to get ready, and he does well in that role. He enjoys it and is a natural. He certainly consults everyone, especially Gregg, about the set lists, but he knows how to talk to Gregg. He knows the right things to say to keep things moving and everyone feeling good.

HAYNES: When we're doing a residency like the Beacon, you have to bear in mind that a certain portion of the audience is there every night, a smaller portion is there multiple nights, but the largest portion is there just one night and those people might want to hear their favorite songs. Nobody is ever going to come to an Allman Brothers show and hear all of their favorite songs but hopefully they'll hear enough of the staples that they'll maintain interest. We have to change it up every night to keep ourselves fresh. It feels like the audience is ready for that.

DEREK TRUCKS: We're past the point of taking any show for granted. What's happening is a natural winding down of things, with only a handful of shows each year and nobody knows what beyond that. It's clichéd to say you should play every time you hit the stage like it's your last gig, but it certainly comes into play.

HAYNES: Somehow we've managed to build this following—combining the old audience with an influx of new fans—that understands what we're doing and allows us to do what we want to. I'm sure if someone comes to one night at the Beacon and it's "jazz night," they might be frustrated. Sorry, but we might play "Midnight Rider" tomorrow and may have played "Melissa" last night.

ALLMAN: The meaning is still there for me when I sing the old songs. All it takes to freshen something up is just put a little bit of jam in, have the intro weave around, add a break. Those things keep it fresh for everyone. A few years ago, Warren and Derek put a whole new spin on "Midnight Rider" and I loved it.

DEREK TRUCKS: We added an extended outro jam and it changed the whole tune. Doing something like that changes the way you feel when you see it on the list. I think we do a good job of knowing when it's time to tinker. I go back and forth about what's right. There's something really nice about getting your hooks in a tune and massaging it over time, but with songs that have been stamped into people's minds so indelibly, I think that it's more important to nail them. No matter how over-the-top great Warren or I play "Statesboro," at least half the crowd is listening to the solo from *Fillmore East* in their head.

Everyone has an internal mechanism that kicks in when a song starts feeling stale. Then someone either has a definitive idea of how to change it or suggests dropping it for a little while so we can come back to it with fresh ideas. I love what we did to "Midnight Rider."

JAIMOE: Rearranging the songs can really keep them—and you—fresh.

HAYNES: I don't think the band would want to exist as a nostalgia band, playing the same shows every night. And the comfort zone we've provided to the audience and ourselves has given us the luxury to be in a situation where we can play what we want and people not only accept it, but also actually dig it. It's kind of amazing.

ALLMAN: I know of a band that plays the same songs in the same order and says the same things between songs night after night. If you ask me, that's a job, no different than being a shock-absorber washer-jammer in Detroit—and not wanting to be one of those is why I became a musician in the first place.

HAYNES: We are not playing together as much and we all have other bands, so when we come together now it's fun for all of us. It's almost like family. In the past, members may have been threatened by playing people's solo material, but now we're actually looking to expand the repertoire in any way possible. It could be a song from Gregg's record, my record, or Derek's record. It could be Van Morrison or Miles Davis; whatever we feel we can interpret and put an Allman Brothers stamp on. Some of it is just the bravery I love of comrades willing to play a song we barely know. We'll get up in front of a sold-out Beacon and play a song we have never played because we have confidence we can pull it off.

And we've just come to terms with the fact that everything we do is going to be on the Internet in some shape or form. In Gov't Mule we have Mule Tracks where people can download the show and many do. You cannot allow this to change how you approach performing. You just have to accept the blemishes and mistakes as part of the music. The kind of music we're longing to make is not about perfection anyhow. All of our favorite records have mistakes if you listen closely enough.

ALLMAN: Probably not a day goes by riding around on the buses that we don't talk about Duane. It's almost like he's with us. Sometimes when I'm on stage I can feel his presence so strong I can almost smell him. I don't want to get too cosmic, but it's like he's right there next to me.

HAMMOND: You can still feel Duane's presence on stage with them. When you talk about Duane with any of them, it's still so fresh and raw ... like he was here yesterday. And I understand because I still miss him. He was such an amazing, dynamic guy.

Brother Duane Allman, 1970.

SANDLIN: I miss Duane so much just because of the way he could get people fired up and moving in the same direction.

BUTCH TRUCKS: Duane was like Goethe's Faust, someone who wanted to experience life, good, bad, or other. He didn't hold back.

RED DOG: Duane once said to me, "All I want to do is leave a mark, that I was here. People will know Duane Allman was on this earth for a while."

ALLMAN: For years I thought that my brother really got shortchanged because he never quite got to see what he had accomplished, but I've slowly come to realize that he left a hell of a legacy for dying at the age of twenty-four.

JAIMOE: You know, the older I get, the more I miss Duane. He was a person who loved to live and he fucking lived, man. He lived life.

CHAPTER

The Final Chapter

*T*HE ALLMAN BROTHERS Band's forty-fifth anniversary in 2014 was supposed to be a milestone for the group, a well-earned victory lap for a singular band, starting with fourteen March shows at the Beacon Theatre. Instead, the year was clouded in confusion before it even began. In an interview with *Rolling Stone* published on December 31, 2013, Gregg Allman said, "Oteil's not with us anymore. I don't know if he'll be back to the Beacon or not. He's gone with Zac Brown."

But this was news to Burbridge, who was shocked when his wife looked up from her phone at a Japanese restaurant as they waited for dinner and said, "I guess you don't have a job anymore."

"It wasn't close to real at all and just illustrates how bad communication can be in this band," says Burbridge.

The next day, Burbridge posted on his blog: *"Wow, what a surprise to wake up on the first day of 2014 to a wildfire in the rumor mill! . . . 2014 will mark the beginning of my 16th year with the Allman Brothers . . . and we ain't done yet!"*

Wildfire number one was quickly put out, but it was a portent of the year to come.

On January 7, 2014, Butch Trucks was talking to about forty people on the Jam Cruise, a five-night musical outing on a ship packed with musicians and ardent fans. They were deep in the Caribbean, engaging in a bull session at the end of Trucks's Music Masters class. Almost as an aside, he mentioned that Derek Trucks would be leaving the Allman Brothers Band at the end of the year and the group was pondering what to do next, including the possibility of adding a new guitarist and carrying on.

The small crowd included a reporter who contacted publicists for the Allman Brothers and Derek Trucks. Reached at home in Florida, Derek quickly decided to release a statement about his intention to leave the Allman Brothers at the end of the year, although it had actually been a group decision to quit touring. The band's three original members would ultimately decide whether or not to continue, so Trucks decided to control what he could: making his intentions clear.

"I started getting these e-mails saying, 'We're going to run with the story. Do you want to comment?'" he says. "It was going to come out that I had decided not to tour with the Allman Brothers after this year, and I wanted to get out in front of it and own this news instead of watching speculation fly."

The only question was whether Derek's announcement would include Haynes. The two guitarists had made an informal pact to go out together, but Trucks didn't know if his partner was ready to go public with this unexpected, rushed announcement.

"I was hoping that Warren would join me, but of course it was up to him," says Trucks. "It all happened really quickly, and I thought it was important to get a release out."

A half hour after receiving Trucks's statement, Haynes called back and said he wanted to change the first paragraph from "I" to "we" and add his own statement.

"It came out that Derek was leaving and didn't mention me, but Derek and I had long been thinking of ourselves as a team and everybody knew that," says Haynes. "It also wasn't about us deciding to leave—it was a band decision to stop touring. Derek and I really felt that this incarnation should be the final one and that when it ends it would be futile to start looking to put together a whole other lineup this far down the line. I made it clear that I didn't want to be in that position."

The band had hoped to keep the news quiet until the summer, allowing for a grand announcement preceding a triumphant final fall run—and at least a chance that the guitarists would change their minds.

Trucks and Haynes issued their joint statement and word ricocheted through social media platforms and music Web sites. Even the most seasoned Allman Brothers observers were surprised by the announcement even if they weren't shocked by the news. The news release unleashed a flurry of articles, making the band more newsworthy than they had been in decades. It also raised more questions than it answered, most importantly: Did this mean the end of the band? Clarification never arrived in the form of a band statement.

Two days later, with the band suddenly headline news, the Allman Brothers came together at Atlanta's Fox Theatre for *All My Friends: Celebrating the Songs & Voice of Gregg Allman*. Derek Trucks, Haynes, and Jaimoe all performed in different iterations, with the whole group coming together for just the final two songs, excellent versions of "Dreams" and "Whipping Post," that made it clear the band was far from done.

The seven members never sat down and discussed the future, near or long term, in Atlanta. The end of the Allman Brothers' glorious, tumultuous career was off to a bumpy start. It couldn't have happened any other way.

"It sometimes feels like there's a cloud over the camp," says Derek Trucks. "There's just always something that seems so heavy and sometimes unhealthy about it. There's always some real weird drama breathing down your neck. Then you have these magical gigs that make it worthwhile—and it seems as if it's been that way from the beginning."

The cloud hovered nearby on February 20, during the filming of *Midnight Rider,* a film based on Gregg's memoir, *My Cross to Bear.* While shooting on a railroad trestle, the production was surprised by an on-coming freight train. As cast and crew ran for their lives, the train hit a bed that had been placed in the middle of the tracks for the shot. A piece of the shattered prop struck and killed twenty-seven-year-old camera assistant Sarah Jones.

It was impossible to predict how any of this would impact the four-teen Beacon concerts set to begin two weeks later, on March 7. The shows already held gravitas as a forty-fifth anniversary celebration but now were heaped with extra meaning. Tickets for the last show were listed on secondary market Web sites for more than $6,000.

The prior year's shows had been a triumph, with Gregg displaying an amazing return to form after a difficult 2012, when he was unable to perform the final show and a half and was profoundly weak all spring. This recovery had once again proven the foolishness of betting against Gregg or the Allman Brothers, both of whom seemed to have at least nine lives. Still, there was concern about Gregg's health when he couldn't finish all the scheduled rehearsals, and the last year had not been easy. Despite strong performances, conflicts were growing, fueled in large part by Gregg pushing to reduce or eliminate instrumentals and curtail the extended jamming the group was known for, a crusade for which he had no allies in the band.

Gregg has always favored shorter, more song-oriented performances over lengthy jams, creating off-and-on tension since the band's inception. The singer's preference can be heard in his Gregg Allman Band, and he had been pushing to move the Allman Brothers in that direction. Haynes and Trucks saw themselves carrying on the proud tradition set by Dickey Betts and Duane Allman, and central to the group's image and appeal.

"The part that's difficult to wrap your head around is we would often end up in the middle of battles that started forty-five years ago and in many ways had nothing to do with what was currently happening," says Derek Trucks. "One time, Gregg got annoyed and asked why 'Done Somebody Wrong' had to have two guitar solos. But that wasn't my decision; there are two solos because this is the Allman Brothers and that's what people come to hear. I said, 'Because that's how you guys recorded it on *At Fillmore East*—ten years before I was born!'"

Jaimoe says that Trucks is correct; some of these conflicts are as old as the band. "Gregory has never liked a lot of that stuff," he says. "He just had no choice when Duane was alive, and that's how it stayed all these years."

Trucks and Haynes believed that was the crux of the problem, that you can't just suddenly change the structure of an iconic outfit like the Allman Brothers.

"It just doesn't work to try and change the entire nature after forty-five years," says Derek Trucks. "You can't make 'Whipping Post' a four-minute song again. That's not what we do well. If you take the firepower out, this is not going to be good. I want to show up feeling confident that I can give everything I've got—not have to second-guess every note we play."

As always, Jaimoe viewed the musical dispute with a historical, philosophical bent. "You can only push solos so far without recycling," he says, noting that perhaps Haynes and Trucks could have reigned their playing in.

"But Warren did what had to be done and somebody had to do it," Jaimoe adds. "It's very similar to Dickey Betts after Duane died, and at other times. Like him or dislike him, Dickey did what needed to be done to keep the band moving and so did Warren. He was basically the musical director and that's how it should be; the person standing out front needs to be the musical director, not someone sitting behind an organ who you can't see half the time."

On March 8, during the second Beacon show, Butch Trucks walked away from his kit before the encore of "Southbound" and Marc Quiñones took

Gregg Allman at the Beacon Theatre, March 2014.

his place. Trucks missed the next show, on March 11, marking the first Allman Brothers show ever performed without the iron man drummer. He was replaced by his nephew, Derek's brother, Duane, and percussionist Bobby Allende.

"I had a bout of Transient Global Amnesia," says Butch Trucks. "Luckily it was during the last song, but I was on stage playing and I had no idea what I was doing. The problem with that stuff is you don't know it. I was smiling at other band members and God knows what I was playing. I had to spend the next three days in the hospital. Good news is that my brain is perfect (no sign of Alzheimer's or anything else) and TGA is very rare and almost never happens more than once in a lifetime. It really hurt that I had to miss that show, though."

Butch returned to the stage after just the one miss. Then the performances fell into a familiar Beacon pattern: horn section and mellower crowds on week nights; more upbeat party shows on Friday and Saturday. But things were just about to get interesting.

Just before the show on Friday, March 21, word trickled out that Gregg would not be performing. The band announced he had bronchitis. He had been hospitalized with shortness of breath and was undergoing tests.

"Neither Derek nor I were entirely comfortable playing the shows without Gregg," says Haynes. "We're good at that sort of thing and have done it a lot and had a lot of great friends who were willing to help out, but it's a daunting task. Putting together shows that would be worthy of the fans paying money became all consuming."

The band was augmented by Kofi Burbridge and Rob Barraco on keyboards, Bill Evans on sax, and Susan Tedeschi on guitar and vocals. Gregg's son, Devon, stepped up to sing "One Way Out." They opened and closed with a towering "Mountain Jam." The show seemed like a triumph, but Haynes bore the burden of its execution.

"Gregg is the voice of the Allman Brothers, period," he says. "We are aware that people paid a lot for tickets, and some have bought airplane tickets and hotel rooms and maybe it's their only opportunity to see the band. Then Gregg's not there. That presents us with two suboptimal choices: canceling or going on in a different direction. We were told Gregg was day-by-day and we hoped he'd be back Saturday."

With Allman out again, the group called on more friends, including Wet Willie singer Jimmy Hall, who flew up from Nashville. The show was a musical triumph that left the departing crowd buzzing with joy. Back inside the theater, however, Haynes and Trucks were lobbying to postpone the rest of the shows.

"Once we realized that Gregg wouldn't be able to perform, there were varying opinions about what to do with the rest of the shows, but Derek and I felt strongly that they had to be postponed," says Haynes.

On Monday, the group announced that the final four shows were postponed. No make-up dates were announced.

The next Allman Brothers Band performances were about three weeks later, April 11 and 12 at the tenth annual Wanee Music Festival, owned

by the group and put on at the lovely Spirit of the Suwannee Music
Park in Live Oak, Florida.

Gregg appeared on stage with his niece, Duane's daughter, Galadrielle, Friday morning, looking happy and healthy. He drew raucous
applause when he said, unbidden, "I want to clear up one thing about
the Brothers breaking up this year. . . . That's a rumor."

The "rumor" had gained traction when Gregg himself said it in a
recent interview. As the crowd roared, Butch chimed in: "We've got a lot
left to play."

The same day, an interview Gregg had given the night before hit
online, with him making similar statements, and saying, "We are
not breaking up. We are replacing Derek Trucks." (In the same interview, he also said that he had been hospitalized due to atrial
fibrillation.)

These pronouncements caught everyone off guard. Gregg's not
mentioning Haynes implied that the guitarist was staying, which put
him in an uncomfortable position. Derek felt blindsided again by the
implication of Gregg's statement.

"All of a sudden this thing that seemed really clear was muddled,"
he says. "I gave three or four years more than I was planning, to get it
to this point, which is fine, because that's how it is in any musical relationship. But then it gets to the end and somehow it's like this one guy
is going off the reservation—it's like I'm quitting. In some ways there's
a target painted on your back."

As confusing as the messages were, it shouldn't have surprised anyone that the Allman Brothers Band was not an easy thing for the
founding members to walk away from.

"Gregg, Butch, and Jaimoe have changed their minds at least twice
about whether they really want to hang it up for good and can you
blame them?" asks Oteil Burbridge. "It's really up to them if it's going
to end. The ABB has been on the road for the better part of forty-five
years. If they want to go out on their shields, who is anyone to tell them
that they can't, other than their fans? I saw both B. B. King and Ralph

Stanley recently. They were both struggling—and I wouldn't trade it for anything."

At the time, Jaimoe said he didn't know what would happen, but he was sure of one thing: if the band wanted to continue, they didn't necessarily need to find two new guitarists. "Everyone says the Allman Brothers are a 'guitar band' but it doesn't have to be so," he said. "Hell, the way Duane loved Coltrane, he might have picked up a tenor and then we'd be a 'sax band.' It was always based around the ideas coming out of our heads, not our instruments."

Butch Trucks, the original member who was the least ambiguous about his desire to continue the band, was beaming as he walked off the stage after his Wanee appearance with the two Allmans.

"Gregg heard the chatter about how good those Beacon shows without him were and he's got something to prove," Trucks said. "He's really focused and ready to go, after a lot of shows where he looked like he'd rather be anywhere else."

Just after the talk, Allman told the band's production team that he wanted to check out the fairgrounds, which he had never done before. He and his girlfriend took off in a golf cart, only to soon return with Gregg bearing a broken left wrist; he had leaned against an idle truck, which then drove away.

The accident added to an overall sense of chaos—of what Burbridge called a "Humpty Dumpty situation." It was unclear just who or what could put the band back together again.

By the time the Allman Brothers Band took the stage that night, Gregg was back from the hospital, his left hand casted. Standing on the side of the stage amidst a gaggle of relatives just before showtime, Butch Trucks shook his head as he loosened up his shoulders. "A broken wrist just as he's ready to go out and kick ass? What rotten luck."

Oteil Burbridge stood next to Trucks nodding his head. "What's next?" he asked, as Trucks walked off to his drum kit. "Me, Derek, and Warren were just talking and said, 'Let's just have some fun playing music together because the other stuff is . . . the other stuff. As it's always been."

With everyone in their places—including Kofi Burbridge on a Hammond B3 set up at the far end of the stage opposite Gregg—Allman sat down at his organ and said, "What a wonderful party. Thank you all for coming." Then he counted off "1, 2, 3!" and the band was off and running into "Statesboro Blues."

The band performed solidly, with Gregg singing three tunes to start the show, then laying low on his organ for most of the night, resting his casted hand above the keys and swallowing pills brought out by his tech. He was more involved throughout the next night's show, which ended with spirited takes of "Whipping Post" and "One Way Out."

Almost immediately after the festival, Allman departed for Australia with his solo band. After two gigs, he canceled his last two shows and returned home, sighting discomfort in his wrist.

Each of the Allman Brothers' remaining appearances had taken on new gravitas, and the anticipation was thick when they reconvened almost two months later, June 8, at Mountain Jam in Hunter, New York. The performance was solid but uninspired. Most of the band looked like they would have rather been elsewhere, which was particularly noticeable after Haynes and Trucks had turned in stellar shows the night before with Gov't Mule and the Tedeschi Trucks Band respectively. Gregg appeared to have lost a lot of weight and took a few hits on an oxygen bottle, an unnerving sight that left many worrying about his health.

Concerns did not ease over the coming weeks as the Gregg Allman Band canceled July shows in the Pacific Northwest and Norway.

During this confusing summer for the Allman Brothers, Dickey Betts was also on the road with his band Great Southern. One sticky August evening, they played the Concert Hall, an intimate spot just ten blocks from the Beacon. The wooden pews of the former house of worship were packed tight and the seventy-year-old guitarist scorched the theater with a focused and fiery performance.

A year earlier, a concert at New York's City Winery had devolved into an uncomfortable, chaotic mess, but on this night Betts conjured up the magic of years gone by. The crowd's intensity was reminiscent of the Allman Brothers' Beacon shows twenty years earlier, when the room didn't seem sturdy enough to contain the passion. There was once again joy and energy reverberating off the walls to the tune of "Blue Sky," "Jessica," and "Ramblin' Man."

Before the show, Betts was relaxed, smiling and friendly, sporting a neatly trimmed full white beard and his trademark cowboy hat. He warmly greeted old acquaintances and reminisced about some of his earliest guitar influences. On stage with his Gibson Les Paul, Betts commanded his six-piece band, playing and singing with confidence. His son, Duane, stood to Betts's right, looking strikingly like Dickey circa 1970.

During intermission, Duane Betts sat in a backstage room, sipping a bottle of water and reflecting on his father's role in the Allman Brothers.

"My father was a founding member of the ABB, wrote some of their most iconic songs and played with the band for over thirty years and no one can take any of that away," Duane says. "It's just weird to think that some of the younger fans may not know about his contributions.

"For years, it was painful for me to even talk about the Allman Brothers. People would come up and tell me they had just seen them for instance and it just stung. It was raw. But my dad has come to peace with it, and so have I. His contributions can't be denied, and whatever happened, happened."

Almost a year earlier, on September 21, 2013, Dickey and Duane had joined the Tedeschi Trucks Band onstage for three songs at the Beacon Theatre, thrilling the sold-out crowd and raising the hopes of many that the appearance would be the start of a detente between Betts and the Allman Brothers Band.

"I had a sense that it probably wasn't going to happen with the

Allman Brothers and maybe it was a bit of a bridge for the fans who had seen so many shows in that building," says Trucks. "It was very meaningful for me and for the audience, and I think it was good for Dickey to walk on that stage and face it down. He spent a lot of time in that place in front of those people and I think to get back there in a family band was important."

The moment was emotionally satisfying for all involved, but nothing more came of it. Still, it would be crazy for anyone who's observed the group's tumultuous, up-and-down career to presume that the final chapter had been written.

"When it comes to Gregg and my father, never say never," says Duane Betts.

For years, the Allman Brothers had navigated a difficult dance in booking shows around the members' other bands' schedules, which is a large reason why their 2014 summer tour only consisted of three festivals. With the end looming and those postponed Beacon dates hanging over them, the clock was ticking. The group had to find a week where everyone was available and the Beacon was unbooked.

In June, the band announced that the postponed Beacon shows would be played in October, along with two additional dates, which would be the final shows. Most close observers and even band members had been anticipating a longer October tour, visiting Atlanta, Boston, Philadelphia, Chicago, and Los Angeles, and culminating in New York, with talk of an extended final run at the Beacon and/or a concluding night at Madison Square Garden. It wasn't to be.

By the time things had settled down enough to plan more shows, there was concern about the ability of the original members, especially Gregg, who had canceled so many summer shows, to mount an extended tour. The Tedeschi Trucks Band also already had dates booked starting October 30, creating a small window of opportunity.

The Allman Brothers Band would end with six Beacon shows, from October 21–28. No venturing outside the city that had morphed into

their home base. No grand finale at the Garden. Just the four resched-
uled shows and two additional performances. It felt like an anticlimac-
tic climax, even to many insiders.

"We all felt that we should do a bigger tour to get to cities that had
been so supportive of the band," says Derek Trucks. "But after doing
the first show ever without Butch and two without Gregg, there was no
confidence that we could just keep booking dates and it's gonna be
fine. Then you add the wildly varying views of what we should be doing
musically, and it felt like a recipe for disaster to add dates thinking things
would get better without any real communication."

The Allman-Brothers played again at their own Peach Music Festival
in Scranton, Pennsylvania, on August 16 and 17. The band seemed
looser and more relaxed than they had at Mountain Jam. The first
night was to feature the band playing *Eat a Peach* in its entirety. As they
took the stage, Allman casually told Holman that due to his injured
wrist, he could not play the piano intro to "Ain't Wastin' Time No
More," the night's first song.

Holman put out a walkie talkie call for Gov't Mule keyboardist Danny
Louis, who quickly made his way to the stage and said he was happy to
play and would do his best, but he didn't know the song. Someone told
him the chords and Derek Trucks walked over to play through the
changes softly. The drummers heard Trucks's playing, thought he had
added a new intro and came in after one time through. The band was
off and running. Thrown into the fire, Louis and the band responded
with an appropriately tight but loose performance.

"You try to play every show like it's your last show; you always want
to play like it's the last time you'll ever play," says Derek Trucks. "But it's
100 percent different when every time you play a song it really might
be the last time you play it with this particular band. You need to make
it count."

Days after Peach Fest, the band's final year gained some unneeded
poignancy when Haynes's longtime guitar tech, Brian Farmer, died

in his sleep at his Nashville home. Farmer was more than a guy who tuned guitars. He was a seemingly indispensible part of this universe, a beloved figure whose name was known by much of the crowd and who was a link back to the Allman Brothers' glory days when the road crew had profiles that almost equaled the band members'.

A week later, a distraught Haynes could still barely speak about the loss of his friend. At their final summer appearance, on September 7 at the Lockn' Festival in Virginia, the entire band wore T-shirts picturing Farmer extending both hands, middle fingers raised.

Original since '69. Jaimoe and Butch at rehearsals for the final shows. New York, October 2014.

In mid October, four days before the first show in the final run, the Allman Brothers gathered one last time in their regular rehearsal space on Manhattan's Far West Side. The only band member to arrive early for an afternoon rehearsal was Jaimoe, who sat behind his kit carefully selecting sticks from a bag, then limbering up with drum rolls. A tech tinkered with the internal mechanisms of Gregg's iconic

Hammond B3 organ, while another checked Derek Trucks's amp settings, and a third tuned a wall of Haynes's Gibson Les Pauls. A fourth crew member sat on a road case waiting for the rest of the band's arrival, his massive Bernese Mountain Dog nonchalantly laying at his feet.

Members slowly trickled in, accompanied by wives, kids, and a few friends, who wandered in and out. Allman looked healthier and less gaunt than he had just a month earlier. The band started working through a knotty section of the instrumental "True Gravity," leading Haynes to say, "I think we got it good enough to have it back in our heads." They moved onto some other transitions.

During a break, Derek Trucks walked around with his iPhone, taking pictures of the mushroom tattoos on the calves of Allman, Jaimoe, and uncle Butch—the ones all six original members had received together in 1971.

Haynes and Derek Trucks were the only band members ever to have not gotten the ink, and the latter had decided to jump on board.

Two days later, on a lazy Sunday afternoon, a Brooklyn tattoo artist showed up before rehearsal and went to work. With just six shows left with the band, it seemed an odd time to make the inky plunge, but Derek seemed anything but anxious.

"I got the tattoo because Jaimoe told me to and I do what Jaimoe says," he explained, reclining on a couch watching a Jacksonville Jaguars game on his phone as he got his first tattoo.

Jaimoe himself stood beside Trucks videoing with his giant phone, taking delight in the whole process.

"Young Blood said he wanted this about two years ago but believe it or not, no one knew a tattoo guy," the drummer said. "I just reminded him about it!"

With Trucks inked up, the band got to work, returning to "True Gravity" and taking a stab at Jackson Browne's "These Days." After about ninety minutes, the room was cleared of visitors and even crew members for a band-only meeting, during which it would be decided that they would have no guests for these Beacon shows.

"There's only six shows left and we decided to go out with just the seven band members," Allman explained.

Butch and Gregg at rehearsals for the final shows. New York, October 2014.

As the shows began, Haynes and Derek Trucks both seemed serene and reflective of their tenures in the band and the decision to quit touring.

"The thing I'm most proud of is that we've been able to carry the mantle of a great tradition, revisit the band's concept and vision and in some ways carry it into the future," says Haynes. "And it was never based on compromise or wondering what the public would expect from a commercial standpoint. It was based on trying to tap into the vision and proud tradition of the original band."

"I want to see the legacy end as it should—at the top—and I think we can do it," added Trucks. "It's a rare thing to be able to go out on top and in great shape. I understand how difficult this is for the original members but at some point, you have to step away. If you can go out the right way, it keeps an amazing story amazing to the end. It might be a hard thing to do, but I believe it's the right thing to do."

Many fans wondered if Betts might make an appearance during one of the final shows. Given his importance to the band's sound, songwriting, and history, it was an understandable desire, if not an entirely reasonable one. After almost fifteen years of no direct contact, the idea of a very public, very dramatic reunion seemed naïve. The fans who craved it for their own emotional healing gave scant thought to the principle's emotions.

Bert Holman and Betts's manager, David Spero, spoke several times about the possibility of an appearance, but it's not clear if any of the concerned parties even knew about it. It certainly never came close to the one thing that would likely be necessary to make a reunion happen: a phone invitation from Allman, Trucks, or Jaimoe to Betts.

On the eve of the run's first show, just before a final rehearsal on the Beacon stage, Gregg Allman stood in the theater's lobby. He seemed at peace with the group's looming end.

"It's been forty-five years," he said. "I think that's about enough."

On opening night, the theater was filled with an air of anticipation and reverence, a step beyond the normal excitement that has always met the band's Beacon performances. They closed the first set with "You Don't Love Me," transitioning at the end into a hard-swinging blues vamp, with Trucks and Haynes trading licks. As that song ended, before applause could swell, Haynes played a plaintive, almost mournful lick, which revealed itself as the melody of "Will the Circle Be Unbroken." Derek Trucks responded with a sacred slide wail, Gregg's churchy organ fell in with them, and the whole band swooped in for a breathtaking instrumental version of the traditional American song of mourning, which always played a special role in the Allman Brothers and which the group played at Duane's funeral.

"Up until Duane's death you could almost call 'The Circle' our theme song," says Butch Trucks. "With that bond we were developing it seemed appropriate, and we used to throw it into jams all the time. Before the first show, I asked Derek to put it into one of his solos. We all just knew that it had to be a part of the farewell."

The next night, the guitarists again started an instrumental "Circle," this time offering up a more jagged, aggressive reading in the jammed out coda of "Black Hearted Woman."

Before the third show, on Friday, October 24, Duane's two Gibson Les Pauls, a 1959 cherryburst and a 1958 or '59 darkburst, arrived from the Rock and Roll Hall of Fame, courtesy of his daughter Galadrielle and appropriately delivered by Twiggs Lyndon's brother, Skoots. They joined the 1957 goldtop that Derek had been intermittently playing since the first show, marking the first time Duane's three primary guitars were all together, and their presence seemed to animate the band, into playing their best show since the fortieth anniversary performance of March 26, 2009. The surge of energy was testament to the remarkable power Duane exerted on the Allman Brothers Band until the very end.

Trucks and Haynes's playing took on more urgency. The two moved closer together, leaning in to better hear and respond to each note. The drummers hit with more force. Gregg Allman was fully, absolutely present, and singing with extra power and precise phrasing.

"Those guitars were inspiring to play," says Haynes. "They are not in the greatest shape after not being played for so long, but the sound is unreal. The tone they generate is so remarkable and distinctive; it is the sound of Duane."

"There was definitely some extra spirit in the room," says Derek. "I think having Duane's guitars struck the original members and was a big part of all of us somehow wrapping our heads around what was happening. At one point, Butch looked down, saw what I was playing and was really struck."

Says Butch Trucks, "It was during 'Dreams' and seeing and hearing Derek play the solo on the guitar Duane used to play it on the first album was very emotional. I shed a lot of tears during these shows and Duane was the cause of most of them. I do still miss him and always will."

During Friday's show-ending "Whipping Post" encore, the band stopped on a dime and went into "Will the Circle Be Unbroken" again, but this time Gregg sang it, a mournful, haunting lament that led right back into the finale of "Whipping Post." The band was flying at a very high altitude.

The Allman Brothers mostly maintained this level for two more nights, with instrumental versions of "Will the Circle Be Unbroken" inserted into "Jessica" and "Les Brers in A Minor," respectively. That left one final show, on Tuesday, October 28.

"The next-to-last night, we had a band meeting to talk about the final show and I just suddenly was hit by how grateful I felt to everyone in the room," says Derek Trucks. "Thank you, Uncle Butch; thank you, Jaimoe. Thank you, Gregg, Oteil, Marc, Warren. Everybody in that room changed my life. You can get caught up in the day-to-day bullshit, but there's been some incredible highs. And not everyone is lucky enough to experience something like that."

The shows had been building in intensity. It remained to be seen if the band could actually pull off Derek's desire to "go out with both guns blazing," which had seemed an impossible dream for most of the year.

Grandiose rumors circulated: They would play four sets. They would play until sunrise, just like at the Fillmore East. They would play an hour-long "Mountain Jam."

Just after the ticketed 8 p.m. showtime, all seven Allman Brothers Band members began to gather in the seventh-floor rehearsal room for one final portrait with photographer Danny Clinch. Derek Trucks and Oteil Burbridge were the first ones there, with Trucks sitting on a couch playing an acoustic guitar as Burbridge sipped a plastic cup of white wine. Allman walked in and said hello.

"It's been a good run," Burbridge said. "A really good five shows."

"Oh yeah," Allman replied. "It makes up for the last one. Those shows in March . . ." He shook his head. "Now we're going to put it all in and leave it on the fucking stage."

Derek Trucks continued to noodle on the acoustic as uncle Butch wandered in, followed by Haynes, holding his toddler son's hand. Quiñones entered the room and they all chatted waiting for Employee Number One; when Jaimoe walked in, everyone found their spots.

The final portrait, in a Beacon rehearsal room, moments before they took the stage. October 28, 2014.

Family members and a handful of friends and management crowded onto the narrow landing outside the room, craning to see in. Butch and Jaimoe's wives stood side by side, their daughters, Elise and Cajai, nearby. Gregg's right-hand man, Chank Middleton, stood by band manager Bert Holman and Gregg's manager, Michael Lehman, in the doorframe. Galadrielle was down the hall. Allen Woody's daughter, Savannah, was nearby. The Allman Brothers were a family affair until the end.

From the first notes, it was clear this was going to be a special night. The reverential, ecstatic crowd was hanging on every note, each of which was played with intent and focus. The band kicked off with a brief reading of the instrumental "Little Martha," transitioning into a "Mountain Jam" that was little more than a tease, then launching into the first songs from their first album, "Don't Want You No More" and "It's Not My Cross to Bear."

Butch Trucks summoned the old freight-train power that drove the band to their greatest heights. Jaimoe complemented his partner's fury with swinging accents and added power. Percussionist Marc Quiñones heaped coal into the furnace. Gregg Allman sang as well as he has in years, while his organ seasoned every song. The front line of Haynes, Trucks, and Burbridge pushed one another higher in an endless conversation of push-pull rhythms and interwoven parts.

Once more with feeling. The final show.

"I had a good feeling from the very first night," says Derek Trucks. "But it wasn't really until the show started on the last night that everything seemed to fall into place and we all knew this had the potential to become something special."

The show largely leaned on Duane-era material, plus three songs recorded after Duane's death but closely associated with him: "Melissa," and "Will The Circle Be Unbroken," which were both played at his funeral, and "Ain't Wastin' Time No More," which Gregg wrote in response to his brother's death. A Haynes-sung "Blue Sky" paid unspoken tribute to Betts. The only late-era song in the playlist, interestingly, was "The High Cost of Low Living."

When the show ticked past midnight, the Allman Brothers were officially wrapping up their career on October 29, the forty-third anniversary of Duane's death. They played an extended version of "Will the Circle Be Unbroken" wrapped in the middle of a massive "Mountain Jam."

After an encore of a high-energy "Whipping Post," the band walked to center stage as the Beacon shook with applause. It was startling to see the seven members together, arm in arm, waving and bowing, because the Allman Brothers have never been a group-bow type of band. Gregg had gone whole Beacon runs without saying much more than "thank y'all," but he took the mic and offered some eloquent words of thanks and reflection. Then he said that they would close out with the first song they ever played together, and every hardcore in the hall knew what was coming. Butch and Jaimoe offered some words, with the latter telling the crowd, "We couldn't have done this without you."

Then they all returned to their instruments and counted off Muddy Waters's "Trouble No More." The whole audience sang along, leaning forward so much that it felt like the theater might tip over backwards. When the song ended, no one on stage seemed to know what to do, lingering by their instruments. Butch and Jaimoe thrust their arms in the air in triumph. Gregg stood and waved. Haynes and Burbridge embraced. Quiñones walked to the front and handed drumsticks to the crowd.

The crowd remained in their seats as a slide show of the band's history, heavy on Duane and Berry Oakley, rolled on screen to the recorded strains of the lilting instrumental "Little Martha." It was Duane's only composition, the notes of which decorate his gravestone. It was also the tune that began this night four and a half hours earlier. The circle was complete, unbroken.

Just after the final note.

When the song ended, the full house erupted again, before slowly filing out with a reverential buzz, thrilled they had been there and dazed that it was all over. Out on the sidewalk, old friends hugged. Tears were shed. Crowds gathered around the back door behind barricades, applauding and chanting the name of each band member as they emerged into waiting vans. Most of the band repaired to a nearby Italian restaurant with friends and families.

"I think the one thing everyone who was in that room could agree on is the night happened exactly as it should have," says Derek Trucks. "I had wanted Dickey to appear and I had wanted the night to be filmed, but there's no way of knowing what impact either of those things would have had. I don't think I would have wanted it to go down any other way.

"There was something really honest and pure and it was a bona fide moment, which don't happen too often on Planet Earth. It was just the band, the seven of us who have done this for almost fifteen years, playing the classic songs. And the fact that it rolled over into October 29, the anniversary of Duane's passing . . . it just ended up working out the way it was supposed to. I don't think those shows would have been nearly as important or that the music, camaraderie, and spirit would have held out had we done a long tour."

By the end of the day, Derek, Warren, and Oteil would all be on their way to other gigs in other cities. Butch Trucks would soon be back at his house in the South of France. Gregg would be home in Georgia, gearing up to receive an award in Los Angeles. Jaimoe relaxed at his Connecticut home.

Reflecting on the shows, Jaimoe paid them the highest compliment, saying they reminded him of that elusive gold standard every iteration had chased like a ghost since 1971: the original band.

"Those dates were a lot like the original six," he said. "We could have kept playing more nights."

At 10 a.m the next morning the bleary-eyed road crew was rolling road crates out the back door of the Beacon, filling up tractor trailers. A handful of fans returned to the theater for one last look, clutching coffee cups as they peeked through the stage door.

The circus had rolled up its tent and was leaving town.

Afterword by Jaimoe

When you have one or more people trying to do something, you either have a team or you have nothing. If someone dictates what everyone else should do, that's not a team. And whether you're making music, going to the moon, or playing football, if you don't think as one mind, then you've got nothing but a train wreck.

The Allman Brothers Band was a team from the day we became a band.

Duane Allman was the guy who had the vision, who saw what he wanted—two drums, two lead guitars, Gregg singing—and knew which musicians could make it happen. There's no question he was the leader, but Duane understood that for it to work, everyone had to have their voice and express their personality. Duane never dictated what anyone else played. He wanted *a band*.

To have a real band, everyone has to be able to express themselves and play what they feel while also pulling for the common good. It's not that complicated; you have to make adjustments to your approach to make it all fit. Some people think this is limiting—that it's about what *you can't do*—but that's not the case. It's about how you do what you do. The personality of a musician is what makes a note different, the only thing that makes any music different from any other, and you have to leave room for everyone to express their personality. And collaboration is what makes a band a band. Real collaboration means real listening and letting what others play change what you were about to play.

Music is like the wind. It drags. It rushes. It's on time. It's off time. Some people cut this off by playing whatever they have planned regardless of what anyone else is doing; they play in such a way that you can't respond. They box you in instead of opening you up. I've played with great musicians who limit what you can play—you can't go anywhere or do anything different, which is the opposite of what music should be. I felt musically liberated the first time I jammed with Duane and Berry, which was the beginning of the Allman Brothers Band.

From that first moment, it was like I had people to really play with, to interact with in such a way that everything opened up. They just freed everything up. And then we set out to find other people who could fit into this puzzle and help us take it further.

Duane had the vision from the start, because Duane could see stuff like he had a crystal ball as big as the earth. It didn't have to be music, either. He understood what was going on with people, and he knew who he was.

Anything worthwhile takes work and everything goes up and down. If you don't really understand those two things, you'll do a million things in life and never find the right thing. You'll always say, "There's no market for this." You have to create something so great that you create a market that didn't exist. Suddenly something no one ever thought of before seems obvious. This is what we did with the Allman Brothers Band.

I used to sit in the music room in high school reading *Downbeat* magazine about guys who had been in Duke Ellington's band for thirty years and thinking, "How in the hell is that possible?" Now I've been in this band for forty-five years.

One thing I've learned in life is hindsight ain't always 20/20. History is complicated and everyone sees it differently, understands it in his or her own way. The Allman Brothers Band history involves a lot of people and there are as many versions of what happened as there are people involved in making it happen. That's why this book gets the history as right as possible; Alan Paul spoke to everyone he could, let them have their say—tell their version of the truth—and then laid it out. You can't try to escape the shit you did in life.

Things just happen in ways you never could plan out and then you accept them and react to them. One indisputable fact is that whatever has happened to, and with, the Allman Brothers Band, we've persevered.

Acknowledgments

Thank you to everyone whose words form the core of this book. I very literally couldn't have done this without your time and cooperation and your interest in making sure I got the story right. Very special thanks to the current and former members of the Allman Brothers Band with whom I spoke, often repeatedly: Gregg Allman, Dickey Betts, Butch Trucks, Jaimoe, Warren Haynes, Derek Trucks, Oteil Burbridge, Marc Quiñones, Allen Woody, Chuck Leavell, Jack Pearson, Johnny Neel, Jimmy Herring, David Goldflies, and Mike Lawler. Thank you Butch and Jaimoe, for your editorial contributions, and Warren, for always answering the call.

Major thanks to everyone else who took the time to speak with me and share their thoughts and memories of the Allman Brothers Band: Bert Holman, Jonny Podell, Kim Payne, Linda Oakley, Phil Walden, Tom Dowd, John Hammond Jr., Reese Wynans, Johnny Sandlin, Scott Boyer, Mama Louise Hudson—and thanks for the vittles—Stephen Paley, Jon Landau, W. David Powell, Gary Rossington, Eric Clapton, Bobby Whitlock, Billy Gibbons, Buddy Guy, Col. Bruce Hampton, David Grissom, Dick Wooley, Kirk West, Red Dog, Bunky Odom, Willie

Perkins, Bob Weir, Steve Parish, Dr. John, Mike Callahan, Rick Hall, John McEuen, Zakk Wylde, Danny Goldberg, Don Law, Skoots, A. J. and John Lyndon, Michael Caplan, John Scher, Jon Landau, Richard Price, Les Dudek, Matt Abts, Jackie Avery, Sidney Smith, and Thom "Ace" Doucette.

Thank you to all the photographers whose work graces these pages, and to Tore Claesson for the portrait.

In loving memory of Duane Allman, Berry Oakley, Allen Woody, Tom Dowd, Phil Walden, Lamar Williams, Red Dog, Twiggs Lyndon, Mike Callahan, Joe Dan Petty, Dan Toler, Frankie Toler, Brian Farmer, and any other deceased member of the extended Allman Brothers family. You are missed every day, Brian.

Managers Bert Holman, Michael Lehman, Stefani Scarmado, Blake Budney, David Spero, and C. J. Strock have been incredibly supportive and helpful in setting up interviews and providing insight and information—in some cases for several decades. Thank you all.

I'm thankful to Kirk West, my brother in all things Brothers, for decades of friendship, support, and serious music raps. He also served as a superb photo editor, and he conducted the interviews with Red Dog and Mike Callahan, the only conversations included in this book that did not involve me.

Kirk and his wife, Kirsten, who have also provided me a home away from home in Macon, did yeoman's work setting up the fabulous Allman Brothers Band Museum at the Big House, which would not exist if they hadn't brought the property back into the family fold. E. J. Devokaitis, Richard Brent, and Rob Schneck have stepped into their shoes in admirable fashion as curators and directors. The Big House Archives provided this book with a tremendous amount of depth and insight. I urge all Allman Brothers fans to visit and support the Big House, and I thank everyone there for their assistance and support in the writing of *One Way Out*.

John Lynskey and Joe Bell of *Hittin' the Note* have been great supporters, and their passion for the ABB continues to amaze and inspire.

Thank you to John, A.J., and Skoots Lyndon for helping bring their brother Twiggs to life and for their overall support and assistance. Linda Oakley was also a special source of information and insight.

Promoting *One Way Out* put me in close contact with Allman Brothers Nation. As Gregory would say, "Y'all are a great bunch." Thanks for the great reception.

My agent, David Dunton, believed in this book immediately and pushed me to think big in all regards. Marc Resnick at St. Martin's has been an enthusiastic, insightful editor from the moment he heard about the idea for *One Way Out*. Thank you both for your belief and support, and thanks to Christy D'Agostini, Karlyn Hixson, and the entire St. Martin's team for their hard work in helping make the book a bestseller.

Guitar World's Brad Tolinski was a major inspiration in the creation of *One Way Out*, which began as a *GW* cover story. Brad has been a friend and mentor for a very long time. He and Jeff Kitts have continued to assign me great stories about the Allmans and others for two decades. Andy Aledort is a great friend and a brilliant guitarist. We have spent countless hours talking about the music of the Allman Brothers. Dickey Betts is lucky to have him. Thank you, to Sam Enriquez, for giving this manuscript a thorough, helpful read, and to Jack Weston, for guidance on art and memorabilia

My wife, Becky, has been a source of inspiration, support, and love forever, or so it seems, and she has never once asked why I was going to another Allman Brothers show. Watching my son Jacob develop a love and respect for the Allman Brothers, and so much other great music, has been a pleasure, and nothing makes me happier than attending a show with him. He, Eli, and Anna are my greatest creations by far.

Thank you to my brother David for turning me on to *Eat a Peach* and so much other great music, and for letting me hang out with the big kids. Thanks to my parents, Dixie Doc, and Suzi, Laura, and Jon Kessler, and my extended family for their unending support. It takes a village to raise children—mine at least—and I appreciate every ounce of help. Aunt Joan is also a crackerjack proofreader.

Thanks to my bandmates in both Woodie Alan (Beijing) and Big in China (Maplewood, New Jersey). Support live music!

Thank you for buying and reading this book.

APPENDIX

A Highly Opinionated ABB Discography

There is an endless array of compilations available, several of which feature liner note essays by me. Most of them will do the job if you want a little taste of the Allman Brothers Band—but you need more than that if you've read this far. I left them all out, in favor of collections that were originally released as albums and official archival live releases. Albums are listed in chronological order of release.

THE PEACHES—THE BEST OF THE BEST

On their second album, **Idlewild South** (1970, ****), the Allman Brothers Band really began to come into its own. Includes "Midnight Rider," the aching "Please Call Home," and the first version of Betts's masterful instrumental "In Memory of Elizabeth Reed," which sounds one-dimensional compared with the live majesty that was soon to come. The entire album is essential listening.

At Fillmore East (1971, *****) captured the band's instrumental glory and improvisatory magic in peak form. Arguably rock's greatest record, the double album holds only seven very long songs—and nary a wasted note.

Eat a Peach (1972, ****$\frac{1}{2}$) includes more tunes from the Fillmore, including the 33-minute "Mountain Jam"—which back in the days of vinyl consumed two sides—as well as great new tunes like "Melissa" and "Blue Sky." I usually start ABB neophytes here, because the album highlights every side of the band. "Mountain Jam" lacks the urgency of the Fillmore cuts, costing this half a star. Everything else is perfect, including the glorious guitar break on "Blue Sky," the song that could end all world conflict.

Brothers and Sisters (1973, ****), the Brothers' first post-Duane album, includes the band's biggest hits—"Ramblin' Man," "Jessica," and "Southbound." You can hear directions changing. Lacks the focused intensity of everything that has come before, but still a great album—and mostly Dickey's album. The 2013 deluxe version, including outtakes and a great live show, is a worthy upgrade.

An Evening with . . . Second Set (1995, ****) provides a good overview of what the band sounded like at the height of their 1990s reunion, when Warren Haynes and Allen Woody helped resurrect the institution. Betts's majestic "Where It All Begins" and the overall slightly stronger collection of then-current songs gives it an edge over the also-strong *First Set*.

FURTHER LISTENING

Sooner or later, you have to own **Dreams** (1989, ****$\frac{1}{2}$), a four-disc collection that does everything a boxed set should.

WORTH SEARCHING FOR

An Acoustic Evening with the Allman Brothers Band & the Indigo Girls (1992, ****) captures the Brothers' acoustic performance at a record biz convention. They hit seven tracks out of the park, from an impromptu "Liz Reed," which later appeared on *Second Set*, to "Seven Turns." The band inexplicably missed out on the early '90s *Unplugged* craze despite being one of the first bands to appear on the MTV show, and one of the few to really shine in an acoustic setting.

WHAT TO AVOID

The Allmans' worst albums, **Brothers of the Road** (**) and **Reach for the Sky** (*$\frac{1}{2}$) were replaced by **Hell and High Water** (1994, **$\frac{1}{2}$;), which, while

still weak, includes some pretty good material and eliminate the worst of-
fenders. Still, there's no good reason for anyone but completists to purchase
this album.

Peakin' at the Beacon (2000, **) is an odd release—the band let Dickey
Betts go because of what they termed subpar playing on his final spring tour,
then fulfilled their Sony contract by releasing songs from Betts's final Beacon run with the band. He sounds OK, actually, but it's a dispirited set—
definitely not a peak.

THE REST

The Allman Brothers Band (1969, ***$\frac{1}{2}$) is a remarkably sure, mature debut filled with songs that have become classics. The production muffles the
brilliance.

Beginnings (1973, ****) combines the band's first two albums in full, making it an excellent choice.

Win, Lose or Draw (1975, **$\frac{1}{2}$) is the sound of a band in free fall. It lacks the
cohesion and fire that marked their first five albums, but includes two great
songs: a ripping take on Muddy Waters's "Can't Lose What You Never Had"
and "High Falls," another stellar Betts instrumental.

People made fun of the live **Wipe the Windows, Check the Oil, Dollar Gas**
(1976, ***$\frac{1}{2}$) when it came out, but the live collection holds up well and is an
interesting snapshot of the version of the band featuring keyboardist Chuck
Leavell and bassist Lamar Williams.

Enlightened Rogues (1979, ***), a comeback album, sounded like the promising start to a new Allman Brothers era. Though uneven and at times a bit
strained, it includes a few lost near-classics and ended up being the last gasp
of a great band struggling to sound like itself.

Seven Turns (1990, ****) was an excellent return to form—much stronger
than most of us expected after the flaccid '80s comeback had petered out.
More than twenty years later, it stands its ground. The album was the group's
best overall studio effort since *Brothers and Sisters*, paving the way for the long
run that has followed.

Live at Ludlow Garage (1991, ***½) is a very solid live set from April, 1970 that is mostly interesting for showing just how much the band grew in the ensuing year before recording *At Fillmore East*. Only essential for hardcore fans.

Shades of Two Worlds (1991, ***½) was less consistent but more ambitious than its predecessor and drove home the fact that the Allmans were back and once again a force to be reckoned with.

The Fillmore Concerts (1992, ****1/2) presented an expanded version of *At Fillmore East*. The sound is superb and it's great to hear some extra tracks, like "Drunken Hearted Boy" with Elvin Bishop, and very cool to hear the *Eat A Peach* "Mountain Jam" follow "Whipping Post," as it was originally played.

An Evening with . . . First Set (1992, ****) captures the band in their early '90s glory, with Haynes and Betts throwing lightning bolts at each other.

Where it All Begins (1994, ***½) is inconsistent but contains some of the best material the '90s Brothers produced.

Hittin' the Note (2003, ***½) is the band's first and only studio recording without Betts and they sometimes miss his distinct songwriting. This is a strong collection, however; a batch of new songs featuring the Haynes/Truck guitar teaming was most welcome.

Live at the Atlanta International Pop Festival July 3 & 5, 1970 (2003, ****) may be the most essential of the secondary live releases, capturing the band as they fully rounded into form. This is a smoking hot two-CD set, and includes some hilarious hippie-dippie introductions from the festival MC.

One Way Out: Live at the Beacon Theatre (2004, ***½) captures the band's Haynes/Trucks lineup in great form on a contemporary set list, heavy with material from *Hittin' the Note*. As always, the songs come to life on stage.

Brothers & Sisters 40th Anniversary Super Deluxe Edition (2013, ****) includes a great-sounding version of the original album; a CD of rehearsals and outtakes, including a half-finished "Early Morning Blues," which became "Jelly Jelly"; and two CDs of a great 1973 show from San Francisco's Winterland.

The 1971 Fillmore East Recordings (2014, ****) includes four full sets from the March '71 performances that were edited down to create *At Fillmore East*, as well as the June '71 final performance at the venue. When it comes to high-quality, well-mastered Duane-era performances, more is more.

Play All Night: Live at the Beacon Theatre 1992 (2014, ****) captures the Haynes/Woody/Betts frontline in glorious fashion and serves as a stout reminder of just how good this unit was at its best.

The group has released a steady stream of their own archival releases, each selected for some historic reason.

American University 12/13/70 (2002, ***$\frac{1}{2}$) was recorded on the heels of two nights and four shows at the Fillmore East and the strain of the road can be heard on the opening "Statesboro Blues"—in Gregg's cracked voice, Duane's and Dickey's occasional flubs, some rhythm section wobble—but then the band pulls together and locks in on a ferocious "Whipping Post" and they're off to the races. This was no doubt also a sentimental choice of manager Bert Holman, who booked the shows as an American University freshman.

SUNY at Stony Brook: Stony Brook, NY, 9/19/71 (2003, ***$\frac{1}{2}$) captures the band six months after the Fillmore shows and just five weeks before Duane's death. This is the kind of tape that used to be traded religiously by the faithful. Bad sound quality for the first few songs is offset by a great performance— and the chance to hear one of the few live Duane versions of "Blue Sky."

Macon City Auditorium: 2/11/72 (2004, ***) documents the band playing as a five-piece and coming to musical grips with Duane's death. His absence is sometimes deafening, but this set captures the band's amazing ability to keep on keeping on. Oakley's bass rumbles with extra fury and Dickey Betts's evolution and ability to start playing slide and step to the fore as the sole guitarist is rather remarkable. Hats off to the cat in the hat, though it's hard not to feel sad at times listening to this recording.

Nassau Coliseum, Uniondale, NY, 5/1/73 (2005, ****) was cut just three months before *Brothers and Sisters* was released and includes "Wasted Words," "Jessica," "Come & Go Blues," and "Ramblin' Man" from the forthcoming album. This was one of the first shows played with bassist Lamar Williams and keyboardist Chuck Leavell, and it illustrates the band's brilliance in reimagining themselves in the horrible shadows of Berry Oakley's and Duane Allman's deaths. You can hear how they beautifully reimagined Dickey and

Duane's harmonies into three parts featuring Chuck's keys and Gregg's organ. This was the start of a short-lived second run at the brass ring.

Boston Common—Boston, MA, 8/17/71 (2007, ***$\frac{1}{2}$) Six weeks after the release of *At Fillmore East* and ten weeks before Duane's death, the band returned triumphantly to the Boston Common, where they had played free shows as an unknown band just two years prior. The highlight is a 26-minute "You Don't Love Me."

SOLO OUTINGS AND OTHER BANDS

Gregg Allman

Laid Back (1973, *****) is probably the best solo album by any ABB member. The soulful, folk-infused rock always resonates. "These Days" and "All My Friends" are masterful interpretations. In retrospect, the fact that Gregg remade two songs from *Idlewild South* just three years after its release was a warning about a coming lack of songwriting productivity, though both "Midnight Rider" and "Please Call Home" shine in their new versions and offer revealing hints of Gregg's own musical vision versus that of the collective ABB.

The Gregg Allman Tour (1974, ***$\frac{1}{2}$) is a great document of GA's ambitious post-*Laid Back* solo tour, featuring an orchestra, full horn section, and sweeping backup singers. Lush and soulful.

Playin' Up a Storm (1977, ***) has some very nice moments, but the L.A. production sheen prevents it from reaching the heights of *Laid Back*.

I'm No Angel (1987, ***) has some worthy tracks, notably the title song, but much of it sounds dated; the same production that allowed the album to be a hit in 1987 has not helped it age well. The album closes with GA's reprise of the ABB's "Don't Want You No More"/"Cross to Bear"—cool to hear him perform live but a pointless exercise to record and indicative of a lack of creative spark.

Just Before the Bullets Fly (1988, **$\frac{1}{2}$) has one standout track—the title cut, written by Warren Haynes, who was soon to help Gregg and Co. resuscitate the ABB.

Searching for Simplicity (1997, ***$\frac{1}{2}$) has a few throw-away tracks, but it is a strong album—Gregg's finest new solo work since *Laid Back*. He once again tackles an ABB classic with the album-opening "Whipping Post," but this time the song is refashioned and driven by Jack Pearson's slide guitar.

Low Country Blues (2010, ***) Producer T-Bone Burnett pulls out a series of blues and R&B chestnuts and Gregg delivers them well, but the album leaves me feeling that it could have been so much more, as hinted at by the excellent cosmic cowboy version of "Midnight Rider" Gregg performed with Burnett's large orchestra for several benefit shows. Backed by horns, pedal steel, and mandolin, Gregg took his old standby somewhere new and it would be great to hear him tackle more tunes in a similar fashion. Burnett went sparse, but Gregg also shines going grand.

Worth Searching For
One More Try (1996, ****) I wrote the liner-note essay and helped compile this collection of outtakes and alternate versions, so color me biased, but it is late night/early morning music at its finest. It's a true shame that this collection, which so beautifully reveals a hidden side of Gregg—vulnerable, acoustic, aching, soulful—is deeply out of print.

Dickey Betts
Highway Call (1974, ****), credited to Richard Betts, was the guitarist's chance to fully indulge his love for country and Texas swing. Pedal steel guitar and fiddler Vassar Clements complement Betts's great songs and sweet, melodic guitar on one of the unsung classics in the ABB musical family.

Dickey Betts and Great Southern (1977, ***$\frac{1}{2}$) is somewhat inconsistent, but includes several standout tracks, including the galloping "Run Gypsy Run" and "Nothing You Can Do" and the gorgeous "Bougainvillea," which can stand up to almost anything Betts has written.

Atlanta's Burning Down (1978, ***) is not as strong as its predecessor, but the title track is a moving ballad about a Confederate soldier's horror.

Pattern Disruptive (1988, **) is significant because it was the first time Warren Haynes recorded with the ABB family. There's not too much else to recommend it, however.

Let's Get Together (2001 ***) was an impressive statement by Dickey. He made clear just a year after he was told he was no longer wanted in the ABB that he was far from done making music. Unfortunately, it sounds like it was recorded in your basement.

The Collectors #1 (2002, ***) was a sweet acoustic follow-up, which included the Irish instrumental "Beyond the Pale," a swinging take on jazz pianist Horace Silver's "The Preacher," and Dickey's version of Dylan's "Tangled Up in Blue." Unfortunately, the sound quality was even worse than on *Let's Get Together*. This one sounds like it was recorded in your grandfather's garage, which is a pity because the tunes are great.

Sea Level

On their self-titled debut, **Sea Level** (1977, ***$\frac{1}{2}$), Jaimoe, Lamar Williams, and Chuck Leavell are joined by guitarist Jimmy Nalls for this hard-swinging set. On his own, without partner Butch Trucks, Jaimoe's diverse work is a revelation and Leavell proves himself to be a solid singer, but the instrumentals carry the day.

Released less than a year after their debut, **Cats on the Coast** (1977, ***) is less to my taste. Though still solid, the expanded ensemble leans heavily toward fusion. Jaimoe's role is also reduced to mostly percussion. This album has not aged as gracefully as its predecessor.

Jaimoe was back in the Allman Brothers by the time Sea Level recorded **On the Edge** (1978, ** $\frac{1}{2}$), replaced by Joe English, and the band seems to be trying to catch some disco grooves. Still plenty of instrumental prowess, of course, and some nice flights of fancy, but not enough of the good stuff here.

Long Walk on a Short Pier (1979, ***) was appropriately titled; it was released just before Capricorn Records went bankrupt and promptly vanished for almost twenty years. That's too bad, because it was an improvement from its predecessor. Still uneven and sometimes too slick, this album has more high points, and unleashes Leavell's rollicking piano a bit more.

Gov't Mule

Gov't Mule (1995, ***$\frac{1}{2}$) announced the debut of a dynamic, heavy group. From the opening a capella "Grinning in Your Face" to the last ringing notes of "World of Difference," this self-titled debut grabbed listeners by the face and didn't let go.

Live at Roseland Ballroom (1996, ****) captures the original band in their full sonic glory. Delivers what the debut hinted was coming.

Dose (1998, ****) is the Mule's finest recording, as the band fully finds its sound. Recorded live in the studio, *Dose* debuted Mule classics like "Birth of the Mule," "Thelonious Beck," and "Thorazine Shuffle" and introduced more dynamics, including the power ballad "I Shall Return" and acoustic instrumentation on "John the Revelator" and "Raven Black Night." It's a powerful work that has stood the test of time.

Life Before Insanity (2001, ***$\frac{1}{2}$) fails to match the brilliance of its predecessor, but not by much. Another great album, as the Mule moves away from its trio base, adding some keyboards, harmonica, and overdubbed guitar tracks.

Live . . . with a Little Help from Our Friends (2001, ****) is the Mule album I go back to over and over. A two-CD set of the original trio powering through fantastic originals like "Thorazine Shuffle" and covers of Black Sabbath's "War Pigs," among others. They are joined by friends like Derek Trucks, Jimmy Herring, and Chuck Leavell for "Cortez the Killer" among many great covers, culminating in a 29-minute "Afro Blue." Nothing makes me miss Woody quite as much as this album, which sums up everything great about the original Mule.

The Deep End, Vol. 1 (2001, *** $\frac{1}{2}$) is Warren's response to the passing of his partner in crime, Allen Woody. He rounded up every guest bassist he could think of, from Phish's Mike Gordon to Deep Purple's Roger Glover and from Cream's Jack Bruce to the Family Stone's Larry Graham to pay tribute. The results are predictably inconsistent, but often great. Woody himself makes a cameo on a previously unreleased cover of Grand Funk's "Sin's a Good Man's Brother."

The Deep End, Vol. 2 (2002, ***) keeps the Woody tribute going, this time with bassists including Phil Lesh, Billy Cox, George Porter Jr., and Jason Newsted. Again, somewhat inconsistent, but often great, and the plethora of guests is a tribute to how highly regarded both Warren and Woody are.

The Deepest End: Live in Concert (2003, ****) was recorded during the 2003 New Orleans Jazz and Heritage Festival and it seems as if everyone from the fairgrounds piled into the theater for a five-hour concert that yielded this sprawling tribute to the late Woody. Jack Casady, Les Claypool, Will Lee, George Porter Jr., Karl Denson, and Sonny Landreth are just the tip of the iceberg. It seemed like Warren needed to produce this blowout before Gov't Mule could resume normal band life without Woody. Long live Cap'n Al!

On **Deja Voodoo** (2004, ***$\frac{1}{2}$), Gov't Mule returns as a quartet with keyboardist Danny Louis on board, along with bassist Andy Hess.

High and Mighty (2006, ***$\frac{1}{2}$) is good but not essential.

Mighty High (2007, **) is a cool idea—reggae versions of the Mule's *High and Mighty* album—that just doesn't quite work.

By a Thread (2009, ***) includes a guest appearance by ZZ Top's Billy Gibbons.

Mulennium (Live at the Roxy, Atlanta, GA, December 31, 1999) (2010, ****) is a three-CD collection that made me miss Woody all over again. More special guests, including the late blues great Little Milton, who leads a six-song blues set.

The Georgia Bootleg Box (2012, ****) captures three shows from April 1996 as the Mule was just really learning how to kick. Powerful stuff, raw and ready.

Shout! (2013, ****) is a stirring album, the strongest collection of songs in years. It also includes a fascinating bonus disk of the same songs with guest vocalists (including Steve Winwood, Ben Harper, and Dave Matthews).

Warren Haynes

Tales of Ordinary Madness (1993, ***$\frac{1}{2}$) was Haynes's solo debut and much of it holds up twenty years later.

Live at Bonnaroo (2004, ***) is a slightly uneven acoustic collection with some very nice moments, most notably the version of "Soulshine" with South African singer Vusi Mahlasela.

Man in Motion (2011, ****) is Haynes's soul album, and it's a good one. Echoes of Traffic and Joe Cocker along with R&B giants. Dual keyboardists Cyril Neville and Ian McLagan create a beautiful bed, where Haynes makes himself at home.

Live at the Moody Theater (2012, ***½) is a two-disc, one-DVD live companion to *Man in Motion*, featuring most of the album, as well as several new Haynes tunes and covers of Jimi Hendrix's "Spanish Castle Magic" and Sam Cooke's "A Change Is Gonna Come." Puts an exclamation point on the fact that no one covers as much ground as well as Warren Haynes.

The Derek Trucks Band

The Derek Trucks Band (1997, ***½) announced loud and clear that Trucks was not your average teenaged guitar whiz. The album starts with the original, 35-second instrumental "Sarod," played on the traditional Indian instrument, and goes right into John Coltrane's "Mr. P.C."

Out of the Madness (1998, ***) goes a bit more mainstream than Trucks's debut, with guest vocals by Haynes and Larry McCray and some hot jamming by Jimmy Herring. This is more of a jam session than a cohesive band album, but it is a lot of fun.

Joyful Noise (2002, ****) represented a big leap for the Trucks Band, with the addition of keyboardist/flautist Kofi Burbridge. Some find the juxtaposition of guests to be chaotic but it works for me because the band gels with everyone: salsa star Rubén Blades, soul great Solomon Burke, blues singer and wife-to-be Susan Tedeschi, and Sufi singing master Rahat Fateh Ali Khan.

Soul Serenade (2003, ***) is a more laid-back effort than its predecessor (which it was recorded before). The title track was one of Duane Allman's favorite tunes, and brother Gregg makes an appearance on Ray Charles's "Drown in My Own Tears," delivering one of his best vocal tracks of the new millennium.

Live at the Georgia Theatre (2004, ***½) is a very representative live album.

Songlines (2006, ****) kicks off with a blast of righteous slide guitar on "Volunteered Slavery" and never really looks back.

Already Free (2009, ****) is a strong collection of focused, low-key Americana, with Doyle Bramhall II, Trucks's wife, Susan Tedeschi, and other guests beginning to hint that Derek was looking past his longtime band. There's a lot to love here, especially the gentle duet "Back Where I Started," featuring Trucks on sarod and guitar and Tedeschi on vocals. It is a gorgeous love song.

Roadsongs (2010, ***) is a very solid double live album that is the Trucks Band's swan song, as the guitarist had already moved on to the Tedeschi Trucks Band.

Tedeschi Trucks Band

Revelator (2011, ***) is a strong start for the new group, but the material does not sound fully gelled.

Live: Everybody's Talking (2012, ***$\frac{1}{2}$) is a double live from the TTB's first full-length tour. All the music comes together here, hinting at what a powerful ensemble this group is becoming, though it remains curiously languid, leaving me longing to hear Derek open up and unwind.

On **Made Up Mind** (2013, ****), the TTB seem to find their groove: Strong, hard-driving R and B and material that feels better suited to the large ensemble.

Jaimoe's Jassz Band

Double Down Grill, 1/28/06 (***$\frac{1}{2}$) The Jassz Band was mostly a local Connecticut band at the time, not playing much original music, but highlighting Jaimoe's swinging drum work and an evolving band with a horn section that alternated between accenting singer/guitarist Junior Mack and taking the melodic lead. The two-disc set starts out heavy on the blues, and then goes deep into jazz on set two, with versions of Wayne Shorter's "Footprints," Dizzy Gillespie's "Night in Tunisia," and a unique, horn-driven "In Memory of Elizabeth Reed."

Ed Blackwell Memorial Concert 2/27/2008 (***$\frac{1}{2}$) More straight-ahead jazz takes the fore at this show dedicated to one of Jaimoe's jazz heroes, drummer Ed Blackwell, but Mack's searing take on Curtis Mayfield's "People Get Ready" is a highlight.

Renaissance Man (2011,****) is a fantastic collection of songs, with guitarist/singer/songwriter Junior Mack really stepping up and riding the groove created by Jaimoe's swinging drumming, Bruce Katz's keys, and a surging horn section playing terrific charts. This is a sleeper album in the Allman Brothers Band family tree.

Index

Photo Credits

Pp. 195, 232, 248, 250, 253, 254, 257, 258, 266, 269, 273, 278, 286, 288, 294, 306, 308, 315, 328, 331, 336, 347, 352, 355, 358, 360, 362, 363, 365, 366, 367, 371, 374, 378, 382, 384, 388, 394, 419, 421: Courtesy Kirk West, www.kirkwestphotography.com

P. 2: Courtesy of the Allman Family Archives/Big House Museum

Pp. 9, 398: Courtesy of Stephen Paley

Pp. 29, 35, 40, 97, 99, 168, 192, 242 (self-timer shot): Courtesy of Twiggs Lyndon

Pp. 45, 67, 129: Courtesy of Toneman/Don Butler Archives

Pp. 76, 95, 100, 113, 118, 144, 156, 175, 182, 183, 201, 202, 207, 220: Courtesy of Sidney Smith, www.SidneySmithPhotos.com

Pp. 93, 194: Courtesy of the Kirk West Collection

P. 111: Courtesy ©Bill Truran Productions LLC

Pp. 130, 131, 132, 133: Courtesy of the Big House Museum and Archives

P. 176: Courtesy © Neal Preston 2013

Pp. 200, 212: Courtesy ©John Gellmamn, www.jgphoto.com

P. 284: Courtesy of the Trucks Family

P. 404: Courtesy of Derek McCabe

Pp. 412, 414: Courtesy of Derek Trucks

P. 418: Courtesy © Danny Clinch